GLOBAL ICONS

GLOBAL

APERTURES TO THE POPULAR

ICONS

Bishnupriya Ghosh

Duke University Press

Durham and London   2011

© 2011 Duke University Press

All rights reserved

Printed in the United States of America
on acid-free paper ∞

Designed by Heather Hensley

Typeset in Chaparral Pro by Keystone
Typesetting, Inc.

Library of Congress Cataloging-in-
Publication Data appear on the last
printed page of this book.

FOR BHASKAR

CONTENTS

ILLUSTRATIONS

ACKNOWLEDGMENTS

When a manuscript has had more than one avatar, indeed the trail of debt is high. *Global Icons* has had many mentors, interlocutors, critics, and enthusiasts. Their circles not only reflect my institutional and personal itineraries of the past decade, but also the varied intellectual contexts in which this project was harvested and nourished.

It seems like just the other day that I was funded by the Rockefeller Foundation for a book on socially transformative female public figures in South Asia, troubled as I was then, as were so many of my feminist compatriots, with the emerging equations between female iconicity, the Hindu right wing, and collective agency. To the Institute for Research on Women, Rutgers University, New Brunswick, New Jersey, I owe a great deal for the early shepherding of my project. In particular, I thank Marianne Dekoven, Belinda Edmondson, Ara Wilson, Kathryn Hansen, Beth Hutchinson, and Bonnie Smith for their insights and enthusiasm. In the years that followed, as I shuttled between the University of California, Davis, and the University of California, Santa Barbara, I was strongly supported by institutions, colleagues, and research initiatives. Many thanks to Dean Elizabeth Langland (at UC Davis) and Dean David Marshall (at UC Santa Barbara) for research funding; the Interdisciplinary Humanities Center at UC Santa Barbara for both my residency (2000–2001) and the later research award; to the Feminist South Asia group (organized by Anjali Arondekar, UC Santa Cruz) and the Subaltern-Popular initiative (organized by Swati Chattopadhyay and Bhaskar Sarkar, UC Santa Barbara). From these coteries, several interlocutors ensured critical turns in the project. A selective list includes Parama Roy, Anjali Arondekar, Geeta Patel, Swati Chattopadyay, Nuha Khoury, and Kamala Viseswaran for their consistent reviews, and Gautam Bhadra, Lucy Burns, David Lloyd, Madhav Prasad, and Sudipta Sen for their memorable interventions. The lively interactions with the "Speculative Globalities" Residency Group at the University of California Humanities Research Institute have continued to enrich my arguments, as have my interlocuters in Kolkata (Brinda Bose, Srimati Basu, and Moinak Biswas).

Courtney Berger, Jade Brooks, and Ken Wissoker: Thanks for your advice and guidance in the often anxiety-fueling review process. My first phone chat with Courtney Berger is not easily forgotten, for she proposed a radical revision to the first draft that really made the difference between a project and a book. I cannot thank her enough for her critical incisiveness, laid-back advice, and gentle nudges throughout the review and editing process, despite tumultuous events, such as the arrival of Elias. The external reviewers of the manuscript were painstaking, precise, and enthusiastic; whoever you are, the book owes a great deal of its current form to you.

Colleagues in the English Department, Cultural Studies Program, and Women's Studies Department at UC Davis and in English, Film and Media Studies, Comparative Literature, and Feminist Studies departments and programs at UC Santa Barbara are difficult to thank with a single stroke, for their intellectual labor cannot be extricated from the affective sustenance necessary for scholarly production. A special thanks to Linda Morris, Seeta Chaganti, Gayatri Gopinath, Elizabeth Freeman, David Simpson, Scott Shershow, Catherine Robson, Greg Dobbins, Claire Waters, Desiree Martin, Joshua Clover, Steven Blevins, Vanita Reddy, and Alyssia Garrison at UC Davis, and to Charles Wolfe, Rita Raley, Russell Samolsky, Julie Carlson, Enda Duffy, Barbara Holdrege, Peter Bloom, Stephan Miescher, Cristina Venegas, William Warner, Carl Gutiérrez-Jones, Yanoula Athanassakis, Rahul Mukherjee, Joshua Neres, Regina Longo, Aranye Frandenburg, Shirley Lim, and Alan Liu at UC Santa Barbara, for conversations of varying intensity. No calculus can quite capture their impact, so these fellow travelers are arraigned in no particular order.

Those who continue to watch over me, my thanks; you impact my senses of the world, and therefore, what I write. To my blood and alternate families now spread over Southern California, New York, the Bay Area, Minneapolis, New Jersey, Kolkata, New Delhi, Bahrain, and Toronto, the thanks you will never ask for: You may be too many to recite by rote, but your care remains memorable. Thanks, of course, to my mother, Ratnabali Ghosh, who continues to put my work before her pleasures; to Afzal Shah, Conerly Casey, and Cesare Casarino for your unlimited love and, specifically, for making many turbulent decisions over the past decade so much easier. And as always, to the volatile, critical, but playful longtime companion who has kept faith with me for twenty-seven years: Bhaskar Sarkar.

"The figure of a woman, her arms upraised, rifle held aloft, facing a vast crowd," recalls Rajeswari Sunder Rajan in *The Scandal of the State* (2004, 213). In this reflection, Sunder Rajan reinscribes a scene from the 1994 news story that in itself harked back to the capture of India's most famous bandit queen, Phoolan Devi, in 1983 and her "moral surrender" to police forces. Controversy over the release of Shekhar Kapur's *The Bandit Queen* and the release of Phoolan Devi from the famous Tihar jail in 1994 jolted memories of the low-caste folk hero who had once negotiated her own terms with the Indian state. That "unforgettable image," as Sunder Rajan (2004, 213) called it, was captured in a widely disseminated photograph that became iconic (figure 1) and later found iteration everywhere: in news stories, on television, and in posters for Kapur's film (figure 2).[1]

The recursive image dense with symbolic accretions—the *iconic image*—would continue to have political impact in time to come. Re-auratized, to use the art historian Kajri Jain's term, Phoolan Devi's commoditized "star" image regained its iconic force among regional Dalit, or lower-caste/class communities, with nascent aspirations to parliamentary representation.[2] So we witness Phoolan Devi's rise to power in 1996, when the bandit queen stood for elections, won, and

FIGURE 1 Phoolan Devi's surrender, 1983. Photo. Courtesy of Sondeep Shankar, Penguin Global.

FIGURE 2 Film poster for *The Bandit Queen*, 1994. Kaleidoscope Entertainment and Channel Four Films.

became a member of Parliament, despite thirty-nine cases pending against her (on charges of murder, arson, and looting). A cynical appraisal of these events would underscore the political machinations that transformed the iconic but forgotten outlaw (who had languished in jail for eleven years) into mass commodity. While *Global Icons* diligently pursues the commodity image of Phoolan Devi, I argue that the bandit queen embodied much more: The woman with arms upraised had become the mediator of a structure of feeling for an emergent collective—possible but yet to come.

As the controversy over Kapur's depiction of Phoolan Devi broke, manifested in highly decorated forms (from figurine to glossy poster), the bandit queen as icon enabled the recognition of collective aspirations with transformative effects. For the media scholar, the social efficacy of the icon raises the questions that inaugurate this book: What cultural work does the icon do in the contemporary world? How do we understand its persistence in manifold guises, from liturgical images to the visual cues blinking on our computers in everyday greeting? The wide scope of these queries aligns *Global Icons* with the many reconsiderations of the icon in recent years, and I will make many excursions into these engaging enterprises as I unfold the theoretical project of this book. A question raised in the catalog for the exhibit "Iconoclash" in 2002, curated by Bruno Latour and Peter Weibel, prompts my approach to the global icon:[3] "Have we not made a long and terrifying mistake about its [the icon's] meaning? How can we reconcile this request for an aniconic society, religion, and science with the fabulous proliferation of images that characterizes our media-filled cultures?" (Latour and Weibel 2002, 2). *Global Icons* takes a hard look at this "fabulous proliferation of images," zooming in on those that attract intense affect, spawn spectacles, or motivate collective action.

The gamble is to renew an interdisciplinary materialist theory of the icon properly attentive to its power in the contemporary world. On the one hand, this encourages a focus on the icon's epistemology, the cultural "framing" of an artifact that transforms it into a familiar sign imbued with symbolic density; on the other, it impels us to consider the icon's ontology, the sensory and affective experience activated by the artifact (historically characterized as its metaphysics). The feedback loop between the cognitively perceived sign and the sensorially experienced artifact explains why icons often appear to function as magical technologies, cultural mechanisms that facilitate articulations of collective aspiration. The force of icons lies in the hydraulic "pull" of an embodied encounter

that is at once multi-sensorial and cultural; consumers/devotees experience an immersion into the "thing" that appears as the object, instituting
a sensible subject. We shall see how such a pull can mobilize the affective
transfers necessary for moving subjects toward a larger social network.
Such a conception of the icon's materiality, I argue, attends to its potentialities as a catalyst for social change. Now, if this book were primarily a
philosophical investigation of the icon's materiality, I would rest easily
with the abstract projection of the "subject" in the thrall of magical
technologies. But, as I have indicated, *Global Icons* began with consuming
curiosity regarding the social transformations made possible through
collective acts of icon adoration or desecration. The historical question
haunted my scholarly reach toward a materialist media theory: Who were
the actors in contemporary iconoclashes? What role did icons play in
these expressions of collective agency? Which actions could we transcribe
as popular mobilization? And which could be read as precursors to social
change? Given this historical imperative, I situated the theoretical project
within a localized context, South Asia, because its rich histories of icon
veneration provided fertile ground for rethinking the promissory skepti-
cism of critical iconoclasm.

Phoolan Devi is not the exception but a paradigm of highly visible public figures whose symbolically dense images and lives circulate at high
speeds in transnational (televisual, cinematic, print, oral, and digital)
media networks. The icons under scrutiny here—Phoolan Devi (the bandit queen), Arundhati Roy (the prizewinning writer turned environmental activist), and Mother Teresa (the face of Christian charity)—are contemporary "global icons," cultural phenomena we see every day but
mostly dismiss as some among so many commodities fleetingly present in
our lives. Until wars break out over images. Until they move us to imagine
a there we want to live in. Until iconomania erupts around us.

Avery Gordon once suggested that ghosts are exemplary figures of social
change, for they assist us in forging social imaginaries yet to come: "We
need to imagine living elsewhere before we can live there" (Gordon 1996,
2). Icons are very different phenomena from these spectral figurative
forms. Icons have unshakeable materiality: They flash on screens, confront us in marble or granite. From the monumental to the ephemeral,
contemporary icons are manifest in physical and virtual domains. But like

ghosts, they are apertures into a there. While semioticians read this movement as an indexical charge that signs continue to carry even after the advent of the digital image, scholars of religion, art history, material culture, and philosophy attentive to liturgical icons suggest icons move us toward a greater truth. For scholars of a different cloth, such a movement would open us to the "plethora of forces in the universe,"[4] a chaotic field of power. Highly decorative, often lustrous, and always designed, these are physically expressive whose elaborate ornamentation speaks to the affective labors of worship. They indisputably qualify as art: culturally framed objects that organize our perceptions and affections, often yoking them firmly to bounded tasks, goals, or actions, as commodities are wont to do. Yet since art also intensifies all sensations, as Elizabeth Grosz (2008) reminds us, these sensuous media can also turn us toward chaos, the natural and social world (or the Other, in the metaphysics of the icon). Hence, icons do not embody the truth; rather, they appear as intermediaries for our movement toward it. "The truth is in the image," Marie-José Mondzain (2005, 180) pithily explains, "but the image is not the truth."[5] Such power, readily celebrated as religious or cultural practice within the anthropological gaze, becomes suspect when it circulates in mass cultural forms such as stars, celebrities, or pop icons—fallen gods who invite iconoclastic severity. With good reason, critics argue that mass-media commodities obscure contemplation, luring consumers into a commodity fetishism that isolates them from social relations. I shall return to what constitutes "mass media" shortly; but my point here is that, despite these allegations, we see these mass media routinely deployed in challenges to hegemonic institutions all over the world; reassembled icons habitually surface in political crises where we witness eruptions of collective aspiration.

Such clashes suggest that there is more to the story of mass stupefaction. Perhaps it is time to bring gods, nature, or chaos into the conversation on the social efficacy of contemporary mass-mediated images. Perhaps a capacious materialist analysis of suddenly volatilized (but hitherto ordinary) icons might explain the operations of these media in times when iconoclasm, iconophilia, even iconomania are on the rise. Perhaps the outbreak of iconocrises all over the world—the types of historical eruptions plotted throughout the book—call for a reconstituted materialist theory accompanied by a historical method that reads icons in mass media as runes of the popular. As key signifiers of collective aspiration, icons that erupt into social phenomena provide further evidence of embattled responses to global modernity amid intensifying global inter-connections.

MATERIALITY

Global Icons "matters" the icon, to invoke Pheng Cheah's (1996) apt tran-scription of certain strains of feminist philosophy (most famously repre-sented by Elizabeth Grosz and Judith Butler). I argue that we need to move beyond strictly semiotic analyses of icons as signs if we are to take full stock of their materiality, the "canvas, concrete, steel, marble, words, sounds, bodily movement, indeed any materials" that Grosz (2008, 5) lists as constitutive of the chaos we territorialize as "art." Certainly, the situatedness of the iconic sign—always culturally familiar, always en-countered in circulation, always eliciting pre-experienced sensations—speaks to the centrality of semiotic theory to icon study. The icon, we might say, requires shared cultural knowledge; it is always an epistemol-ogy. But the material sign is also constituted by non-discursive systems that range from physical infrastructure (such as film studios, cables, or Internet space) to tools and raw materials (clay, wood, or paint), whose components are often glossed over in the purely linguistic analyses of the iconic sign. The latter constitute icons as physically expressive decorative objects whose visual, tactile, or sonorous qualities elicit sensations. If we account for these, as well, icons are best understood as "technologies" that can, on occasion, open, aperture-like, into a social network yet to come. I shall return to this ontology of historical becoming, but first I will qualify my characterization of the icon as technology with a few remarks.

Historical records of material cultures reveal icons to be enduring media that hail back to ancient civilizations and whose new, mutating forms we continue to encounter in our wired worlds. The icon is thus a "technology" in the sense prior to its nineteenth-century reallocation as the practical application of (scientific) knowledge, before its conception as "capital instrument" that dangerously enchants.[6] Even as the Marxist bases of this book compel me to readily grant the ill effects of the icon as enchanting, and therefore luring, commodity, I interrogate any rote in-strumentalization of the icon's social effects. Even as icons organize our perceptions and affections to manufacture consent for existing hegemon-ies, they also can unlock totalizing systems, as the classical *techné* sug-gests, through their capacity as media—a "summoning to action" we see in the "practical arts" or technologies of the popular.[7] If we pursue the cultural biography of icons, we find such unlocking when icons, hitherto circulating as ordinary mass commodities, transform into volatile signifiers of a popular movement against the hegemon. Their materiality in the domain of objects, as Daniel Miller (2005) explains, motivates the study of icons in material culture.[8]

Reconfiguring the materiality of the icon is the first intervention of the book. I directly address present, increasingly orthodox, critical dismissals of semiotic analysis as inattentive to the technological substrates of media. Current media archaeologies (Friedrich Kittler's influential oeuvre, for example); research on media institutions, industries, and policy (for example, the work of scholars like Michael Curtin); and histories of sense perception (as exemplified in Jonathan Crary's exegesis on the carnal density of the eye) compel us to think media materiality in productive ways (Crary 1991; Curtin 2003; Kittler 2010). Returning to the sign, *Global Icons* draws on congruent multi-disciplinary conversations on the icon's technological (substrates such as wood, lacquer, paint), physiological (the sensorial experience), and geophysical (space, movement, depth) materialities to consider its operations as an incorporative technology. We can only understand the social force of the icon when we comprehend *how* it assembles human and non-human matter—wood, skin, incense fume, and street—into its form.

Such assembling points to a second materiality, one that underlies accounts of its magical agency: the materiality of the subject who encounters these decorative, sensation-provoking artifacts. My discussion of the embodied veneration of icons theorizes this second "mattering," one that projects a subject (in its various modes, ranging from the rational contemplative Subject to the living organism) that becomes one with the thing that was once demarcated as object (the icon as material artifact). In this post-Cartesian account, the subject caught in the force fields of sensation loses its sovereign (Cartesian) territory as it flows into matter. The body is no longer the enemy of the contemplative Subject but one fold in the subject's material contiguity with all matter; the flesh no longer blinds perception but is a means for it. If lustrous, decorative "objects" such as icons intensify bodily sensations, as I argue they do, then these artifacts greatly activate an ontological becoming. Scholars of different cloths variously transcribe ontological becoming according to their disciplinary formations and political predilections. My transcription is rooted in feminist engagements with matter—theories of corporeal dynamism where the body, ever the site of struggles over biological reductionism, holds a privileged site. In feminist post-Cartesian accounts that revise the opposition between "intelligent activity" and "brute passivity" (Cheah 1996, 4), the body or the corpus (returning to matter as corpse) is abundant matter, a life force with the potential to undo the violence of territorialization.[9] Hence, in this book I refer to the second materiality of the icon, a sensation-provoking art object that ever enfolds the subject into its form as its corporeality. Looking upon immensely corporeal icons, matter framed as art object, activates becoming the world; it activates an onrush of sensations that are not fully grasped cognitively, but through which we apprehend the world as sensible. The corporeal dynamism of the encounter can undo the secure epistemologies of the icon that rely on stable signification, the code and its law.

The materiality of the icon as a moving technology returns us to the body as a field of power. Beyond the sign, beyond the cognitive antics of signification, the icon activates intense sensations. Or, as theorists of affect might say, as art the icon excites the nervous system, producing impulses in the brain that are folded into the body as sensations. In the epistemological moment of icon recognition, these sensations are channelized into distinct affections and perceptions oriented toward a material object, one that has been demarcated as a thing in itself—quite separate from those impulses in the brain.[10] Since icons are recursive signs, they are inevitably "framed" art objects that are always encountered somewhere else. As such, they elicit pre-experienced sensations organized through material regimes; therefore, despite evoking the combinatory sensorial encounter better known synaesthesia, visuality remains the primary mode of perception in icon veneration. But this is nonetheless an embodied visuality (as we shall see in chapter 2), for icons more often than not intensify sensations so much that sensual perceptions can neither be brought under cognitive control nor localized in a single organ (such as the eye). Rather, these lustrous media activate a tumultuous synaesthesia, stimulating the corporeal dynamism of the body. Any act of perception that isolates an object, Brian Massumi (2002) argues, sets aside something else, a constitutive excess opening the event of representation to the body's constant dynamic movement toward matter. The more objects (like our sensuous icons) stimulate the senses, and the faster the impulses, the more impossible it is for the subject to bring the onrush of sensations under cognitive control—to organize and differentiate sensations into specific perceptions. The heightened synaesthesia of encounters with icons dissolves Cartesian mind–body oppositions and, with it, the sovereign territories of subject and object; those held in the icon's thrall move toward matter. Of course, scholars variously transcribe "matter," rewriting it as greater forces, the absent social, nature, or the divine. For some, icons move us toward a greater truth or divinity, while for others, the icon plunges us into nature. But the icon always opens to an elsewhere—to the chaos of vibrant matter. In this sense, the icon embodies the potentiality of chaos. Following this line of thinking, we might say, if the subject becomes icon, the latter shares the agency of the corporeal subject. No wonder art historians and religious studies scholars have considered icons "magical technologies" that activate desire, speech, and action.

It is precisely this potentialization of ordinary objects that worries critics of commodity fetishism and of idolatry: Magical technologies are dangerous weapons of mass control, mobilizing the power of chaos for hegemonic gain. In the classic scenario, the icon engineers consensus for existing hegemonies. Corporate icons, for instance, regularly guide us down well-established pathways of consumer bliss as the best form of sociality. But under historical conditions of possibility, the icon's potentialities are actualized to forge a popular mobilization against hegemonic institutions, and the moving technology opens into a social configuration that is lived but not cognitively grasped—a social to come that is intuited but not fully perceived. Here icons are apertures into the future, opening pathways for a "people to come" as Grosz maintains; they incite structures of feeling that endure. Those "feelings" endure, despite the forces that lull us into everyday comforts—hence, the fabled potentialities of icons in the contemporary world that motivates this investigation.

In reconstituting the complex materiality of the icon I attempt to bring new insights in media theory, invoking assemblages, networks, and immersive experiences, to the ongoing study of globalization. For theorists of globalization, the "global" has been a productive analytic for organizing the systematic distribution of social, economic, and political power; it illuminates an uneven topography rife with economic inequities (of late capitalist modernity), political imbalances (especially in the wake of failed states), and yawning cultural chasms (as we see in the differentials in faith). Within this topos culture is the placeholder for human activity that, David Held and Henrietta Moore (2009) argue, significantly amplifies, alters, or contests the nature and direction of globalizing processes. Following these conversations, in this book the "global" not only evokes a topography of unevenly distributed inequities, but it further mobilizes a sibling analytic, the local, the requisite critical lens for social communications that remain invisible in the burgeoning research on transnational networks, media industries, and multinational media conglomerates. After all, the burning of a bus or the crossing of police lines, acts sporadically archived in news media, hardly surface in media analysis *as* communication. A mass-mediated sign re-sacralized as icon that in-spires such direct action mandates such a localizing gesture, broadening what we might conventionally view as expressive popular culture.

For scholars of media globalization, the contemporary sprawl of com-munications infrastructures expanding the domain of symbolic produc-tion, increases our sense of cultural proximity to hitherto distant else-wheres; a palpable "global immediacy," as John Tomlinson (2009) names it, pervades everyday life. To say that we live in media-saturated environ-ments bristling with new regimes of images is commonplace by all ac-counts; we live in times in which we are witnessing a "fabulous popula-tion of new images, fresh icons, rejuvenated mediators, greater flows of media, more powerful ideas, stronger idols" (Latour 2002, 3). But how do we understand the social effects of these images beyond their reifying capacities? Icons, I argue, are one genre of signs that enable us to recon-sider the efficacy of these great media flows in forging social bonds, despite their circulation as mass-produced commodities. Arguably, it is their circulation—precisely their historical materiality as intermedial signs we have encountered *before*—that positions mass-mediated icons as fecund "raw semiotic material" (as theorists of the popular name them) for contesting global modernity in public cultures all over the world. A complex materialist critique guides the critic to view affective emergences around icons as articulations of both specific social demands and unmoored desires for a possible sociality—an open-ended sociality that theorists of affect attribute to the body. As intensely sensation-provoking media, icons can catalyze this potentiality. Indeed, we find such potentialization in outbursts of collective aspiration, eruptions that often register as ephemera in the writing of social history.

My argument on mass-mediated signs builds on current conversations regarding the media ensembles (technologies, institutions, and net-works) that we characterize as "global" in their reach. It would be rare indeed to find that remote corner in our times where mass-media flows do not proliferate. Historically the mass media have been understood as communications from a single point of production to a large number of points; often a moniker for powerful corporate institutions (large-scale organizations such as the BBC or Time Warner), they require strong fi-nancial backing for their production, distribution, and delivery. With the advent of digital networks, however, media theorists argue that individ-uals now possess the capacity transmit media content on a scale that was once the privilege of select coteries of mass producers. This puts into question the mass media's famed regulatory power over media content, even as large media institutions continue to monitor consumers' participation via well-developed, finely tuned industrial practices and to tabulate population flows, desires, and motivations (classically through market surveys and, more recently, through user-generated content on multiple platforms). What, then, is the relevance of mass media in these complex media landscapes?[11] In discussions throughout this book, I deploy "mass media" as a critical shorthand for certain kinds of media institutions—broadcast news networks, advertising firms, commercial merchandising companies, pulp print media publishers, and film studios —whose corporate imprimatur we find in the most widely circulating images of the public figures in question. Media "control," in this regard, may be understood as the industrial and technological capacity to distribute, store, and recycle certain images, so that they become the most recursive inscriptions of a public figure. The corporate imprimatur signals the structuring market rationality underlying the authorized "star images" of global icons, logics that persist even in local remediations of these images; as they play to increasingly privatized desires, such public images (of a Mother Teresa, a Arundhati Roy, or a Phoolan Devi) effectively valorize individual rights to spend, vote, or speak.

The major thrust of the book engages with what happens to these corporate images at particular sites of their reception. In the many robust contestations of these images, we glimpse another story of global modernity: one in which mass-mediated images are precisely the widely and cheaply available means for apprehending global interconnections. If our phase of globalization is marked by an increased reflexivity about "being global"—the perception of our connection to multiple "elsewheres" beamed at us every day—then mass-mediated signs that enter and exit local platforms can play a key role in calibrating such perceptions. As we shall see, even at the (often celebrated) peripheries of the world system, mass-media signs are often perceived as originating elsewhere. Therefore, mass-media icons become essential to forging relations to that "elsewhere" populated by those whose needs or resources affect the "here" we perceive as "our" locality. If we understand the icon to be a recursive sign, made culturally familiar through its circulation, it comes from afar, opening us to "globality" as a location—a spatial image of the place where we now live. We shall return to the cartographic function of global icons shortly, but to reiterate the point on global connectivity, I am arguing that mass-mediated signs offer the cultural means for forming or deforming attachments to the "global" as that absent social totality that encompasses us all. On the one hand, those who adore a global icon can become cosmopolitan through mass consumption, living fantasies of universal dreams; on the other, the same icon might be the very symbol necessary to unify an "us" differentiated from a "them" in socially antagonistic acts that are characteristic of the popular. These antagonistic acts exert pressure on the space of the "global" when that moniker seeks to represent the totality of social interests. Given such investments, it should come as no surprise that these media habitually command adulation, anger, grief, fear, debate, and violent action.

Yet global icons remain some of the most under-theorized phenomena of our times. In this book, I read their traces in mass media as hieroglyphics, as Walter Benjamin (1927–40) would say,[12] for the social relations they constitute or destroy. Here, bio-icons, whose images and lives saturate mass media, play a particular role. They are not just significant as powerful signs; they also bear an indexical charge for collectivities that place social demands through them. Their "life story," the formalized *bios*, inductively focalizes the sign and renders it representative of the ordinary (as we see in countless rags-to-riches stories); the icon appears to have been just like us once, a long time ago, despite her later excellence. All of the figures in this book signified by a "name," proper or titular,[13] occupy such a place in historical popular memory; animated in publicity and widely translocated in mass media, they subsequently are annexed as signifiers for collectivities. Hence, their traces in archived mass media content, especially when attracting intense affect, provide glimpses into eruptions of collective aspirations. If one is engaged in writing neither popular histories nor ethnographies, the desire to read icons as social hieroglyphics as we explore the cultural work they do in the contemporary world must attend to a critical method appropriate to the task. In the latter part of the book, I reflexively take up the methodological challenge of "telling" the story of the popular from its not so visible, not so accessible, traces in mass media. The retrospective gaze of the critic rewrites ontological becoming as history.

GLOBAL MODERNITY

If my emphasis falls on macro-scalar change as constitutive of the historical becoming, it is important to take a closer look at the setting of the book. Despite excursions into Byzantine or fifteenth-century India, this book, like many studies of the power of images, insists on a strong historical situation for its selected subjects. For the most part, we dwell in the contemporary. But this is an unbounded "period"; without the comforts of established historical markers, it demands further definition of its spatiotemporal configuration. In this book, the contemporary refers to the turn of the twentieth century: the post-1989 era, with 1989 as the historical marker for a post–Cold War new world order. It was during this time that the pressing questions of this book were asked and answered. Now, it may well be that we are witnessing the demise of the "new world order" in the wake of the financial crash of 2008, in a bittersweet thud echoing that of the Berlin Wall twenty years ago. I finished writing the book in a year of turbulence when this ethos might well have been coming to a halt, as Immanuel Wallerstein recently suggested,[14] so the period in question—the heyday of post–Berlin Wall neoliberalism proving the triumph of Reaganomics—may turn out to be 1989–2008. While the saga unfolds, I focus on existing regimes, still those of the "new world order" of deregulated corporatism (facilitated by the Washington consensus[15]) and military expansionism that found effective mediation in icons ranging from logos to public figures. "Global icons" do cultural work in constituting—in the sense of both instituting and revising—the "world" implicit in the new world order. How can we understand the complex work of these sensuous media in the contemporary world? In what follows, I argue that "public culture," signaling contestations of a single modernity progressing toward the well-defined goals of global capitalist development, offers an effective geopolitical rubric for the question with which we began. On the way, I hope to further refine "global icons" as a distinctive genre of signs that are of considerable significance to global media theories that attend to the "signal and noise" of mass media as it shapes the world.[16]

I begin with the presumption that informational flows are critical to the restructured regimes of global capital whose industrial and financial processes are broadly signified when we speak of economic globalization. Media flows are key to maintaining a sense of geographical connectivity necessary for the efficient functioning of the kind of dispersed production David Harvey names "flexible accumulation." Harvey's (1989, 2005) account of the reorganization of capital as we move beyond Fordism explains why the media have become crucial for the new economy, since "needs" are created (via spectacle, fashion, timed obsolescence) to compensate for the over-production of goods. As communications infrastructures evolve, with the vertiginous proliferation of media platforms as well as of delivery technologies, iconic images move swiftly within mass media networks "selling" the mantra of consumer choice as agency all over the world. Since information must flow fast, N. Katherine Hayles (1993) argues, material constraints (limited buying power, for example) are often turned into consumer options (you can always get the cheaper option)—hence, the experience of the decreasing materiality of this intensely interconnected world and the increased sense of smooth, unimpeded traffic in ideas, lifestyles, information, goods, and people.

Such a map etches the contours of the financial expansionism that underwrites what has been broadly defined as the neoliberal *ethos*,[17] arguably still a hegemonic "aspiration" (understood as the ability to envision a future) after 2008. As commodities, global icons are integral to the smooth functioning of the post-1989 neoliberal economy: They legitimate historically and culturally particular aspirations as widely shared universal ones. It is with Vatican II's new corporatism, for instance, that Mother Teresa's traditional Roman Catholic "charity" becomes encoded as *the* universal form of charity, her embodiment of a universal form of human giving consequently manufacturing consent for Christian missionary expansionism in a new world order. The iconic image now reads as "global," since its universal message projects the global (a social totality inclusive of all) as addressee; its new universalism projects a neoliberal ethos that seems to have won the last war of ideas. It is precisely because of their encoding as a signifier of something global, representative of a globalizing force (a corporate religious institution in the case of Mother Teresa), that some contemporary icons become contentious objects. In historical situations where the lived experiences of neoliberal reorganization produce deep uncertainty, a condition that can be both a debilitating precariousness and a stimulus for change, they attract opprobrium. Exposed in their historical materiality, their globalizing drive, they lose their universal claim to speak for all. Where Coca-Cola once appeared as a drink for all seasons in sleepy Plachimada, as we shall see in the next chapter, a drought (following the Coca-Cola Company's extraction of groundwater) would turn an ordinary commodity into a volatile signifier provoking expressive desecrations of the resplendent red-and-white graphic; with wells running dry, the once universal logo began to appear as the face of a privileged few (as Naomi Klein [2000] has argued for corporate logos) whose needs from afar create want here. Looking at historical situations where icons are potentialized, *Global Icons* avoids the pitfall of reducing neoliberalism to a cultural ethos, to an epiphenomenon; rather, the neoliberal ethos structures the lived experiences of global modernity and, as such, catalyzes interactions beyond semiosis.

The debate on neoliberalism is too vast to be fully discussed here, but I pause to consider a few relevant strands. As a process constitutive of modernity, the globalizing of consumerism, to use William Mazarella's (2003) handy phrase, has elicited substantial attention from the major critics of contemporary globalization (e.g., Harvey 1991; Jameson 1991; Miyoshi 1993). With late capital comes the ubiquitous rise of mass consumerism both in the flow of consumer goods across national borders and in the marketing of the "ideology of consumerism" that anchors the logic of capital in a striated world system. De-territorialized mass-media flows (icons included), which are fundamental to selling "foreign" products in newly opened markets, worry critics of globalizing consumerism, because they threaten to remove people from their concrete life worlds (and thus from immediate social relations) by imbricating them more tightly, more securely, more fully into global systems of exchange.

But this is a story postcolonial theorists, in their variegated pursuit of the un-homely habitations of modernity, know well. In recent years, critical anthropologists have been most successful in refashioning the postcolonial optic to inquire into new wars over global flows in the domain of culture. Clearly sympathetic to the critique of capital, they have embarked on ethnographies of specific regional consumption practices that challenge the notion that mass culture simply reifies one's social relations, thereby bringing fresh perspective to the gloom over unidirectional "global" flows that sell the logic of the free market—"global" because they gather the world, as Fredric Jameson (2002) noted, into the horizon of a singular modernity inaugurated in Europe. When we speak of "global modernity," we often reference this hegemonic historical formation of becoming modern.

In his formidable engagement with the great debates over the origins, locations, and logics of modernity, Timothy Mitchell (2007, 7) asks how we can "relocate" modernity in different global contexts (eschewing narratives of "the West, then the rest"), allowing those contexts "to complicate, rather than simply reverse" the story of (capitalist) modernity. If images are central to the modern world picture, then in their iteration, serialization, imitation, or hyper-linkage we find abundant complication. In battles over stories, graphics, artifacts, and other world-encircling media, we stumble across different stories of modernity from arenas of exchange marked as discrete geopolitical regions (such as Latin America, South Asia, the Maghreb); pursuing them in the itineraries of global icons effectively "provincializes," as Dipesh Chakrabarty (2000) encourages us to do, the Euro-American version of a singular modernity.

Critical anthropologists have been recounting those stories of "multiple modernities" (in the words of Charles Taylor [2004]), the bounded horizons of area studies situating negotiations over global consumerism. One of the most respected critics of a singular modernity, Arjun Appadurai, returns again and again to South Asia to consolidate a specific experience of global modernity; his work in many respects has inspired scholars to pause on local practices of consumption. For media studies in which the "local" is South Asia, such exhortation has produced a vast archive of situated studies that retell the story of global modernity—studies that variously bring cinema, television, calendar art, advertising, and popular print culture under critical surveillance (e.g., Jain 2007; Mazzarella 2003; Rajagopal 2001). The exhortation has had a strong impact in my own trajectory as scholar, moving from postcolonial literary studies to investigations of global media technologies, always with a materialist feminist optic on global capital as it moves more smoothly, and less noisily.

If there are many stories to be told of global modernity, this book offers one plotted through the itineraries of global icons as they reach localized sites of consumption in South Asia. One of the key arguments of the book is to consider how widely circulating "global icons" of high symbolic density flow as commodities; where practices of consumption re-auratize them, transforming them into magical technologies, as Jain has shown in the case of mass-produced sacred icons in commercial arenas of exchange. Jain's *Gods in the Bazaar* (2007) is salient to my inquiries into icons as efficacious media; her rubric of circulation provides a finely calibrated model for how mass commodities are re-territorialized, re-signified in consumption to embody "local" aspiration (which address the global in their re-entrenchments). If we follow John Caldwell's (2008) reconfiguration of participatory "consumption" as new production cultures (especially when user-generated products are fed back into mass-media industries), we are alerted to the images and lives of bio-icons as constantly migrating media content that is constantly repurposed to serve local ends. In every instance of the public icons under investigation here, we see the drive to re-territorialize in mass-produced commodities reassembled as signs of a local modernity. Yet the mass-media flows of *Global Icons* institute a sharp difference from *Gods in the Bazaar*. Apart from a few instances of material culture (figurines, brooches, stamps, mugs, statues, cutouts), *Global Icons* parleys in the transnational traffic in print, audiovisual, digital media (books, pamphlets, films, television shows, news bulletins, photographs, billboards, blogs, fan sites, podcasts). My critical object therefore necessitates the scale of my investigation. On the one hand, if the *global* icon can only be grasped as a mutating intermedial image, then the circuits where we find these global forms cannot be framed within a national context (of the sort we see in Jain's work). On the other, any specific story of global modernity must in fact bind its analysis of consumption to an arena reflexively localized through scholarship. The "local" here is not the one evoked in early theories of globalization,[18] a site that is opposed to the global. Rather, it is a hermeneutic category, much like the East and the West, deployed to mark off a certain arena for studying specific experience of modernity. Obviously, the choice of the arena is guided by my scholarly location in South Asian media studies; hence, in this book we alight on the bustling metropoles or bristling small towns of contemporary South Asia to pursue the annexation of global flows to a local modernity.

By focusing on the bounded arena of South Asia, this book gestures toward the anthropological, but unlike traditional area studies, where the history of the region is given critical primacy, this study focuses on contemporary transnational processes in a period when South Asia is indisputably saturated with globalized media technologies.[19] So while Jain focuses on a single media industry (the production culture of chromolithographs) to track how a public figure assumes global form—that is, comes to be a widely circulated sign embodying universal aspirations—I argue that we must attend to this figure's inevitable intermediality. The local statue that circulates as a photograph that is the blueprint for a painting that legitimizes a televisual biopic discloses the inherent plasticity of these icons, constantly mutating amid media convergences, moving from street rumor to television to poster and back to the street. The scale of transnational networks informs the types of icons I bring together here, figures whose images materialize on multiple media platforms; unenclosed by social networks (such as specific religious or secular constituencies), they are consumed by multiple publics and populations. In short, it is because these icons are "global" in their materiality—embodying universal aspiration and circulating in industrial and social transnational networks—that they are attractive to contemporary scholars of globalization.

So this is not a book about South Asia, for the materialist theory of embodied consumption in public culture elaborated here is not limited to South Asian contexts. Rather, the argument about multiple modernities underwrites the direction of the theoretical gaze to a specific globalizing region, a relocation that implicitly interrogates the self-evident primacy of local arenas such as the United States. I ask readers to engage with the popular consumption of global icons in South Asia to better comprehend the role of mass media in the constitution of global modernity elsewhere in a globalizing world.

Central to this comprehension is a theory of media that explains how potent cultural symbols contest neoliberalism's most stable mantras, in both spectacular and quotidian performances. These might include the collective intelligence of participatory cultures implicit even in individual acts, and I shall certainly attend to these throughout the book. But my primary interest is in the expressivity of actors who collectively articulate their aspirations through global icons. We might pose the question so: How do we understand contestations of neoliberalism expressive in popular culture as collective responses to globalization? The question begs a substantial reply, since there is a formidable critical history to debates on mass culture and collective agency. My critical coordinates as a media theorist are those discussions of "popular culture" that laid the groundwork for thinking about reassemblage as expressive performance, where the searching eye finds evidence of social antagonisms to hegemony. As we shall see, certain strains in those conversations underlie my "readings" of collective agency in the later chapters of the book. Thus, a brief excursion into "the popular" as the scaffolding for the book's historical argument on collective agency may be worthwhile before we turn to the three bio-icons under scrutiny.

THE POPULAR

If in our times of "participatory culture," as Henry Jenkins calls it, consumers increasingly recalibrate mass-media content for their own ends, then we might think of these rituals as expressive popular culture.[20] I do not mean to valorize participatory culture, for the myth of infinite resources certainly matters less to those with little access to media-production or media-delivery technologies. Nor is my criticism of celebratory infinitude simply a gesture, since lack of access is an indisputable reality for many of those who make up the populace whose performative consumption of mass media icons generates iconocrises. Clearly, these are not traditional "publics" constituted by the media they self-reflexively consume, but even in sporadic social actions more characteristic of the subaltern, they seek publicity. Hence, they participate in *public culture*, the descriptor Arjun Appadurai and Carol Breckenridge coined for the spatialized domain of the popular where consumption recalibrates mass-produced media flows. Public culture, they famously argued, was a flexible term that included the popular practices of those who had no access to the modern associational forms of civil society; public culture was that vibrant zone of contestation where mass-produced commodities could be reassembled to articulate a local modernity (Appadurai and Breckenridge 1995).

Like theorists of public culture, champions of the popular have long made the case against the denigration of populism implicit in the degradation of masses, crowds, and populations. Several traditions draw on the writings of the Italian Marxist Antonio Gramsci, whose conception of hegemony envisioned a social totality constituted by different social elements not marked by class belonging from the beginning.[21] Hegemony, for Gramsci, was that constantly evolving process of political reaggregation around a core—always a class core—against an irreducibly absent social that is impossible to totalize. On the one hand, Gramsci's readiness to include classes on their way to becoming proletarian (in his famous "The Southern Question") provided ground for subaltern studies scholars to speak to eruptions of collective agency among the Indian peasantry, insurgent acts elided in hegemonic nationalist accounts of anticolonial movements. Their works, largely inspired by the historian Ranajit Guha, would elaborate methods of reading resistance central to any analysis of collective agency. Certainly when global icons provoke eruptions of isolated and sporadic actions (anger, grief, violence) Guha's propositions for "reading" these as causally linked, as insurgent, are extremely productive. But with the steady influx of mass commodities into South Asia, I shall argue, it is urgent that we theorize a popular flexible enough to capture the expressive cultures of subaltern populations, performances that negotiate mass-media signals to renew social relations. If the popular relies on potent symbols as unifying mechanisms for its articulation, its pursuit must be accompanied by a theory of media. But we often do not find one that incorporates visual popular culture. This is certainly true of early subaltern studies. The written record continued to hold primacy as the archive where scholars find traces of subaltern speech; oral culture (legend, lore, song), considered organic to communal life, also received periodic attention. Visual popular culture, however, remained on the margins of critical analysis, the contagion of mass media (in the hands of political and financial elites) rendering media such as icons suspect as expressions of collective agency.[22]

While in recent years we have seen attempts to attend to potentialities of visual culture with greater acuity, the lure of situated, local, organic communities remains potent.[23] Yet such a focus on traditional popular culture represented by established practices that constitute small-scale artisanal industries, replete with singular cultural histories, cannot account for a repertoire of popular cultural practices that relies on dispersed mass media flows from "elsewhere" as their "clay," as their raw, semiotic material for performances—structured improvisations that reposition mass-media commodities (such as logos) in symbolic ensembles too contingent to take root as subculture.[24] If such (nontraditional) popular cultural practices are the norm these days in our mass media–saturated environments, scholars are compelled to look beyond rooted communities, situated in well-defined locations (a city, village, nation, or region), for evidence of subaltern speech in popular culture.

In this reconfiguration of the popular, we can bring other mobilizations—from micro-scalar negotiations of consumerism to macro-scalar mobilizations against resource extraction—into the same frame as subaltern insurgency. Such mobilizations sometimes work with, rather than against, the logic of democracy. For one, "subaltern" cultural productions make ample use of cheap communications technologies that proliferate everywhere, subaltern speech registering as static on the way to civil discourse. For another, these mobilizations shore up a historical agent not necessarily determined by its class character, even as the traditional left (party cadres, trade unions, student groups) acts in solidarity (rather than as vanguard). To grasp the popular as a dispersion across social elements working with the logic of democracy directs us to a second intellectual trajectory inspired by Gramsci: to Ernesto Laclau's formulation of the popular, in *On Populist Reason* (2005), as an agonistic war of position everywhere democratic institutions are largely seen to fail "the people." The gamble of the book is to bring these two different traditions, exemplified by Ranajit Guha and Ernesto Laclau, to bear on the same social phenomena. While I begin with Laclau's often criticized elaboration of signifying practices necessary for the constitution of the popular,[25] in the latter sections of the book Guha's methods for "reading" collective agency become central to my argument.

In *On Populist Reason*, Laclau argues that "the people" are discursively constituted through signifying practices that harness powerful symbols, phantasmic placeholders "quilting" (as Slavoj Žižek would have it) heterogeneous demands.[26] If heterogeneous social elements are bound through signification, the signifier that unifies also commands considerable affective investment. Hence, potent symbols—culturally familiar, recursive signs with symbolic density such as icons—are obviously ripe for such cultural work. When we do not question their operation as cultural shorthand, they have successfully organized our affections as psychic investment (Laclau 2005, 43). Obviously, such unifying capacities are alluring for both hegemonic and popular forces. For example, Coca-Cola or Marlboro, no longer manufactured by American companies, still signifies a quintessential America. Through them, a powerful social element seeks to represent the entire social totality, binding all differences to the common horizon of a fissure-less society where all others are (or can be) brought into the fold. Conceptually grasping such a totality, Laclau remarks, is "the condition of signification," an impossible task since no social can ever accommodate every demand. Yet one difference takes on the Herculean deed, quilting heterogeneous demands, embodying totality in universal form. Such signification is hegemony, that moving equilibrium where consent is daily sought and sometimes won, but often lost.

We shall see how our three bio-icons are often deployed for such universalizing agendas. Yet they also function as unifying symbols for popular demands, articulated against particular neoliberal initiatives and agendas. We see the surge of the popular when that consensus is fought and an internal frontier appears between the institutional system and the "people" (the *sarkar* and the *janata*, as the opposition is commonly parsed in India). What might begin as an isolated "democratic demand" by a social element not necessarily defined by class accumulates force by forging bonds to other demands; the dispersed plurality, held in a chain of equivalence through signification, is the popular. The "people" emerge as the historical agent of change, with one social element (the *plebs* for the populace in Gramsci) acting as the point of anchorage, their particularity unifying the dispersed collection of agents. Historical becoming reorders the social as a "people to come." As it matures, such a popular articulates a common horizon for "all" differences in the social it represents, and it attempts to change the existing institutional system. In short, it seeks hegemony.

Laclau's conception of the popular enables us to think laterally: to think of transnational social movements as a global popular that eschews the global as a totality in favor of a global as a series of contingent linkages. For scholars of global media, such a conception allows us to think of the potentials of mass media in forging social bonds. But what hegemony spurs such a popular? As I have intimated, in the contemporary period neoliberalism is one horizon of a fissure-less society projected by a privileged few to represent an ultimately incommensurable totality. This regime, institutionalized in various forms, is fought hard on multiple fronts, with the eco-wars over resource extraction in the spotlight. Its face—McDonald's golden arches or Coca-Cola's vivid Spencerian script—

is the global form of the icon seeking to embody universal aspiration masking all differences. Making the case for neoliberalism, one social element places a demand for a free market and its political support ("fair and free elections") as a shared dream of the "free world."

The semiotic economy of the iconic sign lends itself to such a project, since the icon is a highly sedimented recursive sign that has annexed certain symbolic resonance as its "natural" and "eternal" core properties. In this reified form, the epistemology of the icon is secure, seemingly unshakeable. For example, the ever banal Coca-Cola logo, delivered across multiple platforms, lives up to every accusation critics of mass culture have leveled against reifying mass commodities. The iconic logo transfigures particular cultural aspirations into a universal dream, masking social contradictions in the social totality it cannot represent. Since Coca-Cola refused permission to reprint any of its advertisements, I can only describe its allure crafted in a visual artifice that engineers the world, and I assume that my readers have been subjected often enough to the pervasive image culture of Coca-Cola, so that this scenario will be all too easily imagined. Among many others we stumble on every day, one memorable Coca-Cola advertisement depicts a world split in half. The frame divides the cool light white and blue of mountains (signaled by pine trees) on the left from the bright hot gold of deserts (signaled by palms) on the right, with a glistening Coca-Cola bottle running at a diagonal midway through the picture.[27] If Coca-Cola travels everywhere, the ad suggests, it also answers a basic human need: thirst. The well-known caption "Thirst Knows No Season" sprawls across the world picture, turning a specific taste into universal need. Yet if you were to plug the terms "Coca-Cola" and "protest" into Google or YouTube, you would think that vilifying Coca-Cola was just as ubiquitous as the glossy Spencerian Coca-Cola graphic splashed across the globe.[28] We are alerted to these performative desecrations when they become news, and in the news, universalizing logos appear in their historical materiality—someone else's dream. They become news when representation becomes event, the opposition to the multinational's uneven production peaking in varied social actions. Take, for example, an image of one of many protests launched in India in 2003–2006 following the release of a report by the Center for Science and Environment that nearly all cola drinks produced in India contain unacceptably large doses of pesticide. The dynamism of the shot (figure 3), a tiny figure tearing down the towering cutout, only underscores the human agency of desecration as expressive culture.

When we trace this expressive desecration found in mass-media ar-

FIGURE 3 Students protesting pesticides in colas, 2006. AP Photo/Ajit Solanki.

chives to the events that preceded it, we begin to see how local agitation can become a demand for a changed globality that "we," a people to come, would live in common. I tarry with protests against Coca-Cola because, along with desecrations of McDonald's, they are paradigmatic of a genre of contemporary new social movements all over the world, micro-scalar agitations against resource extraction that are gradually evolving into sprawling global alliances. They represent a global popular that is pressing ecological and environmental justice as a common horizon. In these acts of desecration, we see the surge of the popular, holding diverse demands together in a signifying chain, with a clearly marked external adversary embodied in the logo (the "face" of deregulated capital). On occasion, a bio-icon might serve as a placeholder for anti-hegemonic aspirations: Iconic activists such as Wangari Maathai or Ken Saro-Wiwa, for instance, facilitate the placing of ecological demands, while political stars such as Barack Obama and Hugo Chavez channel demands for a new *Realpolitik* that "worlds" differently.

Each of the bio-icons in *Global Icons* undergoes a transformation from a reified "star" to a deeply historical material signifier. These icons are unmistakably plastic,[29] constantly repurposed and reassembled into subsequent avatars. We see such plasticity most clearly in the case of Arundhati Roy, who first exploded onto the global stage when she won the

FIGURE 4 Publicity photograph of Arundhati Roy, 1996. Courtesy of
Pradip Krishen, http://www.nilacharal.com.

Booker Prize in 1997. Roy arrived in publicity as the new and glamorous
face of globalizing South Asia, at once the stereotypically beautiful Indian
woman but also educated and successful—symptoms of a rising middle
class, the force behind India's sudden visibility as a cultural "soft" superpower. She was unequivocally the quintessential writer, the "voice" of the
people. Both ekphrastic descriptions and early recursive photographs of
the writer from the same photo shoot (figure 4) etched the "dancing
curls," "dusky skin," and "bright dark eyes" in public memory, the iterative elements formalizing the iconic image. Pradip Krishen, Roy's partner, proved to be the authorizing figure behind this first image, instantaneously distributed and cyclically iterated in broadcast news media (for
instance, in all the outlets of the Times News Group) and by corporate
institutions (such as publishing houses). The publicity shots from the
same session made their way across media platforms, appearing on the
back flap of *The God of Small Things* (1996), in widely circulating magazines, and (digitally altered) on numerous fan sites devoted to Roy (figures 5–6).[30]

ARUNDHATI ROY was trained as an architect. She has worked as a production designer and has written the screenplays for two films. She lives in New Delhi. *The God of Small Things* won Englands most prestigious literary award, The Booker Prize, in 1997.

FIGURE 5 Photograph of the author on the front flap of *The God of Small Things*, 1997. Pradip Krishen, Random House.

FIGURE 6 Website cameo of Arundhati Roy. Courtesy of Pradip Krishen.

Responding to her "star" image, quickly stabilized in its iteration, within a year Roy publicly reinvented herself as an activist in a series of interpretive gestures (nonfiction, interviews, pamphlets), prompting the formation of a new iconic sign—and a highly contested one. The message of the second avatar, the activist as the face of "global green" soon became the subject of debate over what constituted a popular struggle for environmental justice. Under changing historical conditions—the increasing commodification of the Narmada Bachao Andolan (the social movement against India's Narmada Valley Development Project)—her sign would gather hate or adoration, just as the dropping water table at Plachimada would transform the Coca-Cola logo into a sign of neoliberal interests. Again, such change directs the scholar to the historical situation of the reassemblage to retell the story of global modernity.

Roy's fortunes tell us that global icons are global not only by virtue of how widely they are known, but also because they come to represent global aspiration. The three icons arraigned here are global not only because they traverse transnational circuits of exchange, but also because

they are reflexively marked as representing some shared "global" message, a universal message embodying all who live in a shared "globality,"
that spatial image of social totality. This is precisely why they attract
dissension at a time when all manner of global formations are constantly
contested and renegotiated. Hence, *Global Icons* marks places where global
icons stop their speeding tracks, when their corporate public images are
reassembled and re-auratized. The volatile icon signals the global in a
second sense: as sensible interventions that seek to alter global interconnections, generating frictions along the "chain-link" that is Anna Tsing's
(2004) figuration for contemporary globalization. Those who have not
been historical agents of history, Tsing maintains, have high stakes in
calibrating the abstract universal "schemes and dreams" of modernity to
their particular platforms and agendas. Global connections depend on local
participation in schemes such as "capitalism, science, and politics" (Tsing
2004, 1). In *Global Icons*, we see several efforts under way to recalibrate
these schemes through the popular consumption of global icons. Each of
our bio-icons are inextricable from neoliberal agendas materializing in
varied guises all over the world: For Mother Teresa, the restructuring of
cities into "mega-cities" ostensibly to make space for all; for Arundhati Roy,
the reorientation of protest against resource extraction toward a global civil
society where all can speak; and for Phoolan Devi, the selling of electoral
democracy as the legitimate form of expression for all people. In each
instance, the "scheme"—the projects of the mega-city, of global civil society, of electoral democracy—addresses existing inequities through reorganizations of space, action, or expression along a single "global" paradigm
that would seemingly benefit all. Built on structured inequities, these neoliberal schemes relied on promissory notes for a coming dream actualized
across the world: The path is clearly etched; the goal, unambiguous; the
system, tried and tested. However, in the popular consumption of global
icons harnessed to these agendas we see frictions emerge in the logics of
these global schemes, as cracks appear in the smooth significations of a
fissure-less society. The scheme appears as someone else's dream that un-
settles us; the inscrutable global icon, polished and mystical, disintegrates
into a historical image. Evoking intense sensations, it becomes a volatile
signifier available for re-territorialization. And it often is re-territorialized,
if we look closely at acts of embodied veneration; there we confront the
popular as it seeks to remake globality.

The global icon, then, has multiple functions in the neoliberal era with
its dream of a fissure-less society. Laclau reminds us, since totality is
unachievable fullness, an (ever receding) horizon, it requires radical in-

vestment in symbolic objects; the signifying game moves beyond conceptual apprehension (perceptions) to an affective dimension (affections).
We can see how such an argument prefaces the incitement to a renewed
materialist conception of the icon as a (framed) object that organizes but
also intensifies sensations. For that intensification, galvanizing the present dynamism of the body creates the possibility of new directions, pathways, and connections. If icons are precisely the symbolic objects Laclau
foregrounds, living icons, flashing as beloved phantasms, are prime loci
for affections affected as investments; they are media that relocate us in
the popular through shared (vernacular) cultural figurations of saints,
outlaws, or activists. These figurations, I shall argue, become critical for
the demands for a renewed open-ended sociality that runs counter to the
commandments of personal achievements, investments, or gain. This is
why *Global Icons*, a study that could just as easily pursue the iconocrises
around corporate logos, privileges bio-icons as critical to formations of
the popular.

Since living figures become icons through publicity machines, they are
widely and readily accessible in public cultures: Circulating as iterative
trace in mass media, their global forms are easily available to rich and
poor alike. Hence, they are fecund raw semiotic material for constant
reassembly. More importantly, as I have already indicated, living icons
offer a usable formal graphic for those who emerge as quintessential
"agents" within the popular. They lend particularity to the popular. For
instance, at the anti-Coca-Cola struggle in Plachimada that I examine in
the next chapter, Adivasi (indigenous) women metonymically signify
"the people" as historical agents of change. One face, finding iteration
from movie posters to book covers, emerges as the formal graphic for the
mobilization, but it is not that of the movement's leader.[31] Hence, in this
book I am concerned not with the charismatic leader but with the deployment of a living figure as the embodied placeholder for the mobilization,[32] one that reorients ontological becoming toward the possibility of
a social to come.

CARTOGRAPHY

Crucial to this discussion of global modernity is the cartographic function
of global icons. If, as Edward Said (1983) once argued, social totality has
geographic notation, bio-icons play a key role in the new cartographies of
contemporary globalization with its famous space–time compression.[33]
In embodying (universal) aspirations, global icons institute the "cognitive
maps" of globality (Fredric Jameson's unforgettable formulation of the

impossible imaging of social totality). While Coca-Cola sells "coolness," "sexiness," or "youth" as universal values, it unmistakably privileges a consumer lifestyle to be achieved elsewhere—a place much like America, where all social differences supposedly have been elided, the dream achieved. The vertiginous mobility of global icons primes them as appropriate cartographic mechanisms. Even as we encounter global icons circulating at high speeds in transnational networks, these signs are more often than not re-territorialized to erect an internal frontier between "us" and "them." The treasured Bāmiyān Buddhas offered just such an opportunity for the Taliban intent on forging a jihadist social imaginary. In its studious performances of iconoclasm, the hitherto media-shy Taliban invited Al-Jazeera (the Arabic-language news network) to televise the ritualized blasts on March 26, 2002. The blasts signaled a global iconomanic society, forged through the ex-corporation of the statues from the body politic of Afghanistan. On the other side, a parallel worlding would ensue through Saddam Hussein, the iconic sign of totalitarianism for the United States in search of global economic and military hegemony. Millions watched the tearing down of the monumental statue as mass-mediated iconic sign speeding across screens, its ex-corporation from the "free world" enforcing a hegemonic globality. Channeled through the economy of the icon, a particular historical aspiration—the pitch for economic and military dominance—would begin to appear as a universal longing, the human drive for freedom. All humanity (one image of "the people") would enclose a social totality, even as the cognitive cartography would reveal a world divided between those who had arrived at freedom and those still on their way, still in the waiting rooms of history.[34] Hence, our attention to the icon's cartographic function can expose the very geopolitical divisions the universalizing icon seeks to close, divisions that signal the uneven experience of global modernity.

But these media spectacles, staged by those with access to production and delivery technologies, are a far cry from performative desecrations of Coca-Cola in remote locations considered peripheral in the geography of capital.[35] While images selling corporate or state interests often circulate widely across multiple media platforms, the emergent popular erupts sporadically in the mass media; we notice it only if the performative desecrations register as social antagonism, the articulation of an internal frontier between "us" and "them." These emergences constitute "media events" that are worth a closer look since, to a large degree, they are precisely the iconocrises that motivated this book; in chapter 3, I elaborate important differences between banal media spectacles (the controlled sensationalism of the Taliban blasts) and deep media events (explosions of intense affect in mass media), the latter prompting the epistemological crises of the icon. But if we dally with the cartographic function of global icons, we gain a stronger understanding of why President Obama can become the cultural means for articulating collective aspirations all over the world, even as he remains solidly American in his world making (as so many presidential historians of his speeches note).[36] We see bio-icons habitually straddle such geopolitical contradictions, especially when they signal differentials in power within the region they embody. Is it not the case that in 2008 Obama signaled the continued presence of historical difference within the hegemon, the United States, for a world that always suspected all was not democratic on the American front? Is it not his embodied difference that made him a socially efficacious corporeal aperture for diverse constituencies, ranging from cold Norway to small-town Indonesia, but all desiring of change of the global Realpolitik? Obama's cartographic function is of some salience to the icons I pursue here, if a bit differently. After all, female figures focalize South Asia's position in the world—its time lag of development ever tracked to its successful and violated "women" as national emblems—like nothing else. No wonder that, when *Time* or *Newsweek* promotes India as a cultural superpower, a richly lustrous feminized figure adorns the cover, complete with traditional headgear or flowing fabric and techno-savvy headphones that indicate the good (call center) listener.[37]

My choice of bio-icons is governed in part by their cartographic function: They index South Asia as a distinctive region much in the manner that Fidel Castro affixes a "recalcitrant" Cuba in the geography of the new world order. But one may ask, why these bio-icons, since so many others "locate" South Asia, as well: nineteenth-century stalwarts such as Pandita Ramabai or Swami Vivekananda in their twentieth-century avatars; political stars such as Indira Gandhi (whose cachet effects every other female actor in politics[38]); megastars such as Amitabh Bachchan or Sharukh Khan in their multifarious forms; recycled liturgical symbols such as the virile Ram, the signifier of populist Hindu (right-wing) political aspiration; or, indeed, the elephant in the room, the ever renewing Gandhi. Why, then, Mother Teresa, Phoolan Devi, and Arundhati Roy? My critical agenda, the double imperative to "tell" a local story of global modernity, guides the selection—therefore, my departure from the many figures whom any scholar of South Asian studies would immediately bring to my attention. *Global Icons* is not a taxonomic effort. Rather, I am guided by the specific demands placed through the constellation of icons in this book. They constitute major responses to neoliberalism in South Asia, challenges to economic, political, and techno-scientific schemes.

But beyond such historical motivation, the three bio-icons further signal the epistemological foundations of the book: to think the materiality of the sign in terms of sexual difference. If we understand the materiality of the icon as territorialized chaos, then, in the case of bio-icons, sexual difference is constitutive of that territory. As feminist philosophers have long argued, sexual difference is the primary field of differentiation (mediating biology) for the subject. Since the social processes of historical becoming are central to the book, we must pause on the sexual coding of icons that play a significant role in their social efficacy. In the case of South Asia, cultural forms marked by sexual difference historically have potent cartographic functions (Freitag 2001, 2003; Ramaswamy 2003). If we think about geography in terms of sexual difference, we see that South Asian masculine and feminine icons embody territory rather differently. The feminine icon has long embodied the geographic region (and problematically so, since this effectively secularizes predominantly Hindu iconographic traditions). While my propositions here might easily extend to masculine icons "made" in publicity, the extensive history of the politicized female icon in South Asia makes the gendered female body particularly salient to "fixing" South Asia as a region in the cartographies of contemporary globalization. The symbolically sedimented feminine body as indexical of India (a "geobody," as Sumathi Ramaswamy [2003] names it), available in a vast array of rhetorical forms, renders embodied female icons especially efficacious for negotiating global modernity. Most recently, feminist scholarship on the iconographic force of Hindu right-wing female icons in South Asia (bio-icons such as Sadhavi Rithambara and Uma Bharti) has attended to their capacity to articulate hegemonic aspirations, instigating riots, brutality, and sectarian violence against religious minorities.[39] They bear out my contention that associations of South Asia with feminized figurations persist in postcolonial and neo-colonial imaginaries, lending auratic purchase to symbolically dense female icons in transnational mass media even today.

Such affixing is critical to the neoliberal initiatives that rely on structured global inequities, even as the neoliberal ethos expressed through icons seeks to close the gaps in lived experiences. One particular aspiration comes to speak for all: The world desires a Coca-Cola but will arrive at that cool refreshment already fulsomely enjoyed in the United States. It is a familiar developmental trajectory made good in affixing global icons to specific regions. In this regard, the female body that affixes South

Asia places it in the uneven cartographies of a global modernity; hence, it is equally the target of hegemonic and popular negotiations of globality. We shall see how the embodied difference of these icons work differently in each case, but here I provide a glimpse into their cartographic function through a glance at Mother Teresa: the woman from elsewhere who came to stay; the woman who soon became a hegemonic cultural shorthand for legitimizing "the West and then the rest" divide.

Mother Teresa hit transnational media networks in 1973 when she became the first Roman Catholic nun to grace the cover of *Time* magazine. Despite the dizzying proliferation of her "lives" in the mass media, she is recognized in four or five recursive iconic images. One dominant cluster enforcing perceptions of a selfless missionary who took the dispossessed into her heart, incorporated a helpless dark-skinned baby into its visual design; the combined graphic inscription quickly instituted a racialized geography of giving where the Christian missionary once more appears the benefactor to an overpopulated Third World. The famous photograph, taken by Eddie Adams in 1978 (figure 7), encapsulating the violence of the Third World in an "armless baby" (the caption framing the image), would find wide iteration across media platforms—in a stained glass window at a parish across the world (figure 8), as well as in lithographs, portraits, medallions, figurines, postage stamps, and statues too numerous to be reproduced here.[40] If we remember that Mother Teresa was lionized first in the United States as a global icon, a moment that unassailably produced Calcutta as the city of slums, then the circulation of this gendered mother-and-child inscription comes as no surprise; given the fecundity of the Mother India icon (Ramaswamy 2003), the nun could quite easily embody South Asia for the world awakened to Mother Teresa in the last gasp of the Cold War. The design of the icon therefore would beam a well-known message where the universal gift concealed the expansionist ambitions of Vatican II.

Of course, we know this hegemonic encoding has not gone uncontested in several critical reassemblages of the iconic sign. Most memorable of the exposés seeking to de-sanctify the nun is Christopher Hitchens's widely known *The Missionary Position* (1997), which is still the subject of discussion in blogs where the faithful gather,[41] despite its notoriety. Notably *Hell's Angel* (1994), a film based on the book of the same name, found no distribution outside British television venues, a censoring that speaks to the commitment to neocolonial worlding on the part of financial elites (who head the media conglomerates that would distribute such a work in the historical West). I shall have more to say

FIGURE 7 Mother Teresa with armless baby, 1978. AP Photo / Eddie Adams.

FIGURE 8 Stained-glass image of Mother Teresa, Etobicoke, Canada. Transfiguration of Our Lord Parish, Archdiocese of Toronto, Canada.

about what appears as isolated criticism of this kind, but it is important to note that lone contestations are often revived when the icon is in the midst of an epistemological crisis; as we shall see, Hitchens's exposé returned in full force during the iconocrises of Mother Teresa's beatification in 2003. At this point, we see contestations of the hegemonic message, hitherto inextricable from the icon, accumulate until they establish the historical materiality of the sign; now just a graphic inscription shorn of its hegemonic universalism, the image is reassigned to various, and sometimes wildly competing, messages. It becomes a volatile signifier potentialized in popular culture. Far from affixing the developmentally delayed South Asia, Mother Teresa in her volatile form functions as the saint who protects the heterogeneous "poor" in their own city.

The three parts of this book develop a plural materialism proper to the icon's complex and multileveled relationship to power. Part 1 of *Global Icons*, "Incorporations," traverses interdisciplinary ground to establish the icon's ontology. Chapters 1 and 2 theorize the icon as an incorporative technology, crosshatching its perceptual and affective force that, ultimately, enables subjects to move through the icon into the social. These chapters rethink conventional semiotic theories of the icon to elucidate the phenomenological experience activated by this distinctive epistemological encounter. My effort here is to theorize an embodied consumption (and therein an embodied visuality) that prepares theoretical ground for my historical pursuit of the three bio-icons in the following part of the book.

The bulky middle of the book, "Biographs," focuses on the media networks, technologies, and institutions where bio-icons surface as either ordinary commodities or volatile signifiers—in short, the material culture of icons. Four chapters perform a method for tracking global icons across multiple media platforms sans ethnography. I focus on a few public images, made in publicity (chapter 4), focalized in various formats of the life story (chapter 5), and circulated as institutionally authorized images; emerging as contested images (chapter 3), these are the intermedial templates for popular reassemblages (chapter 6). What emerges in these chapters is a biograph for each bio-icon, a temporal barometer of "multiform and occult postulate of productive activity" (de Certeau 1984, 35); its oscillations mark embattled sites where icons enable negotiations of global modernity.

Finally, the last part of the book, "Locations," returns to history: to the macro-scalar historical shifts that activate ordinary mass commodities into becoming powerful signifiers. In chapter 7, I pause on specific sites of popular consumption where historical actors stake their claims on the three bio-icons; where we witness, once more, a corporeal politics that is responsive to global modernity. In those scenes, where the potentialization of an icon discloses human agency, I return to reading runes—only this time as a precursor to large social transformations. Chapter 8 explores the social logics embodied in each bio-icon, opened to the critical gaze through the analytic categories of the outlaw, the saint, and the activist, to focus on the historical becoming theorized in the earlier parts of the book.

Historical becoming projects a collective subject, a corporeal subject of power whose signs we see everywhere in expressive popular culture—in villages such as Plachimada or Jalsindhi; in small towns such as Mirzapur or Raniganj; in metropoles such as Kolkata or Baghdad. As we hypothesize popular culture in geophysical or virtual locations, we follow the movement of signifiers across scattered media archives. Our look back gathers the temporality of the popular as it disperses to include diverse demands; it gathers icons to assemble sporadic, seemingly isolated acts into the social logics of populist reason. Only such a look explains why mundane signs become explosive phenomena.

PART 1

Incorporations

THEORIZING THE ICON AS TECHNOLOGY

Mother Teresa's beatification, Rome, 2003. Photo. Courtesy of James Hill.

One could begin simply *anywhere*. But perhaps it is best to begin in a place familiar to those who might read this book. Best to begin in the "wired world," which privileged users often mark as "global," where many of us encounter icons every day. The computer screen lights up; we point and click on a graphic inscription. It is one of the many globe-like icons, a graphic likeness to what it offers. It will open into an infinite horizon we know as "Google Earth," where we select a site. The visual fragment inaugurates a subjective itinerary: a home left behind; a friend's house; a reference someone made over dinner; a plot of land we hold in escrow. We could be, and often are, overwhelmed by the immensity of where the icon takes us; we know we cannot ever access those immensities. Yet our increasingly interconnected planetary space—too many pathways, too much territory—is instantly rendered graspable, if in infinitesimal proportion, by the glowing graphic mark.

In our age of mass production, where the producer is no longer easily located in networks of exchange, the artist is missing. It hardly matters who invented Google Earth. What matters is where it gains legibility: the site of enunciation where one recognizes the sign as shorthand legible to digitally networked users with access to personal computing, a network that excludes large swathes of the world's current population.[1] Formally resembling something greater than itself—chaos variously configured as matter, divinity, or nature—the graphic inscription we might think of as the iconic image therefore depends on convention, on one's location in a shared field of cultural reference where one recognizes it as iconic. To gaze on a material object as icon is always an epistemological encounter.

Google Earth is at some level just an everyday icon, instrumental in its capacities. But its familiarity tells us something about the iconic image, a highly condensed formal resemblance to an "original" image—in this case, our imaginary projection of the globe—rendered recognizable by its iteration. Google inscribes the globe, turning it into information; we look through it (and not at it) to enter some other place. Yet our encounter is also an embodied one, as N. Katherine Hayles notes, etching the dialectic between inscription (transmitted from site to site without friction) and incorporation (specific and instantiated sense perceptions of materiality); even in vertiginous flights across the globe, we live as materially constrained embodied subjects.[2] I shall argue that the distinction of the icon as a graphic and minimal, or unfinished, "inscription" makes it reliant on "incorporation" to complete its operations. Incomplete, incorporative forms, icons mandate the study of embodied consumption, and not simply of their production. Toward the close of the chapter, I will emphasize the logic of incorporation as fundamental to this sign, whose corporeality remains somewhat under-theorized in scholarship preoccupied with its cognitive effects. Even as we track and detect in high cognitive mode, the workaday Google Earth calls forth the sensible, both sensory and affective responses.

Google Earth hardly invites the intensity of affective response garnered by the global icons under scrutiny in this book. But the dialectic of the inscriptive and the incorporative in virtual worlds, I would argue, is as salient to bio-icons and, indeed, to all icons—even those (such as liturgical artifacts) most distant from the virtual image. In fact, scholars of religion also speak of icons as minimal inscriptions (of the divine), icon worship opening us into infinite space. If liturgical icons inaugurate an experience of (divine) alterity, when we click on Google Earth we become strangers in relation to all the vast planetary space that beckons.

We reflect on these unconscious habits only when we recognize the materiality of the iconic image—only when the familiar sign is dislodged from its regular function, revitalizing our response to it. Such a tear in the habitual can occur when the icon is deliberately re-focalized for artistic or political purposes. When another virtual icon—the @ sign—was exhibited as one of twelve everyday icons in a show at the San Francisco Museum of Modern Art (SFMOMA) from April 18 to August 5, 1997, its materiality changed because of its framing as art object. Suddenly "@" was historical. The exhibit narrated the origin of the "@," officially known as the "commercial a," as harking back to the early days of a technology that changed the world. Its author was the computer address designator Ray Tomilson, who coined the shorthand while helping to design Arpanet, the predecessor of the Internet, in 1972. In such reassembling of the iconic image in another text, the curator's blurb focalizing the @ for us, the ordinary sign became available for reinterpretation at this specific site of consumption. It became a curiosity of immense significance, a material object that had changed the world. Legitimized by its exhibition at an established institution, the @ became imbued with new cadences so that it would, on the one hand, now represent the elegance of technical prowess that makes complex systems accessible to laypersons, and on the other, enable the fetishistic consumption of a hoary past where computer technology was an eclectic pursuit.

So we begin to see the complexity of the iconic sign. We begin to intuit the formal relations that constitute it: its grammar. Moving further, now into its history, we establish our (subjective) relation to its (objective) materiality: We understand its economy, the organization of relations in dynamic processes of becoming. Central to these processes is the icon's ability to communicate, an ability properly grasped when we look more closely at the formal architecture (design, relations, logics) that governs our relationship to its history and, therefore, to its operations in the social. In short, we begin with its semiotic economy. I will argue that all icons—ranging from the seemingly disembodied virtual image to the physically tactile liturgical artifact—share a distinctive semiotic economy. While "bio-icons" are the genre I pursue here, in this chapter I assemble them taxonomically alongside other types (a diagram, a logo, a photograph) to precisely illustrate the generality of this economy drawn from semiotics.

When we turn to those who have had the most impact on the distinction of the icon as a sign type, two figures loom large: Roland Barthes, the toast of the Anglo-American academy in the heydays of poststructuralism, whose Saussurian semiology continues to inform any materialist

analysis of signs, including the present effort, and the American pragma-
tist philosopher and logician Charles Peirce, whose realist metaphysics
(which influenced intellectuals such as William James and John Dewey)
led to his dismissal by a critical theory informed by Saussurian linguis-
tics.[3] It is only in the second half of the twentieth century that art historians, film studies scholars, and new media studies scholars actively
turned back to Peirce's meditations on the graphic, pictorial, and spatial
figuration of images to recuperate the icon, and shortly we shall see why.
Together the two theorists widen the itineraries of the icon so that it
comes to represent the cultural mechanism we recognize today.

ROLAND BARTHES: THE MYTHIC LURE

Barthes brought the icon, hitherto a material object that had preoccupied
art historians, into the study of mass and popular cultures, even though
he only tangentially referred to the "iconic" message within his larger
exploration of myths (Barthes 1976). References to the icon emerge
throughout his oeuvre, but it compels investigation only because it illustrates the dangerous, yet utopian, possibilities of the optic regime in
photographs. While clearly critical of the naturalizing effects of the photograph's indexicality, in "The Rhetoric of the Image" (1964) Barthes
nevertheless ascribes a certain Edenic state to the photographic message.
Cleared of connotation, the mechanics of photography (a chemical reaction following the passing of optical rays on a real thing in the world)
guarantees the image as a trace of reality.[4]

However, Barthes underscores our grasp of the "non-coded iconic
message" alongside a "coded iconic," one that requires cultural knowledge.[5] In a famous explication of the Panzani advertisement for packaged
pastas and sauces, Barthes noted that the actual photograph of vegeta-
bles tumbling out of a string bag has a continuity with the real world that
renders it "innocent"; writing before computer-generated imagery, one
could rarely intervene in the object photographed—except by trick effects, as Barthes acknowledges. Yet the careful arrangement of the objects in the photograph's frame follows painterly conventions of still life,
imposing artifice even before we get to connotations or "the discontinuous world of symbols" (Barthes 1964, 37). The chaos of "innocence" is
thereby territorialized as art. To communicate "Italianicity" as its "message," the poster relies on cultural conventions: the knowledge of still-life
paintings and the colors—the red (tomatoes) and green (peppers)—of the
Italian flag. The danger of the objective innocence of the non-coded message, in Barthes's view, lies in its capacity to conceal the operations of this

highly conventional knowledge; the indexical charge enables artifice to masquerade as natural. Such becoming natural of the cultural presents rather fecund opportunities for justifying contingent truths as mythic or eternal ones, a recurrent problem, as we shall see, with global icons. We know that global icons communicating particular aspirations as universal ones—a red-and-white graphic signaling that Coca-Coca refreshes, Coca-Cola is for everybody—fulfill a hegemonic function. For this they rely on the stability of the "message" the icon beams telegraphically: an immediate, indisputable, and therefore natural signal whose clarity obscures the artifice of production.

Most memorably, in *Mythologies* (1957) Barthes evokes the image of a Negro saluting the French flag, a "spontaneous" and "innocent" photographic impression "tamed" to represent French imperialism by artifice (Barthes 1972, 118). The photographic image, already a sign ("a black man saluting a flag"), is emptied of its materiality when it becomes a signifier harnessed to "shapeless associations" (in this case, "a purposeful mixture of Frenchness and militariness" [Barthes 1972, 116]) to become myth—a form that "steals" speech, since now the man and the flag's materiality, their histories, no longer matter. Barthes's "Negro," an anthropomorphic figure that conceals its own history, provides a point of departure for an elaboration of the grammatical organization of the icon (its elements, design, and relations). But lest readers wonder why Barthes's analysis of photographs in the pre-digital era might still be relevant to iconic images today, perhaps a closer look at a homologous photographic impression from our post-1989 period is in order. It is a memorable image, widely circulated through mass-media networks (distributed through news agencies such as Reuters for newspapers and picked up on satellite television): the famous photograph of the Tank Man. Now the subject of an entire film,[6] the image of the lone man facing down tanks in Tiananmen Square, captured by Jeffrey Widener of the Associated Press in 1989 (figure 9), is well worth scrutinizing, if only for the stability of the message it is *still* capable of transmitting—a message that participates unequivocally in worlding, in conjuring a shared globality defined by the human drive for freedom.

As the graphic mark of the tiny figure saw iterations in mass-media traffic, Wang Weilin (the citizen thought to be the Tank Man) became an icon. The graphic likeness to human form that made up the core element of the icon's design incorporated a concept (human defiance) that produced surplus value, yet it unmistakably acquired this cadence from an ex-corporated object we might commonly think of as a prop: the tank

FIGURE 9 The Tank Man, June 1989. AP Photo/Jeffrey Widener.

(signifying the totalitarian state). Together, the recursive mark of man and tank naturalized a culturally particular aspiration (the demand for political rights from a regime that had lost its revolutionary horizons) into a universal human condition (everyone wants democracy). As the image circulated, man and tank were incorporated into each other in the grammatical sense, the linguistic union of two parts of speech, but also in spatial connotation. (When the term "incorporation" entered the English language in 1398, it described spatial relations.) Man and tank, black soldier and flag, or Mother Teresa and little brown baby illustrate how elements of the iconic sign are incorporated into each other, yoked in syntagm so that together they become graphic shorthand.

Part of the Tank Man's lure derives from the enduring promise of the news photo. Despite computer-generated images, the news photo is still largely considered indexical: The graphic impression of the tiny figure in the photograph's left-hand corner confronting diagonally placed tanks extending into the shot's depth of field first and foremost had a reality effect as a shocked world looked on, hungry for trickles of news from China. The thrilling narrative of how the photograph was smuggled out of China we find in Charles Cole's sensational account (in the *Frontline* documentary on the Tank Man) would lend the news photo an extreme indexical charge of the real. At one level, the photographic capture of the Tank Man is simply a graphic inscription indexical in its operations: The image refers back to an original image consumers imagine the photographer once encountered.[7] Such a movement back to the image's ground of representation, evoking an "original" image projected on the consumer's imaginary—the sense of being present in Tiananmen Square—is a distinctive quality of the iconic sign. The material sign opens, aperture-like, into its recessed ground of representation.

This is why I characterize the iconic signs as *apertures*. Generally, the "aperture" is the opening in an optical system that determines how a bundle of rays might alight on the image plane. Obviously, my choice of the term is governed by the concept's materiality as physical apparatus: Just as apertures change with technological development, icons materialize in different forms (liturgical support to virtual image) with evolving media technologies. Whether the icon is made in publicity or in the labor of personal adoration, it is a physically expressive sign, incorporating as its quality sensations circling between subject and object and calling forth a decorative eye.[8] Here, aperture intimates the sensory dimension of the encounter relevant to the corporeal dynamism of the global icons in question. Aperture is further appropriate to a graphic inscription like the icon, which relies on an epistemology of looks—that is, even as the icon stimulates synaesthesia, "seeing" remains the privileged sense perception in encountering icons, in an organization of the general experience I shall unpack in greater detail in the next chapter. Since any change in the aperture can fundamentally alter the image projected, apertures are inherently unstable, just like the volatilized icon. Hence, the physicality of the aperture underscores the historical materiality of the icon and the look, the object and its regimes, developed in this book.

The aperture returns us to the Barthesian anxiety over the indexical image. Since the index ambiguously points to its ground of representation (the bullet hole intimates that a murder has taken place), a nuance Peirce extensively develops, we can think of icon consumption as a movement back into a there—the ever receding ground of history. At its most fetishistic, such a "ground"—the reach toward the material relations constitutive of the historical image—is contained, symbolically anchored by a horizon of common good where all historical differences disappear. This is the work of the icon as myth, in Barthes's cautionary tale, its operation as a hegemonic form that conceals its ground of representation and shores up a universal common horizon (everyone wants democracy). At such moments, the consumer luxuriates in the promise of the universal, indulging in the famed passivity of mass consumption. But when this hegemonic form is contested, its conceit laying bare the interests of the few, we open

into the sign's recessed ground; we see it as a historical image, a hegemonic construction limited by its materiality that is hardly universal or
eternal. Hence, the symbolic values it once embodied are rendered historical: They belong to an elsewhere to which we are connected as we "enter"
the sign. In such fissure, the consumer refers back to something beyond
the graphic inscription—perhaps those shadowy forces that define our
materiality. The iconic sign functions as an incorporative mechanism for
moving the historical subject toward its social other.

The moving "elsewhere" gestures to circulation, which, I have argued,
is key to the icon, a graphic inscription that is repeated in order to be
recognizable as shorthand for that "original" image. This is not to suggest that we can, post-Derrida, stabilize one origin for an iconic image.
Rather, the look backward must be understood as a desire to recapture
the original image (what the image maker encountered) and to move
beyond it to its ground of representation (what really happened). Such a
desire may be heightened at specific historical moments, as we see in the
case of the Tank Man.

With the Tank Man, we see an image become iconic sign when it incorporates certain qualities as its natural core "properties." Where semiotics point to "properties" as the naturalized connotations crystallized
into the sign, art-historical and philosophical theories of synaesthesia
characterize "properties" as the qualities of the art object. Sensations
flowing between subject and object, they variously argue, appear to belong to the object as its distinctive quality: You smile at me, but despite
the exchange of sensations, *you* have the lovely smile. In the recursive
sign such as the icon, pre-experienced sensations appear expressive in the
object as its qualities. In Barthes's "black man saluting a French flag," the
viewer's pre-experienced sensations—organized affections expressed as
rousing patriotic fervor—would appear as qualities of the image, folded
into its lines, color, and depth. Hence, the de-historicized "black man"
assembled with the eternal French flag would come to embody, yet again,
the natural properties of patriotic loyalty. This corporeal materiality of
the sign, transcribing the "properties" of the image as both fossilized,
"naturalized" connotations (at the level of signification) and sensation
(at the level of embodied experience) explains why such a cultural shorthand might exert such intense allure. We shall return to the organization
of sensations into affections more substantially in the next chapter, but
here I refer to this double sense of the sign's "properties" to underscore
icons as sensuous media, whose capacity to allure cannot be fully grasped
by tangential references to emotion alone.

If we continue with the icon's semiotic economy, the Barthesian reading illuminates an important process in icon semiosis—the condensation of connotations, or "shapeless associations" as Barthes names them, around a graphic inscription. Condensation ensures a gradual sedimentation of connotations into the sign, an incorporation that engineers a symbolic density. So the Tank Man evokes a frisson of admiration for his heroic defiance, perceived as a manifestation of human will. When audiences first encountered the Tank Man, they encountered the image in (legitimizing) media networks: a "news story" in the *New York Times*, a segment on CNN. And they encountered it focalized in texts that gave it connotative meanings. What was once syntagmatically proposed—if one man could stare down the tanks, surely he exhibited exemplary defiance?—condensed into an adjectivally incorporated quality of the image. The inductive logic of the story would affect such closure. When such a nested image was assembled again and again to communicate the same message, the connotations began to stick, imparting accretive symbolic density to the sign. Predictably, the historical aspirations expressed in those connotations (individualist opposition to totalitarian power) began to assume the shades of natural ones.

Focalized in the first news stories to represent a "natural" human quality, human defiance against great odds, the Tank Man became an instant iconic sign invested with dangerous capacity to conceal a culturally particular hegemonic aspiration (the demand for civil rights) as a universal one. Such deception, which gains power from the imagined link between the iconic image and its original referent, is, of course, the most troubling propensity of the iconic sign. A historically significant news photo such as this can stabilize an ideologically potent message because it is legitimized and disseminated in mass-media networks often insistent on their journalistic objectivity (staging nomenclatures of transparency and balance within news coverage), even as they are controlled by financial and political elites. The recent withdrawing of servers for Wikileaks only further testifies to the political control of networks.[9] The photographic impression of the Tank Man immediately became an iconic image because of China's location in the political imaginary of the United States. Functioning as an iconic sign, the Tank Man embodied a human trait (defiance) that marked him as ordinary, just like us, but he embodied it in such excellent proportion that his act of defiance appeared as exemplary, extraordinary—not quite like us. As we shall see, bio-icons often straddle this ordinary-extraordinary contradiction in their pedagogic functions when they appear to act on our behalf against the hegemon. In his cartographic affixation, the Tank Man would function as a geo-body for China's failed political system; in the face of tanks, the private citizen would aspire to what the West had already achieved. Stuck in the waiting room of history, the Chinese man, embodying racial difference in constant ekphrastic descriptions of the slight man, would affirm the geopolitical unevenness necessary for neoliberalism's vision of progress.

And so the desire for democratic representation now signaled a basic human will to freedom, the iconic sign formalizing the imperial American spread of (electoral) democracy. Hence, the Tank Man is rarely read as propaganda for a culturally localized vision of what democracy looks like; instead, it signifies general human aspiration. After all, the Tank Man was hardly iconic in China at the moment of his iconic rise in the United States. Reporters in China underscored the invisibility of the Tank Man's media traces in China, given government suppression of news; some bewailed the absence of the iconic image while others scorned his celebration in the historical "West." The man representative of China, in other words, was hardly known to (mainland) Chinese publics. Clearly, Wang Weilin was more iconic to the watching world and diasporic Chinese than to the national public—an articulation of the former's desires to "know" the real China condensed in this unique sign.[10]

If the Tank Man exemplifies the motivated sign, estranging us from concrete life worlds, it is because of its universalizing message (everyone loves democracy). As representative of all humanity, the lone figure stabilizes the syntagm of the message. But the Barthesian scheme does not elaborate (an important step in) how the message stabilizes, the inductive mechanisms necessary for linking the image to its connotations. Here a wider genealogy of the icon, one to which I will return later in the book, provides answers. The connotative matrix imparting symbolic density to the icon is garnered through widely circulating stories, the image narrated to inductively incorporate core associations that, over time, come to stay as its natural properties. For "bio-icons," such induction through narration is more pronounced, their "lives" told and retold for instruction; exemplary prototypes, they are often deployed as pedagogy. Hence, outpourings of biographical fragments (biographies, gossip, anecdote, legend, or lore) habitually accompany icons whose message wavers; in the allegations, refutations, and revisions, a wildly oscillating biograph can dislodge the image from its hegemonic encoding. Abundant and contradictory attempts at focalizing the iconic image engender an epistemological crisis that accompanies the potentialization of the iconic image.

The stories focalizing the photographic image were the first to anchor the connotations of defiance that became a part of Tank Man's core iconic image, much in the same way we see nativity tales, hagiographies, legends, or epics focalizing the exemplarity of a liturgical icon. In their unfolding, the news stories of the Tank Man directly or indirectly consolidated a "message" about democratic potentialities, as viewers worldwide watched a lone figure momentarily transcending self-interest in service of a collective dream. In a famous tribute to the Tank Man that appeared in *Time* soon after the event, Pico Iyer (1989) eulogized the act of defiance: "Almost certainly he was seen in his moment of self-transcendence by more people than ever laid eyes on Winston Churchill, Albert Einstein and James Joyce combined." The core image of the Tank Man began to solidify when such a message, originating in mass-media traffic from the United States, was repeated across media platforms circulating in networks with transnational reach. In its iteration, the iconic image gained a density so solid and deep that the core symbolic codes could remain stable even when the image was cut, pasted, remixed in other texts (news stories, artwork, cartoons, or films) in attempts to resignify it. It would always carry within it the indexical force of a news photo of historical significance. I characterize the iconic sign as accretive to underscore its architecture, the loose clustering of peripheral connotations around a few, often unchanging, core properties; throughout this book, the icon with strong core properties are described as highly "sedimented" signs, replete with accretions or core symbolic meanings that stick to them like residue. The Tank Man's residual core was so strong that, despite all efforts to reassemble the image, to interfere with its symbolic coding, when the same photo was printed in *Life* magazine's popular archive "100 Photos That Changed the World" in 2003 anchored to the classic hegemonic message—everyone wants democracy—no one was surprised. And so the Tank Man fossilized into legacy.[11]

I have noted how such stable messages, solidifying because they can circulate widely, serve the interests of political and financial elites who control transnational mass-media networks, even as newsworthy information bits are reassembled, and therefore repurposed, in competing news platforms (consider Jon Stewart's repurposing of CNN news clips every night on Comedy Central). The broadcast mass media's capacity to reiterate the same image so widely and instantly speeds up the processes of mythification: network news, for instance, repeats the same footage as sound bites to quickly solidify the core properties of an image and to establish the syntagm of its message. Harnessed to a crystallized message, an iconic image can become dangerously mythic; it can naturalize the message that transforms it into myth. The Tank Man would reassure the United States of its geopolitical status as the "leader of the free world" by signaling a universal democratic need to "speak," the universal need for civil society.

Myths are comfortable; they reassure. They encourage passive consumption in habitual encounters that cause little discomfort. But when we come across icons that attract a great deal of affective intensity of the sort I shall track in the mass-media biographs (part 2), we might assume that the message communicated through the iconic sign is highly contested. One might think it is only in the esoteric modernist gesture—framing and hanging "@" at the SFMOMA—that the familiar iconic image is unlinked from its function, changing the iconic message. The "@" becomes art, rendered historical in its reassemblage as installation. Beyond such individual performances, however, weighty iconic signs can become raw material for popular culture—and these are the expressive performances that most concern us here.

SIGNS TO PHENOMENA

The Tank Man, for one, came to have many avatars beyond his first appearances in 1989. Some of these retained the well-known stable iconic message of individual defiance as the symptom of a desire for democracy, as we see in songs that mobilize the figure from heavy metal bands such as Anthrax and Skinny Puppy. Others challenged the message re-focalizing Wang Weilin by giving him a singular biography in a novel or a play (a notable example is Stephen Coonts's novel *Hong Kong* [2001]). One memorable reassembling of the Tank Man in mass media, one that assesses the Tank Man's individualism with irony, was an episode of *The Simpsons* that aired on March 13, 2005—long past the wounds of Tiananmen. There the televisual episode substituted parts of the iconic image while retaining its major formal elements—a figure (turned away from us) facing tanks (turned toward us). In the place of the Tank Man, Selma, Marge Simpson's older sister, appeared, confronting the duplicitous tank-driving Madame Wu from an adoption agency (the symbol of the dreaded Chinese state) who attempted to thwart her well-meaning efforts to adopt a Chinese baby (figure 10).[12]

The comedic presence of Selma not only criticized the politics of adoption, it further undercut the lone anonymity of the Tank Man, since her "act of defiance" was neither extraordinary in its ethical reach nor universal in its humanity. A deeply self-interested mother performing selflessness, a middle-class American performing righteous largesse, Selma's

FIGURE 10 Still from "Goo Goo Gai Pan," *The Simpsons*, March 13, 2005.

menopausal drive for a baby, the show's ironic rubric suggested, took on
the hues of a culturally particular ideological view of China—a China
"opening up" but not quite fully, not enough. Far from representing the
will of the people, Selma's unassailably bourgeois whims cut to the heart
of the Tank Man as an ideological projection, an iconic image that had
come to present a specific vision of democracy as individualism that
is more important to Americans than to the Chinese whose "will" he
seemed to embody.

Of course, I am not suggesting that *The Simpsons* revamped the Tank
Man's iconicity. After all, his exemplarity was never in question. Yet the
show's insertion of a situated gaze that codes the iconic image just so, the
act of coding reflexively underlined in Selma's artifactual (cartoon) form,
dislodged the message from its reach into an authentic moment, since
viewers knew clearly Selma had never stepped foot in Tiananmen. The
revision of the message attached to the Tank Man—everyone wants (the
same kind of) democracy—loosened the tie of image to message, dislodging the connotations condensed around it. Through Selma's form turned
away from us, we rethink why the Tank Man came to symbolize what he
did; we see its material history in reflective gaze through the aperture of
the unanchored iconic image.

Such renegotiation in a single (widely broadcast) television show—cutting, pasting, remixing, and thereby freeing the iconic image from its social constraints—might not have a lasting effect. "Goo Goo Gai Pan" did not revise the Tank Man's legacy. So these performances are substantially different from frequent reassemblages that seek to replace the existing message with another in an effort to re-territorialize the iconic image in the name of the popular. Such insistence inevitably wrests a response from those who are most invested in the (now destabilized) message, their reactions often capturing media attention. We see such eruption in mass media with the lawsuit against reassembling the Coca-Cola logo that I touched on earlier. It is worth turning to the case at greater length here to consider exactly how performative resignification works at the level of the icon's grammar.

If icons are generally imbued with accretive symbolic density, there is heightened semantic condensation where gigantic icons such as Coca-Cola are concerned—and especially, for our purposes, given its hoary history in India. The drink that was "expelled" from Indian markets in 1977 was ceremoniously welcomed back in 1997 as the nation embarked on a consumption-led path to national prosperity (following trade liberalization in 1991).[13] In the years that followed, the company invested $1 billion in its forty-nine plants in India.[14] The logo had long signified consumer bliss during the austere period of Nehruvian protectionism. Yet its "return," signaling the consumer revolution, has not gone uncontested. One might say its status as the iconic consumer good has positioned Coca-Cola signs as prime targets in struggles against the privatization of natural resources that are erupting all over India, and especially in wars over water, as one-third of India's villages currently face daily shortages.[15] The experience of living under unregulated resource extraction, a feature of the neoliberal restructuring of the Indian economy, turned the long-familiar face of global capital historical. Coca-Cola's embodiment of the neoliberal ethos (Coke is for everybody, Coke improves standards of living for all) would spur reassemblages of the logo one might retroactively read as expressive popular culture.

The most famous of the anti-Coca-Cola struggles erupted in Plachimada, a remote village in Kerala State in southern India that mostly produces rice.[16] Plachimada soon saw contaminated groundwater (destroying crops) and dry wells when the Coca-Cola Company opened a large factory in March 2000 with a conditional license from the Panchayat (elected village council). When the company started to illegally extract millions of liters of clean water, the water level fell from 150 feet to 500 feet below the earth's surface, affecting water storage and supply. The recent documentary *1000 Days and a Dream* (2007) records the struggle against the corporate giant, which has involved village governing bodies, state courts, environmental and anti-globalization activists, political parties, and nongovernmental organizations, after a small group of resolute nonviolent protestors took their demand for water to the factory gates in 2002. The protests began with several incidents one might consider sporadic until one reads them retrospectively as part of a greater social demand for common resources.

What concern us here are the performative desecrations of the Coca-Cola signs in the village to express protest. The social antagonism of resignification registered in mass media (print and television news before it entered the "blogosphere") when Coca-Cola sued the celebrity photographer Sharad Haksar for trademark infringement. Coca-Cola had been a client of Haksar's advertising firm, and Haksar—for those who know his ads for food, fashion, and cars—was hardly an activist photographer.[17] Moreover, company officials had actually seen the offending photograph three months before raising the sudden cry of infringement. Therefore, the allegations should be understood as Coca-Cola's response to its weakened credibility at Plachimada—and Haksar made note of this in his surprised response to the lawsuit. Given Haksar's credentials as a prize-winning photographer, the incident quickly became national news. As journalists probed further, other unsavory details of Coca-Cola's response to Plachimada emerged, fueling media interest. National newspapers rushed to report that Coca-Cola had gone to some lengths to muzzle the press before the Haksar suit: It had slapped a fifty-lakh rupee ($1,000) defamation suit against a regional newspaper, *Mathrubhumi*, which had covered the anti-Coca-Cola campaign for quite a while.[18] For the media theorist, it is at the moment Coca-Cola cries foul that one spots the slow annexation of the mass media logo in the expressive popular culture of Plachimada; unable to litigate against temporary daily performances, Coca-Cola chose a well-known adversary to take back its logo.

Such controversies provide a point of departure for tracking the itinerary of global icons. Media events such as the lawsuit register in mass media when the frequencies of the icon's trace increase exponentially; if these traces exhibit wildly competing messages, we witness the icon's epistemological crisis and, sometimes, its subsequent emergence as volatilized signifier. It is when icons turn volatile—when they erupt in media events such as lawsuits, happenings that provoke police responses, violent agitation, televised staged spectacles, disruptive "mobs," and so on—

that we notice them anew. In this case, the eruption is the contretemps over an evocative photograph beamed on a billboard to tourists, professionals, and businessmen lodged at the ritzy Taj Coromandel hotel nearby on Nungambakkam High Road in Chennai.[19] But how do we read these eruptions as "runes" of the popular?[20] What kind of divination do they command?

When we read the icon as a reassemblage, retroactively we are able to track its circulation in popular culture. For if we trace the back story of the billboard controversy, we find that the pots that the women placed before the Coca-Cola sign in mute protest endure. Early in the protests, the women at the *dharna* assembled their plastic pots in mute performance of water scarcity; the repetition of such semiotic activity turned an ordinary gesture into the kind of expressive ritual we attribute to popular culture. At the level of expressive culture, the recursive water pot placed in front of Coca-Cola hoardings began to scramble the mass-media icon, and these semiotic acts were carefully archived in news photos and documentary footage (e.g., 1000 *Days and a Dream*, *Bitter Drink, Source of Life*). In these accounts, the pot recurs, always dry, always empty, but it takes different forms, from everyday plastic to (rudimentary or decorated) earthenware. Only the external adversary embodied by the Coca-Cola logo remains stable. We can surmise a plurality of demands at work in the variation of the pots we find in the footage on rallies: For environmentalists, only the traditional biodegradable version will do; for the householders, plastic suffices; for artists and students, the decoration of the pots represent routine aesthetics. By the time we get to the saturated hues of the Haksar billboard (figure 11), the brightly colored pots stark against the yawning Coca-Cola icon have become paradigmatic, and we have learned to hear what they communicate in these daily performances.

Coca-Cola still has the core properties of the iconic sign—it represents an improved standard of living. But this message is disrupted when the bright, cheap, empty plastic pots annex the sign to their fallen state. When its most stable significations—Coke refreshes—are contested, the connotative matrix crumbles, and a riotous polysemy ensues: If Coca-Cola was once for the whole world, now it brings ruin to remote Plachimada; if it knew no season, in Plachimada it spells drought; if it was once sexy, in Plachimada it destroys all life instincts. Every time the pots are yoked to the sign, Coca-Cola symbolizes these life-destroying forces. Every time the stability of its connotative matrix is disturbed, releasing attachments to condensed valences, the icon generates high affect (anger, loss, grief).

FIGURE 11 Sharad Haksar's "Thirsty" billboard, Chennai, 2004. Agence France-Press
Photo/Stringer, Getty Images.

Such reassembled icons surfacing in media events function as "runes"
demanding divination; they propel us back to where it all began—or, at
least, to where we can divine the first demand, singular and isolated.
Tracing the circulation of the reassembled icon (pots yoked to logo), as
well as its frequencies, intensities, and the duration of its deformations,
one can lay bare the social antagonisms at play through establishing
contiguities between media traces—between billboards, photograph,
vigils, actors, rallies. The reassembled icon, no longer appearing as its
culturally familiar avatar, offers a clue to (rather than evidence of) the
popular. It demands that we decode the billboard's visual design, where
empty plastic pots (metonymically representative of a disappearing water table) offer mute protest. Our historical investigation mandates a
media literacy capable of disaggregating complex semiotic arrangements
that cut, paste, and reassemble mass-media signs (advertisements, in
this case). Moreover, methodologically we are compelled to organize a
temporality of signs. Not only the frequency of the trace, but also its
duration, becomes critical to the exercise. The plastic pots yoked to the
logo endure, after all, stubbornly cropping up every time one "looks" for
the back story of the controversial lawsuit. Their endurance tells us that
this is not isolated performance but a repeated gesture that has become

expressive over time; we have chanced on the political theater of the popular. By the time we get to the plastic pots in the Haksar photograph, they are concretely yoked to Plachimada (anchored through written and oral commentaries) and metonymic of water scarcity in southern India (where plastic pots prevail).[21] Our retrospective gaze constructs a temporal arc for the popular, a chain of growing demands that led an influential multinational to flex its hegemonic muscles.

The popular performances at Plachimada relocate Coca-Cola as a hegemonic other from elsewhere. Coca-Cola begins to refer back to something beyond the graphic inscription: to shadowy forms marked as "global," ever receding from the image, death dealing in its effects on the village. Coca-Cola acquires aura, a touch of the infinite, galvanizing the psychic structures of veneration necessary for desecration (or "defacement," following Michael Taussig).[22] Dislodged from the bonds of its most stable message, the iconic sign disintegrates, and the iconic image is potentialized in such popular consumption.

Rather than recognizing the social through the abstraction of critical distance, the corporeal dynamism of the icon affords another mode of perception: a movement of a subject toward other subjects through the force of sensations. In the Plachimada Coke-pots performance we have been following so far, one apprehends not just costs accruing to one's own body but costs that accrue to the social bodies of others—those who placed their pots in front of the sign. In a struggle where the corporeal existence of the body is at risk, such sensuous linkage provides a phenomenological grasp of collective scarcity. We shall turn to the sensorium more fully in the next chapter, but here, as we complete the grammar of the icon, perhaps a look at a bio-icon is in order to move smoothly into the social force of the public figures discussed in the bulk of the book. (In many respects, the book makes a case for the endurance of anthropomorphic attachments to technologies of the popular alongside the proliferation of post-human collective assemblages.) If Coca-Cola can activate the sensorium, the possibilities grow exponentially with bio-icons, the anthropomorphic image of one *just like us* but also deeply other.

For bio-icons, the signifier attaches to an imaginary: Through these anthropomorphic apertures, we "see" an imagined likeness embodying both exemplarity and frailty. In liturgical practice, where the icon is a material image referring back to the divine, the anthropomorphic likeness is regarded as the most excellent form of the icon: saints, leaders, heroes, and all manner of exemplary persons, embodying the best of human qualities, interceding with the divine on our behalf. Through them, incorporated into them, we move toward an "original" image, vibrant in popular cultural heroic figurations whose spark resides in the exemplary bio-icon. When we recast our desire for the Other (for the divine sought in the prototype) in terms of social imaginaries, we stumble on a series of intercessionaries who act on our behalf—for us, and with us. Highly corporeal bio-icons, such as Gandhi, disturb the distance of perceived exemplarity; caught in a force field of sensations, they establish material contiguity with the subject. For South Asia, Gandhi occupies such a place: always exemplary, always seen to act for the common man against hegemonic regimes. He embodies a heterogeneous common rather than a social totality, although he is often reappropriated for the latter purpose. We shall return to repurposing later, but Gandhi is important here because indisputably all bio-icons affixed to South Asia fall under his shadow.

Indeed, if this were an iconographic study, one that traced the semantic relations between icons as signs within a localized field, I would linger a while with Gandhi. But as it stands, this is not a taxonomic work. And yet . . . Gandhi's biograph as a global icon (a transmedial figure delivered across mass-media platforms) is of considerable value to any scholar preoccupied with the communicative capacities of the icon.[23] Gandhi was ever an aperture for a transnational public to envision a world to come, as early ruminations on the sign make clear. The most famous early reflection came from the French writer Romain Rolland, in the essay from 1923 that made him famous. "Did he bring, in the folds of his sackcloth, the word which would free us from the murders to come[?]" (as quoted in Markovits 2004, 17), Rolland asked, questioning the late European empires hotly contested all over the world. He would set in motion an iconic sign that would find public consecration in Richard Attenborough's film *Gandhi* (1982).[24] More important, Gandhi is one of the most corporealized bio-icons we know: His "imagery" is "heavily embedded in physicality"; his body was photographed a thousand times in life and death, inspiring the likes of Henri Cartier-Bresson and Margaret Bourke-White; his meditations have produced theories of the body, with his own as effective political theater (Markovits 2004, 13). Hence, he moves us to think of synaesthetic encounters with icons in more sophisticated ways.

If one were to look for a mythic transmedial iconic image of Gandhi in the contemporary period, Apple's "Think Different" campaign (delivered in television commercials, in print advertisements, on billboards, and on posters) provides a noteworthy instance (see figure 12).[25] Not only was this a widely circulated image, but it also prompted much debate. Most

FIGURE 12   Billboard of Apple's "Think Different" campaign, 1997. Apple Computer, Inc.

notably, Salman Rushdie's short evocative piece, "Gandhi Now," pondered the irony of using Gandhi's image to promote a techno-consumerism that is so deeply alien to the philosophy that made him famous. For its part, Apple reassembled the photograph Margaret Bourke-White took in 1946 of Gandhi spinning while under house arrest, emptying the history of the photographic impression to yoke it to other connotations: of the creativity, of the fiercely individualistic innovation, of the daring of the "forty crazy ones"; the iconic image interpellated transnational consumers to constitute themselves as an alternative (Apple-loving) public through their relationship to Gandhi.[26]

Since Gandhi is a highly auratized iconic image, Apple's use of the icon became notorious for plunging a sacred object into an overtly commercial exchange. After all, computers aside, one could buy the collectible "Think Different" Gandhi poster online for $250. The image is iconic (even if digitally enhanced) in its recursive inscription of a familiar face—the large ears; bald scalp; thin, naked torso; and gold-rimmed glasses. Also iconic is its connotative matrix: To be like Gandhi is to strike out on one's own, on one's own terms. The bright little logo in the top right-hand corner is an added compositional feature harnessing the iconic sign for an alteration in the message: To purchase Apple is to be like Gandhi, a David against the (PC) Goliath. The historical ideology of techno-consumerism is articulated as universal desire through a global icon.

To refute the message, Rushdie re-narrated the exemplary life, albeit in fragments, to resignify the bio-icon. Beginning with an ekphrastic description of the figure in the Apple advertisement, defacing in its unblinking realism, Rushdie describes Gandhi as a thin man with "bad teeth" and "eyeglasses" (Rushdie 2002, 167). Such defacement serves to dislodge the iconic image from its syntagmatic relations in the iconic message beamed by the Apple composition. In doing so, Rushdie reassembles the iconic image, anchoring it through a set of witty vignettes to another message in which Gandhi is a complex and intelligent figure, not a pious saint or an uncompromising individualist. The "lesson" Gandhi conveys as a man of his times, in Rushdie's estimation, is how to survive intelligently in this world, to survive in history with a sense of history: "Gandhi, who gave up cosmopolitanism to gain a country, has become, in his strange afterlife, a citizen of the world. His spirit may yet prove resilient, smart, tough, sneaky, and—yes—ethical enough to avoid assimilation by global McCulture (and Mac culture, too). Against this new empire, Gandhian intelligence is a better weapon than Gandhian piety" (Rushdie 2002, 170). Through the inductive logic of his story, Rushdie refocalizes the iconic message of the advertisement, but not to reiterate the old mantra of Saint Gandhi. Rather, he incorporates the iconic image into a newer connotative matrix, in which Gandhi embodies other human traits and is markedly the ordinary man. The change in the iconic message therefore reinvests the iconic image with a different symbolic resonance; a new or an altered iconic sign emerges that, if reiterated, could solidify as an alternative to the already existing one.

In the case of Coca-Cola, historical contingency governs where and when an iconic sign might be mobilized as semiotic material for reassemblage. With a bio-icon of political heft such as Gandhi, one might say the sign is always available as raw semiotic material for expressive reassemblage. Arguably, Gandhi never quite lost his aura even in the mass production of his commodity image. We see this in posters at antiwar rallies (the "Everyday Gandhis" in Santa Barbara), for instance, where the iconic sign is an aperture into forging community. His image gathers a public in its site of enunciation. More significantly, the iconic apostle of peace is a less embattled figure outside South Asia, retaining his capacity to inspire through narratives of an exemplary life. The most famous reassemblage of this iconic sign in the United States is in Martin Luther King Jr.'s focalization of the iconic image in "Letter in the Birmingham Jail," anchoring it to the message of an efficacious "passive resistance" (or *satyagraha*, as Gandhi preferred to call it). South Africa, Gandhi's political crucible, is the other location outside South Asia where this bio-icon has had multiple lives, Albert Luthuli reassembling the icon for the anti-apartheid movement (Markovits 2004, 65).[27] But in South Asia, Gandhi is constantly "made" and "unmade," the wildly oscillating biograph turning his iconic message unstable, contested; the iconic image seems in perpetual epistemological crisis, with no one signification stable enough to rest easily.

In the sixty-year post-independence period, Gandhi's aura has suffered in South Asia because of his fossilization as a piously moral ideal. While it would be impossible to capture the major shifts in his iconic image in this period, a very short summary of the macro-scalar shifts that affected it might run something like this: The coming of partition, and the critique of Nehru (regarded as Gandhi's protégé) in the decades following independence, cast shadows on Gandhi's legacy. Hindu middle classes, desperate to retain their class status in the democratic polity, accused Gandhi of being a weak leader who sold out Hindus at partition, while heterogeneous Muslim and Dalit communities criticized Gandhi's promulgation of Brahmanical (high-caste) Hindu philosophical doctrines as appropriate for all Indians. Given the changefulness of the symbolic coding of the iconic image, Gandhi became the quintessential volatile icon, always attracting high affect, inviting adoration and desecration. In opposition to the Gandhi harnessed in state projects, we have seen in the post-independence years endless attempts to reassemble the sign in mass culture. I pause on one in which the refocalization of the image would prompt expressive performances of "Gandhigiri," or Gandhian action within India.

Rajkumar Hirani's *Lage Raho Munna Bhai* (Carry on Munna Bhai; 2006) —the third-highest-grossing Bollywood film of the twenty-first century— was one riotous attempt to re-auratize Gandhi. In *Lage Raho*, a sequel to *Munna Bhai M.B.B.S.* (2003), which featured the goodhearted goon Munna Bhai and his loyal sidekick, the main character tries to read up on Gandhi to impress a girl and begins to hallucinate the Mahatma as a person in the "real" world. Munna Bhai, a streetwise and often violent goon, is horrified at the conduct the spectral Gandhi expects of him—offering flowers to voracious real-estate developers, treating corrupt bureaucrats with courtesy—but he decides to follow the strictures to win the girl. On the way, he realizes that Gandhi's way, nicknamed "Gandhigiri (Doin' it like Gandhi)," is actually savvy, realistic, and often effective in situations in which he would normally use brute force. Delightfully tongue-in-cheek and resolutely impious, *Lage Raho Munna Bhai* features a comic actor from the Marathi stage as Gandhi whose makeup and costume imitate calendar-art versions of a ruddy Gandhi. Gandhi in the film, in other words, is literally an iconic image stepped out of the assembled text: the calendar hanging in the dusty library where Munna Bhai goes to look up Gandhi and falls asleep. The calendar image familiar to Indians on a daily basis reappears in the embodied form of the star; intermedial, it carries with it a quotidian kitsch. The hilarity of the hallucination effectively undercuts the extreme piety of the official icon, enabling audiences to revisit the iconic image with its pedagogy of nonviolence; hence, *Lage Raho*'s droll tone attempts to replace the preachy moralism taught at schools with a Gandhism that is simply canny pragmatism in a dog-eat-dog world. While the film obviously establishes psychological realism to ground the ghost in the excessively disenchanted urban space of contemporary Mumbai, for our purposes the film effectively illustrates the process of dislodging the iconic image to re-auratize it.

When Gandhi first appears to Munna Bhai, the goon is impatient, dismissive of Gandhian conduct in a lawless and uncivil Mumbai. He repeatedly questions the universalizing logic of nonviolence that attaches to the iconic image. Rendered volatile by such irreverence and freed from his dull pious message, the friendly, practical, and fatherly Gandhi brings idealism into Munna Bhai's turbulent milieu of real-estate frauds, drug dealers, and trigger-happy mafia.

The poster for the film (figure 13) records the semiotic process involved in icon consumption by presenting the iconic image of Gandhi as the formal reiteration of a graphic inscription (bald head, looped glasses, cloth-clad shoulder) recognizable to many audiences, despite the lightness of the stroke. The strokes glow, literalizing the aura, an always present potentiality in the form of a specter (as Derrida tells us in *Specters of Marx* [1994]). The ethical possibilities prompted by encountering specters, albeit in comic form, is presented through the inductive logic of the film. As Munna Bhai begins to venerate Gandhi, to see his value in quotidian life, the goon inadvertently learns a lesson in ethics as an effective ground for politics. His Gandhigiri leads him to stand up to corrupt real-estate developers or to shame corrupt hospital staff into offering care. Most important, perhaps, the events that followed the release of the film bear out my contention that we must think the icon beyond the sign whose grammar we have industriously explicated so far—indeed, beyond representation. Rather, when an icon motivates social actions whose effects erupt in mass media, the sign can become a social phenomenon. For after its release, *Lage Raho* galvanized "Gandhigiri" all over India: Lawyers offered flowers to corrupt judges; farmers in the Vidarbha region protested with flowers;[28] and demonstrators in Lucknow adopted showers of roses as the expressive popular culture of Gandhism.[29] Almost sixty years after independence, the smiling, ruddy

FIGURE 13 DVD cover of Lage Raho Munna Bhai, 2006. Vidhu Vinod Chopra Films.

Gandhi hanging on the walls of schools, libraries, and police stations hit a collective nerve. What was it about this film that could motivate a return to Gandhi, one might ask, past the aesthetic and commercial success of the film and its massive circulation?

One would have to look at what the graphic inscription of Gandhi incorporates to find an answer—to look at the devotee incorporated into the prophet, the immensely corporealized Munna Bhai played by the blustering, heavily muscular Sanjay Dutt, who sweats, lumbers, and bludgeons his way through the story. The actor himself is rather iconic, his star image anchored by a complex star text. Jailed for running guns and drug abuse for long periods, Dutt is indexically a "bad boy" in addition to being the son of Nargis, the star who came to embody "Mother India" in Mehboob Khan's classic film *Mother India* (1957). Dutt is not glamorous, but he has the muscularity of the angry young man figure set in motion by mega-star Amitabh Bachchan's star body. With an overly muscular body made for harsh urban survival, Dutt incorporates the streets of Mumbai into his form: Scarred by its bewilderingly full streets, dank alleys, and littered piers, he remains relaxed and able in his daily contact with iron and steel. Notions of identification and dis-identification get us only so far in establishing our social relation to this obviously gendered macho body. Rather, as we shall see later in the discussion of the tactility of cinema, we might think of the corporeal star body as an assemblage that annexes certain elements to its form, just as the Tank Man annexes the tank. Dutt's star body incorporates its environment; the object we see onscreen is a corporeal object that is coextensive with Mumbai (the pinnacle and abyss of a globalized Indian modernity) as a phenomenon. If cinema provides a phenomenological experience (as scholars such as Vivian Sobchack [2004] have maintained) that initiates the simultaneous becoming of subject and the world, in *Lage Raho* we are confronted with an overtly corporeal body that intensifies sensations; caught in a force field of that body, the audience, too, inhabits the urban space of the film comfortably. Thus, Munna Bhai attaches the viewer not only to Mumbai but also to the frail old man, half-forgotten by those who acutely feel the harshness of urban survival every day.

The film's reflexive positioning of the devotee as the conduit for the re-auratization of Gandhi is possibly why it succeeds in its project. The film's producer, Vidhu Vinod Chopra, and director have been rather explicit about their pedagogic aim to resurrect Gandhi's message for contemporary youth who often encounter him only as an image on a wall calendar. Not only does Munna Bhai's corporeality draw us into the filmic space, but we participate in the slow buildup to venerating Gandhi because the story focalizes such an act through the humdrum Munna Bhai. Gandhi's words and deeds, his life, are hardly present in the narration; indeed, most Indians have heard too much about that life already. Rather, it is what we are led to induce from Munna Bhai's success, garnered from his growing adherence to Gandhi's friendly suggestions, that compels us to think Gandhigiri as relevant in the contemporary world. Only Munna Bhai can "see" Gandhi, while most of the other characters, including Circuit (his sidekick), remain oblivious to the spectral form. Gandhi is often placed somewhere at a corner in the frame in which Munna Bhai hogs our attention. The iconic image hovers, dislocated until enshrined by the unfolding of events. The formality of the image is underscored in the uncomfortably lush artifactual Gandhi stepped out of the calendar text, intermedially carrying with him the material traces of the art form (ruddy cheeks, draped costume, benign smile). Like other legendary public figures, he activates an open-ended sociality. Thus, a global icon representing a mode of struggle (passive resistance) "approved" in the global North is re-auratized in local sites of enunciation, where he prompts the questioning of legal, financial, and political institutions.

In the viewers who make the world through Gandhi as corporeal aperture, we witness a material contiguity with the "unlivable forces of the universe" (as Elizabeth Grosz [2008] names them). The political act inheres in re-orienting ontological becoming toward a social collectivity, a "liquid social" without boundaries that is lived but not cognitively grasped in a totalizing image. But here we have already moved to the embodied consumption of signs as ontological becoming, a process critical to my later arguments on the social force of global icons. Paradoxically, Charles Sanders Peirce, a semiotician invested in the objective science of signs, saw such potential in the iconic sign. Of course, Peirce's significance to this project lies far beyond such theoretical instrumentality. After all, he is among the few to extensively theorize the icon, a sign whose "natural" connection to its referent rendered it pariah in Saussurian semiology. To a large extent, the Peircean schema is resonant with Saussurian taxonomy in which the symbol is the most arbitrary and conventional sign; in contrast, the icon and the index remain "natural" and "degenerate" sign types, since they are difficult to disentangle from their referents (ontological objects in Peirce). Semiologists who entered the scene later—most notably, Umberto Eco—attempted to revise this schema by forcefully severing Peirce's proposed link between sign and referent and by claiming the iconic sign to be just as arbitrary as the conventional sign. While the underlying historical concerns of my project shy away from the Peircean project of pragmatism—where reality can be empirically "tested"[30]—Peirce's careful parsing of the icon's semiotic economy in his later writings, I maintain, offers a great deal to the study of powerful bio-icons icons who are not necessarily legitimized only through their imagined link to nature or the divine.

CHARLES SANDERS PEIRCE: ICONS AS CORPOREAL APERTURES

Like Barthes, Peirce suggested that the icon generates a reality fix. The icon proposes the ontology of a "thing" similar to (just like) the sign itself and, as such, it motivates an imaginative pursuit of an endlessly receding horizon of the real. But unlike for Barthes, for Peirce the indexical move is charged with ambiguity, for it invites us to inhabit an eclipsed space and time in the present tense. We move into Tiananmen Square caught in an illusion; we are there with the photographer but cognizant of an irretrievable loss. That "place," in other words, remains elusive, inducing stories that inductively locate us just so.

The reality fix preoccupied Peirce from the start. The "early" Peirce, represented by "On a New List of Categories" (1867), is most often cited by critics who are attentive to the ideological dimensions of semiotic analyses.[31] Here Peirce first, and most famously, explicated the taxonomic differences between the icon, the index, and the symbol. Recent scholars on Peirce have argued that this remains the most cited text because of the esoteric (and sometimes idiosyncratic) nature of Peirce's later works. Yet it is in these later works that we see significant revisions of the icon's relationship to the referent, now a series of logical inferences rather than a metaphysical link.[32] In two later pieces—specifically "On the Algebra of Logic: A Contribution to the Philosophy of Notation" (1885) and "Harvard Lectures on Pragmatism" (1903)—Peirce rethinks his philosophical precepts (the passing of substance into being) and psychological speculations (the harmony of the mind and nature), his semiotic categories (natural signs and rational signs) and his adherence to scientific laws.[33]

But I will elaborate on this later work by evoking more familiar terrain: "On a New List of Categories" (1867). There, Peirce designates the process of semiosis (the processes of sign making) in the following way: An object is mediated by a sign vehicle (he named this the "representamen" in 1885), which then proceeds to a mental image (the "interpretant") we understand to be the fully developed sign. He postulates an act of attention that posits a presence of some thing, which appears as an object; this act of abduction (complementary to induction and deduction) is a flash of insight that transforms substance into being. In her insistence on Peirce's semiotic universe, Anne Freadman (2004, 9) notes that Peirce implied that there is no original singularity: "It" is not an object until and unless it represents. Hence, the nominalism of a "substance"—what is present / what exists is subject to internal splitting; the object and its representamen come into being at the same time. In fact, in his later study of signs, Peirce dropped references to "substance"altogether, suggesting that the ontology of the thing can be only inferred; in that inference, the thing is framed as an "object." This closeness of the icon to ontology makes us desire that receding reality whose elusiveness mocks us; hence, the icon is always haunted by the ambiguity of the indexical.

The contours of the icon as a sign type emerge with the Peircean unraveling of the different relationships possible between representamen (the concrete word, image, impression) and (ontological) object retrospectively inferred.[34] A representation just like an ontological object (always inferred) is an icon (e.g., a portrait formally resembles a person's visage); a representation that corresponds to an object is an index (a bullet-ridden body indicates the existence of a murderer in experiential space); and a representation where we impute a relation to an object by logic is a symbol (we impute the word impression such as "man" or "*homme*" to refer to a two-legged creature, if one knows the general laws of the universe). In this early categorization, only the last kind of sign relies on the "imputation," or "thought," that exemplifies human logic (Freadman 2004, 12). Indices and icons are relegated outside the scope of the philosophy of forms.

In this scheme, the relation of the icon to its object is dependent on the representamen (word or impression) that shares the sensory quality of its object (be it the enclosure of lines we call a diagram or a visual sensation of color). The sense of a shared sensory quality motivates the strong perception of material contiguity between subject and object; thus icons heighten our fantasies of physical closeness to the object of desire, intensifying the desire for incorporation into the object behind the graphic inscription. No wonder Peirce characterized the icon as degenerate or natural. The icon is too object-like, and icon semiosis is a phenomenological experience; it is not sign-like enough (not pure thought), not abstraction. It shares this "flaw" with the index, which is also not easily extricated from the laws of "nature" (the Peircean configuration of chaos); if the weathercock's pointing refers to the direction of the wind, it is dependent on natural phenomena. The key for Peirce is the role of the representamen, which, in "Harvard Lectures on Pragmatism" (1903), possesses certain inherent properties that make it "fit" for certain uses. Whether or not the representamen is interpreted as a sign (i.e., whether or not one recognizes a portrait as Mother Teresa), it would still possess these properties. That is, the ontological object shares a physical quality with its representational vehicle and, hence, the icon's irrevocable connection to nature. But such a "quality" is always framed within an epistemology, for the recursive icon always invites interpretation. A geometrical diagram has a graphic likeness to some experiential space-thing, Peirce argues, but it becomes an iconic sign when it is interpreted for certain purposes. Interpretation, or the perceptual act of recognizing a representamen, is a key factor in sign making, and Peirce is at pains to under-line this: "In this sense, a word represents a thing to the conception in the mind of the hearer, a portrait represents the person for whom it was intended to the conception of recognition, a weathercock represents the direction of the wind to the conception of him who understands it, a barrister represents his client to the judge and jury whom he influences" (Peirce 1867 [1867–93], 5). The cultural associations the subject requires complete the icon as sign is critical to overcoming "flaw" of likeness, Peirce seems to suggest. When one sees a sign such as fruit in a still-life painting, the image is a representamen that evokes pre-experienced sensations because it seems to capture a likeness of the object (real fruit)—seems to capture, because the viewer shapes the representamen according other images he associates with it. This turn to conventional knowledge (the iconographic analysis Erwin Panofsky [1955] urges) generates the mental image that completes the sign.[35]

In "On the Algebra of Logic" (1885) and "Harvard Lectures on Pragmatism" (1903), Peirce, more interested in the processes of sign making than in the categorizing signs as entities, moved away from his hierarchical model where the symbol was pre-eminent; he began to "mix" the properties of the signs he had laboriously separated in 1867, claiming the most "perfect of signs" are those in which "the iconic, the indicative, and the symbolic characters are blended as equally as possible" (as quoted in Freadman 2004, 85). Such a mixing of the indexical, iconic, and symbolic in the iconic sign will be extremely pertinent to my analysis, since the icons under scrutiny rely heavily on both the symbolic and the indexical for successful communication.[36] No wonder that the icon, inextricable from a connotative matrix dependent on cultural memory but also turning us toward the ontological, can "sell" historical cultural aspirations as eternally natural ones.

Peirce's later articulation of the icon's "thinghood," lending it the immediacy of "real life," gives the icon the phantasmic aspect proposed in Laclau's "powerful symbols"; no surprise, then, that icons generate affective responses. Already in 1867, the icon for Peirce seems to have adopted a certain "thinghood" in its likeness to the ontological object. The representamen shows some material quality of the object that evokes comparison in the mind of the interpreter. The resulting interpretant, when iconic, appears as a "sensible" sign: It carries the materiality of the phenomenon. The predilection to "thinghood" became even more overt in "On the Algebra of Logic," in which Peirce added algebraic notation, geometry, and maps to his example of icons. In their graphic inscription, diagrams are materially contiguous to objects, but to use them, we must forget that they are not the very "thing" that they represent. Here Peirce alerts us to the dreamlike state contemplating an icon might prompt in the viewer, who forgets the formality of the graphic image so that the "copy" appears momentarily as the real: "So in contemplating a painting, there is a moment when we lose consciousness that it is not the thing, the distinction between the real and the copy disappears, and it is for a moment a pure dream—not any particular existence, and yet not general. At that moment we are contemplating an icon" (Peirce, quoted in Freadman 2004, 26). The icon is phantasmatic, taking on thinghood through its representational ground of likeness; it allows us to hallucinate an object that matches (is just like) the sign itself.[37] It invites a synaesthetic encounter, an embodied consumption that explains the seductive mystique of the icon. One may argue, in the midst of controversies where the iconic sign is deeply contested, the one awakens from the dream to confront history.

By the time he wrote the "Harvard Lectures on Pragmatism," Peirce had become far more attentive to interpretive labor (a word or image has an iconic function when interpreted for certain purposes) and, therefore, to the historical subject (someone who interprets a representamen in this way). Of course, a major departure from Peirce's schema would be to insert the desiring subject (replete with irrational anxieties, aspirations, doubts) constrained by its materiality in the place of interpreter; such intervention radically recalibrates the Peircean subject governed by universal reason. But ironically, as we have seen, in attempting to theorize the icon's inferred "link" to the ontological world, Peirce—the high priest of reason, indebted to Immanuel Kant—had made space for the sensate and affective aspects of the icon. His phenomenological considerations pitched the icon as corporeal aperture, opening us into a space beyond but also one that establishes contiguity with the social space the viewer occupies. The relation between the social and the infinite / real is a sensory one filled with (dis)organized sensations; one space touches the other as the icon awakens and mobilizes our senses. Peirce leads us to understand the conjugated perceptions and affections of icon consumption and therefore to bring disciplinary genealogies (anthropological, metaphysical, and religious) rarely aligned with the semiotic and aesthetic to bear on the icon. In the next chapter, where I elaborate the materiality of the icon as an incorporative technology, I pause at greater length on the icon's ontology. I argue that the embodied consumption icons demand moves us steadily toward a material contiguity with chaos in its varied configurations, and I turn from semiotics to considerations of the icon in the larger domain of visual culture studies, where art historians, philosophers, religious studies scholars, and cultural anthropologists insist on the magical efficacies of the icon. They take us beyond representation into the social, where embodied praxes animate dead matter to make live media.

Icons are ornate, decorative, often lustrous artifacts that can function as apertures to a "truth" beyond their material form. They do not let us rest easily, especially when they are encountered as auratic objects; they demand veneration, the affective labor of worship that transforms sign into an incorporative technology. Alongside these auratic objects, there are those commodities consumers incorporate into themselves as prostheses, in a steady estrangement from the social. These two modalities of incorporation—incorporation into the icon as proceeding toward another subject and incorporation of the icon as prostheses—intimate that icons circulate in diverse, and often intersecting, spheres of exchange. We might well regard mass-produced icons simply as saleable commodities: We transact the expensive Gucci (for $240) or the bio-icon of a celebratory biopic ($9.50) in terminal reciprocity where these are commodities marked by monetary value. But on occasion, an Eva Perón smoldering as advertisement in the virtual world, a Lady Diana flashing on the cover of a magazine, or a Gandhi on a calendar hanging unobtrusively on a classroom wall will motivate a synaesthetic encounter where the potentialialized icon is available for re-territorialization: It demands responses, generates performative acts, engenders happenings. While the book will reflect equally on the different commodity states of the icon, in this chapter I focus primarily on its magical efficacy to earn the theoretical ground for my later analyses of volatile icons that spark collective action. This chapter aims at a redirection of icon theory toward the social; that is, I argue, unlike the index, its semiotic sibling, the icon's genealogies illuminate the role it has historically played as an incorporative technology that orients its devotee toward a social field.

Such redirection, posing icon consumption as embodied praxis, requires an assembling of multiple critical genealogies, not the least of which is a "counter-history" of the icon in Western intellectual thought that is sharply marked by a critical iconoclasm. This book joins a constellation of thinkers who have reflected on the aura of mass commodities—Michael Taussig's (1991, 148) powerful analysis of "the magical technology of embodied knowing" or Susan Buck-Morss's (1992) visual ocularity—without quick dismissals of fleshly fetish objects.[1] Among these, as I have noted earlier, Kajri Jain's and Christopher Pinney's deliberations on such a counter-history provide important points of departure for the study of icons in South Asia. Looking at the "interocular" regimes of visuality in South Asia (from cinema to chromolithography), Pinney rather self-reflexively casts his lot with "the counter-historians of modernity" (specifically, Martin Heidegger and Maurice Merleau-Ponty) to elaborate a "corpothetics" that "can meet, halfway, a different tradition with which it shares much in common" (Pinney 2002, 356). These exhortations inaugurate the effort to conjugate scholarship on South Asia with scholarship on the icon's metaphysics and aesthetics in the historical West; indeed, the bio-icons that are under scrutiny here mandate such conjugation. Such a double gaze carries forward the postcolonial imperative to "provincialize" Euro-American experiences of modernity: first, in elaborating the embodied visuality of the consuming icons that intensifies sensations, provoking ontological becoming; and second, in joining post-Cartesian critiques of the detached contemplative subject, one that would properly withstand the sensuous lure of these highly decorative, physically expressive objects.

If, as I argue, the corporeal dynamism of the icon stimulates the circulation of sensations between subject and object, this chapter projects an embodied subject that expresses those sensations in material culture. If the trajectory of this study moves toward historical subjects whose labor constitutes the social, it is simulated here as we proceed from metaphysics and aesthetics to popular religion, art, and cultural anthropology for a fuller scrutiny of embodied praxes. Embodied praxes further insist on the historical contingencies governing human agency; therefore the chapter closes with a reorientation of this second materiality of the icon to the historical period in question. Following philosophers of corporeal dynamism, I argue that, if bodies are increasingly the loci of control in the full flush of bio-political modernity,[2] then critics of globalization must renew their tryst with the (laboring) body as a dynamic field of power.

To comprehend how icons motivate social action, it is perhaps important to move back to a time when the icon was ever an object of adoration and desecration. This plunges us into multiple genealogies that will receive selective treatment here, given the unmannerly historical and disciplinary scope of icon study. In this sense, this book joins the critical ambition of a well-known tract of icon study, W. J. T. Mitchell's *Iconology: Image, Text, Ideology* (1986), an erudite effort to cobble together a critical genealogy that opens into the fields of art history, philosophy, political economy, semiotics, and literary theory. Mitchell provides a point of departure for this theoretical venture as it attempts to move beyond the iconoclasm so incisively elaborated in *Iconology*.

Taking his cue from the rumination on "iconology" by the early-twentieth-century art historian Erwin Panofsky, Mitchell tracks the rise of iconoclasm in Western (Protestant) intellectual thought and its relation to idolatry and iconophilia. Hence, he starts inevitably with a theological tradition—Greek, Hebrew, and Latin—where such suspicion of the icon is housed. The basic presumption behind such an assumption is that, where the literal image of the divine is pure and abstract, its material likeness in the icon is derivative, improper.[3] Both the icon and the idol, after all, Mitchell reminds us, are etymological cousins in their Greek roots; both the icon (*eikon*) and the idol (*eidolon*) are sensible / perceptible impressions or likenesses of the "idea" (*eidos*) or the invisible / inaccessible "suprasensible reality" (Mitchell 1986, 5). For Mitchell, the etymology is less important to the distinctive economy of the icon than it is to investigate "the idea of image," his primary concern in *Iconology*. The theological iconoclasm he begins with engenders a long tradition in which fear or distrust of images persist, fueled by the Reformation, in accentuating religious difference through the vilification of the Catholic veneration of images. Even when Alberti's "invention of the artificial perspective" in 1435 turned the matter on its head by investing the mechanical material image with the truth of the world in the name of science, reason, and objectivity—a hypotheses that would find a grand culmination with the camera—popular attachments to images and iconoclastic fears about them remained unmitigated. Some years later, in *Picture Theory* (1994), Mitchell follows his sense of the persisting power of images by exploring their regime in verbal representations.[4] Despite attempts to master the icon by *logos*, he argues in this early study of intermediality, the economy of images returns like a repressed memory to intellectual thought and life, an uncontrollable symptom—energetic, invincible, recurrent. The unprecedented power of images at our historical moment, Mitchell insists, fuel fear, phobia, and anxiety, motivating his call for a critical iconology.

In fact, Mitchell (much like Bruno Latour) wryly notes that our times parallel the reign of images in the Byzantine period, where images were the site of struggle between emperor and patriarch, the latter defending images in an effort to protect traditional liturgical practices. Mitchell does not, however, pause on the Byzantine doctrine on icons, dismissive of its essentially conservative agendas that included Christian territorial expansionism. In my view, a closer look at this doctrine is required to distinguish the economy of the icon in contemporary modern life from the general flow of images. In this sense, while Mitchell's work is a valuable resource for this project, I depart from his smooth assimilation of the icon into a general visual economy of images, first to engage with the metaphysics of the icon, and then to reflect on the icon as art—a special kind of technology, as art historians have maintained. In both its metaphysical and its aesthetic guises, the icon appears as (sometimes dangerous) auratic object, a corporeal aperture motivating a synaesthetic encounter.

THE METAPHYSICS OF THE ICON

The Byzantine doctrine positions the icon in a particular economy pertinent not only to scholars of theology, philosophy, or aesthetics but also to those preoccupied with the "ethical and political" fields set in motion by the icon. My discussion, inspired as it is by contemporary iconocrises, commences with theological postulates on the icon as liturgical object. In such return, I follow many other scholars who turn to Byzantine because the crises over icons in that empire prefigure rumblings closer to our time. Notably, David Freedberg's *The Power of Images* (1989) tracks the flaring of violent iconoclasm from the Byzantine controversies to the twentieth century. Freedberg gestures toward a "global history of iconoclasms" by bringing extraordinarily intense episodes of image breaking in disparate geo-historical locations—from iconoclastic violence in sixteenth-century Netherlands to China's repression of Buddhist statues from the fifth century to the ninth century, the knife attack on Rembrandt's *Nightwatch* in 1975, the ripped portrait of the newly married Lady Diana in London's National Gallery, or the tearing down of the statue of Ferdinand Marcos in the Philippines—within the same framework. Freedberg's investigation reminds us that icons were always technologies capable of bringing about something akin to a social movement, as we see in the Byzantine Empire of the eighth century and ninth century. To understand why icons exert such a power, it is crucial to take a closer look at the doctrine that sheltered and legitimized the icon for so many years: theological exegesis that habitually gave way to political machinations.

The Byzantine Doctrine of Icons

The Orthodox defense of the icon generating the "doctrine of icons" that revolutionized the Eastern church brought numerous crises to the Byzantine Empire in the eight century and ninth century. The debates over the status of the icon in religious practice between iconoclast and Orthodox theologians—coming to a head in the first (Iconoclastic Council of 754) and second iconoclastic (the Second Council of Nicaea of 787) crises—irrevocably set in motion suspicion of the icon's mystifying capacities whose lineaments we see later in Freud and Marx, if not in contemporary dialogues on celebrities, stars, advertising, and infotainment. Given such a trajectory, I linger on the Byzantine doctrine of icons, a theological argument that provided the philosophical basis for an aesthetic conception of the icon, and that has been largely ignored in contemporary conversations on the icon.

I have already mentioned one of the most important recuperative attempts to return to Byzantine: *Image, Icon, Economy* (recently translated into English), in which Marie-José Mondzain explains the intellectual contexts in which icons came to be extraordinarily powerful instruments of ecclesiastical politics in the Eastern church.[5] When the center of power moved east from Rome to Byzantine, polemics against religious icons emerged from emperors who sought to restrain the popular appeal of icons. Icons functioned as technologies that enabled participation in a sacral economy, rousing people to celebration and violence. When Emperor Leo III (Leo the Isaurian) first issued an edict against icons in A.D. 726, leading to the dethroning of a popular icon of Christ in the commercial district of his capital city, the officer responsible for the destruction was promptly killed and riots ensued all over the city. The emperor responded by convening the first Iconoclastic Council in A.D. 754, an event that closed with a partial victory for Orthodox theologians (such as John of Damascus and Theodore Stoudios), who won permission for the worship of the images of Christ and the saints (but not of God the Father). John of Damascus's defense of icons is possibly the most cited one among these Orthodox theologians.[6] Mondzain, however, argues that Patriarch Nikephoros, who entered the debate after the first crisis when a second controversy broke out in A.D. 813, presents the most important clarification of the economy that holds together the icon and the image, a figure responsible for bringing theology, which so far had responded to existing practices that had "undue influence" on expressions of faith, into the domain of aesthetics. Since contemporary icons are largely regarded as aesthetic rather than sacral objects, Nikephoros's philosophical arguments on icon composition and worship are more germane to this book than the many other defenses of icons of the Byzantine debates.

But what notion of the icon did these theologians defend? Why was the relation between the icon and the image so central to these debates? The iconoclasts insisted that the veneration of the icon was simply idol worship in another guise. Hence, they closed the gap between the icon (*eikon*, or any image whatsoever), perceived to be an accredited image of spiritual power, and the idol (*eidolon*, or a fantasy image), largely held in disdain as a misrepresentation of divinity. The idol later was to be associated with the "fetish" (emerging pseudo-anthropologically with missionary encounters in Africa, as William Pietz [1985] has explained) and the "totem" (the "uncivilized" representation of spiritual power James Frazer's 1890 tome, *The Golden Bough*, described to a European public).[7] In his insightful unpacking of Pietz's historical unraveling of the fetish, James Kearney argues that the fetish (which came into English via the Portugese *feticio*) quickly became a weapon in the hands of the Protestants who aligned it with the Catholic veneration of objects.[8] The objective was to mark Catholicism as "barbarous and uncivilized" by associating its fetishistic practices with those of Africans (Pietz 1985). Marx's notion of the fetish draws on this anthropological legacy: He expresses wonder at the power of a thing over humans when it is the product of human labor. Freud, too, would relate the totem and fetish to an earlier "primitive" stage of human evolution. Such a history of the fetish invites scholars such as Kajri Jain to renovate the fetish by looking at the work it has done in the European bourgeois-liberal public sphere.[9] The icon is haunted by these other notations of a mystifying power in contemporary deployments of the term in visual culture studies.

The merging of the icon and the idol occurs via an argument over the image. This is why the study of icons always implies a wrestling with an economy of images. For the Byzantine iconoclasts, the icon's materiality —its carnal display of Christ, the Virgin, or the saint's body—intruded on the pure image of the divine that was always invisible in its immensity and only perceived in the abstract. Along with iconoclastic theologians, Emperor Constantine V, whose iconoclastic promulgations prompted Nikephoros to consolidate his theological stance during the second iconoclastic crisis,[10] underscored the failures of the icon to express an image of the divine. The materiality of the image (its decorative, visual form; its tactile surfaces) could never stand in for spiritual essence, the iconoclasts argued, so the icon merely divided divine essence by attempting to capture its infinity in formal inscription. To rephrase this in the terms of the corporeal dynamism I attribute to the icon, the chaos of the divine could never be territorialized in the profanely inadequate image. To worship the icon was to worship matter, not divinity. To such charges, Nikephoros presented a theory (primarily articulated in his *Antirrhetics*) that not only legitimized the icon and sheltered it against charges of idolatry but clearly revealed the philosophical, aesthetic, and political stakes of icon worship.

Central to Nikephoros's argument is a conception of *oikonomia*, or economy, a science of relations that would explain the church's role in the world. If the church fathers believed that the organization, management, and administration of the world should imitate a natural model, a divinely ordained model, the Pauline church saw the realization of such a dream as difficult, given free will that brought with it both evil and suffering. How could the church correct human chaos, redeem wretched management and regulate it to achieve similitude to the natural order? How to generalize the natural economy? What instrument would be pedagogically effective, working across barriers of language and inequities in knowledge? What better instrument, in fact, than the icon, already vibrant in the vox populi? After all, the icon was, Nikephoros argued strenuously, a graphic opening toward the divine—a formal resemblance that established the very possibility of thinking. Here we are close to my designation of the icon as a "corporeal aperture," one that can function as a technology for moving toward the other.

To establish the abstract formality of the icon that the iconoclasts had obviously overlooked, Nikephoros, Mondzain recounts, sets up a relationship between the "natural" and the "artificial" to mark a gradual progression toward the divine: We contemplate the divine through the window of the icon only to realize its infinity, its unrepresentable nature; we are ever aware that the "frame of composition" can barely contain the shards of chaos made strong by the intense sensations icons evoke. Hence, the material of the icon—the image—is never confused as divinity. The divine remains but a horizon. Christ withdraws from us even as we move toward him through the icon. The first entity here is divinity, the prototype accessible in heroic cultural figurations; anthropologists such as Alfred Gell would also foreground the "prototype" as that unreachable thing toward which indexical forms gesture. For Nikephoros, the prototype's "imaginal" (imaginary) nature is shared by the natural image, a consubstantial contiguous economy.[11] The natural image is thus like (similar to) the divine whose essence it shares. The natural image is radically independent of visibility: Its aim is to be not seen. Pure abstraction but sharing God's substance, the natural image is the iconoclast's dream. But it is accessed in the world by the artificial image that formally resembles it, graphically (pictorially or diagrammatically), but never with the hubris of complete imitation. So even as each iconic depiction is historically circumscribed (the materiality of wood, paint, and nails of Byzantine icons replaced by film stock or digital pixels, for example), the inscription repeats a previous remembered inscription (lodged in the imaginary)—ever harking back to the first miraculous image, generating a fertile plastic world of ever morphing graphic inscriptions. Here we already have the psychic structure of yearning.

We can grasp the double relation between images suggested by Nikephoros when we think of the figure of Christ in his human form. The "natural" invisible image lives in hearts of the faithful: It is projected on our imaginary as the Other who inaugurates our deepest perception of alterity. Christ is pure, essential, one with the Father; but he takes human form (*morphé*), arrives in flesh marked as similar to the prototype but not quite. He shares God's substance while he imitates us (becomes like us) so that we may imitate him better. Such a natural image is intuited from its formal resemblance in the icon. This intuition is significant to the semiotic economy of the icon. It means the material support of the divine that is the icon motivates a movement back toward something we have lost, something we desire, but something we can only intuit. The inscription moves us toward incorporation into the Other, sometimes represented by another subject or subjects. If later, in the hands of semioticians, this lost ground of representation is nature (or the ontological world, as we see in Peirce), the icon still motivates us to project into the "origin" of the image—hence, its deeply mystifying, enchanted quality.

But let us remain for a while longer with the dangerous enticements of Christian liturgical icons. To think of Christ in a painting as Christ would be to be a fetishist, to participate only in a carnal economy. But to think that the material image we see is an aperture to the ground behind representation would be to become icon, the artificial resemblance (a painting of Christ) thereby activating a natural image that bears similarity to the divine. Nikephoros inaugurates a mode of consuming the icon that actively moves back to the lost ground of representation, the invisible sky from which the image distinguishes its cutout form (as Jean-Luc Nancy will argue).[12] The icon becomes a window into the infinite.

For Nikephoros, the icon therefore is a graphic inscription that is heterogeneous in its substantiality—that is, it depends on available historical materials as well as regimes of perception, on historical modes of artistry, to achieve resemblance to a similitude with the divine prototype. Twice removed, it has no designs on expressing the divine; in fact, Nikephoros turns to Aristotle's *Organon* to develop a theory of art that describes exactly how the icon is inscribed. The graph, always unenclosed, reveals a fissure that looks back toward the divine through Christ (or a saint) but knows that the origin is never to be achieved. The icon therefore reveals the imaginal identity of the divine. We come to know how God is reached through our imagination facilitated by the images. The lives and works of exemplary figures are those material intermediaries (Christ, the saints, the blessed). Hence, contrary to the iconoclastic allegations, icon consumption is the best historical introduction to abstract thinking. In disenchanted secular times, the imaginal identity of the divine can be replaced by another imaginary, a liquid social in which the gaze of an unlocalized collectivity locates us as subject. I have been suggesting such a place, a there that exists but cannot be grasped by cognition alone.

It is the material form the icon takes that had led to its assimilation into a fetish object, bringing allegations of carnality against it. But how different is its carnality from the flesh/object that conceals presence? Here the redemptive function of the icon promulgated by Orthodox theologians offers grounds for distinction. First, the icon invites a complicated scopic exchange: If the icon is a graphic inscription inviting one to look beyond it to Christ (not only at the image), what we "see" is Christ's gaze, a look back, his thirst for us (for humanity) positioning us as subject. In this exchange of looks, we see hope of redemption for the divine gaze gathers up our frail flesh. In the exchange of looks, while "seeing" involves the other senses, the regimes of perception that organize sensations of icon veneration privilege visuality as one's primary activity. The synaesthetic encounter involves transforming the effects of one sensory mode (visuality) into another (tactility) (Massumi 2002, 35); but the regimes of icon consumption privilege looks, the visual sense organizing the perceptual field even as it is constantly under pressure from the participation of the senses with each other. The ensuing tension is best characterized as an embodied visuality, if we transcribe this theory of affect into the customary critical vocabularies of icon metaphysics.

Embodied perception has received significant critical attention in recent years across several domains of inquiry pertinent to the study of icons. Philosophers alert us to the visual haptology of approaching the Other, as we see in Jean-Luc Nancy's reflections on the "eye that touches,"[13] while art historians underscore the physiological activity of perception, with exemplary instantiation in Jonathan Crary's *Techniques of the Observer* (1991).[14] Moreover, cinema and new media theorists make the case for phenomenological experiences arising from the multimodal assemblages of images, technological substrates, bodies, and physical spaces. Among these fields of inquiry, cinema studies have focused most directly on the icon. I will return to those rich discussions in chapter 4, but here it is worth noting the turn to embodied visuality in cinema studies parallel to the physiological turn in visual culture studies. Following the burgeoning "sensuous scholarship in cinema" (Paul Stoller, Vivian Sobchack, Laura Marks, Jennifer Barker) indebted to Maurice Merleau-Ponty (1962),[15] in an important new work, Jennifer Barker (2009), for example, poses cinema as "the tactile eye," the result of patterns emerging between the spectator's body and cinema (the projector's gate, the long dark hall, word, sound, and image). While touch is linked to a single organ—the skin—it is enacted throughout the body, reverberating in musculature and viscera. Barker's propositions on a double act—the spectator's immersion into the multimodal image and the simultaneous ordering of the world as sensible, where the thing becomes object to reinstitute the subject—not only underscores the hydraulic fluctuations between the epistemological recognition and ontological becoming, but they also emphasize the relatively under-theorized non-discursive materiality of the cinematic sign. Such sensuous scholarship intervenes in poststructuralist theories of image cultures. In the genealogies of the icon tuned to material culture, however, we find references to the phenomenological experience of icon worship everywhere. It would be quite common for a religious studies scholar to describe the combinatory sensory modes activated in icon veneration, an act of embodied visuality (intensified by these physically expressive objects, often rich in color or flecked with gold) inclu-

sive of the aural (the sonority of music), the physical (the crush of bodies), the olfactory (the swirl of incense), and the kinesthetic (dance and
swoon).

This detour into embodied visuality highlights the second factor that
comes into play in the scene of icon veneration: the sensuously made
body of Christ glistening in iconic composition. We remember that the
body promises redemption in its resurrection; its fleshly allure invites a
sense of sensuous contiguity, freeing us, if momentarily, from our constrained mortal social bodies. This sensuous exchange—looking as touching—brings both melancholy (our separation from the divine as Christ
remains Other) and joy (the possibility of return through our contiguity
with Christ's flesh). The intense sensations invoked by the embodied
visuality of icon consumption enables a sense of material contiguity with
the unruly forces of the universe, the abundant matter that religions
configure as the divine. Even in a flamboyantly secular icon—the face of
Greta Garbo I will turn to in chapter 4—these dual axes of promise and
loss remain. Garbo beckons sensuously, irredeemably Other but just like
us in her human loneliness. The economy of the icon, its fabled synaesthetic exchange, I argue, persists in psychic structures of veneration
that we extend to stars, despite all evidence of a disenchanted world.

Nikephoros's theory presents the theological ground for thinking
about the iconic sign as a distinctive one. A graphic inscription recognizable by its iteration, the icon harks back to a lost origin, harnessing our
senses toward a possible ethical encounter with deep alterity. But it is
precisely this ethical reaching that provides dangerous potential to bind
affect to hegemonic political projects. In fact, we see this already in Nikephoros's own expansion into politics as he begins to describe the icon's
oikos, or dwelling. The icon has tremendous power over the container
turned sacred by its touch; it spreads and cohabits (incorporates) the field
that holds it, bringing the profane into the purview of ecclesiastical authority. One can easily see how such a proposition, in iconocratic hands,
can become an instrument for the appropriation of territory sacralized
by the icon. Perhaps this is why so many emperors were the first iconoclasts. In fact, the direct political power of Byzantine icons, legitimized by
theological doctrine, was so great that it persisted beyond the Byzantine
Empire. The art historian Hans Belting, for instance, recounts the fate of
the famous Virgin Nicopeia, considered the most authentic portrait of
the Virgin Mary since it was made correctly, with her cooperation, in the
time of the Apostles.[16] Such a legend no doubt compelled Venetians to
forcibly remove the icon from St. Mark's to St. Luke's in Venice in an

effort to sanctify territory via the presence of the icon. We might think of such happenings—icons becoming phenomena—as persisting in direct or indirect guises in our times, Belting maintains, especially when living public figures can draw on vibrant existing iconographic traditions. For example, the election campaign in Argentina in 1972 mobilized the popular memory of the president's dead wife, Eva Perón, as the Virgin who watched over Argentinean territory, a move made possible by the reigning cult of the Virgin del Amparo. Such phenomena enable both art historians, Belting and Freedberg, to consolidate a formidable archive of icon adoration and desecration in a seemingly "disenchanted" world. They mark explosions of the volatile icon as functioning in a mode similar to liturgical icons, sometimes in liturgical guise, despite the deluge of mass-produced images of the icon in question.

The Byzantine doctrine inaugurates the psychic economy of the icon that would find lengthier treatment in the late nineteenth century and twentieth century. If the icon is crucially a graphic mark that does not attempt mimesis (since divine meaning cannot be enclosed) but works through etching a formal resemblance, the icon must necessarily become legible within a large cultural field of reference. The icon depends on shared knowledge; it is fundamentally a framed art object that depends on a shared epistemology. Hence, Nikephoros presents art historians with a philosophical rationale for thinking about the icon as convention, despite its seemingly naturalizing capacities. The social histories of viewers become key to the study of the icon, as different optic regimes, tastes, and institutional protocols govern the recognition of an ordinary image as an iconic one. But before we move to aesthetics, another domain of the liturgical icon remains salient to the critical genealogy I have been conjugating: icons in Hindu liturgical practice that are still resonant as sacral objects in modern South Asia.

Icons in Hindu Liturgical Practice

Although the iconophiliac liturgical practices legitimized by Hindu theological postulates are seemingly apposite to abstract image worship propagated by the Byzantine doctrines, when one looks carefully at the philosophical arguments about images as incorporative technologies, the differences are narrower than they might first appear. Two texts are critical to such an investigation: Richard H. Davis's seminal *The Lives of Images* (1997) and Diana L. Eck's influential *Dársan: Seeing the Divine Image in India* (1998).[17] Davis offers a rich analysis of how icons have been interpreted by different "communities of response" (his term for inter-

pretive communities) from the sixth century B.C. onward. He is particularly interested in what happens to devotional values that frame objects as icons when those objects (e.g., a medieval South Indian bronze
image of Siva) are transported, with the help of art markets, into other
settings (such as the National Gallery in Washington, D.C.). How might
art historians of the twentieth century, wonders Davis, recuperate the
value ascribed to an icon in devotional practice? Traditionally, priests
oversaw the "ritual establishment" of images in shrines located in temples (and later in homes), carefully orchestrating the material object's
"coming alive" as icon in liturgical settings through a laborious process of
consecration. In the removing of liturgical icons from their shrines, Davis
asks, how we might understand the devotional values they might have
had? What follows is an assembling of theological and aesthetic postulates on the proper use of Hindu icons, as well as a look at the doctrines
that sheltered and those that reviled them.

Hindu philosophical thought is quite clear on the unrepresentable
nature of divinity, the one Brahman who, like God the Father, is infinite
and *nirguna* (quality-less). And like God the Father, divine essence makes
itself accessible to humans through manifestations: If Christ was the one
human likeness who drew us to divinity, in Hindu polytheism, the Absolute has an exuberance of transformations; it manifests *saguna* (qualities)
in multiple forms and names. The primary difference is in the nature of
the manifestation. Where in Christian theology, divinity is finally absent
and the material manifestation (Christ) withdraws from the devotee in
the devotional encounter, in the Hindu schema, divinity has both transcendence (it is beyond form) and immanence (physicality and worldli-
ness). While Christ and the saints (in iconic form) intercede on our behalf, the Hindu devotee can access the divine as presence in the icon,
divinity's material support, under the guidance of priests. Although the
icon is not immanently infused with divine essence, it is a bounded form
animated by *sakti*, or divine energy, when one correctly follows the labors
of ritual worship. Ritual performance enables the agency of the material
support. Eck notes that the image may be considered a *yantra* (device, or
what I have characterized as "technology") that focuses *ekagrata* (one-
pointedness of thought), providing a momentary glimpse through a window. As in the case of the Byzantine icon, the yantra is not a substitute for
the divine; it does not conceal lack but increases one's yearning for the
divine and enables ontological becoming.

As in the case of Byzantine icons, Hindu liturgical icons are not imita-
tions of the infinite but artifactual images that register excess, something

beyond the human form: Siva's third eye and Visnu's four arms are the iconographic markings by which the icon becomes legible. Like the Byzantine icons, anthropomorphic likenesses (distinguished as the *pratima* or *praikrti* form) are the most excellent material supports; Eck characterizes these as icons as opposed to non-human, or aniconic, supports (rock croppings as a form of Siva; a tree as Sati). These forms never capture the infinity of the Absolute; the icon remains an opening to an epiphanic direct encounter with the divine one can glimpse beyond the material form.

The aspect that positions the Hindu liturgical icon as a fetish (Jain interprets it so, following Taussig) is the investing of worldly materials with divine agency. God looks back at you while you strain to catch a glimpse of the icon; you are seen as you see, in the philosophy of *dársan*. The act of encountering the divine is therefore deeply synaesthetic, dependent on matter for its dynamic flows (with the body as its placeholder for the subject). If animating the image depends on ritualized worship, the procedures (ringing of small bells, lighting of incense, singing of hymns, arraigning of fruit and flowers) engage the devotee's body establishing a material contiguity with the divine. The sense perception of the "devotional eye," Davis reminds us, harnesses a sensorium whose aesthetics Pinney describes as a corpothetics, where the devotee sees / touches himself in the gaze of the Other. Lawrence Babb (1981, 400) reiterates the point, describing the act of devotion as unifying a sensorium, an "extrusive reaching where the seer is touched in the act of seeing." Once more, in these accounts, the intensity of the sensations is organized so that the "eye" that touches has primacy. An embodied visuality (transcribed as a visual-haptic encounter in Western metaphysics) names human devotional activity in scholarly reorganizations of the free flows of sensations between subjects and objects. The Hindu icon is therefore regarded as a deeply corporeal aperture that is dynamic in its effects, harnessing the sensuality of the body in distinction from ascetic modes of renouncing pleasure. The affective labor of worship that can sometimes culminate in the trance-like ecstasy of *bhakti* (devotion) that moves the devotee to merge with the divine through one's flesh, not by transcending it. To the colonial eye, such corporeality might have appeared immensely fetishistic. Pietz (1985), after all, establishes how the notion of the fetish (which appeared in 1760) emerged as a means of marking the practices of the colonial other as idolatrous, corpulent. Yet, arguably, even during the ritual the material support or icon is one among *many* enticements to the senses. It therefore does not substitute for the divine. The fire lit during ceremonies or the flame of the *diyas* (lamps), for example, equally represents divine energy, the traces of the divine proliferating in many, scattered traces in the all-consuming religious ritual. Hence, even the most ecstatic devotee in full communion with the Other would hardly perceive only the material support to complete or enclose the exuberance of the divine, the unlivable forces of chaos. The icon remains an unenclosed form, a corporeal aperture opening to divine presence—a technology that moves the subject toward another.

Despite such movement, however, organized religions control these potentialities through doctrinaire rules, conventions, and methods of worship. Situated epistemologies of the icon not only differentiate "cognition" as a nexus of perceptions regulated within a frame that produce the desired effects of introspection (such as self-recognition), but also channel sensations toward specific goals (such as the purification of the self) in a disciplining of chaos expressed in volatile ecstasies. Ritual worship is rule-bound, laborious, and procedural, each act signaling one's love / bhakti for the divine.[18] One marks distance from the divine by such acts; marks those organized relations that Jain characterizes as a "sacred economy." In cases where pilgrims journey to holy sites where the icon historically has been invested with the divine, their arduous journey offers the labor of love that will enable dársan. Devotees learn of such holy sites through an immense roster of narratives that focalize the worldly manifestation of the divine in epics (the later recessions of the Mahabharata and the Ramayana), legends, and folktales; still later, the hagiographies of saints present cases of human excellence as signs of the divine. Biographies not only classify the icon; they teach devotees to learn inductively of divine agency in the world through engaging in semiotic activity. Such focalization is clearly warranted because of the vast polytheistic embarrassment of riches in iconic forms within Hinduism. What the narratives achieve is the consolidation of a symbolic field where the icon is focalized in specific ways, enabling the devotee to recognize the image as venerable.

Scholars such as Jain note it is in fact worship that auratizes an object as divine. When early culture industries marketing mass-produced sacred icons emerge, what was once a commodity image, a gift, or even waste might be become sacral icon when given the labor of worship. This is true not only in public places of worship where one may see assembly-line clay deities cursorily ignored before their proper enshrinement during a particular festival, but also in private domestic arenas where enshrinement animates the iconic form. One buys a clay deity or calendar art, haggles over its price in the bazaar, until ritual transforms it into an object of devotion—once again, the performance of affective labor enabling the agency of the object. The territorial embedding of the icon is therefore extremely important, a liturgical legitimizing gesture that reveals the power of icons. As in Byzantium, priests and kings, recognizing the cachet of popular icon worship, have used doctrinal norms—icons must be territorially established by the intercession of priests—to wield political power and influence. Hence, radical movements such as bhakti were in fact efforts on the part of lower-caste and lower-class Hindus to privatize devotional practice, to approach the divine personally without the intercession of priests.

Images therefore have been at the center of political struggle in South Asia, as in Byzantium, even though traditions of critical iconoclasm entered the subcontinent only in the medieval period. There were some early detractors of icons within Hindu philosophy, notably the Mimansa and Advaita Vedanta schools of the early medieval period. Rather than underscore an abstraction of divinity, the Mimansa school argued that divine agency was simply not necessary to follow the religious conduct prescribed in the authorless Vedas. In years to come, expressions of iconoclasm became the loci of debates over the history of conquest—for instance, the Hindu right repeatedly sought to pigeonhole Muslims as iconoclastic invaders, demonizing Sultan Mahmud's raids of prosperous temple towns in northern and western parts of the South Asian subcontinent in the tenth century. Of these, the Somanatha temple "raid" of 1026 has been the most canonized account, reconstructed histories inductively auratizing the Somanatha idol to harness a hegemonic Hindu popular.[19] In her collation of the "many voices" in the Somanatha temple controversy, Romila Thapar (2004) underscores the subject effects produced by icons—both iconophiles and iconoclasts ferociously arguing over Somanatha, whether or not they believe icons are apertures to the divine.

We can therefore assume that, when confronted by contested icons, iconophiles (Hindu populists) and iconoclasts (Taliban populists) share a structure of veneration manifest in their varied performances of devotion and desecration. David Morgan (2005) makes a similar point as he traverses heterogeneous religious traditions: If we remain attentive to expressive veneration, he argues, we might consider Hindu rituals of lighting incense sticks in adoration as congruent with Muslim pilgrims' kissing the black Ka'bah (al-hajaral-aswal) to repeat the Prophet's gesture. This is not to claim that icon veneration is everywhere; only that heterogeneous expressive practices of venerating apertures into the divine are far more prolific in Protestant, Jewish, and Islamic material cultures than the theological postulates of those religions would have us believe. And, of course, the rich literature on Sufi saints have shown that icon worship has vibrant existence in diverse (often syncretic) Islamic traditions in South Asia (Werbner and Basu 1998). Since we see practices of veneration across cultures as the "sacred gaze" percolates into the secular domain— in the adulation of material artifacts such as photographs, flags, and memorabilia—I deploy the term "veneration" (from the Latin *veneratio*) over devotion to describe the psychic structure that underlies both ordinary and highly theatrical performances of adoration or hatred.[20]

My pursuit of these theological postulates aims to show how icons are regarded across cultures as "corporeal apertures," despite differences in perceptions of the (materiality of the) divine. Most theologies across cultures privilege a scopic exchange, but, as we have seen, many scholars underscore the synaesthesia in icon worship. I join such observations in emphasizing the corporeal labor of icon veneration, returning us to the body as a field of power. The accounts of devotion marshaled here underscore not only the nature of the devotional experience but also the psychic structure of icon consumption. But since both of these generalities urge us to attend to an embodied consumption, we are already in history, where the sacred gaze must be understood, Morgan (2005, 3; emphasis added) insists, as a *"particular* configuration of ideas, beliefs, and customs." Such historical particularity, the material manifestations of general processes and structures, propels us beyond theology to popular religion.

Popular Religiosity: The Sacred Gaze

While scholars of theology focus on the structure of belief, scholars of popular religion are far more interested in variations in the expressive performances of veneration. They move into the "physical domain of religious belief" (Morgan 2005, 5) littered with liturgical supports but also flags, pins, key chains, calendar art, and kitsch figurines that accumulate as junk until re-auratized by historical contingency. Hence, they redirect us from the generality of metaphysics to localized sites of icon consumption.

It is well-nigh impossible to present an account of icon study in popular religion, so I highlight one important treatise: Morgan's *The Sacred Gaze* (2005), which directs us to situated icon consumption. Morgan's exegesis is not only wide-ranging in its treatment of the material culture of religious belief, but it is also interdisciplinary in scope (trafficking in art history, philosophy, literature, and theology) and inclusive of several popular religious traditions even as popular Christianity remains its primary preoccupation. Such range is again evident in Morgan's look at the media ecologies of an iconic image. Music, architecture, and literature, he argues, are as important to the "covenant" of belief the icon commands as is the actual liturgical support. Hence, he establishes the dependence of the iconic image on a field of "interpretations" that gives it psychic force, echoing Peirce's sense of the icon's indexical ambiguity that invites consistent inference.

The notion that different kinds of covenants govern the eye of faith further suggests we read the visual-haptic encounter proposed in theological accounts historically, as embodied praxes that are contingent on context. No Hindu or Christian theology, following Morgan, can account for heterogeneous social practices of belief; it can only explain the logic behind the experience of worship—in this case, the logic of incorporation. Morgan's social history of the devotee, exemplifying scholarly work on popular religion, elaborates the heterogeneity of cultural forms in which we see belief at work, from embodied "speech" of ritual to spectacle, procession, teaching, or commemoration. We can see how such flexibility allows us to consider the persistence of devotional psychic structures and cultural forms in secular life, and especially in the veneration of bio-icons whose "graphs" we shall pursue with greater acuity in chapters to come. Morgan's traversing of multiple media platforms further anticipates my perusal of the media ecologies of icon consumption in chapter 4.

Of course Morgan, too, underscores the embodied visuality of the sacred gaze as ultimately moving toward another subject. The devotee visualizes himself in the deity by activating these incorporative technologies. Such a suggestion, which emerges from religious studies, has been instructive to scholars in visual culture studies, media theory, and anthropology concerned with viewing practices in general and with (collective) spectatorship in particular. Within South Asian studies, "devotional structure" (emerging from bhakti[21]) has been influential for studies of spectatorship in cinema, as well as for the viewing practices associated with newly crafted mass-produced images in South Asia. First extended to poet saints, bhakti soon came to political leaders in South Asia with Mahatma Gandhi (often characterized as a "living saint") as the most obvious example. Historians such as Shahid Amin (1984) have shown how Gandhi came to be treated as a god; how his image was auratized so that people customarily went for Gandhi dársan. Art historians such as Pinney have focused on the political work of visual practice (chromolithographs, in Pinney's case) in "enchanting" a public figure. Like the radical bhakti poet-saint, Gandhi strayed from upper-caste norms. By 1933, he had come to speak for the poor, especially low-caste Hindus and "untouchables," with the establishment of his newspaper *Harijan* (Children of God). Quixotically, Gandhi came to function so much like a liturgical icon that, in the 1930s, poet-saints began to draw their sacral charge in relation to him. The art historian Geeta Kapur (1993) notes how the popularity of the mythological Marathi-language *Sant Tukaram* (1937), a film about a bhakti saint, drew on Gandhi's iconicity through national hagiographies (Kapur 1993). Jain makes a similar argument about the *ugra* (virile) Ram icon mobilized by the Hindu right in its visual practice in the 1990s. This traditional iconographic image drew its political vitality, Jain argues, from the muscularized masculinity of the mega-star Amitabh Bachchan, who is adored by lower-class, often disenfranchised young men (the legendary lumpen proletariat). In a shuttling between commercial and sacred arenas, the auratized political image (Gandhi) could render a mass-produced cinematic image (Sant Tukaram) legible as divine, or an auratized cinematic image (Amitabh Bachchan) could revitalize a traditional liturgical image support.[22]

Already here we are confronted with expressive performances of veneration that enable the political efficacy of icons. Already we have moved away from the abstract ideal devotee to historical actors who use icons as incorporative technology for contingent participation in the social. Already we have moved to the center of the book: the "biographs" of the three icons who variously facilitate the popular. But we are ahead of ourselves, for there is still one more disciplinary excursion to be made if we are to fully grasp how the material artifacts we have been considering came to be understood as "signs" transacted as commodities in different spheres of exchange—an excursion into art history, where the efficacies of the icon have been a grand preoccupation ever since Byzantium.

THE AESTHETICS OF THE ICON

One might say that theology is to religious studies what aesthetics is to the study of art. But it is critical to designate just what kind of aesthetics we are concerned with here. For although we are concerned with the icon's formal lineaments and its relation to the ontological world (be it the divine, nature, or the social), we will not focus on philosophical aesthetics per se. As Michael Kelly (2003) reminds us with instantiation in Jacques Derrida, Theodor Adorno, Arthur Danto, and Martin Heidegger, philosophical aesthetics are less invested in the experiential encounter of the devotee (see Kelly 2003) than with the nature of truth illuminated by the technologies of art. But truth is important in this book only for the ground toward which the icon gestures; more significant is the nature of the aesthetic experience, the synaesthetic encounter now reconsidered from perspectives in art history. Here again we are confronted with an (ideal) subject who exerts aesthetic judgment through a removal from the body as aesthetics evolves into a modern science—an "anaesthetics," in fact, as Susan Buck-Morss (1999) maintains in her archaeology of aesthetics. Returning us to the original field (the Greek *aisthitikos*), Buck-Morss reminds us that aesthetics proper had far more to say about sensory viewing practices that inevitably proposed an embodied viewer; it is the numbing shocks of modernity, she argues, following Walter Benjamin, that reified a detached contemplation removed from the human sensorium. On might say that art historians have rejuvenated this older sense of aesthetics in several strains of inquiry, but here I (selectively) follow the conversations most relevant to understanding the embodied aesthetics of icon study.

Iconology and Iconography

No scholarly itinerary of icons would be complete without a discussion of Erwin Panofsky's incitement to stir beyond formal or aesthetic study to a much wider interdisciplinary domain. Touching on the icon first in "Perspective in Symbolic Form" (1924), Panofsky elaborated his concerns in *Studies in Iconology* (1939), a book that proposed the study of icons as a science.[23] His pursuit of two kinds of study prompted by the icon—iconography and iconology—compels us to consider not just the formal, but also the social and political, dimensions of the visual arts.

Panofsky distinguishes three levels of meaning that engage the viewer of a picture. The first of these involves a perception of compositional elements such as color, line, and relations between entities, sensations that become expressive in art. An analysis of Leonardo da Vinci's *The Last Supper*, at this level, would identify the color, line, and design of thirteen men around a long table. A second level involves registering artistic motifs, themes, and concepts. We see the figure of Christ but recognize him from a culturally known gesture, pose, or location within the painting. To "know" Christ means to inhabit a larger cultural field of "stories and allegories" (Panofsky 1939), an iconographic endeavor where the "graph" is recognized by its repetition of a prior image known to the artist and viewer. This reminds us of Mondzain's suggestion that, as artificial images, icons are heterogeneous in their substance: They use the materials of their time to endlessly repeat, albeit in somewhat changed form, a semblance of the original miraculous natural image. The repetition of iconic trace—the inscription—implies that the examiner of the painting must catch it, must know it just as one knows a code, within a larger cultural repository. Here, like scholars of popular religion, Panofsky sees icon semiosis as participation in shared cultural knowledge and practices. While this book clearly is not an iconographic study, these observations are important to historical situations explored later when, harnessed through existing cultural figurations, bio-icons orient ontological becoming toward the social.

But Panofsky is invested in the authority of the art historian—that someone who can describe and classify iconic material in a painting much as the ethnographer describes and classifies races (Panofsky 1955, 31). The art historian's interpretation is the legitimate discourse to be followed by laypeople. In strictly aesthetic terms, as a graphic inscription, the icon is "found" through the proper identification of the primary iconographic trace (the "correctly" made four arms of Visnu, or Christ marked by gesture), even as compositional arrangements and styles may vary. Traditional icons therefore rely on highly regulated forms of knowledge disseminated through institutions and other legitimizing discourses; a religious body or established scholars in a discipline have the authority to ratify an icon. In Hindu practice, we can read bhakti as a move to wrest the right to authorize icons from the intercession of priests or kings, an attempt to destabilize legitimate knowledge production. Such a struggle over cultural (religious and political) authority is instructive to the study of icons that circulate in the secular domain, as well, and it is particularly pertinent to the global icons under scrutiny here, since contestations of their hegemonic iconic messages are just such moments of negotiation—attempts to wrest the icon from its legitimate global form, reassembling it as a technology of the popular.

Aesthetic identification, Panofsky maintains, is followed by the third level of meaning construction, an interpretive moment that propels this practice in art history into what we might think of today as cultural studies. Paintings have intrinsic meaning or content—what the German philosopher Ernst Cassirer (1923–29) would name symbolical values, Panofsky suggests. Drawing on Cassirer, Panofsky explains that these values reveal the basic attitude of a nation, class, or religious / philosophical persuasion. In such a scheme, *The Last Supper* would exemplify Leonardo da Vinci's personal take on Christ and, by extension, that of the high Italian Renaissance. Most important, Panofsky insists that this meaning may be present with or without the artist's conscious intention, an assertion that prompts debates over ideology in later art criticism. This is the iconological move, the analysis that explores the logic of the icon and produces a synthetic rather than analytic moment for Panofsky. But how might the scholarly synthesis of "the artist and his age" escape the subjective eye? Through a strong historical focus, Panofsky maintains, where every work of art would be substantially located back in its historical moment and temper. Where iconography leads us to cultural history and semiotics, iconology opens the study of visual arts into social psychology, anthropology, political science, and history. Of course, Panofsky unifies the moment of production by designating certain "essential tendencies" of a historical moment, and he does not differentiate between viewer positions. Such elaboration would come much later.

Panofsky's attention to the icon found iconophiliac response in Ernst Gombrich some years later, where the icon is deployed rather differently. Gombrich's *Art and Illusion* (1956) and *Symbolic Images* (1972) position pictures as natural signs (echoing Peirce) easily accessed by the child, the savage, the illiterate, even the animal (see also Gombrich 1981). Such a move slips easily into the long history of iconoclasm Mitchell was at pains to explore in his treatise on iconology. Gombrich's pursuit of the image stems from a nature–convention divide in which pictures inhabit the domain of the natural—we are biologically "programmed to scan the world," an optic ability that attaches the picture to nature (Gombrich 1956, 20)—as opposed to words, which rely on conventional knowledge and involve indirect and circuitous routes to cognition. Gombrich's stylized schema allows him to expand and extend the visual formula garnered from the study of paintings to popular culture. In his hands, the study of icons enters discussions of comics and pinups (Gombrich 1956, 9). Here we are already in more familiar territory: The Virgin Mary is proximate to Madonna (the pop star) who repeats the Virgin's lineaments, albeit as form of parody. In this sense, Gombrich moves us into popular culture, with its dispersed variations of cultural expression.

The conventional art-history discourse on the icon we see in Panofsky has a corresponding canon of aesthetics in Hindu iconography, initially catalogued by historians and religious studies scholars. Here, too, devotees recognize an image as an icon because they share cultural knowledge of aesthetic iconographic strictures. An image is not Siva without the third eye; it is not Durga without ten arms equipped with identifiable weapons. Eck notes that *silpins*, or artists, were given strict iconometric and iconographic instructions for making the most excellent image support they could, rules that later were catalogued by art historians such as

J. N. Banerjea (1974) as a theory of art. Once again, the repetition of original material is key to the icon, even if the ornamentation of the trace might vary. Likeness or livingness (*sajivta*) was the primary requirement and not realism, Jain argues, leaving room for exuberant ornamentation and stylization of the images—but always made to correct specifications. In terms of synaesthetic exchange, the exuberance of ornamentation is fundamental to the icon. Whether made for publicity or liturgy, icons are always decorative, resplendent in glitter, texture, color, and style. Sensations, shared between subject and object, become heavily expressive in the icon: expressive as the devotee's art in the *bhava* of image making (traditional popular culture), and expressive as the qualities possessed by these highly ornamental objects (made of textured fabrics, clay, wood, and rich metals, often).

Jain notes that bhava, or excessive ornamentation, reflected the insufficiently contained private sacrality, so that the space and time of the image world became coterminus with the world of the devotee through artistic composition; the devotee further found his or her image within the frame of the picture in groupings of figures around a central image. She returns to the figure of the devotee, variously configured elsewhere as the consumer or the spectator, as well as the culturally embedded viewer so central to Panofsky's gaze. And it is one that has grabbed the lion's share of attention in studies of icons in South Asia. No wonder anthropologists have engaged passionately with what might have otherwise remained largely pursuits of art historians.

Jain is one among many historians and media scholars who are preoccupied with popular practices of consumption from religious life that make their way into the consumption of modern media such as film and television or of mass-produced products such as calendar art. Kapur, for instance, has persuasively demonstrated how Hindi-language popular cinema invokes a frontality of address—that is, the spectator is incited not to see the film text as made from raw material as in classic realist cinema, but to read the iconographic language of *mise-en-scène* through their sedimented knowledge. Sant Tukaram's miraculous visage is worshiped because of the presentational aspect of supporting iconic material from Hindu religious practice; the divine, after all, has immanence in the material culture of the world. Hence, a viewer interpellated by iconography will be encouraged to worship the cinematic image. The film theorist Ravi Vasudevan (2000) extends this commentary on ritual worship to suggest that iconographic material in popular commercial Hindi cinema can be understood as a kind of "condensation of the image," so that a whole elaborate world is encapsulated in the robes, gesture, and props surrounding Sant Tukaram in the 1937 film (Vasudevan 2000, 137). It is to this world the viewer returns through the icon. No wonder, then, that when Dadasaheb Phalke's film *Lanka Dahan* (Burning of Lanka; 1917) was screened in Mumbai, viewers who recognized the god-hero Ram took off their shoes.[24] Such auratization is precisely what Indian realist cinema will disavow. Kapur contrasts the presentation of Tukaram in the famous popular mythological with the reflexive attack on frontality and its suggestions of divine presence in the hands of art cinema auteurs such as Satyajit Ray, whose famous critique of Hindu orthodoxy in *Devi* (1960) disparages the deleterious effects of a devotional psyche. While I would argue that the music in Ray's film celebrates the affects of devotion but seeks to remove them from liturgical orthodoxy,[25] I am in general agreement with Kapur—and, later, Jain—that urban literate bourgeois art practice is marked by a reflexivity that is more recognizably "modern" than the (equally modern) popular practices enshrined in popular cinema, calendar art, chromolithographs, and many other visual practices.

In these studies of popular culture, coteries of consumers already gather. They prompt us to ask: Who auratizes the icon, and what historical motivation lies behind their devotional performances? Such questions, emerging as they do from the itinerary of the icon in art criticism, register a larger historical shift in the field, a redirection of critical attention toward the social histories of the "receivers" (of the iconic message), a categorization that suggests a turn to semiotics. Hence, the incorporative technology we have explored so far becomes understood as a sign that communicates a message, if we have the media protocols to receive it. Within art history, on the one hand, icon veneration receives renewed attention from practitioners such as Robin Cormack (whose work revitalizes the study of Byzantine icons and the society that produced them); on the other, newly conceived investigations in semiotic theory begin to reshape art-historical questions regarding the efficacy of the icon. The latter elaborate an embodied aesthetics of icon consumption, marking a turn into the social, and consequently, into the popular.

Popular Aesthetics

In a short co-written piece, Mieke Bal (a narratologist who brings rhetorical analysis to bear on art history) and Norman Bryson (an art historian known for his attention to the social history of art practice[26]) explain what pressures the interdisciplinary terrain mobilized by semiotics puts on art history, Bryson still attached, in the 1980s, to a positivist view of knowledge (the identification and explanation of visual elements and art practice). As one arena of cultural activity among many in the worlds of sign making, art history could hardly remain untouched by the testing of fact, truth, causality, and proof that had revolutionized semiotics. If the artist had become a "sender" of a message breaking free from the shackles of authorship, the idealized viewer multiplied into a vast array of people marked by different social histories, and the context became the "frame" that imposed coherence on a text within a discursive field (Bal and Bryson 1991).

Bal's own work reflects this turn. In *Looking In: the Art of Viewing* (2001), her major treatise on art practice, she emphasizes the materiality of the work present at its reception. The exact spot on the wall where a painting is hung is the enunciative context that frames matter, composes it for the viewer. Instead of the past, the present animates the material life of the painting, the slight dent in the wall's plaster now contiguous with the meaning the receiver assembles of a seventeenth-century painting. The physical materiality of the image is irrevocably in the present, the image becoming icon in consumption. The painting's potential is activated by the social history of heterogeneous viewers bringing a multiplicity of codes to the visual message. Hence, "the work of art enters networks of semiotic transformation as volatile and tangled as the glances of a crowd in any minute of its life" (Bal and Bryson 1991, 187). Such a differentiated sense of viewers, in Bal's view, is the legacy of the "feminist turn" in semiotics in which the gendered nature of the field of vision imploded the concept of an idealized viewing perspective and insisted on different modes of reception (Bal and Bryson 1991, 188). Her focus on the heterogeneity of viewers (their needs, memory, access to codes, taste, subjection to institutional protocols) bypasses the scholarly activity of piecing together only those elements that might move toward a coherent plausible formal explanation of an artwork.[27] Gone is the art historian's need to exhibit scholarly analyses of a work's production history, as *Looking In* poses the semiotic questions: What elements of a painting are "focalized," or rendered meaningful, from a particular point of view? How do heterogeneous views create conflict around a single artwork? What histories do the viewers bring to their consumption of paintings? We might extend these questions further, keeping in mind the earlier conversation on metaphysics: How does the frame of composition territorialize chaos? When do the intense sensations provoked by the art object dissolve the frame?

Such questions have been addressed most directly in the anthropology of art, represented here by the striking, if controversial, contribution of Alfred Gell, an anthropologist whose semiotic theories of art as technology speak to the genealogies of the icon we have already traversed (and who has had considerable influence on the two major theorists of South Asian icons, Christopher Pinney and Kajri Jain).[28] Gell caused quite a stir with his essay on the enchantment of technology (Gell 1992), but his theory of indexes received sustained elaboration in his posthumously published *Art and Agency* (1998), in which he advocated a methodological atheism necessary to theorizing the reason behind art's "magical" efficacy.

Two points from this work are particularly salient to our concerns. First, in suggesting that artifacts can function as animate objects (while eschewing theories of animism), Gell develops a substantial theory of fractal personhood. If, as I have suggested, a semiotic economy implies an organization of subject–object relations, Gell argues that artifacts mediate social relations between prototypes (what the artifact seeks to represent) and the "recipients" (those affected by indexes but who can be effective themselves). Positioning recipients as outcomes of mediated practices, Gell underscores a "distributed personhood" shared by prototype and recipient. Such fractal personhood suggests a networked materiality in which consumers are neither simply swallowed by the objects they incorporate within them (I become Barbie) nor singular agents acting freely on commodities (I live free of Barbie). Rather, they live a shadow life of objectified personhood dispersed into the world of objects that seemingly are external to them; they live between chaos and territory, incorporative technologies such as icons only exacerbating the experience of shuttling between the two.

Gell's theory of fractal personhood applies most extensively to indexical artifacts that have abductive agency. Here we remember Peirce, who also insisted on abduction (rather than induction or deduction) as the process behind icon semiosis, even though, as we shall see, Gell moves beyond signification as communication. The logic of abduction transpires when both induction and deduction fail to account for material entities in their transformation into signs. The failure, in Gell's account, inheres in the index that is always cognitively indecipherable. Smoke might indicate a fire in accordance with natural laws, but, Gell remarks, smoke can also be made without fire (our cultural knowledge tells us). As artifact, smoke is therefore not fully decipherable, compelling synthetic inferences that remain ambiguous, unstable. Therefore, we infer that a smoke signal has an agency we normally ascribe to people. As technology, it enchants with its magical efficacy in the world; as aperture, it directs us to the natural or social world, incorporating us into it through its material form. Most important, it prompts the recipient of the signals to respond in performances that, for Gell, are not necessarily invested in communicating with other subjects. Such a theory rather obviously provides the logic for happenings that icons can prompt, for the repertoire of expressive performances (including the artistic theatricality of icon desecration) we understand as popular culture. My only reservation remains with the unshakeable instability—"volatility," in my vocabulary—of such magical artifacts, for, as I argued in the previous chapter, the speed (and frequency) of icon transmission ensures that certain inferences, synthetic as they are, may well stabilize as the legitimate account. They often focalize a graphic inscription to communicate a stable message. But this is the situation with mass-mediated images beamed from a single point to a large field of reception. Gell was hardly addressing mass media. Rather, his theory of the abductive agency inherent in auratic objects analyzes consumption in everyday performances (with their requisite singularity) of a fractal personhood.

Indeed, the performativity of consumers has been a source of fascination for scholars of all cloths, including those who scrutinize mass media such as Hollywood cinema. Early Hollywood cinema's attractions, too, invoked an embedded social world through spectatorial activity such as sing-alongs, as Miriam Hansen (1991) has argued, but these activities soon disappeared with the standardization of Hollywood cinema, when the abstract spectator replaced an imaginary community held together by cultural reference and sociality. In such studies of mass media, social history returns with force, inspiring other forays into the popular we shall encounter in chapter 4. Briefly, in the case of Indian cinema, Vasudevan (2000) has shown how the sociality of collective consumption persisted even as cinematic norms stabilized; the devotional structure was formalized into the language of cinema—a dársanic organization of looks—well after so-called mythologicals (films based on stories from the Hindu epics and *puranas* [Prasad 2004, 102]) disappeared, sacral enchantments living a shadow life in the cinema. One may add the *kirtans*, or hymns, in mythologicals, as well as the melodic popular music continues to transmit a devotional sensorium familiar to audiences. Popular medleys of cinema attenuate the yearning for the divine as the cinematic iconography opens one into the space of devotion and to the divine beyond. Such audiovisual language constitutes an imaginary community at once.[29] Such an aural dimension to the ocular can indeed be regarded as a "counter-history" of visuality, especially if we remember that Indian

films are often distinguished by the inclusion of song-and-dance sequences as part of the narrative.[30] Cinema sets up a force field of auratized images; therefore, its potentialities can be actualized into image
constituencies that are widely exploited in the sphere of "cine-politics"—
that is, image constituencies that often are mobilized as electoral voting
banks when stars cross over to politics.

While I will focus more centrally on cine-politics later in the book, it is
worth noting here that these studies of collective spectatorship, reception, and fandom—staples of popular culture—argue for a mixed economy of auratic and ordinary artifacts. Icons may have the kind of abductive agency Gell attributes to art, giving them auratic charge. But they
might also lapse into ordinary junk piled in an attic, hoarded in a shop, or
discarded as trash. Christopher Pinney's *Photos of the Gods* (2004), for
example, offers a wide range of such mass-produced images endlessly
morphing into miraculous and alluring figures at certain critical junctures. Sometimes the transformation, the aesthetic salvaging of elements
from an already known "divine" original reassembled within a realistic
scene, fulfills well-conceived political agendas. Gods come to reside comfortably in fields filled with tractors driven by industrious modern farmers or along national borders infested with armed soldiers.[31] Historical
contingency ensures that certain symbolic meanings, garnered from inferences transmitted within their media ecology, stabilize. They become
incorporated into graphic inscription, and the iconic sign accrues density.
It is this accretive symbolic density that is most useful to politics, in
Pinney's view, enabling the ideological capture of the traditional philosoph-
ical/liturgical object. The mother goddess therefore sanctifies Mother India in a series of lithographs (as well as songs, speeches, and poems) in the
nationalist's capture of the iconic trace.

Yet such messages often come to be contested over time. When they
are, the image, dislodged from its connotative matrix, regains what Pinney calls its "figural power." It turns volatile, in my terms, when it can be
accessed as aperture once more. Through his ethnography in Bhatisada
(in India's heartland), Pinney (2004) supports his argument about this
turning figural by showing how lower-caste denizens who are not interested in the artist or why the icon was produced often respond to mass-
produced icons to excavate its future potentialities, its ability to lead the
worshiper elsewhere. The icon with abductive agency bringing good fortune enables the devotee to imagine a there where they want to live.

We have moved far indeed from detached contemplation of aesthetics
as a modern science to a robust popular where material artifacts function

as corporeal apertures to something beyond representation. Hegemonic populism seeks to bind the ambiguity of this indexicality, re-territorializing unleashed sensations to a common horizon where all subjects exist in equivalence. But the popular articulated against hegemony deploys icons as technology for incorporation into a collective unbound by commonality: There is no general aspiration; there is only a linking of diverse demands. Since the collectivity is indeterminate, it remains a "there"— peopled by other subjects, no doubt, but not those who can be defined by cultural or natural laws. The indeterminacy of the social ensures that the icon that quilts heterogeneous social demands still exists as potentiality; volatile in its magical efficacy, it enchants with its agency even as its animated form incorporates us into the world.

As I close the discussion of the synaesthetic encounter and its social consequences, it is best I disclose the stakes of this genealogical reflection clearly. With embodied consumption, posed here at the micro-scalar level of the subject, I have elaborated a plural materialism that is key to understanding the potentiality of the icon to which I shall return. But the selectively assembled genealogies also signal a politics of embodiment that I see as crucial to any intervention in the conversation on global modernity, where the accumulation of "biocapital"[32]—offering surplus "life," as Melinda Cooper (2008) has argued—has become important to the techno-scientific ambitions of neoliberal regimes that extract, buy, sell, and redistribute blood, tissue, organs, plants, and indigenous knowledge. Theorists of new media assemblages (such as Mark Hansen and Eugene Thacker) have rigorously criticized the turning of biological materiality into information, recoding the subject and the world. While these conversations are not part of this book, they certainly lend new urgency to my focus on corporeality. When enfolded into the icon (as a moving technology capable of unlocking totalizing systems), the same body that is constrained and appropriated by capital can become the means for the subject's incorporation into a liquid social. Corporeality is therefore a potentiality,[33] shared by the icon and the adoring subject, that can turn consumption into contingent embodied praxis.

In theorizing the corporeal dynamism of the icon, I have attempted to designate a second materiality for these objects. Such "mattering" follows a philosophical tradition that includes Spinoza, Deleuze, Lingis, Nietzsche, Bataille, de Certeau, and Massumi and that parleys in the logic of abundance, where chaos is a plethora of forces. This is appropriate to the logic of exuberance crucial to the metaphysics of the icon that I seek to bring into conversation with studies of its material culture.[34] Some theorists of affect—notably, Brian Massumi and Steven Shaviro—advance an incorporeal materialism in which the body is a dynamo that is constantly moving toward matter. But in the living organism's "becoming," or taking form, Massumi argues, the body, its excitations increased in its interactions with other objects, is consistently brought back into the grid of law, code, and signification that label it as particularized subject. And yet, if we consider its basic dynamism, its consistent capacity to adapt (mutations that are often the purview of natural sciences), then something always remains unanchored to a particular perspective (Massumi 2002, 15). Therein lies its potentiality.

In part 3, where I return to the question of collective agency against a (bio-political) global modernity, one can see how this potentiality can be rethought as the body's open-ended sociality. If the body is always opening to matter, it is always social in its movement toward material contiguity with the collective. This is not its "pre-sociality," Massumi maintains, but an unassailable lived sociality that is always arrested when subjects are divided into groups or, worse still, individualized. The potential of the body to change becomes the possibility of social change, as the closing chapters of the book show. One might say that the formation of the popular—the harnessing of the "taking form" or becoming—is one moment of capture, but it draws its energy from (and exists always in tension with) lived sociality, the affectivity of the absent social.

To conclude my framing of the icon's corporeal potentiality, a word regarding my critical location within these theories of sensation and signification. As I indicated earlier, my point of entry is through the work of feminist philosophers who are not always cited as theorists of sensation and who have long insisted on the force of bodies—especially bodies marked by difference—as a potentiality. In conjunction with this philosophical tradition, which is ever attentive to difference, I build on decades of work in gender studies, postcolonial studies, critical race studies, and queer "body criticism." While my epistemological debt to this work is vast, the direct inspiration for this book is Elizabeth Grosz's call for an "energetics of signification" (Grosz 1994), one that poses representation to be one event among others—hence, the body is a force to be reckoned with, not simply a sign to be read.[35] If we consider the body debates in feminist theory, the work of philosophers such as Moira Gatens (1995), Genevieve Lloyd (1994), Rosalyn Diprose (2002), and Rosi Bradiotti

(1994) appear alongside Grosz in their varied emphases on the body's potentialities as the ground of feminist ethics. But it is Grosz's focus on corporeal dynamism in *Volatile Bodies* (1994) that remains most influential to my feminist project, even as her *Chaos, Territory, Art* (2008) informs my emphasis on the body as a field of power.[36]

In her post-Cartesian critique of a surface-depth schema, Grosz prompts us think of the body–mind articulation as the Möbius strip, where both surfaces (interior and exterior) are at once legible.[37] A physical experience (an accident, a wound, a beating) shapes the psyche inasmuch as psychic experiences (visual objectification or being the target of hate speech) leave imprints on the body. Such a perception may be regarded as a corporeal conception of the "subject" shaped equally by law, right, requirement, social imprimatur, custom, and habit as by the biological, technological, or the ecological. The corporeal incorporates the psychic and physical constitution of raw flesh into a "body"; it establishes the body as a technology, as Michel de Certeau (1979) would insist, coextensive with the world of objects but marked by messages that separate it from the social Other. Such a conception allows us to think of incorporative technologies such as icons as capable of forging social bonds, joining subject and object through their lustrous and alluring forms. The icon can activate ontological becoming even as it reorients the subject toward an unrealized possible social.

These scholarly trajectories remain critical for my argument on the icon's potentialization under historical conditions of possibility. They bring the force of the body to bear on struggles over global modernity in which global icons habitually surface. In turn, these glittering forms indicate that "globality"—that place where we now live—is increasingly experientially corporeal. Our bodies become heavy with missed flights in overcrowded airports; the young lift telephones during long night shifts that rewire their bodies to different time zones; the jihadist turns from lost oil wells of wealth to fight the new world order by imploding his body. Hence, the icon, which activates intense sensations, becomes fundamental to grasping the phenomenology of the global.

PART 2

Biographs

THE MATERIAL CULTURE OF GLOBAL ICONS

Arundhati Roy by the Narmada River, 1999. Ian Berry, Magnum Photos.

Global icons are deceptively smooth. Their hard, commoditized shine blinds us; they move fluidly, effortlessly in mass
media. Culturally, particular messages packaged as universal
mantras stream from a single point of production, often
backed by strong financial conglomerates. They materialize
in a "global footprint," the geographic contour encompassing
a large number of sites of reception that is transnational in
reach.[1] For many, the compromised commoditized Gandhi or
Nelson Mandela, yoked to the great "cause" of consumerism,
seem now aligned with those very forces—of capital, of
metropolitan racialized power—they once fought. One of
the global icons under scrutiny here, Arundhati Roy, rumi-
nates on the deeply destructive effects of iconization in general, responding obliquely to her own material life as mass-
mediated sign:

> It is interesting how icons, when their time has passed, are
> commodified and appropriated (some voluntarily, others
> involuntarily) to promote prejudice, bigotry, and inequity
> they battled against. But then in an age when everything is
> up for sale, why not icons? In an era when all of humanity,
> when every creature of God's earth, is trapped between
> the [International Monetary Fund] checkbook and the

American cruise missile, can icons stage a getaway? The three high priests of nonviolent resistance. Together they represent (to a greater or lesser extent) the twentieth century's nonviolent liberation struggles. Today the elites of the very societies and peoples in whose name the battles for freedom were waged use them as mascots to entice new masters. (Roy 2006, 69–70)[2]

Roy's point is both simple and elegant. Icons exist in synecdochal relation to the many, shoring up part for the whole. Yet their star image captures an individuated figure wrenched from the very social relations that gave it ethical charge: The icon is illustrious, extraordinary, imbued with human qualities that common people lack. Such reification is especially disturbing when the icon in question spent most of his or her life working for the very social world that gradually has been eclipsed by the gigantic shadow of individual greatness.

In this classic form of the commodity fetish, as Marx intimated, the (iconic) sign appears as a *social hieroglyph* that speaks to the abstraction of labor within a total system of exchange. As both Theodor Adorno and Walter Benjamin would variously argue,[3] it invites scrutiny of its secrets; made hyper-visible through publicity, it surfaces as an inscrutable mystical object soliciting the critic's gaze. Gandhi as mascot for Apple's "Think Different" campaign, for example, presents an ironic figuration in which the commodity fetish services not only a techno-consumerism the living figure emphatically challenged but also a consumer economy whose costs accrue to the very poor whose desires transformed Gandhi into (the beloved) "Bapu" (an affectionate term for "father"). Yet the irony is only apparent when the appropriation of Gandhi elicits criticism, releasing the message of capital this "imagistic correlate" (as Adorno might have described it) conceals, hides, and encrypts.

More than Adorno's, Benjamin's elaboration of the commodity as social hieroglyphic is most relevant to the economies of the icon I have proposed so far. His observations on the critical gaze motivated by a certain commodity image do provide a well-established critical framework for thinking about social relations through mass-mediated signs. Much like Benjamin's allegory, the dialectical image that motivates us to return to an original meaning, the icon, also can lose the "phantom-like objectivity" of its commodity form to reveal its historical materiality. Like Baudelaire's rage-filled allegory (as Benjamin reads it) transforming a vacuous Cupid-on-the-candy-box into the "becoming human of the whore" (the prostitute as the first image of the wage laborer), a mystifying Mother Teresa keychain can be transformed by embodied consumption into a historical figure, a lackey for Vatican II.[4] But beyond its general function as a wish image, I have argued, the icon is a rather distinctive mass commodity: a framed object that is heavily reliant on a secure epistemology, its decorative form intensifies sensations, provoking an ontological becoming. In short, the icon's distinctive operation enables the transformation of this sign into a magical technology of the popular. While in its hegemonic circulations as mass commodity an icon might well provide a glimpse into existing social relations, as volatilized signifier it alerts us to demands for social change. When the icon volatilizes, we "see" it in its historical materiality. Now a dialectical image, the icon appears heterogeneous, a rebus, entering the crisis of signification that is a controversy. Hence, scholars of the popular remain ever attentive to emergences we recognize as "media events" where multiple and competing significations of an icon peak, generating high affects. Other images of the bio-icon, entering mass media networks from less objectifying interchanges, make ephemeral appearances. Their entry troubles the waters; contestations of the icon's universal message signal that an epistemological crisis is at hand.

If we follow the propositions of the preceding chapters, epistemological crises disturb the organization of perceptions and affections that stabilize the sovereign territories of subject and object, dislodging the subject's orientation toward the goals, tasks, and activities expressive in the mass commodity. As sensations flow freely between the icon (a lustrous object unassailably intensifying sensations) and the subject (the devotee/consumer), the icon volatilizes; it provokes an ontological becoming. The autonomous flow of affect flowing freely between subject and object, however, confronts us in mass media as merely one among many sensational events. Two difficulties arise: on the one hand, the problem of locating affect, and on the other, the ubiquity of sensationalized media events. For in the mass-media capture of autonomous affect, sensations are often *re*located to the subject, which now appears as pathologically delusional, hysterical, or delirious. When such a subject is collective, we have the famed fear of mobs, of uncontrollable crowds that are no longer rational subjects. Any actions these mobs undertake are sporadic and historically inconsequential. Moreover, sensations packaged as hyperbolic word, sound, or image and splashed across the news as cryptic headline, alluring sound bite, disturbing (and repeated) footage, or enticing "tweets," hit us so often that we are numbed to their affect. But if we remember a constant tension remains between the flow of sensations (autonomous affect) and its arrest (captured affect as emotion), then sensational events, even commercially motivated publicity stunts, are worth investigating for what they can catalyze.

The task at hand is to discern when to pay attention to sensational controversies as signs of the popular—to stabilize relevant controversies amid the infinite traces of our durable bio-icons. After all, our bio-icons have robust presence in mass media. They dazzle us in everyday celebrity culture; the frequency of their media traces peak when they receive recognition (accolades, prizes, institutional status). But these moments hardly direct us to their social efficacy as magical technologies of the popular. When do these glittering images function as corporeal apertures for popular contestations of hegemonic aspirations? When are they social hieroglyphs for contestations of macro-scalar historical changes? If, as I have argued, the neoliberal ethos is one hegemonic aspiration that is consistently negotiated in public cultures, the controversies surrounding our icons most relevant to this discussion are those in which the stark historical materiality of the icon destroys its capacity to embody universal aspiration—the icon enters an epistemological crisis, an iconocrisis with lasting effects. One of the methodological challenges of reading the popular is to discern which controversies accompany a deeper epistemological crisis driven by macro-scalar change.

Iconocrises are hardly new phenomena, as the curators, editors, and scholars of *Iconoclash* remind us. Joseph Koerner (2002) provokes us to think of the fervent desecration of images in the Low Countries following the Reformation; these iconoclastic acts prompted several artists (such as Albrecht Dürer) to sanctify the fall of images in their works. But in doing so, the artists acknowledged the power of the icon. Their artworks—at once iconoclastic and witnesses to iconophilia—can be read as one of the many "iconoclashes" that have rocked the world since the Byzantine controversies of the eighth century. We are invited to place the events of 1566 alongside those of 2001, when the Taliban destroyed the Bāmiyān Buddhas. As ever, the ritualistic desecration of the Buddha statues as a partial transformation into an aniconic society, Pierre Centlivres argues persuasively, only motivated a proliferation of giant Buddhas—hitherto neglected colossuses now restored for future generations in Tadzhikistan and China and new ones built in other parts of the world (most memorably, a gold one in Thailand that is much larger than the Afghanistani Buddhas).[5] Despite the historical continuity established by the "Iconoclash" exhibit, one striking difference persists between the peaking iconoclasm of the Reformation and the iconoclashes of our time. Iconocrises of the present are often well-orchestrated media events with calculated global coverage, as we have seen with the Taliban and the carefully controlled Iraq war footage (making leaks all the more subversive). If icons are often deployed in such meticulously planned media spectacles, in the rote staging of politics, how are we to weigh the significance of the iconocrises of the three bio-icons in question?

The iconocrises that concern us may be characterized as deep (media) events that govern our understanding of large historical forces or movements, as Mrinalini Sinha (2006) describes them. These are substantively different from "banal events," which Wendy Brown (1997, 1) argues are the regular contemporary media controversies that have become a part of everyday life. In her meticulous reconstruction of the controversy over Katherine Mayo's book *Mother India*, published in 1927, that erupted through the 1930s, Sinha situates the *Mother India* affair as the most massive international controversy before the controversy of *The Satanic Verses* broke in 1989. Sinha's historiographical intervention calls for a rethinking of the "event," which is necessary to reposition the *Mother India* controversy in the histories of colonial India informed by an imperial-nationalist framework. While the publication of *Mother India* did not mark a historical rupture, a clear before and after, the cascading waves that emanated from the debates produced an unpredictable event: a break in dominant British colonial understandings of Indian society (2006, 4–5). The *Mother India* affair might therefore be considered the kind of "creative event (*événement matrice*)" that facilitates historical shifts in semantic domains crucial for political mobilization.

The iconocrises of our three bio-icons are neither as global in scope nor as effective in activating deep ruptures as the *Mother India* or *Satanic Verses* affairs. But we need to be careful of too cursorily dismissing contemporary media events, to be more painstaking in parsing their reach and effects. Consider two recent global media events concerning the Bollywood actress Shilpa Shetty. A mediocre actress, Shetty hit transnational media networks in 2007 as the target of hate speech on the British show *Celebrity Big Brother*.[6] While the incident was insignificant, as Shetty was at pains to note, the "waves" created by the controversy marked it as an event: The show received calls from hundreds of viewers; Tony Blair apologized on behalf of the two women who had misspoken; and the Indian government offered the culprits a free trip to India that might revise their racist misconceptions about Indians. Commentators were quick to regard such responses as the mark of a change in British relations with India as an emerging economic power, the controversy both a symptom of a historical shift (governed by large historical forces) and constitutive of the shift, although on a much smaller scale than the creative event of *Mother India*. Shetty's appearance in the *Celebrity Big Brother* affair is fundamentally different from the cameo role she played the same year when she was kissed by the actor Richard Gere at an HIV/AIDS awareness event and right-wing Hindu troops burned effigies of Gere afterward. This banal media event, orchestrated by a Hindu right that was desperate to jolt the middle class into national chauvinism, was elaborated as an affront to Indian womanhood (despite Shetty's sharp protests to the contrary). The tired cliché did not really capture any existing semantic struggle; it merely attempted to revitalize a languishing conservative social agenda. The banal event simply illustrates just how much convening media spectacles have become a part of everyday life in India.

The bio-icons in this volume have often been in the midst of both kinds of controversy. When Phoolan Devi "surrendered" to Indian police forces in 1983, her negotiated terms, as Rajeswari Sunder Rajan (2004) has so eloquently argued, fueled a controversy over the failure of the postcolonial state's politico-juridical stability. Coming close on the heels of the Emergency period (1975–77), already a serious blow to the postcolony's project of democratic self-rule, the controversy might be considered the tailspin of a long historical shift. Phoolan Devi's life story, splashed across the nation's major news venues in 1983, only underscored just who had reaped the fruits of freedom. If an eleven-year-old girl could have been brutalized—married off to an older widower, beaten, raped, and abducted—into becoming an outlaw by virtue of her gendered caste status, surely something was rotten in the postcolonial state of India. By 1994, when controversies erupted over Shekar Kapur's film *The Bandit Queen*, the furor over Phoolan Devi's representation as a Dalit subject captured the structure of feeling of a rising Dalit social movement with aspirations to democratic representation. While these two controversies were indeed creative events in which the bio-icon had turned volatile, other controversies that have dogged Phoolan Devi have erupted and faded as many banal events: the soap-operatic tensions with her sister; her arraignment in court; her numerous confrontations with publishers, lawyers, filmmakers, and journalists. Several chapters will discriminate between the two kinds of media events that erupt along the biograph, the cultural biography, of the icon.

We are concerned here with those oscillations of the biograph that register contestations of the icon's global form as it embodies hegemonic globalizing aspirations. As the international "face of charity," not only did

Mother Teresa effectively legitimize the financial and political expansionism of Vatican II, but her widely disseminated iconic sign virtually obscured vibrant social work under way in the "city of slums" that gave her
global purchase. The epistemological crisis around the nun, which arose
from efforts to package Kolkata's neoliberal restructuring as a "mega-
city," would conjure cultural figurations of the popular saint whose image
could not be yoked to either transnational (Roman Catholic) or local
(Kolkata) agendas. The heated outbursts over the value of the saint would
illuminate an auratic object whose unproductive expenditure could not be
subsumed within regimes of charity. In the "Locations" (part 3) section of
the book, I will return to the historical denouement of the media events
discussed in this chapter. I will argue that the epistemological crises
around the saint, the activist, and the outlaw, whose auratic charge explodes their capture in global forms, arise from neoliberal transformations under way that are fiercely contested. If the mega-city, which reorganizes urban spaces through foreign investment, is one macro-scalar
change we see as part and parcel of neoliberal regimes all over the world,
then global civil society as the only mode of political activism against state
and corporate power, along with electoral democracy as the only workable
political system, are two other projects of contemporary modernity managed through the global icons arraigned here. If Arundhati Roy's glamorous image signaled a "networked" transnational green politics, the
exemplary global civil society, environmental activists in India worried
whether the cost of global legibility might entail the elision of situated
social (environmental) movements, calls for distributive justice taking a
backseat to deep ecological critique. And when Phoolan Devi's commoditized image as a legendary outlaw—whose entry into parliamentary politics signaled the triumph of India's electoral democracy—made a splash,
commentators in the national press saw it as deleterious to vigilance
against continuing state violence aimed at subaltern populations. In each
of these cases, the saint, the subaltern, and the activist become packages
that conceal the social contradictions that arise in the face of these global
projects. Well-crafted, lively, and entertaining narrations of the icon's
"lives" manage antinomies that stabilize the epistemology of the icon.
They appear as representative of a new, now global, social totality.

These recursive global forms continue to circulate; polished, mythic,
and recursive, they endure until the unbearable weight of global modernity exposes their historical materiality. Certainly, neoliberal restructuring produces deep uncertainty that is apparent in the manifold crises of
our times. But despite precarity, if the human subject is constantly dyna-

mic—adapting, mutating, or evolving—then we can posit outbreaks of affect around the reorganizations of spaces, bodies, and resources as a demand for new pathways to change that are unpredictable in their outcomes. When these outbreaks surround global icons that embody particular neoliberal aspirations, we can review this basic capacity in historical terms. Epistemological crises, in other words, provide indices well beyond a shift in signification; they can register creative, dynamic forces at work beneath the well-charted road to progress. These shifts, folded into representation, appear as one among many controversies in mass media. It is only in the retrospective critical gaze, such becoming is writ as historical contestations of global modernity; only in retrospect, the controversy appears as a deep (creative) media event.

In the balance of the chapter, I stabilize three controversies we can read as contestations of the neoliberal consensus, where the global form of the bio-icon appears especially alienating: Roy's highly publicized turn to activism in 1999; Mother Teresa's globally telecast beatification in 2003; and Phoolan Devi's widely reported assassination in 2001. All three controversies are not simply disagreements that erupted in media but creative events—dissension that spiraled into heated exchanges (demonstrated in sensational speech or gesture) that intimated furious negotiations of neoliberal agendas materializing a global modernity. In these iconocrises, we plunge *medias res* into the biograph, into wild oscillations that record increased frequencies of mass-media traces as sensationalized events direct us to the volatile signifier in the eye of the storm.

SCENE ONE: THE OCCASIONAL ACTIVIST

We know that Arundhati Roy burst on the global stage when she won the Booker Prize, Britain's most prestigious literary prize, in 1997 for her only novel, *The God of Small Things*. Shortly thereafter, Roy turned to nonfiction writing in sustained intellectual solidarity with environmental and economic justice movements in India, quickly earning the unwieldy appellation "writer-activist."[7] Perhaps Roy's legitimacy as an activist is most closely linked to her participation in the Narmada Bachao Andolan (NBA), a worldwide mobilization against the building of the Narmada dam that launched one of Roy's first nonfiction pieces and to which she donated her Booker Prize money. We shall return more substantially to Roy's activist engagements with the NBA later in the book; but here, such involvement is important because her designation as an "activist," one who not only fights the local war but also translates that struggle for transnational audiences, is precisely what has been most vociferously contested in the Indian national media.

The child of a Bengali Hindu tea-planter father and a Syrian Christian mother, Mary Roy (the inspiration for the sensuous portrait of Ammu in *The God of Small Things*), the activist icon Arundhati Roy had her early education in her mother's informal Western-style school in Ayemenem, in the southern Indian state of Kerala. After a few years of boarding school, Roy, at sixteen, began to study architecture at the Delhi School of Planning and Architecture. Then she famously "dropped out," disturbed by the thought of catering to the demands of the elite for the rest of her life. In fact, her earliest written work—the screenplay "In Which Annie Gives It Those Ones," which became a national-award-winning film in 1989—features a maverick architecture student whose eclectic urban plans attempt to ameliorate the living conditions of Delhi's many non-citizens dispossessed by the government's aggrandizement of public space. Just a few years earlier, Roy had played a sultry "tribal woman" in Pradip Krishen's film *Massaey Sahib* (1984), a successful venture that culminated in Roy's marriage to the director. Yet her own screenplay for the film *The Electric Moon* (1992) was not greeted with enthusiasm. But Roy persevered with her writing, dedicating four years to her debut novel, *The God of Small Things*, a publication that catapulted her to fame overnight.[8]

The rest is history. The book turned out to be a milestone in the world of Indian English letters, only paralleled in its international cachet by Salman Rushdie's novel *Midnight's Children* (1981). Made restless by her sudden fame, Roy embarked on a series of nonfiction pieces in the year following her Booker Prize for *The God of Small Things*. Already in these early polemics she betrayed suspicion of mass media's ruinous Midas touch. "*The God of Small Things* became more and more successful and I watched as the city I lived in grew blacker," she says in the seemingly direct but carefully crafted prose that has won her fame. "The cars became sleeker, the gates grew higher and the poor were being stuffed like lice into crevices, and all the time my bank account burgeoned. I began to feel as though every feeling in *The God of Small Things* had been traded for a silver coin, and if I wasn't very careful I would become a little silver figurine with a cold, silver heart."[9]

But the glamorous writer's turn to activism met with real opposition when the ubiquity of Roy's star image made her *the* global face of the NBA, often eclipsing charismatic leaders such as Medha Patkar who were instrumental in the grassroots mobilization of the organization. I will return to the question of activism in the NBA later but here I provide a quick gloss to the social movement (see also Ghosh 2009). Amita Bavishkar's excellent scholarly study of the indigenous communities, or Adivasis, involved in the NBA suffices as a beginning.[10] Bavishkar's *In the Belly of the River* places communities affected by the dam (upstream and downstream) who have mobilized against unfettered "development" in the Narmada Valley as the central actors of the struggle. She describes the NBA as a social movement against the Sardar Sarovar Project (SSP), one part of the greater Narmada Valley Development Project, the single largest river-valley hydro-irrigation project in India, involving the building of 30 major, 135 medium-size, and 3,000 minor dams. The Narmada Valley Project was inaugurated in 1961; in 1985, the World Bank agreed to fund it.[11] Proponents of the project argue that it will bring irrigation, power generation, and drinking water (added as an afterthought) to vast populations. According to government estimates, 152,000 people will be affected by the project, 37,000 of them Adivasis from the villages of Gujarat and Maharashtra.[12] Such a techno-scientific spectacle is part and parcel of the neoliberal state's voracious appetite for energy.

As Roy's nonfiction began to circulate transnationally—first in a series of reprints in international newspapers, and later in small-press publications of "pamphlets"[13]—scholars who had been writing about the NBA warned her against her tendency to make large, sometimes oversimplified, claims on the behalf of the movement. The sociologist and human-rights activist Gail Omvedt, for instance, criticized Roy in an open letter for her wholesale dismissal of "big dams" and development for rural peoples and for her misrepresentation of the massive NBA global alliance as a "small ragtag army" confronting a Goliath state.[14] Later, when Roy was jailed for a day in 2002, others were vociferous in their criticism of her for paying 2,000 rupees in exchange for three months in jail. Paying the fine, they argued, not only validated the trumped-up charges brought by the state against several activists but also singled out Roy from those who faced the penalty but could not afford the fine. Even reports that seemed supportive of the "new Arundhati Roy" adopted a sardonic slant. "She had shaved her head and stomped around swathed in her multicolored scarves along the sands of the Narmada," declaimed Malathi Rao (2002), highlighting the sensuous appeal of the star icon. "She added colour to the movement."

If these voices appeared suspicious, one critic attacked Roy in no uncertain terms: the social historian Ramchandra Guha, who is known for his extensive accounts of environmentalism as a global social movement articulated as a series of regional struggles. Quite soon after Roy's first pronouncements on the NBA, Guha accused Roy of unthinking self-indulgence in her antinuclear polemic, "The End of the Imagination" (1999). Guha's trenchant critique prompted a sustained debate on the Roy's activism in the Narmada Valley in *The Hindu* and in *Frontline*, an English-language magazine run by the *Hindu*.[15] Attacking Roy's political statements in *The Hindu* in November 2000, Guha argued that Roy should have stuck to writing novels because her vanity effectively devalued the work of more serious activists on the Narmada dam project. The cause was just, Guha believed, but Roy's grandstanding on its behalf served only to turn her into a spectacle at the expense of the anti-dam movement. To a large extent, Guha, Omvedt, and others took pains to "correct" Roy's speech acts because they had such wide transnational circulation; but for our purposes, their criticism corrected the symbolic cachet of Roy's iconic image, as well. Indeed, Guha declaimed extensively on Roy's many slips. In making disparaging remarks about the judges when India's Supreme Court was hearing a case filed by the organization she sought to support, Roy was careless, Guha maintains, and harmed the NBA as a consequence.[16] Others were gentler in their opprobrium. In late 1999, when the National Law School in Bangalore convened a meeting on the Narmada issue, the eminent legal scholar Upendra Baxi suggested that it would be wise for the NBA to disassociate itself from Roy because Roy's speech and actions could have a tremendous impact on the movement.[17] With *The God of Small Things*, published in a hegemonic language (of governance), Roy was already legible as the reified glamorous "voice" of Indian democracy; multinational media representatives followed her to the banks of the Narmada, to the Supreme Court, to her one night in jail. Once the "voice" of social critique against caste discrimination—a subject that still exerts considerable fascination for the historical West—the literary star now legitimized green politics.

The controversy over Roy's alliance with the NBA in November 2000 highlighted Roy's global form as the "green activist." The widely recognized articulate icon feted in the world of letters could be depended on to render a complex and unfamiliar local struggle in the global South intelligible to transnational publics through her actions and speech acts. But our preoccupation here is less with Roy's performances than with how she is consumed as an activist. On a larger scale, one might argue that the affective response to how the activist mediates—voices, represents, captures—a regional or local movement is one indicator of the many negotiations over global modernity. If modernity signals a conception of politics where states are accountable to their peoples, the NBA is without a doubt a modern enterprise; questions of compensation, redistribution of land, relocation of the affected communities, affordable electricity and drinking water, and a living wage have always been central to the movement's political agendas. Yet local, regional, and national intermediaries between affected communities and the state have been ever wary of the NBA's insertion into transnational financial, legal, and media networks. They fear the hijacking of regional and national agendas to a global green project, a concern that emerges from a perception that the "global" encapsulates a certain style of mobilization based in the global North that masquerades as representative of all environmentalist struggles. The mass-mediated commodity image of Arundhati Roy, in its particular valence as the "activist" who acts as transnational intermediary, not only revived that fear but also provided an occasion to negotiate the geopolitical imbrication of the NBA. In other words, the activist icon became an effective site for rethinking the NBA's global connections—and particularly the social movement's incorporation into a global modernity, where not all demands against resource extraction, one of the key features of neoliberal expansionism (expressed as both land grabs in special economic zones and the capitalization on energy resources) would be heard.

Indeed, Guha's own scholarship has been critical to understanding such geopolitical differences of green. Perhaps this is why he has been so suspicious of the global forms of activism Roy's commodity image embodies. Sorting through the variants of contemporary environmentalisms—defined as the resistance of ecosystems' people to omnivores—Guha (1997, 4) captures differences in their reach, critical targets, and, most important, modes of activism that enable national and global legibility. One variant of global environmentalism, "the environmentalisms of the poor," is vibrant in the global South. These movements in India, Brazil, and Kenya, among other locales, rely on techniques of direct action, on traditional networks of organization (the village or the tribe), and on traditional forms of protest (the *dharna*, or sit-in demonstration; the *bhook hartal*, or hunger strike by a heroic or exemplary figure; and the *jail bharo andolan*, or the "filling-the-jails rebellion"). By contrast, Northern-style environmentalisms rely on methods of redress from the courts, lobbying of legislators, and exposure in newspapers or on television. The NBA is a successful mix of the two variants, showing its strength through hunger strikes, economic shutdowns and hartals, and sit-ins, while equally engaging in strong media campaigns, court cases, and lobbying of key players such as the World Bank (Guha 1997, 13). A third variant of environmentalism links ecology with questions of human rights, ethnicity, and distributive justice. Here, the defense of a particular locality, rather than the human-as-species relationship that is so central to Northern environmentalism, is the issue at hand (Guha 1997, 18). Some elements of this third variant persist in the NBA struggle, since, as we shall see in a longer discussion of the movement, the Adivasi communities of the Narmada Valley are key actors in the struggle.

The strength of the NBA derives in part from its dexterous interlinking of these different modes of environmentalism so the struggle is made legible everywhere;[18] hence, the necessary cultural translation into a commonly held value-laden framework that scholars of transnational networks such as Sidney Tarrow describe as the astute global framing of mobilization. The Battle of Seattle in 2000 (waged against the WTO meetings), for Tarrow, epitomized an optimal global framing that enabled networks (linkages with a common purpose) to become coalitions (collaborative endeavors), and then to become movements (sustained interactions between challengers and authorities on matters of policy). Obviously, the NBA has managed to calibrate such a chain of linkages, translating complex, strange, and unfamiliar clashes between ecosystems' peoples and police, mobilizing local idioms of protest to register under the common parlance of green.

But such global framing has met with strong criticism in India. Most participants readily acknowledge the gains of being legible under a global green banner; after all, international currencies clearly affect national, urban publics' perceptions of local protests. Yet activists, including Roy, worry with a characteristic postcolonial suspicion of dependence that the presence of benevolent nongovernmental organizations (NGOs) serves to defuse political anger, thus turning folks into dependent victims.[19] NGOs, after all, are not wholly free of governmental processes and procedures, Upendra Baxi reminds us.[20] Therefore, they transform the modes of social action undertaken by those who stand to lose the most and pass organizational power into the hands of intermediaries. Given her perpetual media presence, Roy worries about the spectacularization of protest—"colorful demonstrations" and evocative banners—that serve to make struggles visible but shift our attention away from "real" political action, which is "when soldiers stop fighting, workers refuse to load weapons, and people stop funding companies that make them" (Roy 2004b, 39). Still others criticize the mythopoetic capture within national and global media—the eternal dyad of Medha Patkar and "her" Adivasis —of a rapidly morphing movement. The NBA has changed immensely since its first local stance, when it forcefully asserted, "The dam will not be built" (Kak 2004, 327). It has moved from local resistance to a formal critique of large dams, to a broader inquiry into accepted models of development and, more recently, multiple engagements against privatization. But the cost of global legibility has been the fixing of the first moment in the public imagination, now a static iconic image of the movement. Finally, one of the clear problems of mobilizing the green banner as a grid of global intelligibility is the distilling of certain elements of the movement that now stand in for the whole. The NBA now reads as a struggle against the destruction of the biosphere, environmental injustice against indigenous communities, and the problematic of national "development." Guha emphasizes this third variant, which does not receive extensive media coverage, as focusing primarily on local constellations of power (the alliances between rural elites, politicians, bureaucrats, and the police) engaged in local struggles over ethnicity (the cultural characterization of advasis), human rights (the right to redress against forcible evictions or violence in police custody), and distributive justice (who represents non-citizens and citizens who have almost no political voice). Hence, these resistance groups within the larger alliance are neither well funded nor protected from the violence of the state in the ways that other NBA activists and participants are. Only those who speak in "civil tongue" register as activists worthy of politico-juridical protections against rapacious corporate and government initiatives.

The individuated figure of the (environmental) activist icon has been a point of translation of local struggles for transnational audiences. On the one hand, his or her speech acts make local stories intelligible; on the other, the icon's embodiment of the struggle morally sanctions and legitimates local actions (including violent insurrections that might otherwise register as sporadic hooliganism). Here we see the global form of the activist icon: Historically, particular speech acts (e.g., Roy's translation of local claims into the civil-legal discourse of rights) have become universal messages (e.g., of "green" action for the earth) in which a glamorized middle-class figure comes to embody resistance in South Asia. If we take Guha's provocation to think global modernity along a North–South axis, the parallel case to the NBA is the legibility garnered by the Movement for the Survival of the Ogoni People (MOSOP)—a mobilization against the Royal Dutch/Shell Oil Company in the Niger River delta—after the entry of writer Ken Saro-Wiwa. In his work on "marketing rebellions," Clifford Bob demonstrates how Saro-Wiwa became crucial for transnational awareness of the MOSOP. When Glenn Ellis and Kay Bishop, a husband-and-wife freelancing team originally interested in the Etche minority in

the Niger delta, decided to make a documentary on the Ogoni, Bob maintains, they did so because they had found the articulate Saro-Wiwa, whom
they could harness as translator and icon.[21] Saro-Wiwa's explanation of
the Ogonis' struggle, in a fifteen-minute documentary segment for the
BBC, doubled support for MOSOP and turned the repressive Nigerian regime into an international pariah. Roy functions in a similar way for the
NBA. Her star image, speech, and actions give the NBA wide coverage in
transnationally networked mass media. One might recall the documentary *Dam Nations: Damage* (2002), was funded by the BBC, in which Roy
reigned as the protagonist even after the BBC refused to fund Franny Armstrong's *Drowned Out* (2002). In the latter film, Roy makes only the brief-
est of appearances as the saga unfolds of Luhariya and Bulgi, two Jalsindhi villagers who stand to lose their home to rising waters. Such a
choice of what mass-media institutions such as the BBC will produce—and
distribute, for that matter[22]—goes a long way in revealing how collective
struggles are consumed through individuated icons who embody them,
often in "global forms" that seek to universalize in the name of solidarity.
The "global" institutes a unifying perspective that other locative designa-
tors such as the translocal eschew.

Guha is explicitly critical of the process of individuation that is required for the NBA, a large social movement, to be globally legible. Hence,
he is particularly scornful of Roy's self-styling as a beleaguered dissident.
Her only fears of violence to her person came from her unassailable
position as a citizen, Guha points out, whereas many in the NBA face state
violence every day without much hope of legal redress. Roy (1999b, 108)
insists: "When I told my friends that I was writing this piece, they cau-
tioned me. Go ahead . . . but first make sure you're not vulnerable. Make
sure your papers are in order. Make sure your taxes are paid." Irritated at
this elite concern at a time when blasts from nuclear tests in Pokhran
were affecting the bodies and lives of many in the area who had no
channels for such flamboyant dissidence,[23] Guha asks sardonically: "A
month before Ms. Roy sat down to write her piece, 400,000 adults had
marched through the streets of Calcutta in protest against the Pokharan
blasts. Were their homes all raided by the Income Tax Department?"
(Guha 2000a).[24] Of course, Guha was responding to Roy's earliest, and
admittedly most self-involved, tract of passion; in the trajectory of Roy's
nonfiction writing, "The End of the Imagination" is perhaps her weakest
and most sensational political pitch. Yet its historical place in Roy's now
burgeoning body of nonfiction must be remembered. It was one of the
first nonfiction ventures from a writer who has constantly reinvented

herself in the face of such criticism—stabbing at the glamorous façade, cracking the hard sheen of her star body. To confuse media objectifications of Roy with Roy's objectification of herself (her "self-indulgence," as Guha puts it) is precisely to resort to oversimplification, a charge her staunchest critics level against her.[25]

If Roy's global form as a star activist for a green NBA is contested in the debates of 2000, how is her commodity image cut, pasted, and remixed in such revision? One central commodity image of Roy as iconic activist circulating in the mass media represents her as a "voice," in a fetishistic capture of her speaking for "the people." As early as 1999, after "Greater for the Common Good," Roy's first nonfiction piece on the NBA, was published, photographs of her caught in mid-speech—mouth working, hands (if visible) in expressive gesticulation—began to circulate in (print and online) magazines, on websites, in broadcast-television news footage, in documentaries, and in interviews. Mass-media traces of the "speaking Roy" peaked in 1999, when she was glimpsed at the highly publicized "Rally for the Valley" for the NBA, an event she helped organize in August 1999.[26] The widely circulated images became almost ubiquitous after she received the Lannan Award for Cultural Freedom in 2004. In a series of photographs underscoring her value as a voice, photographs that generically are quite different from the highly stylized shots taken when she won the Booker Prize, Roy habitually appears at a podium or behind a microphone (see figure 14).[27] One may even say that the microphone and the podium become material objects incorporated into the icon's body, iconic prostheses for a star activist.

This mass-mediated commodity image carrying an iconic message— Roy as the voice of the people—has become a point of contention in Roy's alliance with the NBA. One of the opinion pieces prompted by Guha's polemic against Roy, "The Arun Shourie of the Left" (Guha 2000a), directly attacks the fetish of "voicing," effectively cutting and remixing these ubiquitous visual images of the speaking Roy for new ends. In a thoughtful inquiry, Neera Chandhoke (2001, 1), a longtime associate of the NBA, questions the iconic visuals in which Roy appears to speak for those who stand to lose their homes and livelihoods because of the dam.[28] Chandhoke does not embark on a refutation of anything Roy has to say about the losses incurred by the dam-building project but questions the politics of translation involved in making legible the particular plight of subaltern subjects.[29] Chandhoke approaches the historical materiality of the global icon, situating Roy as a middle-class, educated subject who shares cosmopolitan class-based affiliation with those who

FIGURE 14 Arundhati Roy at the Riverside Church, New York, 2003. Photo. Sari Goodfriend.

read her as a representative of those who, as Gayatri Spivak has famously argued, "cannot speak" (i.e., do not have access to communication). It is not that Adivasis affected by the Narmada River Valley Development Project are incapable of representing themselves, Chandhoke explains, but that they simply do not have access to the specialized languages of legal entitlements, rehabilitation and resettlement, and compensation—the languages of modernity that govern Indian state and civil society.[30] Chandhoke illustrates this incommensurable language divide, the tragedy of modern India, through an evocative story:

> [A] revenue official surveying land holdings in the valley for the purposes of assessing the amount of compensation asked a tribal about his land holdings. The tribal, pointing towards an area of land, claimed proprietorship of that land. Expectedly he was asked to show the relevant papers that establish land ownership—the *patta* [deed]. Equally expectedly, the tribal did not possess any such *patta*. "How do you know in this case that the land is yours," asked the revenue official. "The bones of my forefathers are buried along the boundaries of the land," answered the tribal. (Chandhoke 2001, 2)

Since such a claim cannot be supported by the state, the revenue official leaves without a record of this Adivasi as one deserving resettlement. The impossibility of translation between two languages expressing two entirely divergent understandings of the social world is clear in this example. When Roy becomes the voice for such a man, Chandhoke argues, the icon inevitably condemns that other life world to extinction: "The control over translation, recollect, is hers and hers alone" (Chandhoke 2001, 2). Chandhoke remains sympathetic to the loneliness of the translator's voice; hers is a systemic critique of the specialized languages deployed by the state against its own people. But the critique is effective, a performative desecration that wrests the iconic image away from its link to "the people." Roy is no longer the ordinary citizen raging against the state but a privileged subject with a keen sense of rights and obligations. In this respect, Chandhoke is not so far from Roy's criticism of her own iconization as a voice, a position Roy inhabits with some discomfort. Refusing to be the "voice of the voiceless," Roy draws our attention to the systemic silencing that generates a notion of voicelessness in the first place: There are no voiceless peoples, only those "deliberately silenced, or the preferably unheard."[31] In such refutation, the icon's reflexive speech acts join in the cutting, pasting, and reassembling of her mass-mediated sign.

The controversy over Roy's alliance with the NBA reveals deep tensions over regional and local incorporation into transnational (often corporate) financial, legal, and media networks. Activists, writers, scholars, ecosystems' peoples, and journalists participate in this battle over the iconic sign in an effort to refute the global form of a local struggle. Environmental justice as a universal "global green" obliterates many fronts in the NBA where distributive justice and not saving the earth (the focus of deep ecology) is the key concern. The controversy further illuminates the prevalence of mass-mediated signs as *the* sites where such negotiations increasingly take shape. In dislodging "the people"—the diverse, and regionally dispersed, constituencies held together as the NBA—from the icon, Roy becomes an aperture into the popular. Through her now clarified historical relations with the NBA, we glimpse those who will not speak in the tongue of a global civil society.

If such performative desecration releases the iconic image, the image in our contemporary mass-mediated public spheres more often than not is quickly re-territorialized to embody localist or nationalist hegemonic aspirations. This is most evident in the articulation of "difference" among enthusiasts of the free-market economy in India, those who are ferociously pleased with India's post-1991 trade liberalization. An article in the *Times of India* ("Image India," 2005) maintained that Indian icons of sports, cinema, spirituality, food, information technology, literature, music, business, and fashion are fast becoming "global icons," selling

"Brand India" as a cultural soft superpower to transnational audiences. Indeed, as William Mazzarella (2003) documents, national difference is now a vaunted product in global markets that are too savvy to parley directly in exotica. India's historically particular relationship to consumer goods, Mazzarella argues, pursuing the local negotiations of global flows, govern how contemporary ideologies of consumerism have been managed since the opening of markets in 1991. Consumer goods (products manufactured in Britain) were the target of national economic self-determination (*swadeshi*) in the freedom struggle; a strong sense of nationalist difference persists even since the consumer revolution of the 1980s, which was speeded up by trade deregulation and changes in the communications infrastructure of the 1990s (Mazzarella 2003, 13). Mazzarella examines how Indian advertisers manipulate their global address to mark consumer goods as both global and distinctively Indian, creating a genre of signs that just cannot be read as the homogenized versions of signs originating in the global North. One might think of Indian models/ beauty queens as manifestations of such re-territorialized signs: Their streamlined bodies, gestures, dress, hair, and make-up meet the standards of the multibillion-dollar transnational beauty industry, even as a reified Indian "flavor" flaunts national difference for transnational audiences (see, e.g., Reddy 2006).

To read this genre of signs that cannot be flattened into one global regime of signs, Mazzarella argues, one must grasp the re-territorializing of mass-mediated signs marked as global within local sites of consumption. In local productions of global icons, especially those that rely on new communications infrastructures and technologies, we often see such re-territorialization. But let us consider the process further with a closer look at a second bio-icon, Mother Teresa. The furor over her beatification in 2003 illustrates one such local negotiation, in which the denizens of Kolkata rose up in arms over Vatican II's appropriation of Mother Teresa as Christian missionary par exemplar. Amid refutations of the global form, we see the emergence of a "local saint," re-territorialized to give the city she served an international facelift.

SCENE TWO: THE MIRACLE

October 20, 2003: Incense fumes mingle with the heavy scent of white tropical flowers. Women clad in distinctive blue-bordered saris dot the crowd of 300,000 in St. Peter's Square. Bengali songs punctuate somber Latin hymns as the three-hour beatification ceremony for Mother Teresa unfolds on a bright autumn day in Rome. Clearly, the Vatican had acquired an "Indian flavor," as one journalist writing in the Indian English-language press noted, in full pursuit of Pope John Paul II's policy of "inculturating" local idioms into Roman Catholic church practice (Saba Naqvi Bhaumik 2003, 25). That the Vatican would once more mobilize Mother Teresa as its cultural ambassador came as no surprise to either her admirers and or her critics. Nor was her beatification an exceptional event for a pope who had beatified 476 saints in twenty-five years. In this case, he had waived the requisite five-year waiting period after the person's physical death for beatification proceedings to begin. Commencing briskly after Mother Teresa's death, the petition for the dispensation for sainthood and the concomitant diocesan enquiry had been set in motion already in 1997; by 2002, the pope had ratified the nun as "Blessed Teresa of Calcutta," just a rung below canonized saint.

But this was no customary beatification, for at the heart of the globally telecast media spectacle was the charismatic figure, both adored and reviled, whose sainthood millions all over the world (and certainly in her country of residence, India) had eagerly awaited. Here was a radical nun who had once left the church, choosing exclaustration and insisting that she could hear God's command without the mediation of her ecclesiastical superiors, but also one who, by the end of her life, had become the compassionate face of a modern Roman Catholicism and the first Roman Catholic nun ever to grace the cover of *Time* magazine. Perhaps the split-screen color photograph on the front page of the *New York Times* the next morning laid a finger on the nature of all the "fuss" over Mother Teresa (figure 15). On the left half of the photograph's frame, we are presented with a congregation of cardinals, backs turned toward the viewer, resplendent in scarlet ceremonial garb; organized, grave, inaccessible, they seem absorbed in the task at hand. On the other half, we see a crowd sprinkled with some sari-clad Missionaries of Charity, Mother Teresa's order, interspersed among common citizens (one of them, a man clad in a cheap windbreaker, possibly of South Asian descent)—all looking out beyond the frame toward the cardinals.

The press of the crowd is evident: elbows jostling, necks craned, eyes screwed up, faces raised in anticipation. One woman raises a pair of binoculars as if to measure the distance between her and the icon turned theological object. The right side of the split screen fittingly indexes the way in which female viewers are placed at a distance from the male clergy, a religiously gendered division unerringly captured on camera. The split screen stages the two Mother Teresas who had come to trouble each other in years following her Nobel Peace Prize in 1979: The "saint of the gut-

FIGURE 15 Onlookers at Mother Teresa's beatification, 2003. Photo. Courtesy of James Hill, *New York Times.*

ters," a highly volatile auratized icon alive in popular hagiographies, alongside the global icon the Vatican II harnessed for its vast lines of cultural, social, and religious credit. Together, they make her an inscrutable commodity inviting the critic's gaze.

With her beatification, Mother Teresa seemed fully incorporated into the Europe of her birth. Born Agnes Gonxha Bojaxhiu to Albanian parents in 1910, she left her native country just as she turned eighteen. Bojaxhiu's first call came at the young age of twelve, leading to her emigrate to Ireland to join the Loreto Order in 1928 before being sent to the land of her dreams, India, as a novitiate. Starting as a geography teacher, Sister Teresa received a second call in 1946, prompting her to leave the Loreto Order and to found her own congregation. As we shall see, the break from conventional Roman Catholic practice was not easy; it would haunt the radical missionary even after she was completely reabsorbed into Vatican II. With hard-won permission from the pope, Mother Teresa opened her first house, Nirmal Hriday in Kalighat, in 1952; by 1960, several other establishments had begun to crop up all over India. In the years that followed, international renown came to the radical missionary from official quarters, culminating with the Nobel Peace Prize in 1979. Further, in 1978, Pope John Paul II, a fellow Eastern European, came to head the Vatican, and Mother Teresa's international credentialing gathered momentum. The post-1979 period is the most controversial in Mother Teresa's life. As her order grew internationally, she became a commodity par excellence for admirers who advocated an upgraded and modern brand of Christianity, as well as a target for critics who decried the proselytizing propensities of colonial missionary work. In 1989, the much traveled, much embattled icon had her second heart attack and tried to resign as head of the order. But the sisters voted her back into her position as leader, persuading her to stay until early 1997, when, after handing the reins to Sister Nirmala, Mother Teresa succumbed to failing health. She died on September 5 of that year. The beatification ceremony we are following here came six years later.

To be sure, the process of turning the missionary into a saint—a living saint, as she was widely claimed to be, into a beatified one—did not go smoothly. Where Mother Teresa had been ubiquitously mourned in her passing, her beatification brought rumblings of discontent from many quarters. Orthodox Catholics grumbled about this early manifestation of the pope's policy of fast tracking to sainthood, suspicious of a laxity in canonization procedures; secularists, leftists, and social progressives protested that Mother Teresa hardly needed the stamp of church approval, given her unassailable position as a local saint in Kolkata, the city she had made her home.[32] More virulent attacks came from the usual suspects, such as the Hindu right in India. The Rashtriya Swayamsevak Samiti (RSS), the parent body for many right-wing parties, including the Bharatiya Janata Party (BJP) and the Vishwa Hindu Parishad, launched an attack on the beatification in the special Diwali[33] issue of its mouthpiece, *The Organiser*. In an effort to reduce Mother Teresa's work to the lowest common denominator of proselytization, *The Organiser* argued that to glorify this saint would be to glorify conversion and to ratify the troubling iconic message that anchored her image: that the universal human ability to give is best exemplified in the Christian expression of charity. But this was simply predictable criticism against the Vatican, which the RSS saw as a theocratic organization with a global ambition similar to its own. Hence, when Pope John Paul II visited India in 1999, the RSS burned effigies with "conversion" scrawled on them in one of its many banal media events.[34]

But the rumblings of discontent about Mother Teresa's sainthood continued to grow, shaping into a deep controversy. It was not as if the nun was a stranger to controversies; but this was a big one, where her encryption of the popular was at stake. Beyond the political grandstanding, murky facts about the Raniganj (or the Monica Besra) "miracle," which had been used as evidence for her beatification, had begun to emerge. Such news appeared sporadically, often tucked away in newspapers that celebrated Mother Teresa. For example, contestations of the miracle made up a small news item in the international section of the *New York Times* sporting a photograph of the beatification ceremony examined here. Yet the reports were persistent and nagging. Then another face emerged from the shadows cast by the bright glare of beatification: that of a thirty-two-year old Santhal woman, Monica Besra, who insisted that the touch of a medallion carrying Mother Teresa's image had cured her abdominal tumor. Besra's claim would corporealize the saint for transnational audiences as details of tumors, cures, nursing, and physical pain dotted news reports. As Besra acknowledged the miracle, other voices vociferously debunked it and the processes of miracle making. The doctor under whose care Besra's tumor had disappeared produced medical reports of her treatment; Besra's husband, Selku Murmu, who at first denied the miracle, changed his story under pressure from the Missionaries of Charity; and the Left Front government of West Bengal, which generally had been supportive of Mother Teresa's charity work, discouraged the turn to "superstition." All these actors contributed substantially to the litany of press exposés, public challenges, lawsuits, and political rancor, and the global icon began to gather high opprobrium and adulation.

Despite the vilification of the miracle, Mother Teresa's beatification followed rigorous procedure. Beatification mandates an ideal candidate who led an exemplary life. Whatever the criticism of Mother Teresa's notorious silence on injustice, genocide, or embezzlement, the case for exemplarity is easily, if not effortlessly, made. More problematic was the second important qualification for sainthood: evidence of the subject's powers of intercession with God on behalf of ordinary folks.[35] At the heart of the process lay the "miracle," a most vexed event, given the adulation saints habitually garnered in their daily lives. How might it be possible to adjudicate between what might be the delirious fantasy of a devotee and the sacral reality of an event? As the definition runs, the miracle "can be witnessed by the senses, but is in apparent contradiction to the laws of nature."[36] How could the church verify the truth behind an apparent contradiction and not rely on the idiosyncrasies of adoration? One nomenclature stabilized over time: the "cure" of a medical problem that defied the laws of nature, a headlong confrontation between religious and scientific truths and, hence, the formation of the Consulta Medica board of the Congregation for the Causes of Saints that, paradoxically, relies on the latest, most sophisticated medical technologies (e.g., CAT scans, pharmaceutical regimes, medical reports of treatment) to make their assessments. In fact, the current board is headed by Rafaelle

Cortesini, a heart-transplant specialist who claims to have personally witnessed as many as 500 miracles.

Mother Teresa's beatification made its way down the customary routes. The diocesan enquiry was convened in Kolkata from 1997 to 2001, headed by Archbishop Henry D'Souza and Bishop Savaldore Lobo, with Brian Kolodiejchuk as postulator. (The latter would later publish Mother Teresa's "private writings.") The tribunal compiled a formidable document in which one hundred witnesses responded to a survey with 263 questions to produce 35,000 pages of testimony in an eighty-volume report. The archives are housed in Rome but closed to the public. The second phase was completed in just over a year, and the pope, following the board's recommendation, ratified Mother Teresa's sainthood in December 2002. There were several miracles to choose from here: A Frenchwoman with broken ribs in the United States found herself healed when she placed a medallion embossed with Mother Teresa's image on her body; a Palestinian girl insisted that Mother Teresa's appearance in her dreams had cured her cancer. Closer to home, a Catholic nun, Rita Mascharenus of Purulia (a village 250 kilometers from Kolkata), allegedly found herself able to walk after suffering from partial paralysis from the waist down following botched surgery; she had rubbed a cloth touched by Mother Teresa's body on her lower parts when a voice commanded her to walk—and she did.

Yet the definitive miracle chosen by the tribunal was Monica Besra's troublesome one, for reasons that bear elaboration here. First, Besra was a local case but outside the media-infested urban space of the metropolis. As a transnational order run from Kolkata, the Missionaries of Charity, as well as the order's fellow male Roman Catholic clergy, rightly thought it fitting that an articulation of faith should come from Mother Teresa's home culture. But cynics alleged that the Missionaries of Charity deliberately chose Besra because of her obscurity and the difficulty of tracking her down to the remote village of Nakore, 500 kilometers from Kolkata. Certainly, Besra's identity was kept secret until a journalist from the United Kingdom "found" her in 2001. Further, Besra had converted to Christianity—a soul gained and saved—from her tribal Santhal religious roots. Santhals are indigenous peoples in West Bengal who often occupy the lowest rungs of the Hindu caste ladder, qualifying for the post-independence legal category of "Scheduled Tribes."[37] Hence, Besra epitomized continuing inequities in Hindu religious organizing for which Christianity seemed to offer a restorative.

Finally, Besra's treatment records were in disarray. She had been admitted to both the Balurghat hospital in South Dinajpur, West Bengal, and the larger North Bengal Medical hospital in 1998 for treatment of tubercular meningitis, a disease that often results in tubercular tumors. Under the treatment of two doctors, Ranjan Mustafir and Tarun Kumar Biswas, Besra developed sharp pains later in the year from a tumor in her lower abdomen and checked herself into the Missionary of Charity hospital at Patiram. There, two of the sisters had prayed with Besra all night as she writhed in pain, one of them pressing a medallion given to her by Mother Teresa on Besra's abdomen. The corporeal touch of the saint seemingly arrested the growth of the tumor and ameliorated Besra's pain. Such an event appropriately took place on September 5, 1998, the very day that marked the first anniversary of Mother Teresa's death. No wonder this was the chosen miracle and Besra, the blessed devotee.

Here the story of the miracle disintegrates into unsavory trails. The two doctors testified to treating Besra with medication that supposedly reduced the tumor to a cyst; its disappearance, they argued, was no miracle but good medical practice. The West Bengal government filed a case based on the doctors' testimony (both employees at a government-run hospital) in the district court of South Dinajpur, where the presiding magistrate, Gautam Ghosh, pronounced the miracle a hoax. As the controversy swelled, Pragriti, a rationalist society based in Orissa, filed a case against the pope; West Bengal's minister of health appeared on local television to present the medical findings of the government's case; and Prabir Ghosh of the Science and Rationalist Society, known for his "guru-busting" of god men and mystics, was unrelenting in his media exposé of the Besra case.[38] Responding to pressure, Besra approached Sister Betta of the Missionaries of Charity for the requisite files on her treatment, but neither Sister Betta (who had been transferred out of the Patiram facility) nor the files could be found. So one cannot tell what record of the treatment was forwarded by the diocesan enquiry to the Consulta Medica board, or whether, with the classical metropolitan disdain for rural sectors, the tribunal took those records seriously as valid proof of a medical cure. And if the records were forwarded to the Consulta Medica board, how were the reports, from a small, unknown, rural "Third World" hospital evaluated? Given the Roman Catholic church's tendency toward secrecy, judicious answers to these questions are hard to find; we only know that too many facts did not fit comfortably into the narrative of a curative miracle. Finally, while several news reports first featured disdain of the miracle expressed by Besra's husband, Selku Murmu, he later changed his story to what a Mother Teresa loyalist, Navin Chawla, characterized as a forceful statement of a miraculous cure. Besra, however, remained un-shaken in her belief that a miracle had indeed occurred.

The truth of the miracle is less important here than the deep contro-versy provoked in its wake. The most obvious face-off occurred between materialism and spiritualism. The miracle was, after all, beyond the "laws of nature," beyond economic and scientific rationality. In a miracle, "You can touch the supernatural," Cortesini once famously said.[39] But more important, there were those who were not directly involved in the beatifi-cation proceedings who argued that Mother Teresa was hardly a spiritual exemplar because she was completely co-opted by a transnational re-ligious corporation and was suspect in her financial arrangements. Here Mother Teresa's global form was clearly at stake for those troubled by the continuation of colonial-style civilizing missions in the post-colony. The "universal mother" turned chilling historical, with an inescapable mate-riality hitherto claimed only by isolated voices such as that of Christo-pher Hitchens. The choice of a low-caste Hindu convert to Christianity only highlighted Mother Teresa's role as a missionary whose loyalties lay elsewhere—with the image management of a transnational corporation, not with the local needy. These views were challenged by others who insisted that Mother Teresa had been appropriated by corporations, do-nors, and governments, and this had little to do with her own deeply spiritual reasons for her work. By 2003, it seemed that efforts to harness Mother Teresa as a Roman Catholic saint had backfired with those she had served all her life. The local denizens of Kolkata refuted the very grounds of her official sainthood—the miracle.

If Vatican II struggled to territorialize Mother Teresa by incorporating her into its official canon, it was poaching on someone else's territory, for in this period in the city of Kolkata, the city government was making ongoing attempts to re-territorialize this powerful sign to forge its newly emerging connections to global capital. These official efforts were given new life in 2003 when local media joined in the call to re-territorialize Mother Teresa. The short film *From Saint to Sainthood* (2004), by the journalist Payal Mohanka, exemplified these efforts by forwarding a local polemic against Mother Teresa's global reputation. "For the Vatican, Blessed Teresa of Calcutta is just a step away from Sainthood," Mohanka intones, referring to the beatification process that had made a splash in Kolkata. "But for Calcutta, she was always a saint."[40] If the global icon had become a means for the Roman Catholic church to embark on a new religious and financial expansionism (as we shall see in chapter 8), this globalizing drive met another—the neoliberal restructuring of the hitherto left-oriented state of West Bengal, with Kolkata's transformation into a mega-city leading the way—in a head-on collision.

Such re-territorialization of Mother Teresa as a "local saint" had been under way ever since the well-orchestrated media spectacle of her funeral in 1997. The funeral became one of the first media events for the hitherto Marxist state government of West Bengal—known for its opposition to the opening of local markets to globalizing economic forces—to launch its "new Kolkata" campaign. Although the change in name from Calcutta to Kolkata did not concretize until 2002, the new Kolkata was already on its way by 1997. Under the regime headed by Buddhadeb Bhattacharya— whom many middle-class Bengalis, disapproving of the Left Front's pre- vious regime, applauded as a "gentleman" or *bhadralok*—a concerted effort has been made to invite foreign investors to build housing, manage waste, and revamp the traffic infrastructure. This has met with consider- able economic success. The World Bank, Asian Development Bank, World Health Organization, and Department for International Development (in the United Kingdom), along with multinationals, transnational organiza- tions, and foreign-funded nongovernmental agencies—none of whom are accountable to the affected electorate—are now enthusiastic participants in the government's land redistribution and urban restructuring projects and in its cleansing drives to improve the city's image.[41] Mother Teresa's funeral was one of the state's first media campaigns to use emerging infotainment networks to attract foreign investors to Kolkata. Mother Teresa's commodity image provided a ripe opportunity to beam a newer, brighter, more cosmopolitan image of the decrepit colonial city to trans- national broadcast and satellite television audiences. The localist hege- monic aspirations of the Bhattacharya regime are even clearer today, after several confrontations between the "Left Front" government forces and farmers who refuse to see their land scheduled for reassignment as special economic zones (enclosures for setting up factories, industrial plants, and ancillary businesses).[42] Mother Teresa became one of the first "faces" of this capitulation to flexible accumulation.

While the world mourned the living saint, the Left Front government launched its new image via the funeral as media spectacle, a spectacular and laborious affair that included representatives of her order and of the Roman Catholic church, government officials, and foreign dignitaries. As the funeral cortège wound its way down streets recently repaired and spruced up by private corporations such as ITC and Exide, the city sur- reptitiously flaunted its "Calcutta Beautiful" image under the guise of mourning. The colonial "City of Slums" that had been produced as the

Roman Catholic missionary's necessary prosthetic would now masquerade as a mega-city that had arrived in the twentieth century sans poverty. Neither the exalted Roman Catholic nor the local city saint would direct our gaze to the famous poor the nun had served all her life. Flamboyantly wrapped in national colors, Mother Teresa once more became a mobile cipher, this time as a local leader testifying to the city's cosmopolitanism, civility, affective labor, and social welfare. Soon after, the city government turned Mother Teresa into a bona fide attraction in its bid to attract foreign investors and tourists to the historic colonial capital of India by insisting on converting the Mother House on 54 Lower Circular Road into a Heritage House amid protests from the Missionaries of Charity. A corollary controversy erupted over the renaming of Park Street (a major commercial street that attracts shoppers and restaurant goers) after the beatified saint (Banerjee 1997, 1). By 2002, Mother Teresa had been voted one of the "greatest post-independence Indians" in a poll of middle-class Indians conducted by the English-language weekly *Outlook*. Who could sell Kolkata's makeover—an image of a "new," progressive, globally connected city—better than Mother Teresa?

Such negotiations of global connections foreground points of friction where capital flows are translated, negotiated, or contested. As I intimated earlier, here we have a transition into mega-city facilitated by the global icon that met with unexpected opposition, as we shall see in the closing chapters. The poor would turn out in hordes; they would interrupt the stately procession down city streets. Their physical claim on the saint's body as it made its way to the official site of the state funeral would underscore the corporeal potential of the volatile signifier that is so crucial to becoming an icon.

Once more in the press of crowds we become aware of a biopolitical modernity in which bodies are biologically, legally, and economically aggrandized for commercial gain. No wonder the manifest corporeality of the icon gains renewed force. If the icon is an incorporative technology, the body establishes a material contiguity between devotee/consumer and chaos. The flesh of the saint incorporates the flesh of the poor, and the body of the activist at risk assembles the biosphere into its fold. The more volatile the icon, the more enhanced its corporeality. We see this most clearly in the case of our third bio-icon, most firmly a signifier of the popular. In controversy over Phoolan Devi's legality following her assassination, we shall see how the corporeal public memory of the fallen bandit queen becomes critical to renegotiating her global form. With such corporeal signification, the global icon begins to regain its transformative potentials in deep controversies where the commodity image is contested, disrupted, or renegotiated.

SCENE THREE: BIGAMOUS BODY

One of the innumerable eulogies in national print media extolling Phoo-lan Devi's incalculable gift to her "people" (the dalits of the Indian heart-land) imagined an encounter at the pearly gates. "What did you do?" she would be asked, and the petite Phoolan Devi would grandiosely reply: "I gave my people dignity" (De Sarkar 2001). Such enumerative rumination on India's most fetishized and infamous bandit queen was quickly suc-ceeded by vociferous debates on Phoolan Devi's tenuous legal status, her powerful iconicity and, of course, her legacy.[43] Appearing in late July 2001—right after her assassination at her residence in New Delhi by Sher Singh Rana and three accomplices—flamboyant accolades nestled un-comfortably against riveting whodunit narratives struggling to explain Phoolan Devi's violent death in terms of general and pervasive lawless-ness, the availability of small arms, rampant crime, and political conspir-acies in New Delhi. "Guns Cast Shadow over Bandit's Queen's Life" read the headline on an editorial in an English-language daily in which the bandit queen's assassination soon became an example of a political and legal system in crisis (Bhattacharjee 2001). In such wildly disparate ac-counts, no commodity image of the bandit queen—neither the global fetish (the wronged girl who rose above her circumstance so popular among transnational audiences) nor the national success story (the out-law whose redemption proved things had indeed improved for India's democratic minorities)—would stabilize in print and audiovisual mass media. In the many meditations on the bandit queen, something from the past, something lodged in public memory, could not be erased: the corporeal traces of the subaltern returning to haunt all attempts to an-chor the iconic image to a stable iconic message.

Though already legend in the Chambal region of the Indian heartland, the poor dalit girl (more specifically, a Mallah, a subcaste designated "Most Backward Castes" in state parlance) came from the village of Gurha ka Purwa in the northern Indian state of Uttar Pradesh.[44] Born in 1957, married at eleven, raped, abducted, and beaten in police custody, Phoolan Devi became a notorious outlaw, earning the moniker "bandit queen" with the infamous Behmai massacre of twenty-two Thakurs (members of a particular caste) in 1981. Shortly thereafter, hounded by police forces and fearing the wrath of the Thakurs, she made news again when she negotiated a historic surrender with state representatives. I shall return to this event in much more depth in chapter 8. For eleven years after the surrender, Phoolan Devi seemed to disappear from view; yet while she was in prison, she remained a vibrant subject of testimonials, biographies, and films. With the changing electoral caste fields of Uttar Pradesh, Phoolan Devi emerged from jail in 1994 and entered politics in 1996; by then Shekar Kapur's widely distributed film *The Bandit Queen* (1994) had turned her into an international celebrity. In the two decades before Phoolan Devi, India's best-known bandit queen subaltern, was gunned down in late July 2001, she had been rapidly translated into a global fetish and seemingly was incorporated into the logic of democratic politics in her post-1996 role as spokesperson for "minorities" in the Indian democracy.

In the days following her assassination, as details on the police inquiry, the distribution of Phoolan Devi's considerable estate, and the contretemps over her funeral poured in, two bodies of the dead bandit queen emerged in the national imagination. One was Phoolan Devi, the legal object of investigation, the twice-elected member of Parliament whose rise to political power indexed the rapidly changing political landscape of the Indian democratic polity. Alongside it was the second: Phoolan Devi, the legendary outlaw, the symbolic avenger of an unjust socioeconomic system symptomatic of the postcolonial state's failure to protect its most disenfranchised populations whose extraordinary life had circulated in mass media ever since the Behmai massacre.[45] The two bodies habitually interrupt each other.

The first body—the dead one in the autopsy room—projected Phoolan Devi as a rational abstraction: the legal subject, the citizen and parliamentarian who had possibly become an expendable political pawn in a larger electoral game of wooing the votes of regional Other Backward Castes,[46] but also a common criminal who still had thirty-nine cases pending against her in lower courts and was therefore denied a gun license. The dead body bore legal and familial inscription as daughter, wife, sister, and self-professed "housewife" and "agriculturalist"; the whodunit narrative that circled it followed a suspenseful line of deductive reasoning in tracking conspirators, motives, the getaway car, and the SMS cards (often used to track illegal activity).[47] As a legal object under investigation, the corpse generated a chain of signifiers that positioned the dead Phoolan Devi as a citizen-subject: The unsavory minutiae of legal wrangles over her assets and fierce disagreement over her familial loyalties splashed on the front pages of major national newspapers read like any tabloid worth its salt. Journalists and Samajwadi Party leaders decried the lethargy among investigators. The Central Bureau of Investigation seemed suspiciously slow; the Thakurs, suspiciously happy; the BJP, suspiciously unconcerned —all pointers, reporters argued, to a larger political conspiracy. "Phoolan Devi's murder is in the classic Indian whodunit tradition," alleged a reporter in *The Statesman*. "The more the police investigate, the murkier things become" ("Phoolan Case: Cops Settle for Revenge Motive," A4). A typical follow-up to the bandit queen's assassination read: "Meanwhile at Phoolan Devi's 44 Ashoka Road residence, relatives are battling over the distribution of her assets. Yesterday at a press conference, Mr. Umed Singh announced that he was forming a trust to handle Phoolan's assets. Phoolan's sister, Mrs. Munni Devi, alleged that Mr. Singh wanted to acquire her dead sister's money through the trust. She said she would take the matter to court" ("Pankaj Has Criminal Record, Say Police" 2001). The rhetoric of these accounts was low-key, skeptical, the cops brazenly but not surprisingly buying the Thakur revenge theory. Moreover, a clear note of cynicism echoed through these reports. A news item in *The Statesman* provides an emblematic instance: "The 'utility' of Ms. Phoolan Devi in the caste-driven and explosive political fields of Uttar Pradesh will not end with her violent death. The 'Bandit Queen' is bound to be resurrected in the run-up to the crucial Assembly elections" ("Pankaj Has Criminal Record, Say Police" 2001).

At first glance, the unsavory minutiae of the legal wrangling over Phoolan Devi's assets—the proceeds from Kapur's *The Bandit Queen* and from the biographies and testimonials written about her total several lakhs;[48] she also had several real-estate holdings, including a house in New Delhi's elite Chittaranjan Park—seem to be fairly conventional, though the coverage read like any sensational soap opera. The players on the scene were many: Umed Singh, her present husband; her mother and sister; her brother; and Shiv Narain, perceived by many to be the proper heir to her estate. No one agreed on where Phoolan Devi's last loyalties lay: Knowing her fierce loyalty to her filial family (their move to Gwalior from her birth village of Gurha ka Purwa was, after all, a key condition for her surrender), should the family be her legitimate heirs? One Samajwadi Party worker attested, "Didi[49] brought in names of her mother, sisters, and nephew as heir to accounts and locker" ("Pankaj Has Criminal Record, Say Police" 2001), while Phoolan Devi's mother accused her son-in-law, Umed Singh, of exploiting her daughter (12 lakhs or $27,000 in loan and his registering the family car in his name). Kamini Jaiswal, the feminist lawyer who had secured Phoolan Devi's release from the Tihar jail in 1994, reported that Phoolan Devi had not only anticipated her own death but had wanted to make a new will disinheriting her husband. In his own histrionic performances, Singh insisted that he would place Phoolan Devi's assets in a trust and launched a dharna outside police headquarters, pleading for proper legal justice for his wife. These disputes revealed the slippages of familial inscription on the body of the bandit queen: She seemed not to belong to any single kinship structure or caste affiliation. Here was a commodity par excellence whose secrets were not easily revealed, a social hieroglyphic for caste-based social relations. The inscrutable commodity would haunt the careful plotting of the whodunit. Hence, emotional declamation or strangely comic episodes would interrupt the rote recounting of events—for example, a concise report on the assassin Sher Rana and his accomplices in *The Statesman* on August 7, 2001, was suddenly jostled by a paragraph-long sketch of a moment at Phoolan Devi's cremation when the bandit queen's mother and sister took exception to Umed Singh's *pagri*-tying, insisting that this was not their "family tradition" ("Phoolan Supporters Come to Blows" 2001). Volatile and powerful, the iconic image would escape all attempts at re-territorialization. In death, Phoolan Devi could hardly be aggrandized to signal electoral democracy—aphoristically christened "free and fair elections"—as the political marker of successful egalitarianism.

If the familial inscription would not stabilize, neither would the state's legal hold. For one, Puttilal (Phoolan Devi's first husband) petitioned her assets on August 24, 2001, at a civil court in Kanpur. According to their Hindu marriage in 1972 (which does not require civil certification but is legally recognized by the Indian state), Puttilal was the legal "heir," given their lack of a formal divorce. But this legal claim was at odds with the very moral codes (of justice and redemption) that transformed the female "outlaw" into a legal citizen-subject. Further, if by romantic logic "husbands" are of the heart, Phoolan Devi's *only* husband was Vikram Mallah, who, by her own admission, had "married" the destitute Phoolan Devi in the "eyes of God." Therefore, neither Puttilal nor Umed Singh, the "legal" husbands, qualified as the "true" heir. Into this bigamous morass came allegations that Umed Singh had a secret marriage to Sunita Singh and that they were never formally divorced. The nation watched as the real-life drama, the stuff of Bollywood, spilled onto the national stage. "Three Husbands and Phoolan's Mother Battle It Out for Her Crores" said one of the quieter headlines to run in a major newspapers (the *Times of India*), while tabloids offered more spice on the spiraling illegalities.

The middle-class soap opera–style accounts, attempts to re-territorialize Phoolan Devi as a subaltern turned lawmaker (evidence of the success of Indian democracy), overtly pitched their stakes against the eulogized "outlaw" prevalent in transnational media. Some biographical essays recounting Phoolan Devi's life refer to this global form of the bandit queen by placing her on a roster of other global outlaws such as Bonnie Parker and Belle Starr rather than tracing her regional genealogy to the original Chambal bandit queen, the one-armed Putlibai. Yet in both types of narration—the heightened celebrations of the legend and the low-key legal whodunit—the thrills and sensations of Phoolan Devi's life were conveyed in a thickly visceral tongue, in the rhetoric of bodily excess. "Phoolan stuck out like a blown-off arm in a society where men call the shots," feminist commentators exclaimed (Kakaria 2001), while other articles in magazines and newspapers dwelt morbidly on blood, guts, and gore. Blood seemed to infuse the accounts of her death: the blood of Behmai, where the outlaw had supposedly shot twenty-two men, splashed across newspapers and magazines and on television news,[50] while *India Today* referred to her murder as an appropriately "Bloody Finale" to a bloodier saga. Another telling caption trailed the present crime to a history of violence: "The Bullet-Riddled Biography" in *Outlook* magazine (Mukherjee et al. 2001) offered a litany of dead bodies to close its chapter on the outlaw, casting the shadow of Behmai on the respectable Mrs. Phoolan Devi. Here Mala Sen, the author of Phoolan Devi's best-known biography (*The Bandit Queen* [1991]), underscored Phoolan Devi's own inability to move beyond that shadow. "I was born into a violent life," declaimed the bandit queen in an offhand comment to Sen weeks before her death, a remark duly emblazoned on the magazine cover. "I will have a violent death" (Mukherjee et al. 2001). Sensational as they are, these glosses achieved an important function: They graphically superimposed a remembered subject, the corporeal subaltern, onto the citizen's body under the forensic gaze. Omens and portents infiltrated rational deduction; disinterred body parts exploded onto the decorously laid out and garlanded dead member of Parliament surrounded by family members; theories of blood feuds and vengeance clashed with hypotheses of political conspiracy; and the laws of the Hobbesian state of nature entered the capital city of lawmakers.[51]

These instances demonstrate how the legal body of the dead bandit queen was constantly destabilized by the phantasm of another body: a corporeal body, a bigamous body of indeterminate kinship alliances, a body that incited both (public) violence and tears, a bullet-riddled body standing as a reminder of Phoolan Devi's long history of violence. As Stanley Theodore (2005) maintained, Phoolan Devi remains a "sign of her times," a symptom of decolonized India's political and socioeconomic dysfunction. What would the Mahatma say, asked the author, if he were alive to hear the ballads about her? From his tone, we can assume that these ballads recount a gory lore, a memory from which there was no escape in all the attempts to lay Phoolan Devi to rest.

If corporeality captures the singular historical materiality of a subject's lived experiences, then the corporeal significations of the bandit queen's dead body spoke of violation and social injustice garnering collective outpourings of grief. No wonder some commentators were tempted to read this emblematic body against the legal object (the pride of the state) and the legend (the global fetish). Undercutting the commodity image of the individual hero infused with extraordinary feminine force, on the one hand, Madhu Kishwar, the editor of the pioneering feminist 'zine *Manushi*, dryly noted, "Phoolan was no durga [Hindu goddess], she was just a battered woman."[52] On the other, commentators reminded the national public that Phoolan Devi was no anomaly. Inserting class differences into the equation, they read the corporeal body as a social hieroglyphic for "the predicament of many in our society, especially rural India" (Agnivesh and Thampu 2001). Corporeality would return historical materiality to the icon, once again manifest as the girl from the Chambal still socially and economically distant from the metropolitan middle class who mourned her in mass media. In contestations in mass media, the iconic image could no longer serve a rags-to-riches story in which the global icon would at once signal the backwardness of the (caste-ridden) "East" even as her "rise" absolved transnational audiences of any need to intervene in this other world. Nor could the iconic image of Phoolan Devi anchor the iconic message dear to a national public congratulating itself on the success of a democracy in which an indigent dalit could become a parliamentarian. The corporeal body brought trouble to both these messages, dislodging the iconic image and turning icon into volatilized signifier.

In these three controversies—Arundhati Roy, Mother Teresa, and Phoolan Devi—are social hieroglyphs that invite critical scrutiny. In each case, the heat of the moment exposes the historical materiality of a commoditized star image. The glamorous green activist appears as a well-educated middle-class subject whose voice points us to a collective still silenced by the languages of power; the face of human charity appears as an employee of Vatican II whose body is claimed by the poor; and the rags-to-riches girl reminds us of populations in the Chambal where her fortunes remain an anomaly. In each case, we witness awkward and creative calibrations of global modernity—be it of capital, science, or politics

—where in the ever-widening fissures of shiny commodities we begin to glimpse social transformations that are under way.

Beyond the "friction" between parties in controversies, we might think of these points of negotiation as friction along paths of global connection—those "awkward, unequal, unstable, and creative" points that, Anna Tsing (2004) maintains, relocates the "global order" as a series of negotiations. Universal dreams and schemes are "charged and enacted in the sticky materiality of practical encounters," Tsing (2004, 1) argues, bringing friction to the otherwise smooth and unimpeded flows of people, goods, and money. We know that friction on the road slows traffic even as it facilitates flows; hence, we must think of global connections in coteries of those who facilitate the flow of capital and those who seek to renegotiate those flows. Global forms in which universal abstractions such as capital, science, or politics appear productively enable different publics to articulate their stakes in an ever-mutating global order. We have seen each of our bio-icons embody universal abstractions, specifically those that garner consensus for neoliberal regimes. Therefore, they are precisely sites for such productive friction. Those who seek to re-territorialize these signs cut, paste, and remix to articulate their global stakes. When no re-territorialization is possible, when no significations will settle, when growing fissures dislodge the iconic image from any stable message that might anchor it, the iconic image becomes available for either adoration or desecration. We see the volatile icon emerge—unstable, awkward, and creative. In such a war of signs, icons spiral into events: Crowds gather; newspapers flash flaming graphics; statues are desecrated; embassies are mobbed; and riot police huddle behind glass and smoke. The sparks from what might first appear as a semantic struggle explode into social phenomena.

We all partake in the glittering life of public images. Made in publicity and sold through multiple media channels, they conceal their own production within a larger system of exchange. They appear unique, without equivalence, even as they are standardized in relation to other, similar objects; they appear singular even as they are mass-produced commodities generating financial, social, or cultural surplus value for large-scale organizations, institutions, and industries. Their ubiquity stems from the technological and industrial capacity of the mass media, specifically the broadcast news media and commercial publicity machines, to beam a well-tailored image from a single point of production to a large number of points of reception—these days, all over the world. The "public images" of our global icons indicate those widely circulating images that carry corporate imprimatur, and are often authorized media content designed for publicity; the qualifier "star image" underscores the artifice of these images that become most representative of our global icons.

Culturally familiar, often multimodal, and always recursive, as these images move swiftly across multiple media platforms, they often carry the materiality of the media format in which consumers had encountered them *before*. For example, when we encounter the Eddie Adams art photo of Mother Teresa and the armless baby remediated in a personal devotional blog, it brings with it not just a discursive message but also the institutional legitimacy, traces of print photography's visual substrates, and the media formats of the high-end magazine platforms. The intermediality of the global icon's "star images" partly depends on how widely circulated and legitimized they are. It would follow that such "star images" made for publicity are released by institutions with the financial, industrial, and technological capacity for wide distribution. If as successful corporations large and complex media institutions are structured by the prevailing market rationality, then at the level of culture they sanction cultural myths that sustain this rationality. As we saw in chapter 3, some of the most accessible, widely circulating images of our global icons fulfill specific neoliberal agendas and are therefore subject to controversy. Hence it is no stretch to argue for the structural agency of the market, its rationality underlying the messages syntactically attached to highly publicized images of global icons. This chapter investigates the managerial drive of such "star images," first by a close look at the financially robust media networks that publicize (produce and distribute) them. However, as we venture further into the media ecologies of these images, we shall see how they are constantly remediated by the creative industries of local production and consumer enclaves. Here we are back to social relations by the close of the chapter: what effects do these widely circulating commodity images have on social relations? Does consuming the intermedial star image isolate devotees or activate forms of collective membership?

Such consideration of the materiality of the icon's star image historicizes the deceptively mystical, universal, and seemingly eternal commodity, on the one hand, and enables us to comprehend the apposite social efficacies of the same icon, at once a luscious commodity (reinforcing hegemonic perceptions) and a luminous aperture (compelling social action against hegemonic institutions), on the other. We follow the transnational itineraries of lustrous star images because they bind us so firmly to hegemonic aspirations—in our case, a universal mantra of free choice (often expressed through consumerism) that smoothes over inequities that emerge from the restructuring of global capital. Indeed, in our age of communicative capitalism, we witness in these images a world-making corporate drive. From the hard, gleaming, defined contours of star images we move, in the chapters that follow, to their dispersions refracted in expressive culture.

Understood as products of "publicity," a constellation of practices aimed at managing popular perceptions of people or ideas, star images direct us first to production—to those media institutions that, more often than not, are financially robust multinational corporations with global networks,[1] even as social practices (action, knowledge, memory) remain crucial for consuming star images as signs. No critical discourse has been more attentive to public images—both regimes of publicity and the publics constituted by encounters with star images—than "star studies." Practitioners in this interdisciplinary domain increasingly proclaim the death of the star in the shadow of celebrities big and small. Yet the material economy of the *star*, marked as exceptional, exemplary, enduring myth, teaches us more about how icons operate as technologies for yoking collective dreams. These conversations are of salience to our global icons —Mother Teresa, Arundhati Roy, and Phoolan Devi—that, as we shall see, approximate stars in their sensuous allure.

All three have vibrant lives in the glossies, garnering social and cultural capital. When we think about Arundhati Roy, we effortlessly remember her as the Booker Prize glamour girl; when we think Phoolan Devi, we recall her widely publicized "life" as the bandit queen in Shekar Kapur's famous biopic. But we rarely think of Mother Teresa as having the same sensuous lure as a star. Yet the wizened nun, who deliberately chose the cheapest and plainest garment (a mill-produced cotton sari) as the mark of her order, became a regular in the glossies after she was splashed on the cover of *Time* magazine in December 1973. Before 1973, we find a few scattered images of Mother Teresa that had transnational circulation: a 1968 appearance on BBC; a 1969 BBC-funded biopic (Malcolm Muggeridge's sentimental *Something Beautiful for God*) carried on networks in Britain and the U.S.; and a photograph of Mother Teresa accepting the Templeton prize in London, 1970. A scarce visual archive of images that surface with scholarly digging (accessed through specialized news engines such as Google's "news archive search," but then available for a fee payable to particular news media databases where these are domiciled), these are neither recycled, repurposed, nor reassembled. But the *Time* magazine spread, introducing Mother Teresa to transnational audiences as a "Living Saint," would change all that, as Mother Teresa began to edge out Jackie Kennedy, Madonna, and Queen Elizabeth II as the "Most Admired Woman" to grace *Good Housekeeping* magazine. The stage was set for the arrival of the highly credentialed Eddie Adams photograph from 1978 (Adams, by then, a Pulitzer Prize–winning photojournalist[2]) that would become one of the most enduring inscriptions of the nun. Once more, his institutional base at the Associated Press would enable quick and wide distribution of the image. By this time, Mother Teresa had gained the equivalence of a star: for example, the Norwegian newspaper *Aftenposten* eulogized the nun's plainness, the "star without false eyelashes and makeup, without jewels and fur coats, without theatrical gestures" in 1979 (Alpion 2007, 4). The comment is intended to highlight the saint's plainness in contrast to the glitterati, but the association with the opulently pleasing star image, paradoxically, catches the degree to which Mother Teresa's image has a sensory impact. More important, it measures the graphic inscription in terms of its equivalence to the standard image of the star, with false eyelashes, makeup, jewels, and a fur coat—the accoutrements that establish a standard for an image to count as a star and that convert a singular figure into generality (it can be now exchanged for a series of "star" counterparts). Being shorn of those invariable traces of the star, in this case, increases Mother Teresa's moral value; the repetition of a plain, spartan look (encrypted in the blue-and-white sari) makes asceticism one of the distinguishing traces of Mother Teresa's star image in years to come.

We shall see how sophisticated media technologies transformed all three living figures into stars. But star studies, and the adjacent field of celebrity culture analysis, has engaged in such endeavors for some time, developing a richly nuanced apparatus to consider critically how living people operate as mass-mediated signs.[3] I pursue the materiality of the star image in this chapter through productive entanglements with star studies in its early, as well as more recent, transnational evolutions. First, elaborations on the star image—its design in visual, audiovisual, and print media—offer insight into the social function of the forms living people take in mass media. How exactly the star image commoditizes living figures, marketing an image measured against other standard objects of equivalence; how such a star image manufactures consent through its iteration in circulation, the constant repetition of invariable features stabilizing the syntactical relation of image to message; and how star images attain either singularity or standardization within large media ecologies becomes eminently clear.[4] These facets of the star image are the bread and butter of my claims regarding the social function of the public images of the bio-icon in mass media as legitimizing cultural mechanisms for hegemonic agendas.

Second, close attention to the production, distribution, and exhibition of star images in particular media platforms (from documentaries, to tabloids, to coffee-table photo essays, to cheaply produced pulp biographies, and talk) and through specific media institutions (often large-scale, complex organizations that legitimate an image) establishes how a star materializes at a certain historical juncture. While "alternative media" (small-scale production such as cable-access television, local radio, or fan 'zines, as well as modest distribution systems) might well reassemble an intermedial image, the "public images" (indicated by the corporate suffix "Ltd.") I explore here are largely distilled, calibrated, distributed, and delivered in broadcast news media and by commercial merchandising (e.g., busts, posters, stickers, etc.). Broadcast news media, with its capacity to instantaneously and cyclically reiterate a single intermedial image (e.g., a tabloid photo of Justin Timberlake flashed on CNN's headline news cycle) can effectively distill one graphic inscription as the most representative of the icon. But this corporatized signal is never the fully stabilized because, as we shall see, star images are constantly "remade" in embodied consumption. It is in this gap of the never quite that we see the expressivity of the popular.

Third, the material culture of the star image discloses perceptions and affections that explain the lure of the star; and it presupposes a consumer subject swallowed by the object he or she consumes, an extreme instance of objectified personhood projected in theories of passive (mass) consumption. We shall see how attention to spectatorship has substantially complicated such presumption, motivating propositions of a fractal personhood (in which a consumer partially incorporates the star image as animate prosthetic) and an enduring interest in the collective spectatorial performance as an unremarkable fact of mass consumption.

THE STAR IMAGE

Icons are the ilk of stars: They have polysemic "star" images; they inspire hagiography; they lure spectators to fantasy. While icons have been around for centuries, stars are phenomena of the last century. Yet star systems affect contemporary global icons, the historical form with which we are concerned, in important ways. In some contexts, they actually render icons legible to heterogeneous audiences. Thus, the rise of stardom has more than critical lessons to offer those who study mass-mediated icons.

As we know from the many critical considerations of Hollywood stars, the star was not born with cinema. It was not until the 1910s that viewers came to know the name of the Biograph girl, Florence Lawrence, and with burgeoning interest in the careers of Mary Pickford, Douglas Fairbanks, and Charlie Chaplin, a full-fledged star system was soon in place. Critical analysis of the star phenomenon followed much later, with Edgar Morin's look at French stars in the 1960s (*Les Stars*, 1969) inaugurating the turn to star theory.[5] In their comprehensive introduction to star discourse, Lucy Fischer and Marcia Landy (2004) note that it was the revaluing of popular culture in the 1970s that led the way to a series of exegeses on stars. The star came to be regarded not simply as a bankable artifact produced by studios for profits; instead, the "star image" took different turns in its distribution, exhibition, and reception. Richard Dyer's famous *Stars* (1979), one of the first full-length studies of the star as a cultural phenomenon, is often regarded as a critical threshold, followed by *Heavenly Bodies* (1986), his analysis of stars (such as Paul Robeson) who had crossed over into media fields other than cinema. There the intermedial star image would mandate a wider cultural knowledge; there the star morphed into celebrity or icon.

Hollywood stars initially dominated critical discourse on stars. Several anthologies offered a smorgasbord of stars, while studies of major stars (such as Marilyn Monroe and Mae West) appeared both in collections and as single case studies.[6] Attentive to the materiality of the heterogeneous, multichannel "star image," its visual, verbal, aural, and tactile streams, many of these early works looked closely at the technological and industrial (including the financial, economic, institutional) production of the "star text"—that meandering "biograph" whose smooth façades concealed the secrets of producing the image. Reaching for a critical language to explain the magic of stars, commentators underscored the "making" of the star image through studio promotions (television shows, websites, advertisements, tie-ins, and memorabilia), publicity (hagiographic productions of romances, scandals, and politics), and commentary (critical evaluations and awards), even as the stars themselves struggled with the studios (in vertically integrated Hollywood) over control of their own image. The story of star studies as an emerging discourse has been well documented (e.g., Fischer and Landy 2004; Gledhill 1991, 2003), so I will not belabor the historical unfolding of critical landmarks here. Rather, I want to focus on particular moments in this larger discourse that bear on the study of the icon, beginning with the constellation of practices we call publicity as it animates the star image. In a direct sense, publicity incorporates design, marketing, and value formation (via common terms of monetary and cultural exchange) and, more indirectly, the formation of public fantasy.

Publicity

In the most obvious sense, the field of star studies has consolidated a formidable framework for considering the formal, narrative, and cinematic composition of the star image (character, gesture, posture, dress, placement in mise-en-scène, lighting, camera angles, film stock, acting styles, and so on), along with considerations of technological and industrial affordances.[7] Such discussions of how a star image is carefully calibrated for profit are highly salient to the best-known images of our bio-icons who serve hegemonic functions; looking at the production of particular images as publicity illuminates the structural agency of these ostensibly innocent products. I have already noted how Mother Teresa's image, for one, has been carefully controlled, with most publicity photographs (taken by contracted photographers or freelance star photographers) ratified by the Missionaries of Charity before release and circulation as public images on multiple platforms. The most famous photographs, such as the many (hagiographic) collections of Mother Teresa's daily life by the photographer Raghu Rai, all bear the marks of corporate authorization.[8] While she was alive, Mother Teresa kept the reins tight on her public image, as it was increasingly remediated in transnational networks all over the world. For instance, there are several accounts of her refusal to be interviewed or photographed by those she perceived to be non-believers in her cause. Sunanda K. Dutta, the editor of an English-language daily and by no means a critic of Mother Teresa, recounts how Mother Teresa once had him replaced with the overly sympathetic Desmond Doig for an event on Kolkata television because she wanted to tailor the interview.[9] Nor was this an isolated event, as her detractors demonstrate: Mother Teresa and her order—and, later, the Vatican—would keep a watch over the iterant star image. In such vigilance, the frail missionary was not so different from the Hollywood star of the studio era, desperate for control over the publicity that produced her.

But this is also true of a bio-icon without such obvious institutional backing but who nevertheless captured mass-media attention. If we look closely at Arundhati Roy's stylized star image in 1997, we find that it, too, was highly manufactured for publicity—both for *The God of Small Things* and to sell "Indian writing in English" as a global product. Before 1997, Arundhati Roy made the news in print on few occasions: first in sporadic reports of her activities in indie publications such as *The Green Left Review*, and second, with her controversial defense of Phoolan Devi's rebuttal of the film *The Bandit Queen* (1994).[10] Post-Booker win, two kinds of

FIGURE 16 Aurundhati Roy, the author of *The God of Small Things*, 1996. Photo. Raghu Rai, Magnum Photos.

star images began to circulate widely: highly stylized images of a pensive writer in repose and equally stylized but seemingly suddenly snapped shots of the writer caught in the bustle of the humdrum, a writer no different from the average middle-class Indian. The former were characteristically beautifully lit compositions by famed photographers such as Raghu Rai or photojournalists such as Pablo Bartholomew. A photo by Bartholomew that made the rounds caught Roy, demurely dressed in a cream-colored top, in silhouette, eyes downcast, in a strong interpretation of the literary star as meditative and thoughtful.[11] Another, a classic Raghu Rai shot, is a softly lit black-and-white glossy that further feminized the usually bubbly activist (figure 16).

In this genre of authorized photographs, Roy the writer appears as an isolated genius, a myth supplemented by another slew of images, now ephemera that has turned the exception mundane. The settings for these are deliberately intimate—Roy caught shopping, relaxing at home, walking past a bookstore. They are mostly full-body shots featuring a casually dressed (often jean-clad) Roy as the Booker Prize winner who looks like any other young woman in metropolitan India.[12] In these, publicity's hubris is clear: Through publicity, we gain access to the intimate secrets encrypted in the smooth façades of the star image. We know how (and where) the star lives; later, where she shops, works out, runs, speaks, or works. Together, both kinds of photographs designed a lustrous "star image" aimed at intensifying aesthetic pleasure, as dress, pose, gesture, depth of field, lighting, mise-en-scène, and film stock combined to style highly aestheticized compositions. These images found, and still find, wide circulation, easily accessed through popular search engines and are often digitally reassembled in web art.

The single-channel visuals are often embedded in written texts (in print or digital media) that turn the star image heterogeneous; the intermedial star image, however, continues to carry its *prior* materiality (the sanction of a Raghu Rai photograph, for example). The stories that accompany Roy's publicity photographs quickly focalized her as the new middle-class "princess of prose" (the title of the issue of *India Today* published on October 27, 1997, which was partially devoted to Roy).[13] The "story" about the new star established her as an extraordinary voice and intellect but also as a very down-to-earth, ordinary soul whose beauty was an added bonus. The seemingly supplemental value of beauty would ameliorate deep-seated sexist fears of the sharp-tongued female public intellectual. To garner social value, the story further focalized specific contours of the star's body that generated sexual excitement (conveniently displaced onto the English "establishment"): "Slim-hipped Roy, her carelessly curled hair casually cascading over her face, her nose-ring twinkling with naughtiness, and her language flapping with originality, excited the stodgy English literary establishment."[14] Likewise it drew our attention to the plain, checkered bedspread on which Roy sat, the everyday blue jeans, and her unassuming manner despite obvious celebrity. In the easy threading of the extraordinary (in talent and beauty) as rather ordinary (the everyday girl), we have a unified public fantasy closing over social antagonisms that would locate Roy as representative only of a metropolitan intelligentsia.

Standardization

Publicity works through standardization: the production of value when the star image is measured via common terms of exchange, propelling the singular into generality. The priceless commodity Phoolan Devi can be transposed as a Belle Starr or a Bonnie Parker, a revaluation that recasts the icon into "universal" frames of reference. And so Mother Teresa is considered on par with Saint Francis of Assisi and Gandhi; Arundhati Roy, with the "green" activists Medha Patkar and Vandana Shiva. One stellar moment that illustrates the processes of standardization through which value is produced occurs in Mary Ann Weaver's description of Phoolan Devi's famous surrender, an intermedial image (recalling the format of the "original" Sondeep Shankar photograph) remediated equally in visual and print media. Iterations of the iconic image—a woman with her arms upraised, rifle held aloft, facing a crowd—directs us to the "original" outlaw who brought the state to its knees, who drew large crowds of the worshipful and the curious. The invisible trace of this figure would remain potent even when the face of Seema Biswas (the actor who played Phoolan Devi in Kapur's film) effectively replaced Phoolan Devi's visage in the stylized movie poster. So in 1994, after Phoolan Devi's release from the Gwalior jail, Weaver would recount the scene once more for the (transnational) readers of *The Atlantic* (with a digital version made widely accessible on the Internet):

> Phoolan climbed the wooden steps of a twenty-three-foot high dais, shaded by an awning of red, green, and yellow cloth. Hindi film music blasted over a public address system. She was dressed in a new khaki police superintendent's uniform and a bright-red shawl, and she wore a red bandanna on her head. . . . Defiant and truculent, she flashed a cheeky grin. Her red bandanna gave her the appearance of an Apache. . . . [T]he Beautiful Bandit, the Bandit Queen, was really a wisp of a girl: less than five feet tall, with high flat cheekbones, a full flat nose, and slit eyes. She looked like a Nepalese boy. (Weaver 1996, 1)

This is an eminently mythic portrait, and a highly corporealized one. The iconic image (with the red bandanna) is now subjected to the liberal feminist gaze that focalizes Phoolan Devi's resistance to the gender systems that inscribe her. The figure ascending the dais is feminized (a "wisp of a girl") and eroticized (the resonance of the boy) while remaining masculine (dressed in a uniform, forcefully "truculent" and "defiant").[15] The reference to Nepal, which is often at political odds with the Indian nation-state, and to the Apache quickly transcribes the regionally situated Dalit female subaltern into commonly known figures of disenfranchisement. Within such a universal parable, Phoolan Devi's star image accrues social capital.

Such widely iterated public images of our bio-icons, accruing capital through their equivalence with other bio-icons, often function as intermedial templates for a range of expressive reassemblages that directly address the "original." Images from broadcast news media are habitually redesigned in small-scale do-it-yourself (DIY) media in "convergence culture," to use Henry Jenkins's (2005) descriptor for transfers of media content across platforms. As we shall see, these reassemblages often cite authorized images to recode them in popular culture; quixotically, popular traffic in these established authorized images only maintain their massive circulation (search engines like Google, for example, store images according to the traffic). We come across endless artistic reassemblages of the original news photographs of all three bio-icons, displayed on canvas, woodprint, sketch, or lithograph. Phoolan Devi, for example, is standardized not only through a stable set of photographs (the three or four famous snaps taken during her surrender in 1983), but also through style. We stumble across bright, glossy mutations of those public images everywhere on the Internet—frowning behind bars, scratching her head shyly with gun in hand as she walks toward the pavilion to surrender, or staring defiantly at the camera wearing a red shawl and red bandanna. These intermedial images straddle high art and commercial enterprise alike. For example, Phoolan Devi in the red shawl becomes the template for high-art works such as the internationally known artist Vasan Sitthiket's portrait of her in the series "Vasan's Women," exhibited at the Valentine Willie Fine Art gallery in 2007 (figure 17). Accompanied by corresponding portraits of Aung San Suu Kyi, Simone de Beauvoir, Kathe Kollwitz, Ulrike Meinhof, and Gudrun Ensslin, Phoolan Devi is relocated via her translation, through the common term of the female rebel, into a global feminist pantheon. The exhibition bears the telling caption, "*We come from the same way.*"[16] But we find the same image commandeered for commercial merchandise, as well: One can choose it as the visual design for coffee mugs, T-shirts, and stick-on tattoos bought from the Postpunkkitchen.com website for individual self-expression through consumerism.

These photographs of the armed outlaw remain some of the widest circulating ones of Phoolan Devi, despite the many later photographs of her as a respectable member of Parliament. Effectively transposed as the female rebel, she continues to inspire artists whose interpretations are expressed in their style of portraiture: bright colors, folksy broad strokes, and minimal realistic detail. While they use news photographs as their drawing board, their portraits (in oil, mixed media, or virtual media) both reiterate and negotiate the public image of Phoolan Devi by recasting it in mural style, standardizing her as a "people's" icon—a translation into the common term we see in both DIY personal media and works of high art.[17] Figure 18 provides one striking example: Erin Currier assembled her feminist hero from another photograph (a full frontal shot featuring the bandit queen, cartridge belt slung across the torso) for an exhibition at the Parks Gallery in Taos, New Mexico, in 2006.[18] Her explicit location of Phoolan Devi in a pantheon that included those who fought political institutions, such as Aung San Suu Kyi, Wangari Maathai, and the Mothers of the Plaza de Mayo, standardized the bandit queen's value; at the same time, the expressive style of the "mural" aimed to intensify visual and tactile modalities, heightening the bandit queen's efficacy as incorporative technology.

In Currier's strong emphasis on the bandit queen's symbolic cachet, Phoolan Devi is no longer wearing a khaki uniform but, instead, a yellow shirt with a picture of the mother goddess imprint—a *mise-en-abyme* for the outlaw's wrath-fueled demand for social justice. Like other expressive reassemblages, the virtual mural remains attentive to Phoolan Devi's historical location, and yet, like some well-known biographies, the mural interprets Phoolan Devi as the embodiment of divine justice (the virago goddess Kali, a source of fascination in the historical West).[19] My point is that these remediations in DIY media, as opposed to those in mass media, reflexively undercut the message of the intermedial original image (Phoolan Devi as the victim/virago from the unruly hinterland) to re-standardize the global icon for transnational consumers. But here we have already strayed from publicity and the role of corporate media institutions in this foray into expressive culture. So I will return to the public image in order to elucidate perhaps the most important feature in the process of icon formation—the repetition of a pre-existing trace.

Repetition

Publicity works through the repetition of certain graphic inscriptions, making them as the definitive ones, the most culturally familiar images of a living person. Thus, the backstory of industrial and technological production of the star image becomes quite central to grasping its historical materiality. Richard Woodward's (2002) investigations of Monroe's publicity photograph for the film *The Seven Year Itch* (1955), for instance, relates a curious story about the famous inscription—the star straddling the subway grating with white dress whirling. It was an image beamed in gigantic fifty-foot form in Times Square for the movie's promotion; an

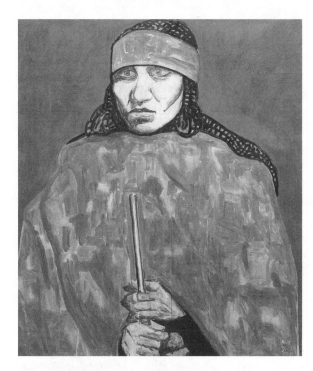

FIGURE 17 Vasan Sitthiket, *Phoolan Devi*, mixed media on canvas. Courtesy of Valentine Willie Fine Art.

FIGURE 18 Erin Currier, *Portrait of Phoolan Devi*, mixed media on canvas. Courtesy of Erin Currier, www.erincurrierfineart.com, represented by the Parks Gallery.

image that many saw as instrumental in unraveling Monroe's marriage to the baseball star Joe DiMaggio. Woodward notes that the idea for the photograph came from Sam Shaw, a friend of Monroe's, who had taken a similar photograph while clicking sailors with their girlfriends on Coney Island in 1941 for *Friday* magazine (Woodward 2002). Shaw's cinematic eye saw the sexual possibilities of the suggestive pose; hence, he offered the photograph as a prototype for the Marilyn image, resetting the star image in (Manhattan's) public eye. Woodward explains what became common gossip: the doctoring of the original and the underground circulation of a sexier "original" once the Monroe photograph had passed into mass circulation. The photograph, re-enacted in *The Seven Year Itch*, is a classic example of successful publicity as it stabilizes a single image as the most iconic one. Once the image was successfully redesigned to resemble the original (now a repressed trace), Monroe became instantly famous. As the intermedial image (recalling the "shot") continued to be reproduced and circulated in varying delivery technologies (movie posters, billboards, playbills) as the definitive trace of Monroe, the star passed into icon.

Massive circulation and consistent reiteration are therefore fundamental to the transformation of a star into an icon. The repetition of a pre-existing trace—the Coney Island photograph as the "natural" image of sexiness that Monroe later embodies—tells us how mass-produced images can follow the same proscriptions of icon representation followed by master artists. Constructed star images draw on conventional culturally salient codes (exposed women's legs and underwear as sexual stimuli); they draw on public memories of other semantically congruent graphic inscriptions. On the one hand, the publicity photograph fashions a graphic trace like the natural image of the singular actor imagined by the audience; on the other, the heavily stylized star image harnesses a culturally situated symbolic domain that turns the star into a motivated sign. Monroe could be instantly sexy because she jogged the memory of girls on Coney Island; Roy could become instantly a glamorous writer when she jogged the emerging images of Indian women in beauty pageants that were exploding in global markets as India "opened up" after 1991. While the public images of our bio-icons experience such hardening through repetition, Roy is the one who shares the frame with Monroe as sexual commodity. Not only would Roy motivate phenomenal visual expressivity—unlike Salman Rushdie of lore or Aravind Adiga, most recently, as corollary winners of literary accolades—but even verbal accounts of Roy teemed with ekphrastic eulogies to her "curls" and "collarbones." Over time, these graphic traces would acquire symbolic density.

The collarbones would underscore an appropriately delicate femininity made more attractive by the joie de vivre of the curls. Such publicity capitalizing on pre-existing cultural references would turn celebrity star into icon, a symbolically loaded graphic shorthand that could be quickly mobilized for commercial or political promotion.

Condensation

One of the effects of publicity is to condense a heterogeneous star image into an invariable trace so that it can function better as a shorthand that embodies some universally recognized quality. In this case, icons and stars operate slightly differently even as both depend on hagiographies for their focalization. Hagiographic discourse habitually attempts to imagine a space behind the star image (the private person standing behind the actor). The private person reassures, scandalizes, or surprises, often inciting identification or dis-identification from the consumer. Such a reach beyond the image to a fictitious ground of representation simulates the economy of the icon, but with one important difference. In the case of the movie star, the "private person" behind the public image works to consolidate a star image that is contingent, temporary, and variable. But when the reach beyond involves linking an invariable graphic trace (some aspect of the material image) to an unchanging ("universal") quality (James Dean's slouch connoting rebelliousness), a link that is possible only through iterative symbolic accretion (or "semiotic depth" [deCordova 2001, 26]), we might surmise that the image is an iconic one. Stars quite often carry symbolic weight; their rise and fall is symptomatic of specific historical events or changes. Britney Spears's splayed legs might have caught the temper of wearing no panties, but this is a time-bound expression of exhibitionism—a marked departure from the invariable association of James Dean's classic slouch with a basic human quality of young rebellion.

The auratic appeal of iconic images derives from the effective condensation of symbolic secretions around a single graphic trace so that, over time, the trace comes to exemplify the universal attribute of the icon. The quality of selfless giving condenses in the formal lines of a wizened face framed by a blue-bordered sari. It is not that this pose, as opposed to the inscription of Mother Teresa with the baby, explicitly signals giving. But because the symbolic valence of selfless giving has condensed into this graphic image, any imprint of the nun would evoke that invariable quality as its core property.

Figure 19 is a classic sketch in pencil by Mariola Paini that is available

FIGURE 19 Mariola Paini, "Mother Teresa." Pencil sketch. Mariola Paini, Saint's Gallery.

for sale online at the "Saint's Gallery."[20] While the circulation of the image is restricted by its price (measured in monetary value at $299), this composition of a barely visible profile underscores the point I have been making about the minimal aesthetic iteration (the unenclosed form) required to produce an iconic image or to invoke its ground of representation. The sketch repeats a culturally familiar gesture of repose, symbolically encoding the image as connoting pious reflection.

Beyond their embodiment of an invariable quality, icons are exemplary figures—they represent human excellence in some form. Hence, the movement back into the image's ground of representation jolts a projection onto our imaginary, jolts a sense of awe but also of loss. When stars invoke such spectatorial activity, we are in the domain of the icon. Consider the Hungarian film critic Béla Balázs's rumination in 1945 on Greta Garbo's face, in which he suggested why the globally famous star might be an icon. Behind the glamour, behind the constructed face, behind cultural

traditions of beauty that prompt us to think of Garbo as extraordinary
lies a perceptible hint of sadness that comes from her estrangement,
Balázs maintained. Garbo's "suffering" arose from the all-too-human experience of loneliness, a sense of radical alterity (Balázs 1970 [1949], 4).
So even while specific spectatorial enclaves may fetishize Garbo's form as
standing in for normative white beauty, her mystique has wide reach,
given the vast cross-cultural secular and religious engagements with the
human experience of our metaphysical alterity, the basis of loneliness.
Since star icons are enchanted objects inviting sacralization, they simultaneously naturalize and universalize historically particular traits (Monroe's sexiness, Garbo's feminine beauty) and insert spectators into contemplative metaphysical economies (in Garbo's case, of estrangement
and loss). On the one hand, the star icon's lonely fame formalizes our own
estrangement, as the film texts speak in the modern historical languages
of familial discord, financial failures, or sexual debacles. On the other, the
star icon appears as deeply Other, distant from us, opening us up into the
experience of metaphysical alterity. The star icon is therefore fundamentally paradoxical—both extraordinary, and therefore lonely, and belonging to the public, beloved by virtue of the universal quality he or she
embodies. When we see such an enigma motivating the spectator into
yearning for the infinite, we see—as Richard Dyer's "heavenly bodies"
suggest—the one spectacular form in which the sacred survives in the
disenchanted, secular, post-aristocratic world. This is why the image of
the star icon habitually appears enigmatic, even inscrutable, despite fervent (and often repeated) attempts to "explain" the star's mystique—and
to dispel it. We are reminded once more of Adorno's allegations against
the mass cultural image, his incitements to decode it as social hieroglyphic. Yet we are at a point in industrial history where "mass media" of
the culture industry thesis has substantially changed, perhaps most in
the mode of distribution. Perhaps a more sustained focus on distribution
is in order to gauge the efficacy of the publicity photograph whose ideological operations are challenged in expressive popular cultures.

DISTRIBUTING THE PUBLIC IMAGE

Our global icons materialize as mass-produced artifacts in films, newspapers, magazines and tabloids, television, radio, books, websites, billboards, pamphlets, stamps, and other commercial merchandise (figurines,
brooches, and key rings). They are transmitted across wide networks (e.g.,
broadcast television networks, news agencies such as Reuters and the Associated Press, publishers such as Random House) and are increasingly deliv-

ered as multimodal images (news photo emplaced in a documentary, a handwritten letter embedded on a hyper-mediated blog). Each transcription of the intermedial star image affects its sensory modalities, while changing media formats (tailoring a famous pencil sketch as ancillary trace in a televised interview) and genres (the insertion of the same image in the news as opposed to a melodramatic biopic) continually re-design it. And then there are the media with more limited reach: local and regional cinemas, local-access television, low-budget documentaries, theatrical performances, live public speech acts, songs, legends, folklore, newspapers and other print media limited by language use, memorial sites (graves or statues), paintings, calendar art, photographs, and ornamental objects (medallions or figurines), to name a few. These media with limited distribution also produce public images, but sometimes only accessible within closed social networks (a stained glass window with Mother Teresa at a local church). These public images often make short-lived appearances in the broadcast news media that constitute my archives for "reading" expressive popular culture, and we shall turn to them substantially in chapter 6. But here I will pause on the broadcast news media, institutions that are the backbone of publicity—and therefore of the star image.

Media Institutions (People, Organizations, Networks)

At the smallest scale, we can locate powerful media people who make things happen. They can be well-known studio heads; credentialed photojournalists; famous artists, writers, or scholars whose personal cachet legitimizes a certain image as "true"—the best capture of a famous icon. Their cultural value reinforces the artifact, sometimes spilling over onto the icons they admire. In the enormous visual archive on Mother Teresa, whose austerely unglamorous figure once invited vacuous comparison to Lady Diana's glamorous image, Raghu Rai, India's leading documentary photographer (associated for periods with major media platforms such as *The Statesman* and *India Today*) occupies such a space.[21] Rai, a devotee of Mother Teresa, has several collections of photographs of her to his name; his highly stylized images, collected and reprinted as photo essays, are some of the most widely circulated media on the nun (not only in collections, exhibits, and magazines, but also in postcards, pamphlets, and prayer books). Several of his photographs (accessible on the Magnum Photos website at http://www.magnumphotos.com) catch Mother Teresa in brisk action, caught mid-stride, stooping to comfort, purposefully rounding a corner, or looking up with a quick smile as the camera snaps. These photographs focalize the nun at work in the city, and they were

FIGURE 20 "At Nirmal Hriday," 1979. Raghu Rai, Magnum Photos.

first serialized in collections on Mother Teresa before they were recycled in commercial merchandise as cheap postcards or expensive coffee-table books.[22]

A photograph of Mother Teresa taken by Rai during her evening prayers at Nirmal Hriday in 1986 (figure 20) highlights the interiority that motivated the nun's public works. For Rai, the gesture of unconscious devotion—the hands further scrunching the well-known, deeply lined face—signals Mother Teresa's rich interior life. Not only is the viewer guided to interpret the graphic trace as a formal resemblance of an imaginary projection (the image of faith), but the glossy, beautifully framed, soft-contrast photograph also renders the icon deeply sensuous; the crossing between the visual and tactile modes, prompted by the soft gloss of the black and white, motivates synaesthesia. This photograph would become an iconic one in national memory, circulating in art collections and on cheaply produced postcards. It also becomes the visual epigraph for Rai's hagiography *Mother Teresa: A Life of Dedication*, in which he describes his photographs as "paens" to the nun, anchored by an accompanying pedagogic message from Mother Teresa: "If we pray, we will believe / If we believe, we will love / If we love, we will serve" (Rai 2005).

In time, Rai's photograph would be inserted into a visual public history of India. It would become a collectible among other iconic photographs selected from the nation's post-1858 history (after India came under the

British Crown), an institutionalization that would yoke the nun to India as a localized topos. These were collected in the volume *The Definitive Images: 1858 to the Present* (2004), consolidated by the photo editor Prashant Panjiar.[23] Sondeep Sarkar's snapshot of Phoolan Devi also made it into the collection, as did Sanjeev Seth's shot of the Meenachal (better known as the cover image for Roy's *The God of Small Things*[24]). No doubt, Panjar's choice of photographs was governed by the fame of their photographers and the wide circulation of the images (with numerous iterations), which ensured their currency as the representative signs of India. But to be so collected (in event-based publications or serial ones such as *Life* magazine) auratizes these mass-produced images, underlining them as iconic. In each case, the cultural status and industrial clout of a media institution selectively legitimates an iconic photograph bearing a very particular message that is rendered iconic in iteration. There is no hegemonic intention to be located here; only a structural agency. If large-scale, complex media institutions are corporate bodies controlled by financial and political elites, we may assume that the sanctioned "message" will be capital-friendly, generating surplus value (monetary, cultural, social) that ultimately rationalizes prevailing industrial regimes.

But the question of controlling media content in its multifarious migrations troubles easy equations between the broadcast media and market rationality. This is because the processes of broadcasting these days involves the streaming of media signals through organizationally complex, layered, and interlinked matrices—a distribution sprawl, we might say, within whose nodes media content is negotiated and re-negotiated on a regular basis. Increasingly, when we speak of an image having a "global" footprint, we are confronting a constellation of media linkages— for example, large-scale media organizations (such as MTV), subcontracting distribution, exhibition, or delivery through subsidiaries (such as MTV India) or local collaborators (cable-access television). In other words, as Michael Curtin's (2003) evocative notion of "media capitals"—the switch point for mass-media flows that originate from locations in the global North (for our purposes here)—suggests, media content from a single point of production undergoes several revisions when tailored for local or regional markets.[25] Varied negotiations along a chain-linked connectivity routinely determine what media content is appropriate, what sells, and how it should be evaluated.[26] This is not to say that local constellations are above market logics; on the contrary, they are canny players to local, regional, or niche markets. Hence they also participate selling the neoliberal ethos (with its characteristic emphases on consumer agency, individual potential, innovation, civil speech, and electoral democracy), but calibrate it to suit local taste and temper. The intermediary and local pathways impacting any media stream encourages critics like Amit Rai to privilege the media assemblage over the cultural product: In his persuasive transcription of Bollywood as a media assemblage, Rai discloses multiple pathways for audiovisual streams, speeding through Kenya to Trinidad, Iran, Kansas. These vertiginous flows, he argues, should direct critics to the temporary and partial relations that form where these media stream, where they "catch on" to bodies of globalized consumers (Rai 2009, 3). We will pause on where the public images "catch on" to consumers shortly, but let us stay with the complexity of broadcast.

Since our bio-icons stream in multiple media, it would be impossible to stabilize one media assemblage that broadcasts their public images. However, one can single out important media constellations where the public images gather their core properties, where their cyclical iterations crystallize a stable message. For our bio-icons, who are constantly "in the news" (sometimes even after their death), broadcast news media (with its infinite platforms) is one constellation worth a closer look, especially if we are attentive to the localizing practices that re-territorialize these global icons. One may argue the public images of these bio-icons carry with them the authenticating stamp of the "news photo" (disregarding the fact why the photograph was taken in the first place), a material trace that lends them a classic reality-fix even when we encounter them in unquestionably fictionalized media formats (such as the Hallmark biopic or BBC-funded feature film, as is the case with Mother Teresa and Phoolan Devi).[27] This intermediality, the lingering visual memory of the news photo, naturalizes (this really happened) and legitimizes (this is objective truth) subsequent remediations. Such a reality-fix saturates the icon, unlike the celebrity whose capture by paparazzi we often dismiss as idle speculation photo-shopped into existence.

If news coverage worldwide now stretches more deeply into areas with expanding communications infrastructures; if we are witnessing increasing numbers of local editions of national newspapers, new television channels, and the "reincarnation" of radio with the latest FM technology, and this is especially true of India (Sinha 2006, 121). Although newsgroups have recently diversified their outlets,[28] and we are seeing more media convergences (a single news corporation owning several media platforms),[29] newspaper reading remains a vibrant social practice. Newspapers (which celebrated 400 years of publication in 2005) have the second-largest circulation worldwide in India at 72 million, just after

China at 85 million (Sahay 2006a, xvii). As Robin Jeffrey (2000) has shown, India's linguistic history has much to do with the survival of this social ritual even since the introduction of television broadcast and local access news and the Internet.[30] In his view, improved technologies of production, distribution, and delivery; steadily growing literacy; expanding purchasing power; and aggressive publishing driven by profit contribute to this new explosion in news media (Jeffrey 2000, 17). Local newspapers channeled in print (digital only in metropolitan areas), representing local events or the interests of specific linguistic communities, not only have sustained Indian languages, but they have also grown in number, readership, and popularity, especially after the censorship period under Indira Gandhi in 1975–77 (Jeffrey 2000).[31] In the year 2000, about 60 percent of Indian adults were literate in their mother tongues, a class of potential readers that numbered close to 500 million. Indians buy about 50 million newspapers each day; only 6 million of those (less than 15 percent) are in English.[32] Such data gives us a sense of the reach and clout of this medium; it illustrates the numbers involved when we speak of regional circulation.

The larger point, however, is far more important than consumer data culled from media institutions. Despite what we perceive as corporate mass media, communicative capital encounters friction everywhere it travels. This has a quixotic effect on the ubiquity of the star image. It is certainly true that the large corporations with national investments in high-circulation magazines that offer feature articles, short stories, and serialized novels also own many of the local publications.[33] In fact, much like Rupert Murdoch's conglomerates, Jeffrey notes, in 1993 twenty families and a single public company controlled more than 70 percent of the audited daily publications in India, and among these, three families owned 11 percent.[34] More important to our concerns with the star image is the curious tension around the truth-effects of the news that impacts the hegemonic functions of the star image. On the one hand, the newspaper revolution has seen the staging of objective journalism (transparency, balance, evidentiary data gathering) in local papers; the embedding of already well-established iconic images imbued with institutional value (Roy's Booker photos, Mother Teresa classics, the Phoolan Devi surrender photos) serve to legitimate localized media stories on these figures. On the other, magazines and newspapers have moved steadily toward extensive coverage of gossip and hearsay, pinups, and sensational stories, the "page 3" celebrity culture where private lives are avidly followed. Many see this as the "magazinification" of newspapers (and the news in general); the *Times of India* was one of the forerunners, but local publications have followed suit. Hence, mythic star images of icons who seem to constantly stimulate controversy are of greater interest to the local news (Sahay 2006, 9). Local publications interlinked with broadcast media (and local narrowcast media, which is not our concern here) often play to their home base, facilitating a prism effect in which editors and writers deflect national or multinational interests encrypted in the star image.[35] So the star image of the global icon is often deliberately re-assembled, its syntactical relations to a stable message disturbed, in efforts to re-territorialize it. In some cases, these modulations become local negotiations of who "owns" the traffic flowing through transnational media networks.

Mass-mediated images embedded in these new matrices still reinforce the status quo, offering varied reassurances to varied publics who read the news. Part of the equation is to consider how they are in fact read or viewed, and the social regimes and practices of consumption finally grant these media their social efficacy. Without the social practices of embodied consumption, there can be no icon—hegemonic or popular. If we bring back the social, we need to think of the star image as nested within a larger media ecology in which the broadcast of the star image is only a part of the icon's itinerary.

Media Ecology

In his influential book *Media Ecologies* (2005, 15), Matthew Fuller addresses radio to make a larger point about studying the objects and processes of the media:

> So here's a list: Pirate radio: transmitter, microwave link, antennae, transmission and studio sites; records, record shops, studios, dub plates; turntables, mixers, amplifiers, headphones; microphones; mobile phones, SMS, voices; reception technologies, reception locations, DJ tapes; drugs; clubs, parties; flyers, stickers, posters.

The list, performatively highlighting its heterogeneous, multi-scalar composition in modulated combinations of commas and semicolons, suggests that sound waves find completion in the sociality of the club only when we take into account all else that falls between them. The fact that the polyphony of pirate radio traverses the signal, for Fuller, underscores "connective disjuncture" as a crucial term of composition. We might think of the star image in these terms: a distilled designed image beamed widely but always performatively received; a controlled message refracted through local subsidiaries, molded in diverse delivery technologies, tailored to the tastes of local publics.

Here we return to star studies and its preoccupations with the "reception technologies" and "reception locations" of mass culture. One aspect of reception, the argument goes, concerns the (localized) knowledge one brings to the consumption of the star, as Richard deCordova's (2001) magnificent work on the shift from "picture personality" to star persuasively explains. Picture personalities of American cinema that emerged between 1909 and 1914 were constituted by three kinds of knowledge—of their names, their roles (viewed in films and in journalistic discussions), and their careers (professional and otherwise). The star was something different, as the star's private life increasingly became a source of fascination. In deCordova's account, the star relies on a cultural paradigm in which public and private spheres are autonomous; access to the star's "private life" in tabloids, magazines, or publicity materials had the quality of a secret revealed, a secret that could better explain the star onscreen. Scholars of national cinemas who have followed deCordova's emphasis on regulated knowledge systems observe that the American "concept of the star" traveled with its culturally particular paradigm of personhood to other public cultures, where it was substantially modified. Neepa Majumdar (2009) demonstrates how the "star" became a reflexive form of knowing screen personalities through the calibration of an imported form of the (American) star to nationalist projects of image making. Majumdar's analysis further emphasizes the heightened reflexivity involved in recognizing an image as a star image.

These conversations underscore the centrality of public knowledge to the full transmission of the iconic image. Star systems regulate the knowledge of screen personalities by invoking the star as a certain kind of text, garnered from films, posters, publicity materials, television shows, magazines (reputable or not), and—by now—websites, blogs, web 'zines, screensavers, and so on. By contrast, icons are rarely "sold" to publics as icons. Rather, a mass-produced image becomes iconic when it is recognizable as an iterative one, when its epistemology engages the viewer in a specific semiotic economy. Hence, the star image of stars and icons may flow in the same media networks, but the icon demands knowledge beyond that mandated by stardom. To know Gandhi as an icon, for instance, might require aesthetic recognition of a graphic trace, but also situated social, cultural, political, and religious knowledge that renders his image legible.

The wider epistemological reach of the icon means we can find icons' star images in media other than those that lead down the conventional pathways of stardom; my digressions on the news photo was an effort to suggest the broader cultural field of these bio-icons who are not movie stars, even though they participate in the rich iconographic canvas of female film stars of the Bombay-based silver screen. All three bio-icons travel in news media; well-known media institutions more often than not legitimate their star images. Global icons that have no institutional backing, little social standing, and even less political clout are particularly reliant on the social efficacy of prevailing viewing regimes for public images to become iconic. Among our three icons, Phoolan Devi, the low-caste folk hero, fits the bill. We know that Shankar's photograph of Phoolan Devi facing a crowd on February 12, 1983, became the definitive graphic trace of bandit queen. We might note as Shankar's fame grew (he rose to become the general secretary of India's Working News Cameramen's Association), so did the value of these pictures.[36] Taken before the digital era, this shot still has truth effects that theorists of photography habitually decry.

The photograph was particularly coveted because the bandit queen hitherto had circulated in oral rumor, gossip, and lore. While she was being remediated in print news media, she escaped visual capture. Shankar mythologized the photograph by reporting how difficult it was to get the shot, as the hounded, reclusive, "hunger-stricken," and "ill-tempered bandit queen" lashed out at journalists waiting for the perfect shot as she gave up arms. News photographs such as this one often constitute an "originary" trace that is later cut, pasted, and remixed for publicity. We see a remixing of the Shankar photograph in the poster for Kapur's film: The bandit queen, now in color (complete with the famous red bandanna described in the news stories of 1983), still faces the crowd—surrendering in the name of the populace, as the picture suggests—but bears a gun and has her back to us (see figure 2).

To grasp the power of this iconic image, we would have to consider the social rituals of viewing news photographs within the local context where the image took root in the public imaginary. Generally, news photography still has what Roland Barthes (writing before digital photography) named a core of analogical solidity. News photographs are widely considered the "guaranteed witness" of actual events, as John Tagg (1988) has noted, and as theorists such as Allan Sekula (1982) and Victor Burgin (1982) have long established, news photos conceal the conventional nature of photographic communication. R. Srivatsan (2000) calibrates these general observations on news photography to a localized site of consumption—India—insisting that we remain attentive to the specificities of this media's materiality. Unpacking the social rituals that determine the visual field, Srivatsan recounts his shock when confronted by an unidentified dead woman after the riots in Hyderabad in December 1990, a shock of the "real" soon managed by a series of discussions of whether the victim was a Hindu or a Muslim. Such an immediate semiotic thrust, the turning symbolic of the indexical image, Srivatsan argues, reveals how scopic regimes (image and word) operate to gain control over disruptive events. In this case, the photograph restored his sense of order in that, if it could be taken, surely things were not so bad; moreover, the identification of the corpse as Hindu or Muslim could ameliorate distress, girding sensational image with the rational historical narrative of periodic violence between the two communities.[37]

To view such a photograph so means to participate as a national public, a collective consciousness critical to the consumption of global icons. This reaching for the truth—for the "real" behind the graphic trace—may be regarded as one such move (Srivatsan 2001). We might think of Sarkar's photographic capture of Phoolan Devi in these terms: It enabled national publics to gain scopic control over prevalent lawlessness, containing it within a geographic region (the "backward" Chambal Valley) and an isolated, anomalous, inevitably gendered body.[38] Such a move would cartographically fix Phoolan Devi to India's heart of darkness.

Already with this media ecology, where viewing regimes contribute to the making of star images, we are plunged into the social history of viewers. Histories of stardom, with their rich archives of spectatorship, fandom, and reception study, have obviously contributed greatly to this question. They direct us to localized arenas of reception where our global icons are consumed. In fact, given my proposition that the iconic image is always incomplete, requiring inductive narrations, reception technologies, and locations—as media ecologists suggest—assumes centrality in icon study.

For icon study, iconic images gain their purchase from their synchronic relations with other objects of equivalence, movie stars among them. Certainly, female icons are standardized in terms of female stars. This is why localized histories of stardom—in South Asia, for our purposes—are so crucial to grasping the values icons accumulate in their mass-mediated lives. Such synchronic relations would shore up the power of star images as they soak the energies of other objects circulating in their force field, objects whose fates are largely determined by the vicissitudes of public memory. When we focus on star images, we are in the thrall of objects that relate to each other through the rituals of consumption; social practices of consumption, along with corporate institutions, govern the economy and value of objects. So as we conclude our perusal of mass media, I will focus more closely on the "media fields" inhabited by the global icons in question, traditionally the loci of iconographic study.

Media Fields (Iconography)

The study of stars in Indian cinemas has been patchy, at best, especially when considering the transnational reach of star images.[39] In their early exegesis on three female stars, Behroze Gandhy and Rosie Thomas (1991) locate the beginnings of the star system for commercial Hindi-language cinema in the 1920s, with stars as contracted employees of large studios. With the breakdown of the studio system in the 1940s, however, and with the coming of the war, stars were pursued by private financers and thus became closely tied to commercial interests. Majumdar (2009) imparts greater depth to the Indian star system, carefully laying out the media platforms—films, posters, and film magazines[40]—that consolidated the Indian star by 1925. By the 1940s, movies had become star-centered products, and the earlier reticence to gossip about the star's private life had been overcome in a burgeoning public *filmi* culture. Movies could now maximize their profits based on the presence of stars in films.

Majumdar's exploration focuses on the female star as the site for negotiating indigenous conceptions of stardom. As the Indian star system began to mobilize the American concept of the "star" for profit, symbolically loaded feminine images dominated the anticolonial national public sphere. A fecund Hindu cultural nationalism imagined a "free India" in feminized form, drawing on rich iconographic traditions. In recent years, art historians, visual culture scholars, historians, and anthropologists have extensively catalogued the political imprimatur of the iconographic mother goddess, disseminated in secular prints during the nationalist period (see, e.g., Pinney 2004; Ramaswamy 2003; Uberoi 2006). Pinney argues that visual culture industries predating cinema were so popular that the colonial government sought to repress certain seemingly religious but overtly political prints—for instance, the Bombay Presidency government banned Raja Ravi Varma's chromolithograph of the eight-armed mother goddess (Ashtabhuja Devi) killing two butchers who slaughtered cows on grounds of sedition, as the mass-produced visual image aroused passions during the Cow Protection debates (Pinney 2004).[41] Clearly, an alternative cultural sphere of imagining the nation had mobilized mass-produced visual works; thus, the female deity embodying *shakti* (power) that sacralized the cartographic space of India meant that feminized figurations would garner considerable political affect. Sumathi Ramaswamy (2003) intimates that by 1909, the regal Bharat Mata (Mother India) had become India's sacralized geo-body, commanding the citizen beholder to save her from colonial persecution; much later, the Hindu right in India would mobilize such a figuration again, this time to inscribe India as a specifically Hindu political space. The work of these visual culture theorists is crucial to comprehending how a geographical space—South Asia—can become closely associated with iconic female figures. Yet, as Majumdar notes, such figuration inevitably meant that female actors in the public sphere operated under strong social constraints placed on their speech, gesture, or display of the body. So even as female stars easily invoked psychic structures of veneration, their gesture, speech, and action as public figures, as well as what could be said about them, was severely regulated within the bourgeois nationalist framework. The private lives of women, nationalists ever protective of the untouched "home" argued,[42] was not an appropriate subject of public consumption; nor should female bodies be easily displayed without responsible censorship. Hence, the female star exerted powerful allure but met with social censure.[43] It would take several decades—well into the 1950s—for female stars to be considered "respectable" women. Majumdar marks the rise of Durga Khote and Nargis as two prominent indicators of this turn.

Female public figures such as our contemporary global icons also avail themselves of the high symbolic purchase of these religious and political iconographic traditions. In general, the iconographic force field of an icon heightens its accretive density. Margaret Thatcher draws on Golda Meir and Indira Gandhi even as Al Gore gains energy as documentarian from Michael Moore. The female icons in this volume all benefit from the force fields of Indian female stardom, informed as it is by popular iconographic displays of politicized female bodies. One such star drawing her symbolic cachet from her role as Mother India was Nargis, a sex bomb known for her many love affairs; her performance in Mehboob Khan's classic *Mother India* (1957) transformed her into the quintessential Mother India, Indira Gandhi's glamorous double in years to come.[44] A role of a lifetime, *Mother India* further auratized Nargis's star image, enabling her to move effortlessly into parliamentary politics (she was nominated to the upper house, the Rajya Sabha, in 1980).

Nargis's itinerary from the glitter of cinema to political podium anticipates the fate of both Phoolan Devi and Arundhati Roy, bio-icons catapulted into the business of politics through the (commercial, cultural, and social) purchase of their public image. More important, the female icons in this book directly draw from the iconographic force of Mother India—with Mother Teresa as the most direct beneficiary. Catholic religious organizations were able to capitalize on Mother India in selling Mother Teresa as a familiar Madonna/Mother figure legible to differently situated consumers of the "living saint." We see this in the iteration of one iconic image, taken after she won the Nobel Peace Prize, in which a child always accompanies Mother Teresa, an assemblage I discussed earlier in the book. One of the famous photographs of Mother Teresa taken by Raghu Rai, which shows her cradling a baby against her breast, turned slightly to her right to protect the infant, recurs across material culture.[45] It is as much the source of painterly homage—for instance, in Judy Jones's celebrations of Mother Teresa's life and work (figure 21)[46]—as it is an imprint on commercial artifacts such as Indian postage stamps (figure 22). The image on the Indian stamp found iteration on stamps in African nations such as Chad, Djibouti, Uganda, Gabon.

Roy is a rather differently gendered icon: sexual, glamorous, brainy, and modern. Roy's iconic sign arose at the confluence of many overlapping markets for South Asia. A beauty industry was in full swing as South Asian "beauties" entered world pageants en masse. At the same time, a second wave of pop feminism had created global markets for the "woman of color." (One website celebrated Roy with "three words: Woman of Color. A unique critique from the non-western world."[47]) And an equally pop multiculturalism set in motion a bazaar for non-Western goods. As if the stars were not yet aligned, India was celebrating its fiftieth anniversary of freedom from British rule. What better time, asked the cynics, for a "daughter" of India to be crowned the "princess of prose"? Roy epitomized the new face of globalizing India. It was an India one could live with, one that signaled the success of market deregulation through its flamboyantly antigovernment icon of free speech. Even when accounts sympathetically reported Roy's protestations of her star image, they inevitably returned to the gendered star body with obsessive ocularity. While conveying Roy's entrapment in infinite reflection, an interviewer for *The Independent*, for example, proceeded to ekphrastically reinstate the famous close-up: "Everywhere she went, her own image was stalking her: staring from every bookshop window, the gorgeous smoldering photograph, all elegant collarbones and untamed curls." The article went on to replace this early image with a second one, positioning Roy in a different, yet equally glamorizing, chain of signifiers. "Shearing off the long hair,"

FIGURE 21
Judy Jones,
Mother Teresa.
Digital image.
Courtesy of
Judy Jones.

FIGURE 22
Mother Teresa
postage
stamp. India
Post.

the journalist noted, the activist Roy has now adopted "the current gamine Audrey Hepburn crop."[48] If such an image could arise transnationally at the confluence of several markets, in India changes in female stardom had laid the groundwork for nuances of this feminization. Like Majumdar, Gandhy and Thomas argue that, by the 1970s, feminist screen idols such as Smita Patil and Shabana Azmi—who share the badge of "activism" with Arundhati Roy—had legitimized and glamorized images of modern, young, successful, and vocal actors in public life.[49] Roy's cachet as glamour girl capitalized on the prominence of these two stars of "alternative" or new-wave Indian cinema.[50]

Perhaps the most direct inheritor of star power was Phoolan Devi, the bandit queen, who holds an eminent place in cinema history (beyond Kapur's internationally known film). By the 1970s, stars were highly coveted products; it was a decade that saw the emergence of Amitabh Bachchan as a cultural phenomenon whose superstar magnitude had not been witnessed before on the subcontinent. I would argue this is precisely because his image quickly became a technology for imagining anti-establishmentarian desires, especially on the part of those who felt left out of the electoral calculus. In this sense, Bachchan is a star aperture whose popular appeal far surpasses that of the more traditionally iconographic Nargis. Precious little has been said about Bachchan, perhaps because of this complexity. Jain's (2007) recent treatment partly makes good this oversight, but a full-length study on Bachchan remains long overdue. Lalit Vachani's essay on Bachchan's failed move into politics offers one description of his rise following his entry on national screens as the quintessential "outsider" in Prakash Mehra's film *Zanjeer* (1973). It is this iconic outsider status, Vachani argues, that disabled Bachchan's move into state governance, despite the actor's close friendship with Rajiv Gandhi; after a brief stint in the 1980s, Bachchan retired from parliamentary politics, describing the arena as a "cesspool" (Vachani 1999). Vachani's analysis suggests that Bachchan's presence as a vibrant outsider in an alternative public culture inhabited by lower-class viewers who often feel unrepresented in the political process (the parties, organizations, and civil institutions of modern associational life) may be why he was able to make a comeback in Hindi-language films. In his sixties, Bachchan enjoyed new popularity as an unelected godfather-like figure, enshrined in Ram Gopal Varma's remake of the Francis Ford Coppola classic, *Sarkar* (2005).

Bachchan's rise as the disenfranchised hero is most relevant to the discussion of Phoolan Devi's star image. For one, Bachchan's many portraits as an angry young man whose sense of justice was above the law (most notably in the mega-hit *Deewar* [1975]) quickly legitimized and glamorized outlaws on screen. Rumors of bandit queens had been around in local print and audiovisual media since the early 1970s. The journalist Taroon Bhaduri, for example, had published a wildly popular book, *Chambal: The Valley of Terror* (1972). The very same year, Ashok Roy made the film *Putlibai*, based on the original "bandit queen" of the Chambal, singling out the feminine figure from her many male counterparts.[51] In the meantime, the Bombay cinema dream factory had begun to churn out populist romantic bandit heroes, monumentalized in the blockbuster *Sholay* (1975), starring Amitabh Bachchan—reportedly the first film Phoolan Devi saw in the theaters. Fascinated with the female outlaw, Ashok Roy went on to make the Bengali-language film *Phoolan Devi* (1984), followed by the Hindi version *Kahani Phoolvati Ki* (1985), which aimed at a larger national audience. Both of these popular melodramas starred Reeta Bhaduri (Taroon Bhaduri's daughter and sister of the Bollywood actress Jaya Bhaduri/Bachchan[52]). These were succeeded by the equally populist *Daku Hasina* (1987), featuring the siren star Zeenat Aman, after the infamous massacre at Behmai and Phoolan Devi's surrender. By 1987, as she languished in jail, Phoolan Devi had become a national legend, in part drawing her cultural purchase from the gloried infamy of these fictional social bandits. It is such an iconographic field that explains Phoolan Devi's stardom.

But it was the Kapur film that crystallized that image for transnational audiences, a film that drew Phoolan Devi's ire for what she saw to be an exploitive depiction of her rape and abduction. Funded by the BBC's politicized Channel Four, *The Bandit Queen* (1994) catapulted Phoolan Devi into transnational celebrity. The film came out after Phoolan Devi had completed her eleven-year jail term, and it was immediately banned in India. Not only did Phoolan Devi attack Kapur's transcription of her "life," which led to her fallout with Mala Sen (her biographer, who also wrote the script for Kapur's film) over Sen's participation in the project, but scholars, critics, artists, and journalists all joined the furor over the film's representation of "India" to the "West" and the sensationalization of rape (Fernandes 1999; Longfellow 2002).[53] As Leela Fernandes notes, Kapur was certainly aiming at social critique, at social realism rather than melodrama, and the film did largely seek to disrupt the hegemonic national image of India's successful transformation into a consumer capitalist economy, given that its most disenfranchised could find justice only outside the law. Yet the film only reinforced an existing neocolonial opposition between the "West" and the "Third World," where the Third World's monstrosity only continued to enrich the West's sense of civilizational supremacy. Scholars such as Fernandes worried about the film's emphasis on "the problem of Indian culture," including the usual litany of woes (child marriage, caste system, gender inequality) indicative of a failed modernity (Fernandes 1999, 125). In India, the middle class responded sharply to the politics of displaying the naked subaltern body that denied Phoolan Devi the rights of decency extended to middle-class Indian women (though the naked body in the film, as Fernandes notes, is actually that of the male rapist).[54] Kapur's film projected the global form of the subaltern turned icon: the classically dispossessed caste-marked subject (the caste system always the focus of titillation in the historical West) who reinforces the fragility of the rule of law in the historical East.

Nor has the depiction faded from public memory. A recent two-minute thriller inaugurating an expanded twenty-four-hour Hindi movie channel, Zee Cinema, combined Phoolan Devi's saga with iconic images from *Sholay* as an advertisement.[55] The thriller, *Paap Ka Anth* (The Limits of Sin), repeats the iconic trace of the bandit queen—arms upraised, rifle held aloft, and red bandanna draped over her hair (figure 23)—that we remember from Kapur's film poster. The most commoditized star image of the bandit queen as a stereotypically disadvantaged female figure (a "brown woman") requiring rescue (by "brown men") is therefore, in this case, directly produced in cinema.[56]

And the saga continues, for Kapur's text has returned as a contested object in Krishna Mishra's *Wounded* (2007), a film about Seema Parihar, India's new self-proclaimed "bandit queen." Parihar agreed to star in the biopic only if Mishra would strive for a realism nowhere to be found—in Parihar's view—in *The Bandit Queen*. Strikingly, when the police in Mishra's *Wounded* find Seema Parihar (who stars as herself) living under a false name, they do not haul her away to the police station; rather, they invite her to a public surrender. Inevitably, Parihar arrives dressed in a khaki uniform with the characteristic red bandanna (not the black jeans and black bandanna she dons in the rest of the film). She raises her rifle over her head before handing it over to the police. She folds her hands to greet the crowd. The specter of Phoolan Devi lives on in this ritualized reenactment.

Finally, the excursion into the economy of star images we have pursued here brings me to the question of genre, the social pacts that point us to reception locations, to the embodied consumption that traverses the mass-media signal. They are therefore crucial to a consideration of

PRESENTING INDIA'S FIRST 2 MINUTE THRILLER.

FIGURE 23 Film poster for *Paap Ka Ant*, 1989. Gautam Bokadia.

the media ecology in which the feminized global forms of our bio-icons dwell. With genre, following Fuller (2005), we have moved to people swallowed by stars, incorporated into the sensuous form of the star image. In their consumer activity we find the secrets of those social relations encrypted in mass-mediated signs—secrets we have begun to decipher in our restoration of the icons' historical materiality.

OF SOCIAL RELATIONS

Star studies have always been preoccupied with social relations that produce, and that are produced through, star images. The losses or gains made in contact with stars, icons, or celebrities preoccupy most theorists of stardom, debates cast in terms of subject–object relations. Devoid of historical materiality, stars appear as inscrutable objects that charm, incorporating subjects into their animate forms; their inscrutability is further accentuated when they are frequently translocated and diverse publics seek entry into them. Kwai-Cheung Lo's thoughtful essay on Hong Kong martial arts stars such as Jackie Chan and Bruce Lee (Lo 2004), whose star images flow as wildly and freely as those of our global icons, compels us to consider why someone as famous as Jackie Chan might appear awkward on the David Letterman show with its massive global footprint.[57] (The Indian press went to town regarding Aishwarya Rai's coyness on the same platform some years later.) Despite Jackie Chan's fame, Kwai-Cheung Lo argues that the highly muscled bodies of Hong Kong's male stars, passing from the comics to the screen, remain inscrutable to American audiences. They remain fantastic, flying through the air, astounding audiences with a super-human capacity that fails to represent Hong Kong's suture of Chinese cultural tradition with Western influence at the level of realism. Such a failure, Kwai-Cheung Lo insists, comes from the changeful, unstable, and fast-paced lifestyle of the former British colony; the non-transparency of the hero's hyperbolic body captures this indeterminacy. That body can be "filled" by a historical sense of Hong Kong from the viewer's perspective. So the body itself—the graphic inscription—is an empty space, a "hole" or opening that invites us into the space of history that mobilizes it. When we are unable to read such a body historically, the star appears strange, awkward in his manner, and therefore enigmatic. Despite cutting, dubbing, and re-editing, Jackie Chan does not seem to "fit" anywhere; he can be neither safely stereotyped nor celebrated (Gallagher 2004).

Christine Gledhill furthers the notion of the aperture-like star in her remarkable *Reframing British Cinema, 1918–1928* (2003). Gledhill insists that the 1920s were a critical period in which British cinema sought to consolidate its roots in popular visual narrational traditions while situating itself in relation to Hollywood and European cinemas. The star became the key for envisioning the future of British cinema, the acting styles of Edwards or Guy Newall distinguishing the British predilection for "underplaying" from the American "playing from the heart." To combat the "bogey" of the Hollywood star, the British star marked the deployment of skill through his style—that is, the ability to underplay a role. The performativity of the star drew spectators to the space behind the star— the private, "real" person given to avoiding excess, given to well-bred restraint. Gledhill reads such a gap between audience and performer, and between performer and the "real" star, as structurally relevant to middle-class British audiences in a society marked by social distance and demarcation.[58] The star image, when iconic, opened the spectator into the space behind which one could consume being British in a combination of restraint (of style) and passion (the sincerity of acting to the best of one's ability). Here the iconic British star facilitates the spectator's will to become part of a collectivity by consuming the star image.[59]

Gledhill's star foregrounds an object—the iconic star—through which subjects move toward others.[60] Here the star operates as a technology for forging social bonds, its incorporative processes substantially altering personhood. But this is the most utopian scenario; not every star image facilitates such movement. A more modulated sense of the exchanges through which icons are transacted calibrates the range of social relations that star images encrypt in their material lives in mass media. As Igor Kopytoff (1986) maintains, while we find increasing homogenization of objects and subjects (commoditization through standardization) in complex public cultures, these are mixed economies inclusive of smaller networks that simultaneously singularize or re-singularize commodities. The biography of "things" (objects or people for Kopytoff; iconic images in our case) reveals a shuttling between singularity and generality, neither of which is a pure state, for while singularity is usually attributed to people, the history of slavery speaks of the translation of people into goods.[61] And while things are widely regarded as objects valued in terms their equivalence to other objects, in gift exchange they can escape their generality. In multicentric economies, where there is no single universe of value ascription, most things have mixed fortunes: They may be saleable items that later become collectible, priceless, or worthless. Therefore, we need to attend to the temporality—duration and frequency—of icons, Kopytoff surmises, so we can properly comprehend their deactivations and reactivations as efficacious media.

Where Kopytoff insists on the temporal, the "biograph" we shall take up more substantially in the next chapter, Arthur Gell dwells on the question of agency posed in a mixed economy of commoditization and singularization. Given that people can become objects, and vice versa, Gell notes that both are capable of agency at different stages in their "biographies" (Gell 1998). If we are asking what we might make of the relation between the classic star image and the consumer, Gell's notion of a "fractal personhood" provides a capacious rubric—a personhood earned through incorporation into the star that first appears as excorporated object.

Fractal Personhood

The corporeality of the star image is well established in critical discourses that speak to reified and fragmented star bodies. Of course, star images unavoidably are assembly-line products that serve markets' needs; of course, they will sell whatever is perceived as enticing. But beyond publicity, images of movie stars can serve other social needs at particular historical junctures. For example, Jane Gaines (2000) has explored how Betty Grable's legs came to be associated with the Second World War through a series of wartime pinups. By aligning linguistic and sexual economic exchange—the mystical commodity fetish embodying magical natural properties that concealed the labor of production—Gaines argues that Grable's legs drew on pre-existing cultural associations: Women's legs equal sexual enticement. Hence, the legs could fetishically promise the lure of the girl at home to soldiers engaged abroad; legs brought comfort, the concealing capacities of the well-polished fetish, never bringing into question the objectified fragmentation of the female body—its historical materiality.

While the corporeal attraction that is the privilege of the star can clearly estrange us from social relations (the labor of production), I have been suggesting there are occasions when the intensification of sensations aroused by the embodied, lustrous, and designed star image can turn object into incorporative technology; the star disappears as object, inciting an ontological becoming that can move subjects toward the social. For André Bazin, this incorporation combats of our sense of morality in continuing the "existence of the corporeal body" (Bazin 1967, 9); hence, stars seem imbued with magical agency. Much like their theological counterparts, the saints, stars inspire reliquaries where their corporeal substance becomes treasured fetish, sometimes with miraculous power.[62] We remember the posthumous kidnapping of Charlie Chaplin's corpse,[63] following a long tradition of grave robbing and body manipulation of dead icons (Abraham Lincoln, Che Guevara, Eva Perón, Patrice Lumumba, among others), as testament to the lure of magical star bodies that promise material continuity with the universe.

These varied senses of incorporation into the star image hint at divergences in the icon's social efficacy, a technology at once capable of reifying and enabling social relations. On the one hand, we can think of fractal personhood as the movement toward chaos as one is enfolded into the icon. Here, certain media forms, such as the melodrama, facilitate the collapse of Cartesian body–mind dualisms as sensations disinter the sovereign territories of subject and object. Kapur's The Bandit Queen (not to mention Ashok Roy's bandit films), for instance, are highly melodramatic texts. Melodrama is one of the three body genres Linda Williams (1991, 143) places beside pornography and horror as a mode of representing where the body is "besides itself" with "sexual pleasure, fear and terror, or overpowering sadness." All three modes erect a zone of fantasy in which de-subjectified subjectivities oscillate between self and other, subject and object. In melodrama, the oscillation makes the icon's image volatile so that viewers enter into the excessively present, constrained, violated, weeping body. Whether one sees melodrama as a mode of representation or, in a more Deleuzian vein, as an affect-modulation machine, one can hardly ignore the manifest corporeality of melodramatic depiction—a corporeality that energizes the viewing subject's incorporation into the iconic image. In melodrama, the mirrored image of affect as emotion increases the gravitational force that moves body into the media stream. Yet on the other side of flow lies binding, the re-attachment of the subject to the star image as a firmly framed object, a prosthetic that territorializes the subject who enters it. Lost in the media worlds of celebrity, the frame composing chaos into territory remains firmly emplaced. Michael Warner (1993) advances such a proposition in his astute analysis of contemporary public spheres saturated with mass media, where icons offer a kind of membership to a public.[64] Warner explains that images and texts are meaningful to a public when they have a "strategy of impersonal reference." To become public in the eighteenth century required routine self-abstraction, disembodiment. Yet the positivity of the body would make its way back in the libidinal economies of the public sphere, as both Warner and Lauren Berlant (1991) have reminded us, the subject's body interjected into the public arena through a prosthetic object. Mass-mediated stars, icons, and celebrities are some of the most enticing prosthetic objects, their overexposed bodies hotly contested, desired, or rejected. Warner evokes multifarious fantasies about Ronald Reagan's body that incited public aggression (e.g., the abundant imaginings of Reagan's anus), fear, desire, or enchantment. At the moment of desiring the icon, we witness a "we"—*our* sports, *our* lingo, *our* music, and, more recently, *our* president. For minority subjects unable to escape the positivity of the body, the prosthetic object is precisely a means of controlled disembodiment: By disappearing into Michael Jordan's body by buying sneakers, one enters a stratified "we" even as one enjoys the positivity of one's own body through the specularized star body. Here the thing that holds us firmly in its grip, the frame that territorializes, imparts pleasure. The subject is re-territorialized as the unique image, its flow toward chaos arrested.

But what kind of collective membership does the icon offer in the hydraulics of binding and release? Theorists of stars and celebrities note that the move toward collectivity is achieved by the star or icon, but rarely by celebrities.[65] Unlike the icon that acquires value over time, celebrities can be manufactured instantaneously in "pseudo-events" (Daniel Boorstein's term for pure media events manufactured to consolidate the media image of a person). Here the person might not even be an actor in the public sphere, let alone one who has achieved excellence in any sense; the private lives of people are the main draw in celebrity culture. Stars can, of course, be instant celebrities; becoming an icon is a lengthier and more complex process. In this sense, the celebrity is at the opposite end of the spectrum from the icon. Where the icon is closer to the heroes of lore, as Leo Braudy (1990) explains, the celebrity is rather ordinary—an extremely fabricated image, not exemplary except at a momentary and contingent juncture where his or her private life is the subject of media coverage. Stars live celebrity lives that rise and fade from view every day. No one remembers what Tom Cruise ate for breakfast or what he wore to the Oscar gala unless those acts express some special quality the actor symbolizes. But the exemplarity of stars, reiterated in invariable traces over time, can turn them into icons.

These differences have much to tell us about the social bonds that are enabled or disabled in encounters with star images. Where the star icon can motivate collective adoration in different forms of spectatorial activity, celebrities are usually consumed in isolation. They are purely commodity; their lives substitute for what is missing in ours. They engage us in dangerous "para-social" relations in a world of increasingly fragmented family, kinship, and community ties; although they are deceptively similar to icons in enchanting the consumer, celebrities do not open us to another. Rather, as Richard Schickel (1985) reminds us, celebrities bind us in false structures of intimacy that move outward to an individual whose media image is mistaken for reality. The invisible threads of this imagined intimacy become suddenly visible when, for example, a pathological stalker appears to stake his or her claim.[66] For many theorists of celebrity culture, this is the most enervating aspect of celebrity. As a part of the "culture of distraction," Chris Rojek (2004, 90) notes, celebrities engulf us in faux ecstasy, deflecting our attention from structured inequalities. By contrast, at their most auratic, icons mobilize incorporation into the social, often through forms of policed collective membership demarcated by "us" and "them," the internal frontier that constitutes the popular.[67]

To recapitulate the argument: Gell's fractal personhood can be conceived as a continuum in which we have complete dominance by the ce-

lebrity who swallows us, often leading to disorientation or social estrangement (sometimes pathologically expressed) on one end and the
forging of subject–subject relations through a disappearing object (often
leading to collective bonds) on the other. In ontological becoming, the
boundaries of personhood begin to disappear altogether. But such becoming can be arrested when the perceived boundaries of the object (into
which one has disappeared) hardens in the cultural form of a famous
individual. Neither of these processes determines the kinds of social
action that might ensue; rather, we might say, they can indicate whether
one acts individually or collectively. I shall turn more substantially to this
question on individual and collective veneration when I consider the
work of the icon as volatile signifier. But there is still a process central to
materializing the icon that must be considered before turning to the
volatile icon: narration, a process that "fills" or "opens" the space behind
the public image, reactivating received truths or stimulating creative
speculation.

Pursuing the historical materiality of the star image directs us to the
different spheres of exchange where these images are harvested, revised,
or dismantled, localized sites of consumption we traverse in the next two
chapters. There we move to fleeting, ephemeral, short-lived traces of the
icons in expressive public culture from the hyper-visible star images animated in broadcast media. In this chapter, we began with publicity to
shore up the industrial, technological, and social processes that "make"
the best-known public images of our bio-icons. Since publicity is best
understood as a constellation of practices, structures, and regimes—since
it has to be grasped not only as production, but also circulation, distribution, and consumption—it tells us that encounters with icons are not
simply the epiphenomena of capitalist development but are constitutive
of its logics.

Publicity relies on public fascination. We are cynical about publicity,
but we crave what it gives us. We know that the smooth surfaces of the
star image are artifice, but we desire the "real" that it conceals. As Jodi
Dean (2002) reminds us, in the belly of the beast—in the myth of full
disclosure as successful publicity—lies secrecy. Dean's concerns are the
massive expansions of communications infrastructure that underlie a
"global information society"—concerns quite removed from the situated
analytic gaze of this book. But the hyperbolic publicity of chat rooms,

cyber-salons, and e-zines that Dean describes, where everyone is celebrity, has a certain salience for the historical, post-1989 period of icon consumption with which we are concerned. Clearly, publicity is the currency of our time; hence, the emerging notions of communicative capitalism. Value seems to lie less in the object than in our ability to know everything about it; we are fascinated by the process of leaking rather than what the leaks reveal. And clearly, our hubris at getting at the "truth" that is evidently "out there" is the prevailing public fantasy of full disclosure that covers over the "gaps, antagonisms, inconsistencies, and lacks that pervade the social field" (Dean 2002, 8). These are observations to which I will return shortly, but as we proceed to the next chapter, I will highlight one of Dean's most provocative claims: that the secret, suggesting a world of withheld relationships (economic secrets, military secrets, sexual secrets, secrets to power—the list is endless), fuels publicity (Dean 2002, 10). Secrets direct our energy to a world of social relations rendered mystical because it is hidden from view; secrets invoke fantasy; secrets provoke speculation. In our scheme, the incompletion of the iconic sign has always prompted story, the inductive logic of story enabling us to fully grasp the sign. If icons prompt story, highly public icons—whose publicity generates secrecy—instigate enormous speculation in gossip, rumor, legend, and lore as necessary supplements to established biographies, biopics, and hagiographies. We turn to these animating inductive forms to understand the scale of affect these corporeal bio-icons command, to the biograph that bears witness to the social efficacy of the icon.

Where glittering images dazzle us, the telling of "lives," the quiet but inexorable animation of these images, hover on the edges of icon study as ancillary process. The distinction of the bio-icon, however, whose public image depends on its *bios*, formalized as a "life story," mandates a closer look at the process of "telling lives" as it constitutes the social materiality of the icon. At the simplest level, the many narrations or "lives" circling a bio-icon focalize it as a sign so that it may efficaciously transmit a message. Telling "lives" can activate an image to become icon, a saleable item to become gift, a person to become a thing. Such narration continues to animate bio-icons long past the physical death of the living figure. Hence, telling lives is one of the central social activities to consider in an icon's cultural biography. The performance of telling lives, reorganizing intense sensations released by icon veneration into affections and perceptions, constitutes the icon's social materiality that this chapter explores further. We shall see how the performance of the tale—its intensities, it provocations, its partial truths, its secrets and elisions—can reveal competing social demands central to the formation of the popular. If this is our central concern, we must attend to how "lives" make apertures from a universe strewn with images.

Much of this chapter will focus on how narrating lives can commoditize or singularize an iconic image, acts that inexorably move us toward hegemonic or popular aspirations. Narrations are the major social practices that assemble the iconic image within a connotative matrix so that it may begin to carry a stable message; in narrations we are often shown, not told, of the icon's extraordinary deeds through the unfolding of story. We learn by example, not prescription. Of course, this is precisely why powerful institutions wage wars over regulating the proper narration of public lives, legitimizing those that convey their worldview. Hence, it is critical that we look closely at how such regulation works through publicity: What are the mechanisms of control? What procedures sanction the hegemonic capture of a bio-icon?

I argue that powerful cultural figurations that express social actions as their excellent qualities (incalculable giving as generosity, fearless protest as sacrifice) reorient the ontological becoming activated in encounters with icons toward the social. I consider the potentiality of these figurations vibrant in popular lore more closely in chapter 8; here, I introduce the subject to underscore how institutions can harness their force for hegemonic purpose. Hegemonic institutions (e.g., the Vatican) seek not only to brand a particular personage (e.g., Mother Teresa), but also to patent the general figuration (the saint) through elaborate legal procedures. The saint becomes a standardized common term in the tortuous processes of miracle confirmation, and Mother Teresa becomes the institutionally sanctioned stereotype. A cultural figuration heterogeneously manifest in popular lore is brought into the calculus of measurement. We see such a process in public narrations that focalize the Christian saint as embodiment of charity, the civil activist as the voice of the people, or the low-caste reformed outlaw as the emblem of democratic progress. Since "lives" animate living people into signs, these public narrations impart value, bringing historical bio-icons into equivalence with others of the same caliber—often a company of the elect who are far, far, indeed, from the unruly popular. This has important consequences for the living person yoked only to the standardized figuration; reduced to one exemplary trait, she becomes a classic stereotype. Stable public narrations develop reassuring stereotypes: Phoolan Devi's inevitable rags-to-riches story reassures the bourgeois of their working democracy.

Authorized biographies across media platforms enable standardization, bringing the bio-icon into equivalence with her peers through the process on focalization; the more heavily institutional they are, the more didactic the purpose. In these cases, we witness a negation of the creative force of figuration that is unstable in its many cultural manifestations. Uncertainty, the effect of unsettling macro-scalar change, can activate the often dormant figurations in social memory, generating the epistemological crisis of the icon's global form. In chapter 3, we encountered some of these moments in three controversies in which the stereotype is destabilized by the onslaught of competing "truths." If institutionally sanctioned biographies standardize excellence, binding consumers to the fantasies of a unified social (where Mother Teresa embodies charity for all) or to a closed membership (Christians of faith), when these hegemonic forms invite opprobrium, there is an exorbitant influx of remembered popular avatars. As speculation spirals and as inventive playful rumor, lore, gossip, and hearsay accumulate, we witness attempts to retell the story—to re-focalize the sign. This is exactly why narrations of the icon's life are where battle lines are drawn and tents are pitched for long wars over the meanings of a singular life. Hence, the scholar of the popular must attend not only to the well-known public narrations of bio-icons but also to surges in gossip, rumor, or exposé that disrupt iconic "message." For those are occasions when the image is up for grabs; volatilized, it can become a magical technology of the popular.

I delved into the historical materiality of the iconic image in the previous chapter. Here, we pause on the logic of its narration. Publicity facilitates the movement, since the performance of full disclosure depends irrevocably on the tidbit, the fragment, or hearsay that will enable re-focalization of a well-known public image. As the chapter proceeds, we garner a more complex sense of publicity through its Other: secrecy. And secrets, as always, bring trouble to smooth narration; they gather energy only to explode. We shall see how the "lives" of icons are dotted with the hidden, the half-concealed, the recessed, or the forgotten. Two stories—Mother Teresa's secrets and Phoolan Devi's forgotten lives—illustrate the effects of concealment. Whatever is secret erupts; whatever is recessed returns.

In some respects, this is the law of genre: Derridean exorbitance in the face of regulation. But if we understand "law" structurally, as Derrida always encourages us to do, then the "secret" arrives because publicity is regulated—controlled, governed, instituted. To put it bluntly, when publics begin to suspect that some*one* (a faceless "they") actively hides or conceals certain truths of a life from (a formless but exuberant) "us," there is already a fracture in the (hegemonic) fantasy of a unified public.

Secrets reveal regulation at work; they generate exorbitant meaning in endless speculation. In the cascade of "lost fragments," the iconic image emerges as historical, volatile, provoking retellings of its story. Retellings that destabilize received truths of the icon and its universal message can initiate the epistemological crisis that precedes its volatilization.

THE LIFE STORY

How do we take a plunge into the complex domain of narration? The "life story," one form of controlling *bios*, provides flexible scaffolding for the many forms of telling lives: sanctioned biography, autobiography, hagiography, collaborative testimonies, and sketches in interviews, as well as gossip, rumor, and lore recounted in print, digital, and audiovisual media. The life story may take multiple forms even as it is produced and delivered in multiple technologies; the only stable characteristic we might presume is the life story's inductive logic that guides us to focalize the iconic image in specific ways. We can be induced to think of the icon as extraordinary in authorized and legitimated proto-hagiographic productions (from the Hallmark biopic to institutionally sanctioned print biography), while exposés and gossip columns (tabloid press to reported lore) rife with private scandal compel us to contemplate the ordinariness of the icon, exposing the "fiction" of its exemplarity.

Inductive narration, which is highly performative, always finds completion in reception, where the listener variously grasps the message—a "connective disjuncture," to recall Matthew Fuller (2005), that no publicity machine can regulate, despite an arsenal of controlling mechanisms (from embedding testimony to "authentic" footage and parataxes such as prefaces and glossaries, interviews, and so on). Such sociality enriches our understanding of the icon's rich materiality. When "secrets" erupt, biographical fragments of a lost or recessed time, scene, or event proliferate, often bringing ruin to the efforts to regulate the iconic message. As speculation intensifies and fragments accumulate, the iconic image is seen as stereotypical, limited, historical. As what it signifies becomes contested, it brings about quarrel. The chapter heads in this direction: toward the secrets that fracture the perceptions of a unified social, fueling the social antagonism at the heart of the popular.

It is only when we grasp the investments in "lives," in the social pact of disclosing the "life story," that we are able to comprehend the force of the secret and intuit the depth of betrayal, opprobrium, or mistrust such failures might provoke among consumers. The hue and cry over secrets conveys the degree of affective investment in an icon, especially when the icon is regarded as "belonging" to the public. The more a living figure is animated in publicity, the more sensation it provokes, the more intense the affect of revelation—the more her "life" (or, at least, the disclosed fragment) is subjected to repeated and strenuous reanimation. If the visual design of the iconic images makes for the icon's sensuousness, the rhetorical and narrative capacities of the "life story" constitute its affective charge.

But such capacities are governed by the mode of telling lives. A biopic might draw on a melodramatic mode to provoke sentiment, while gossip often enacts intimacy for its emotional draw. As a customary manner of expression, the "mode" of telling selects, organizes, and distills the iconic sign with the presumption of a shared sociality; hence, the specific mode of "telling lives" always points to a localized context of reception. Here our global icons posit some difficulty, since many of the biographies that constitute their global form originate in the mass media (print, audio-visual, and digital) in the global North before making their way into South Asia. Thus, social practices of "telling lives" in both locations are equally relevant. Since it would be virtually impossible to offer an in-depth discussion of all the modes of telling in these arenas—always a challenge for "global media studies"—I undertake a selective commentary before launching into the two stories that illustrate the work of focalization.

Minor Lives

Life stories have a long history within South Asia across mass and alternative media. We are largely focused on mass media—it is our archive in this book. What we find in mass media (e.g., pulp print biographies or biopics aired on national networks) has a longer history as a mode of narration across media practices, technologies, and platforms in South Asia. All of the major religious traditions have a variegated repertoire that circulates, reworked, in visual, written, and oral media (Arnold and Blackburn 2005). Premodern life stories were chiefly hagiographical oral and written accounts of the lives of saints, deities, kings, cultural heroes, and poets; these existed in (elite) classical Sanskrit and popular forms (as we see in the collected legends of the *bhakti* saints). In the case of highly venerated icons such as Mother Teresa and Phoolan Devi, we see a persistence of these older forms of telling life stories: Mother Teresa's life story is often recounted by someone else, as is traditional in the lives of saints, while fragments of Phoolan Devi's life were transmitted in oral and theatrical culture (songs and *nautanki* performances on Phoolan

Devi's *biraha* [sorrow]) as early as 1983. Another stream of life stories entered the subcontinent with the coming of Islam, in the forms derived from the Middle East: the lives of Sufi *pirs* or *ghazis* (spiritual guides/teachers) available at tombs or disseminated in oral performance; oral and written forms of religious biographies with a pedagogical aim; and the great autobiographies of the Mughal emperors (the Baburnama and the *Akbarnama*).

By the eighteenth century and nineteenth century, these earlier traditions were partially supplanted and recast by a whole genre of "modern" life stories that recounted the lives of those with "high character," or *carita*, and commercial printing in the nineteenth century was largely responsible for this flowering. Autobiographical speech, as Sudipta Kaviraj (2004) demonstrates with the example of Sibnath Shastri's *Atma Carita* (1918), was predicated on the moral caliber of the speaker. The biographical/autobiographical mode established the prototype of a "high moral character," yoking it to a historical manifestation; those worthy of animation in these forms were brought into equivalence, into commodity, with others of high character simply through a mode of telling lives (the full-fledged biography, autobiography, or memoir). Men of high caste or class positions, modern men with reformist zeal, were first to turn to the form, while women found autobiographical narration attractive but difficult. By the early twentieth century, political autobiographies (especially those written while in prison), such as Mahatma Gandhi's *The Story of My Experiments with Truth* (1927–29) and Jawharlal Nehru's *Autobiography* (1936; its original title was *In and Out of Prison*), had become staples, and autobiography had become political history by the time Indira Gandhi projected herself as the secular embodiment of India.[1]

If the evolution of this social practice indicates how iconic images of those whose lives are worthy of telling might be focalized, and what roster they would inhabit, female icons (especially those not legitimated by a powerful male figure) would gain their right to publicity—to a narrated life made public—with the rise of women's political biographies during the nationalist movement. As Purnima Bose (2003) notes, highlighting Kalpana Dutt's *Chittagong Armoury Raid Reminiscences* (1945) and Margaret Cousins's *We Two Together* (1950), these widely circulating print biographies had an unmistakable legitimating social function. Dutt promoted the heroic nationalist body of the freedom fighters of the Jugantar group in a language of corporeality that celebrated not only the endurance of pain but also courageous aggression against a violent colonial state (possibly, Bose suggests, to combat the enervating portrait of effeminate Bengali men of the time). Autobiography became a mode of witnessing bodies as they were shot, arrested, and beaten, well in keeping with the group's strategy of spectacularizing highly publicized acts of physical violence. Many biographies of women would retain this testimonial dimension, projecting the "event" of the body in action, well past the nationalist movement. We see this most directly in Phoolan Devi's "lives," but also in the many sketches of Arundhati Roy's highly corporeal image as it acts for the disenfranchised on the banks of the Narmada. The practice of focalizing a corporeal female image, a body in action signaling agency, was soon well established in the freedom struggle, and since autobiographies narrated subjectivity, they became crucial to the formation of individual female nationalists who could use their generic capacities to establish agency. Such an impulse is certainly at work in the Irish suffragette Margaret Cousins, who threw herself into the movement for women's rights in India after emigrating in 1915. In her "autobiography" *We Two Together*, co-written with her husband, James Cousins, Margaret Cousins paints a heroic picture of her role in the Irish suffragette movement in its most militant, window-shattering phase. Here the corporeal female body in jail—weighed, force fed, restrained—emerges as political spectacle.[2] These tales of embodied actors underscore the cultural work of the "life story" in focalizing female icons as corporeal apertures.

On the other side of the world, approaching the historical post-1989 era, debates on life stories exploded in the wake of the poststructuralist turn to "minor" subjectivities. On the one hand, the practice of female autobiographies in different local contexts received critical attention from scholars of diverse political persuasions;[3] on the other, scholars agonized over the "representation" of autobiographical voices from the "Third World" by editors, biographers, and critics based in "the West."[4] The life story emerged as an extended (auto/biographical) narrative—selected, ordered, transcribed, detailed, edited, and sometimes even narrated by the interviewer—that offers a chronological reconstruction of a life, maybe even a fragment of one. Critics who focus on the "life story production" of minoritized or subaltern subjects, unlike those who focus on the private autobiography of privileged bourgeois subjects, are careful to unpack the necessarily collaborative nature of these practices. Carol Boyce Davis (1992) positioned these collaborative practices on a spectrum: dual-authored life stories (Alex Haley's *The Autobiography of Malcolm X*); collective life stories, where one life refracts many (Leila Khaled's *My People Shall Live*); individual life experiences punctuated by discursive interactions with an editorial voice (Fanon's life recounted by Isaac Julien in *Frantz Fanon: Black Skin, White Mask*); and the interview or conversation model of consolidating a life (Fatima Mernissi's *Doing Daily Battle*). All three of our global icons are consumed in at least one of these collaborative forms.

Made in Public

The scenes sketched so far foreground the autobiography and biography, published in print (and now digitally) or envisioned onscreen, as the most widely prevalent modern mode of telling lives. Often these are authorized documents subject to regulation—sanctioned publicity, as it were. Of these, the collaborative *testimonio* (a narrative related by a first-person narrator as protagonist or witness) has the highest credence as representative of "minor" subjects,[5] just as hagiography articulates sacralized icons or the back story etches the star. Often attempting to singularize a commoditized star image, such narrations, however, shore up prototypes, bringing iconic images into equivalence with their historical or contemporary counterparts.

The testimonio, for one, performs (before the consumer as jury) a public witnessing where the illiteracy of the disenfranchised generates truth effects for events in the story. Looking at testimonios across Latin American contexts, John Beverley (1992) remarks that, despite the obvious socio-cultural disparities between the person whose story is narrated and the collaborator (biographer, critic, or editor who witnesses in the religious and legal sense [Beverley 1991][6]), the testimonio can be regarded as a formalization of political solidarity. Building on these insights, Caren Kaplan (1992) notes how women's testimonios, therefore, should not be treated as autobiographies but as anti-literary works, "outlaw" genres, that signal the presence of transnational feminist collaborations. In this sense, the life story is almost always regarded as representative of a social group, and the protagonist becomes a shared cultural figuration. We see this come into play most clearly in the reception of the many "autobiographies" of the illiterate bandit queen, where the first-person narrative is transcribed from taped oral narration and interview responses are recorded by a series of biographers while Phoolan Devi served her eleven-year jail term. As in the case of the testimonios Beverley examines, the most famous among them the controversial *I, Rigoberta Menchú* (1983), Phoolan Devi's biographies/autobiographies are also a combination of interview segments, eyewitness accounts, journalistic reportage, confession, and oral history.[7]

The most widely discussed among these life stories are Mala Sen's *Bandit Queen* (1991) and Marie-Thérèse Cuny and Paul Rambali's *I, Phoolan Devi* (published in French and English in 1996); some less-well-known French publications are Richard Shears and Isobelle Gidley's early *Devi: The Bandit Queen* (1984) and Irene Frain's fictionalized *Phoolan* (1992), both later available in English translation.[8] Cuny and Rambali's "autobiography" replicates some of the problems of popular testimonials, including a publisher's note that vouches a trifle too strenuously for the authenticity of the piece. The publisher begins with the "problem" of writing an autobiography for the "illiterate" subject but solves it by proof of labor and Phoolan Devi's consent. The "story" is captured on audiotape transcribed into 2,000 pages, shortened to 460 pages (and translated, we would imagine), and then read to Phoolan Devi, who "approved every page with her signature, still the only word she knows how to write" (Cuny and Rambali 1996, vii).[9] Here the publisher betrays his anxiety about speaking for the subaltern, while the actual overwriting of Phoolan Devi's taped voice is quickly camouflaged. Who, for one, translated the original tapes into the 2,000-page written text? What were his or her credentials? Who selected the shortened text (read back to Phoolan Devi) and on what basis? In the absence of answers, the "autobiography" relies heavily on authorizing parataxis for its reception as authentic tale, unassailably focalizing the iconic image along an axis of disenfranchisement. Just as in early-twentieth-century South Asia being a subject of biography translated the living figure into a person of "high moral character" (*carita*), the testimonio form authenticates the subaltern.

Even more troubling is Frain's eulogy (following her earlier commercial success, *Le Nabab*), featuring another divine avenger. *Phoolan* is pieced together from prison diaries, interviews, and news reports in which Phoolan Devi is mythologized as a feminine sacrificial force known as the unpredictable, untamed goddess Kali. "She is sweating," Frain recounts in her third-person fictionalized biography. "It is the black sweat of the goddess" (Frain 1992, 145).[10] The bandit queen is now distilled into sheer mythical energy, a universal metaphysical "feminine" attribute. These popular testimonials largely turn Phoolan Devi into a commodity envisioned through several distorting lenses: a "voice" recorded on audiotape, transcribed by multiple, and sometimes unqualified, translators (as Mala Sen acknowledges), a "life" rewritten, and later visualized, in mass media.[11] But with Phoolan Devi's translation into the Kapur biopic, the telling of the bandit queen's life met with opprobrium, since now the local legend had a transnational audience. In the look back from the historical West, the global form of the icon would face debate, and the telling of lives would give way to certain reflexivity about commoditizing disenfranchisement. Attacks on the stereotyped bandit queen would revise the terms under which an outlaw's story could be told. Hence, Krishna Mishra's film *Wounded* (2007) would commence with a contractual meeting between Seema Parihar (the newly anointed bandit queen) and the film crew, who agree to "witness" her life on her terms. In the aftermath of Kapur's film, the commoditized bandit queen would be re-singularized into a historical subject who struggled against the violence endemic in her life.

In sharp contrast to these testimonio-style life stories, Mother Teresa's biographies perform strong adulation or desecration. The biographies in print media span many languages, their circulation obviously circumscribed by the reach of a particular language. One cross-section of these resembles traditional hagiographies of saints, in which particular fragments of the saint's life are narrated to illuminate moral values. Lush Gjergji, Mother Teresa's Albanian countryman living in Kosovo, has been one of the more prolific among this variety of biographers; his *Nëna jonë Tereze* (Our Mother Teresa; 1980) is a strongly devotional text that nevertheless offers interesting materials on the nun's early life. Gjergji was the first biographer to animate Mother Teresa's childhood in Skopje, but the biography had limited circulation until the English translation was published in 1991. Another slew arrive in Mother Teresa's second home, Kolkata, where hagiography intensified affect; in these, Mother Teresa is more often than not positioned as mother to Kolkata's poor. These range from small-press productions in the Bengali language with limited regional circulation, such as Sukanta Kumar's *Biswajanani Mother Teresa* (Mother of the World, Mother Teresa; 1997), to glossy coffee-table books such as Gautam Ghosh's *Mother Teresa: The Apostle of Love* (2002), where photographs of and messages from Mother Teresa act in concert with the biographical narrative.[12]

The heightened sensation in the hagiographic production of Mother Teresa prompted sharp reaction to such adulation, compelling refutations of the sanctified image on several occasions and from many quarters. One of the first to cry foul was Susan Shields, a sister who had left Mother Teresa's order because she was discomfited by the unhygienic conditions in Mother Teresa's homes. But Shields's manuscript recounting her experiences, *In Mother's House*, found no publisher. The fate of that biography reveals the force of regulation as it produces the secret. No wonder Shields's story would provide grist for a biography of sterner stuff, a performative desecration through telling lives: Christopher Hitchens's infamous *The Missionary Position* (1995). Written at the height of Mother Teresa's fame, this well-known exposé followed on the heels of Hitchens's "The Ghoul of Calcutta," published in *The Nation* in 1992 and the screenplay he wrote in 1994, *Hell's Angel*, a film that never found distribution in the United States.[13] Hitchens is, of course, not a lone voice; others join him with varying opprobrium.[14] Most notable among these, perhaps, is the vituperative but well-researched treatise *Mother Teresa* by the Indian doctor Aroup Chatterjee, which appeared in 2003 from a local press. It offered a fairly laborious critique of Mother Teresa's overt social conservatism, evincing suspicion at her "charitable" giving.[15] The works by both Chatterjee and Hitchens overtly deface the public image, releasing it from the hegemonic message of the global icon (Mother Teresa as the face of charity). They induce other interpretations of the nun as a canny, publicity-loving, colonial-style missionary in it for the soul count. The radical instability of meanings accruing to the iconic image, affect-laden in the ferocity of claim and declamation, rendered the image auratic —singularized when wrenched away from the company of the (equivalent) great.

Hitchens's text illuminates how biographies work to contest (ideological) "messages" naturalized by the commoditized iconic sign. In an incisive analysis of Mother Teresa's political instrumentality, Hitchens pursues her suspect political alliances, most famous among them her link to Haiti's notoriously genocidal Duvalier family, as well as her "deliberate" use of celebrity to legitimize the Roman Catholic church's political interventions. Further, Hitchens attacks Mother Teresa for her proselytization, an agenda that endows her care of the needy with surplus value, as well as for her socially conservative views on abortion, homosexuality, and other such party-line Vatican stances. Such selective love, Hitchens would argue, hardly expresses a living in common, a possible social to come. It is in Hitchens's account that we discover the article in the British medical journal *The Lancet* (September 1994) in which the physician Robin Fox recounts his consternation over medical operations in Mother Teresa's health facilities, including the reuse of hypodermic needles, widespread misdiagnosis, the administration of inappropriate medications, and the lack of analgesics to control intractable pain. So the Hitchens biography becomes a reassemblage—cutting, pasting, and remixing already existing, if obscure, texts on the nun such as the (unpublished) narrative by Shields and the article by Fox. In marshaling evidence for transnational readers who do not have access to these recessed documents, Hitchens draws a social divide between an "us" (transnational publics) hoodwinked by "them" (the league of the powerful that authorize Mother Teresa).

Responding to this debate over Mother Teresa's star image, a third cluster of biographies deliberately perform a balancing act. Some of these are clearly authorized, resolutely "objective" in rhetoricity and narrative restraint but also highly sympathetic: Katherine Spink's *Mother Teresa: The Complete Authorized Biography* (1997) and Navin Chawla's *Mother Teresa: The Authorized Biography* (1992, with several reprints) are stellar examples. Spink's friendship and Chawla's adoration of Mother Teresa are well known. Chawla's biography begins with the reproduction of a handwritten note from Mother Teresa whose words hint at the hagiographic dimension of the work. "Let your book be love for God in action," writes Mother Teresa, sanctioning the biography and intimating, perhaps unintentionally, that a narrative of the exemplary saint's life might constitute divine revelation (Chawla 2002, iii). After her death, efforts to balance adoration and critique increased, as we see in Anne Sebba's *Mother Teresa: Beyond the Image* (1997), Emma Johnson's *Mother Teresa* (2003), and Gëzim Alpion's *Mother Teresa: Saint or Celebrity?* (2007).

Even in these more balanced re-assemblages we find highly personal investments in the project, indicating that the most reflective meditations on the nun might still invoke her as an object of veneration that one can only touch gingerly—and only by disclosing the biographer's own ethics. Alpion's biography, in particular, is rather self-reflexive about the project, placing its assessment of the celebrity saint in relation to other biographies; Alpion thereby analyzes the equivalence of the biographical form even as he assembles his purportedly elusive subject. In fact, Alpion rather self-consciously tries to rectify selective depictions and to restore lost narrative fragments of Mother Teresa's life that have not received much public attention: His take on Mother Teresa's early life (1910–28) growing up in Skopje, the controversy over claims about Mother Teresa in both Albania and Macedonia, and the rupture with the Loreto Order make lively reading. His biography, late to the table, demonstrates exactly how an icon can enter and exit different kinds of exchange; how it can be singularized, commoditized, then re-singularized in the complex overall "biograph" that endures well after the person's physical demise.

Most important, perhaps, it is the circulation of these life stories that turn global icons into contested objects. *Where* the icon has been has much to do with how it is reassembled (cut, pasted, remixed in another text) in specific public cultures. The outcry over the Raniganj miracle in the controversy over Mother Teresa's beatification, for instance, responded to her transnational circulation as miracle maker, for Mother Teresa's very first entry into mass media was closely connected to a so-called miracle. Scholars argue that it was Malcolm Muggeridge who first "discovered" the radical nun quietly at work in Kolkata, catapulting her to global fame in an interview with the BBC in 1968. When he followed this up the next year with the lachrymose *Something Beautiful for God*, a biopic that focalized a relatively unknown Mother Teresa for transnational television audiences, he widely broadcast news of a photographic miracle: The film stock was inexplicably able to capture Mother Teresa's image in the absence of sufficient light, a miracle Mother Teresa never denied (Chatterjee 2003, 50). The film's story focalized the nun's image, symbolically coding it as exemplifying the human capacity to give in its most excellent form, but since Muggeridge's film sought to demonstrate the superiority of a Christian faith that could inspire charity, a culturally particular worldview attained universal form in the iconic sign, giving rise to a global icon. Of course, in some polemics against Mother Teresa, we are repeatedly informed that while Muggeridge was waxing rhapsodic about the "divine light" that illuminated the dim shooting location, his cameraman knew it was simply new Kodak film stock that had enabled the capture—a story Ken Macmillan, of the company that produced the film, corroborated in 1994. But the divine legitimization of the Muggeridge miracle remained resonant in public memory and was finally contested only when the controversy over the Raniganj miracle broke in 2003. Clearly, the responses to the Raniganj miracle had less to do with questions of veracity than with the iconic form the figure known for her works in a local public sphere (Kolkata) had taken: The politically disinterested face of (Christian) charity laboring in the name of the poor, reminiscent of colonial civilizing missions in South Asia. The miracle stamped Mother Teresa as an "official" saint in an adoring city that had christened her its popular saint. No wonder miracles raised hackles. With the Raniganj miracle, ratified by the church, Mother Teresa was once more embattled precisely because of the global purchase made good by her final reintegration back into the church.

Muggeridge's biopic signals the importance of this genre as a mode of telling the life stories of the global icon. Earlier I paused on the melodramatic, corporealized mode of telling Phoolan Devi's life. Mother Teresa's biopics, by contrast, are highly sentimentalized hagiographic productions. The teleplay *In the Name of God's Poor*, which was produced by Hallmark and premiered on the Family Channel on October 6, 1997, just a month after Mother Teresa's death, for instance, waxed lyrical even as it aimed at a balanced perspective. Co-written by Dominique Lapierre and Carol Kaplan, the film focused on four to five years of Mother Teresa's life (when Mother Teresa left the Loreto Order to found her own congregation), and then jumped thirty-four years to her Nobel Peace Prize award ceremony in 1971. The hard years of getting there are achieved in quick edits so we can jump ahead to the successes and accolades. Like other biopics—notably Richard Attenborough's *Gandhi* (1982), with its famous elision of Subhas Chandra Bose—the Hallmark production's selectiveness and deliberate simplifications drew a fair amount of criticism. Mother Teresa reportedly sanctioned and then withdrew consent for the film three times—a fact that horrified Geraldine Chaplin, who played the young nun in the film. Lapierre repeatedly insisted that Mother Teresa had agreed to the final cut and that it was the sisters in her order who later withdrew their consent.[16] Of course, Lapierre is hardly well regarded in Calcutta since his novel *City of Joy*, released in 1987 and which formed the basis of Ronald Joffé's film of the same title in 1992, crystallized for transnational audiences the image of Calcutta as the city of slums. Neither *In the Name of God's Poor* nor *City of Joy* could be filmed in the city because of vociferous protests against such depictions. Many in Kolkata's local press decried the fact that *In the Name of God's Poor* had to be shot in Sri Lanka, leading to several noticeable historical discrepancies in the portrait of the city in this purportedly realistic biopic.[17]

As Lucy Fischer and Marcia Landy (2004) note, biopics more often than not are saturated with the codes of melodrama, effectively condensing affect around the iconic image. The biopics of Mother Teresa have repeatedly reinforced her global form as the (Christian) face of charity by harnessing a vision of Kolkata as a city of slums to the iconic image of Mother Teresa. The Kolkata of *In the Name of God's Poor* is necessary prosthetic, as much a part of the iconic image as the tank is to the lone figure of the Tank Man. This recursive composition has been highly contentious with regard to the shadow the religious superstar casts on the city of slums. The bodies of the poor stand in for Calcutta, where the destitute "lived like animals," Muggeridge once surmised, until rescued by Mother Teresa to "die like angels." No wonder the Roman Catholic saint would become historical—*someone else's saint*—when Kolkata embarked on a path to becoming a mega-city. For the city's poor, the fight over the "city of slums" as the icon's prosthetic would hardly be relevant; only in *local* broadcast media would the image (frozen as Mother Teresa

FIGURE 24 Girl at street
parade with Mother
Teresa's picture, 2005.
H. Vibhu, Hindu
Images Photo.

and brown child) present irony (as we see in the tongue-in-cheek photo,
figure 24).

In no major (hagiographic) biography do we ever find mention of the
Ramakrishna Mission, the Nari Sebha Sangha, or other venerable religious and social organizations that have been long at work in the city,
some dating back to the nineteenth century. Aroup Chatterjee, in fact,
compiles a list in a well-researched chapter of an otherwise shrill exposé.
In 1969, the BBC-sanctioned, culturally familiar script of a callous Indian
society and the angel of mercy had already begun to emerge with Muggeridge's *Something Beautiful for God*; we would see another sentimental
BBC biopic twenty-eight years later: *Mother Teresa: A Life of Devotion*
(1997), in which a tribute to the nun ensues with a series of medium
close-ups of Calcutta's by-now-famous frail and destitute bodies. In fact,

Karen Stone's brief introduction to the BBC documentary (distributed through the Arts and Entertainment cable network) positions Mother Teresa as a benefactor to "lepers, beggars, and unwanted children," thereby reinforcing the syntactical assembling of the saint with her gutter. The surplus value provided by the bodies of the poor for the social capital accruing to the iconic Mother Teresa finds a far more horrifying articulation in pedagogic tools that highlight moral lessons. One example illustrates the norm: Paolo Gherladini's wittily titled Italian-language book for children, *Mother Teresa: The Missionary of the Impossible* (1997), which features Mother Teresa, surrounded by cowering villagers, fighting Indian jungle creatures with a burning log. When questioned about such an unreconstructed colonial portrait of a civilizing mission, Gherladini asserted that it was just the "sort of thing readers really like" (as quoted in Chatterjee 2003, 117).

The biopic is the most traditional genre in audiovisual media technologies where we see mass-mediated global icons emerge.[18] By contrast, Roy's status as an "activist" has made her the subject of documentaries, often with fairly limited exhibition, distribution, and delivery platforms. Since documentaries have historically been seen as acts of solidarity with social movements, this comes as no surprise. Some of these pay overt homage to her work; some collaborative pieces foreground the icon to consolidate transnational networks of solidarity, much like the "testimonials" of the bandit queen. In documentaries such as *Dam Nations: Damage* (2002), funded by the BBC and featuring Roy as protagonist; Paolo Brunatto and Angela Fontana's Italian-language homage *Arundhati Roy: The Goddess of Small Things* (2002); and Aradhana Seth's reflexive *DAM/Age: A Film with Arundhati Roy* (2002), Roy's star body plays a key role in contestations over her image as activist, since the currency of the body at risk is often the measure of the activist's commitments. Each documentary presents struggles over how much risk Roy will, or agreed to, take on to emerge as an activist—a body in action. The narrations evoke a common cultural figuration, the activist, to measure this contemporary materialization: Roy's dedication, endurance, and capacity to suffer are constantly measured against other historical manifestations, such as Medha Patkar and Baba Amte, and Roy is always found wanting. Hence, unlike the affect-laden narrations of Mother Teresa and Phoolan Devi, Roy's "life," these sketches and interviews offer a deeply historical subject who performs the limits of excellence. We shall see how her difference from the two other bio-icons positions Roy certainly as a less auratic, but no less a technology for the popular.

The social economy of the narrations—what could be revealed, what had to be concealed, what had to be forgotten for new inventions of the sign— reveals the exorbitance of the embattled iconic sign. Too many meanings chafe against each other; regulation (through re-territorialization) of supplementary intransigent narrations are doomed to failure. The ex- orbitance of value the icon accrues primes it for forging, negotiating, or rending existing social relations. In the lives of two of our global icons, Mother Teresa and Phoolan Devi, we see such exorbitance rising from the secrets, ruptures, and recessed fragments of their life stories. What is withheld gathers energy, coming back to haunt the smooth surfaces of hegemonic narrations.

EXORBITANT SUBJECTS

One fundamental sign of exorbitance is the outbreak of biographical fragments that induce heightened semantic and affective activity around an iconic sign as it is dislodged from its hegemonic message. Sometimes a recessed aspect of the icon spurs debates over icons' value. An elision, a secret, a gap, a slip can return to undo the hegemonic iconic message in the right historical moment. At others, an abundance of recessed frag- ments can create unruly textual exorbitance, fissuring the smooth, hard surface of the commodity image. Here I pursue two stories in a fair amount of depth to show the work of the secret in publicity's glare. These are life stories that focalize the exemplary hegemonic images of Phoolan Devi (the sign of democratic progress) and Mother Teresa (the face of charity).

My intention is hardly to identify—as biographers often do—the veri- dical figure standing behind the text. Quite the contrary: I only recon- struct the "life" of Mother Teresa or Phoolan Devi strategically to disclose what is exorbitant to each icon. Because of Mother Teresa's institutional backing, her biographies are highly reticent texts. Their gaps and elisions provide glimpses of a repressed text—literally a "missing" part of this tra- ditionally exemplary life—that fuels the common veneration of Mother Teresa as a popular saint in Kolkata. Here exorbitance is literally the dangerously elided supplement, recursive, always exerting pressure on hegemonic performances of the life. Phoolan Devi is a rather different case—an icon who endures, but in radically changed guises. Here exorbi- tance is abundance, the piling of different, sometimes competing, iconic images that begin to blur the boundaries of the stable commodity at particular historical junctures.

Secrets and Lies

The uproar over Mother Teresa's value as a saint prompted one incisive comment that went to the heart of the matter: "The vitriolic bitterness of her critics, on the one hand, and the increasing adoration of her followers on the other underscores a contemporary dilemma which will come into focus after her beatification: what place can supposed saints have in the age of satellite television and the Sensex?" ("Saint in the Making" 2003). The offhand remark suggested that "saints"—not the official or the semiofficial "local" variety but popular saints—are anachronisms. They have little or no chance of being understood as religious revolutionaries because of the reifying propensities of mass cultural productions. Eyewitness testimonies more often than not are performed for news cameras, even as diocesan enquiries remain closed to the public. Traditional hagiographies more often than not are disregarded as enchanted discourse; they certainly are not regarded as authoritative perspectives on the icon. Despite this state of affairs, in the heat of the beatification controversy, an anachronism came to life in emerging perceptions of Mother Teresa's popular sainthood: her incalculable gift unfettered by institutions and states who sought to re-territorialize her. Such re-singularization as enchanted object was largely fueled by a persistent biographical fragment that made several returns to the public eye: the lore of her rupture from the Roman Catholic church that was a well-kept, but not forgotten, secret. It would remind both devotional and secular publics in Kolkata, where apocryphal tales circulated in local print media, that the religious celebrity had once been a radical revolutionary—singular in her departure from the church. Like all secrets, this rupture gathered energy; it invited speculation, giving rise to many tales about Mother Teresa's famous stubbornness as well as her championing of the poor. In concrete terms, the rupture materialized in the temporal form of a missing chapter in Mother Teresa's life.

To identity the "hole" in this otherwise intensely documented life story, a quick sequencing of the famous life is in order. We know that Agnes Gonxha Bojaxhiu was born in August 1910 in Shkup (Skopje) to Albanian parents. At the time, Skopje was a Turkish province within the Ottoman Empire; later, it became a part of the Yugoslav Republic, and it is now located in the independent Former Yugoslav Republic of Macedonia. These ethnic, religious, and geographical fault lines—Mother Teresa's Albanian ethnicity versus her origin in Macedonia—have motivated efforts on the part of Macedonian Slavs to lay claim to the expatriate saint (Mukherjee 1999, 1). In June 1980, Mother Teresa was declared an honorary citizen of Skopje, but the erection of a statue honoring her soon after her death drew protests from Albanians who saw Mother Teresa as ethnically Albanian. Hence, on the eve of the beatification, Albanians decided to put up their own statue in the capital's square, organizing a people's marathon to remember Blessed Teresa in the fall (Alpion 2007, 51–56). As hegemonic public singularization that generated aura for state power, the battle of the statues speaks to well-established social divisions between Macedonians and Albanians. The "life story" would be deployed to "correctly" focalize these public images.

Such wrangling over origins came as a shock to city dwellers in contemporary Kolkata, who simply saw her as unequivocally "our" Mother Teresa. Hoping to scuttle the "origins" debate, they pointed to the nun's departure from Skopje at the young age of eighteen and her subsequent choice to make Kolkata her home. Therefore, the argument ran, theirs was the right of singularization. One of her most judicious biographers, Alpion, argues that the murder of her father, a political activist, motivated Bojaxhiu's religious turn, as the adoring young daughter replaced him with the figure of Christ.[19] Her first call came at twelve (in 1922) and led her, in 1928, to emigrate to Ireland to join the Loreto Order. During her sojourn in Dublin in 1929, before being sent to the land of her dreams (India) as a novitiate, Bojaxhiu completed her religious training; it is there that she chose the name "Teresa," or "Little Flower," from the modest, less-well-known French nun Saint Thérèse of Lisieux.[20] By 1931, Sister Teresa found herself teaching geography at a girl's school in Calcutta, a city she would make her home for the remainder of her life. The elaboration of the proper name points to Mother Teresa's "life" beyond the physical life of the historical person; like the bandit queen, returning palimpsest-like as imprint on the lives of future female social bandits, Mother Teresa now assembles fantasy, fiction, and eulogy alongside biography and history.

While attentive to historical particulars, the lives of saints often seek to realign their subjects in terms of "universal" frames of reference; as I suggested earlier, a standardized cultural figuration brings about such realignment. The more institutionally backed the public image, the more elaborate the procedures for measuring exemplarity through miracle (the labyrinthine process of Mother Teresa's beatification), civil speech (via technologies of recognition for Roy's speech), and enfranchisement (political analysis of Phoolan Devi's electoral success)—gold standards for bringing saint, activist, and outlaw into equivalence within a global pantheon of the select. Yet, as we shall see in the next chapter, all of these cultural figurations are avowedly anti-institutional in popular lore, where they circulate in the varied historical guises of the *virangana* (female hero), *sataygrahi* (nonviolent protestor), or *sant* (saint). Their popularity precisely relies on their actions against established moral, social, and religious codes; they appear to act on "our" behalf, and against the hegemon. When the global form of the bio-icon is contested—the iconic image becomes historical, and the stereotype explodes as false truth—the force of these widely shared cultural figurations return as unrealized potentiality.

Religious studies scholars often underscore the magical efficacy of saints who evoke a "morality beyond morality," saints whose popularity lies in their revolutionary departures from the institutions that once housed them. Such popular saints, along with outlaws and activists, I would argue, are apertures for the expression of collective aspirations for a living in common that undoes living with hegemonic rule, stricture, or norm (e.g., of charity or civil speech). John Hawley (1987) notes that the saint's "morality beyond morality" remains vibrant across religions in the varied genres of hagiographic practice that assemble saints as exemplars.[21] Narrations recounting the saint's transcendence of ordinary moral codes put into question established codes of religious, moral, and social life.[22] Devotees articulate their personal bhakti, or devotion, without the intercession of priests through telling the lives of those who stray from institutional norms. Despite her Christian inscription, Mother Teresa was often considered "our mother" in hagiographic discourse (articulated orally or in print) of Hindus, Muslims, and Christians, practices greatly facilitated by the widespread and still vibrant adoration of exemplary figures unbound by religious institutional constraints.[23] Such perceptions and affections of the missionary as belonging to the people, on this side of the internal frontier, are organized by the secret—in the form of the missing chapter of her otherwise well-recorded life story.

The period between 1945 and 1950, which marks Mother Teresa's exit from the Loreto Order and formation of her own congregation, is the episode that has excited most speculation—a period of mystique when Mother Teresa heard a call within a call (a call to keep her vows but to change her vocation), a period of mystery whose records are obscure. In August 1946, on the eve of Indian independence, Calcutta erupted in Hindu–Muslim riots that were transformative for the young Sister Teresa. Several biographers note that she left the order exactly on August 16, 1948, the two-year anniversary of the "great killing" in 1946. Eileen

Egan (1986) locates the riots as the traumatic moment that led to the nun's call while unwell and traveling to Darjeeling on a train that year, and some biopics on Mother Teresa's call feature the archbishop of Calcutta's first reading of Sister Teresa's request to leave the convent as a traumatic response to violence.

The events that followed became one of the many controversies that were to hound Mother Teresa. Alpion's and Chawla's biographies devote a substantial amount of time to discussing these events. Chawla's biography, simply titled *Mother Teresa*, is an example of a local hagiography—a well-researched but personalized portrait of an idealized "living saint."[24] Hence, Chawla's text rarely speculates, offering a circumspect account of the famous "rupture." Shortly after Sister Teresa's second call, "the call within a call," she asked her mentor, Father Celest Van Exem, for advice on how to proceed. Until the formation of the "Brothers" in 1963, a unit of the Missionaries of Charity, the relationship between the Loreto nuns and the male clergy in Calcutta was largely paternalistic, a "Father–Sister" rubric in which nuns would approach Rome first through their superiors in the Loreto Order and then through the male clergy. Sympathetic to the visionary nun, Father Van Exem advised Sister Teresa to write to Mother General Gertrude Kennedy of the Loreto Order at Rathfarman, Ireland, while simultaneously consulting Archbishop Ferdinand Périer of Calcutta on the ecclesiastical laws governing the conduct of nuns. The process that ensued is less interesting than a core issue that emerged within it: the uncertainty about whether or not Sister Teresa could "leave" the Loreto cloister by virtue of "secularization" or "exclaustration." Secularization would mean Sister Teresa would become a laywoman, a social worker, while exclaustration would enable her to keep her vows while serving the poor outside the enclosures of the Loreto Order.[25] Obviously, the devout Sister Teresa, who had given herself to Jesus, found secularization abhorrent. The notion of "social work" unattached to a divine purpose was to become lifelong anathema to her, perhaps in memory of this early negotiation.

It was the archbishop of Calcutta (who in 1977 recounted the young nun's "queer ideas" but amended that to "unusual ideas" in 1986 [Alpion 2007, 203]) who recommended that Sister Teresa write to her superior for secularization. Certainly, his first response was not sympathetic. The made-for-television film *In the Name of God's Poor*, which, many argue, dramatizes one of the most persuasive scenarios that ensued from Sister Teresa's request,[26] portrays the archbishop as ready to dismiss her vision as a traumatic response to the riots, at least initially.[27] No wonder, then, that the young Sister Teresa was sent away from Calcutta to Asansol (a small town 175 miles northwest of the city) to recuperate and meditate on her second call for a whole year. Recent commentators note that the Loreto nuns had become suspicious about Mother Teresa's closeness to Father Van Exem, leading to the decision to send her away from Calcutta (Kolodiejchuk 2007, 55). But by the end of 1947, Mother Teresa's famous stubbornness showed its colors: She held to her request, quietly but firmly. Moreover, Sister Teresa now had permission from the head of the Loreto Order, the Mother Superior at Rathfarman, to write to Rome, with one amendment: Her superior recommended that Sister Teresa ask for the "indent of exclaustration," not secularization.[28] Perhaps Gertrude Kennedy was worried about what might befall a young female foreigner in a country in the throes of independence, without the protection of religious vows to guide her and mark her as sexually and socially inaccessible—a colonial logic, no doubt, that can be understood as a sympathetic, protective gesture at this historical juncture. Given the young nun's position within the Roman Catholic power structure, Sister Teresa dutifully ran her own letter addressed to Rome by the archbishop. Ratifying everything else, he once again asked Sister Teresa to change her request for exclaustration to secularization, and once again the nun complied, albeit with a sinking heart. The request wended its way to the Apostolic Nuncio in Delhi before making it to Rome. Egan suggests that the archbishop in Delhi may have changed the request back to exclaustration,[29] for in August 1948, Rome sent word: Sister Teresa had been given the indent of exclaustration.[30] Certainly, in the popular imagination it was the young nun's departure from the order, her anomalous position "outside" the established congregation—her extreme independence in striking out on her own, her extreme faith that challenged established codes of behavior expected of nuns—that drew curiosity, criticism, and admiration. In short, her departure from the Loreto Order made her a legend, made her enter a roster of popular saints (Hindu and Muslim) widely venerated by rich and poor in Kolkata.[31]

Biographers complain that exact accounts of Mother Teresa's rupture from the Loreto Order are missing: She kept a much discussed "lost" diary in this period, which she might have destroyed when she became an internationally renowned figure. Chawla (2002) notes that many witnesses recall seeing Mother Teresa handing slips of paper recording her call to her mentor, Father Van Exem. In recognition of Mother Teresa's many journals, poetry, and letters, it is perfectly plausible that she kept a record of those tumultuous years—many of them spent in breathless waiting for permission from Rome. But the diary is nowhere to be found, leading Alpion and others to speculate that Mother Teresa destroyed it.[32] Kolodiejchuk insists that Mother Teresa wanted the documents relating to the founding of the Missionaries of Charity to be destroyed because she feared she would be given a prominence that belonged to God alone. He reads secrecy as an act of faith. But if we remember that he is, after all is said and done, an institutional man who in "revealing" the private life of a religious superstar only transcodes her once more, placing her in a pantheon of Christian saints, then these "full disclosures" must be understood as publicity's endgames. Within the biographical arc, the rupture from the Loreto Order still holds a mystified place. Since secrecy always garners energy by virtue of repression, the missing records have generated endless speculation on what might really have taken place in those years, on the nature of a rupture so strong that an older, and far less radical, leader of a congregation might want to destroy all evidence.

The veracity of the record is less important for our purposes than what it suggests about the icon: her break with institutional and established codes, signs of the "morality beyond morality" that is the mark of a popular saint. But before I turn to this, two points require further elaboration. Both proceed from the patchy narrative that can be hypothesized from the little evidence that does exist, and particularly from the gaps and elisions in idealizing biographies authorized by Mother Teresa (Spink's and Chawla's works among them). First, there is the notion of a rupture, and not just a polite departure, from the Loreto Order—a conflict that was always emphatically denied by Mother Teresa, ever faithful to the order she left, and by Loreto nuns interviewed by Chawla and others.[33] Here Kolodiejchuk does provide new evidence in the form of letters in which Mother Teresa despairs of her increasing difficulties with the Loreto Order (its refusal to grant her stay at an empty house in Tengra; whispers at Entally that she was engaged in devil's work; rumors that students at Loreto were forbidden to join Mother Teresa).[34] These published confidences in part corroborate the circumstantial evidence gathered in the biographies that produced energetic speculation on Mother Teresa's rupture/departure.[35] More telling is the legendary tale in which Mother Teresa is believed to have started her first "school" in the sweltering slums of Motijhil, scratching the Bengali alphabet with a stick into the earth for an audience of five enthralled street children. As we know from the lore of the Kalighat stories divulged in the next chapter, these early starts—the vision of a young foreigner surviving through a sheer act of faith—reinforced Mother Teresa's auratic value even after she became a celebrity.

Where there is no speculation, there is hasty concealment by her most loyal biographers, such as Chawla. If, in fact, Sister Teresa's departure was amicable, it is not clear why she found herself with no resources to start her work. In an interview with the sympathetic Chawla, a representative of the Loreto Order insists that the order helped Mother Teresa with furniture and gave her four sisters to assist her in her new enterprise. But when exactly did the sisters join her? We know that the first to join Mother Teresa were her former students. Chawla hurriedly insists that the order generously gave Mother Teresa daily tram fare to and from her Creek Street residence, uncertainly adding it might have given her more "had she wanted it" (Chawla 2002, 42). If Mother Teresa had no shame in accepting alms for the poor from controversial figures later in her life, why did she not swallow her pride and beg for start-up money from the order as she began her new vocation among the poor in 1948? Was it simply a self-devised test of her capabilities? Or had there been a rupture that made it impossible for her to approach her fellow sisters with equanimity?[36]

There are just enough contradictions to hint at a deeper rupture than the official record claims. Traumatized or not, isolated or not, the young nun must have been sufficiently driven to leave her only contacts in a strange country in major political turmoil to form her own order. The timing of Mother Teresa's request to Rome—in the violent period following Indian partition, with Calcutta as one of the most troubled centers—makes the archbishop's insistence on secularization all the more curious. Kolodiejchuk's commentary suggests that Mother Teresa herself insisted on secularization, and the archbishop simply conveyed her request. But this does not fully explain the archbishop's decision. Why would he want her to renounce her vows as she embarked on her own in a turbulent city? Is it because he thought Rome would never grant the indent of exclaustration? Or did he see Sister Teresa as straying too far from a religious hierarchy designed to protect her, a hierarchy where obedience to God was inextricable from obedience to the church? Exclaustration would mark the nun as a separate and independent Roman Catholic church emissary in a city where Archbishop Périer guided the institution's work. Could his insistence on secularization have been punitive? Like the truth of Mother Teresa's rupture with the Loreto Order, the archbishop's intentions are impossible to pin down. Hence, they invite curiosity. It would not be straying too far to think he was at least dismissive of the call within a call, dismissive by not thinking it worth exclaustration, dismissive by intimating that Sister Teresa could easily give up that which was clearly most precious to her: her vows.

As soon as the letter from Rome arrived, Sister Teresa packed her bags and left the Loreto cloister, where, as an Eastern European, she was already an anomalous denizen, a stranger among strangers in a strange land they had made their own.[37] Archbishop Périer watched her activities closely for a year, finally requesting a constitution for her congregation in 1950 and personally carrying Sister Teresa's successes to Rome. By this time, Kolodiejchuk notes, the archbishop had become an admirer of the recalcitrant nun. In 1950, the pope granted the nun permission to head her own congregation. She was now Mother Teresa.

Emerging from this period, and taking Indian citizenship in 1950, Mother Teresa opened her first house, Nirmal Hriday in Kalighat (commonly known as the Home for the Destitute and Dying) in 1952. By 1960, she had opened her first house outside the city, in Ranchi, and several other establishments cropped up all over India soon after (Chawla 2002, 87). The rest is history, and a well-documented one, unlike the missing "chapter" from 1945–50. In the years that followed, international renown came to the radical missionary from official quarters. In 1962, she was given India's Padma Shri Award by Prime Minister Jawaharlal Nehru (who named her "koruna dutta," or "merciful giver"), re-territorializing her as national treasure. The Decretum Laudis (Decree of Praise) from the Second Ecumenical Council (1962–65) followed in 1965. With the inception of Vatican II and its drive to intervene in state politics, and the postconciliar development of "feminine spirituality," the quiet rebel in Calcutta had become a hot commodity—one whose secularizing missionary work could now legitimize the Catholic church's role in (what was seen as) the developing world. A decree was issued in 1965 that made Mother Teresa's congregation a Society of Pontifical Right, allowing her to expand internationally. By 1990, although India only had 16 million Roman Catholics, Mother Teresa had 476 branches all over the world. Her international celebrity soon followed: Muggeridge's interview in 1968 catapulted Mother Teresa to fame, while his film (1969) and book (1971) presented the "living saint" to the world. A religious superstar was born.[38]

I have suggested that the extreme secrecy surrounding large aspects of Mother Teresa's life has prompted curiosity, speculation, and numerous hypotheses. The records may be missing, but the story of Mother Teresa's abandoning a single religion to serve the poor across class, caste, or creed was a memory that endured. Never a rebel or even theatrically inclined—

unlike Saint Francis of Assisi, to whom she is most often compared[39]—Mother Teresa, in her early rupture from the Loreto Order, was positioned at a tangent from the church in hagiographic practices that revere her, motivating her popular sainthood. Much like Phoolan Devi, whose subaltern past remained a memory evoked in corporeal exchange even when the bandit queen became a political pawn, Mother Teresa's "morality beyond morality" could not be erased despite her later emergence as perhaps the most famous religious celebrity of the late twentieth century.

In fact, it was the Vatican's efforts to shelve Mother Teresa safely in its roster of saints, garnering equivalence through (the gold standard of) the miracle that came under attack during the beatification process. Those who claimed her as a popular saint offered multiple historical instances for judging excellence. Like the bhakti saints, went some stories, Mother Teresa rose above institutions to command private devotion; like the universal mother, she offers refuge for her devotees; like the goddess, she embodied the energies of gift. The exuberance of figurations in popular culture focalized in the multiple and competing life stories failed to stabilize a standard iconic image, re-singularizing Mother Teresa through symbolic excess. Volatile, she turned auratic, commanding veneration.

Return of the Recessed

The resurgence of a (deliberately) "secret" generates multiple and competing life stories and, thereby, an exorbitance that disturbs the well-regulated tale. But secrets do not always point directly to a hegemonic institution or regime; they might arrive as recessed or forgotten biographical fragments in the wayward unfolding of the biograph. The force of the forgotten fragment, and the iconic image it focalized, is especially potent when such a fragment returns after a long lapse—sometimes well past the physical death of an icon. Sally Hemings returned as Thomas Jefferson's well-guarded secret (fictionalized in Barbara Chase-Riboud's *Sally Hemings: A Novel* [2000]); a flirtation with National Socialism returned as Paul de Man's albatross; a sexually active gay lifestyle returned Rock Hudson's other life (beautifully stitched together in Mark Rappaport's *Rock Hudson's Home Movies* [1992]); Pakistan returned as Jinnah's "mistake."[40] These secrets matter mainly because these are durable icons who still have social efficacy. If the durable icon has a historical form that is contested at a particular time—as our global icons clearly have—then the explosion of secrets can draw a line in the sand between "us" and "them."

Durable icons that have lived through radical changes of fortune, through radical reinventions, fall prey to this genre of secrets. In their disjunctive biographs, they appear and disappear as public images. When they are in the public eye, they can be commoditized or singularized in various ways; when they disappear, they fall into worthlessness as commodities. We see this most directly in the case of Phoolan Devi, who was periodically forgotten as she languished in jail or lost elections but who always galvanized the cameras in her many, often well-orchestrated, returns to the glare of publicity. With each return, a tumble of recessed biographical fragments creates an exorbitance of significations of the new iconic image that make it impossible to stabilize the syntax—and, therefore, the iconic message. Among such returns, Phoolan Devi's death proved a climactic instance of such instability, as we will see in chapter 6, irrevocably volatizing her iconic image.

But this is no surprise. The death of icons has always rendered them volatile, since dead bodies are always densely symbolic signs that pull us into their orbit in their intimation of our own mortality. Despite all attempts by religious and secular organizations to re-territorialize a figure, famous dead bodies are known to arouse passions and, sometimes, to initiate semantic struggles at moments of political and economic transformation.[41] We might remember that Evita was the most expensive corpse ever, given that three wax copies of her body, costing a total of $200,000, had to be made to delude body snatchers. Imre Nagy, the Hungarian leader who was hanged and buried in an unmarked grave for attempting reform in 1958, elicited a huge reburial ceremony in 1989 as Hungary evolved into post-socialism. And, of course, we know the fate of Che's body: hands cut off to prevent identification, killed by Bolivian soldiers and secretly buried in 1967, then ceremoniously reburied in Havana in 1997. In *The Political Lives of Dead Bodies* (2003), Katherine Verdery reads such bodies—when they die and when they are buried, excavated, reburied, mourned, and memorialized—as ciphers for large political transformations, illustrating how the singularized corpse can function as a politically efficacious technology. Death rituals, in Verdery's argument, provoke embodied consumption, a repertoire of expressive public performances of the kind I will turn to in the next chapter. The performances tell us their lives again and again, seeking the restfulness of the stable iconic message so it might pass into legacy.[42]

Moving back to the textual economies of narration with which we are concerned here, when the icon dies, many avatars of the icon come cascading back, focalized in obituaries, eulogies, biographies, paens, hagiographies, and so on. Such exorbitance of narrations produces multiple

significations that provoke violent debates on the icon's legacy. If the icon
was particularly given to radical reinvention of his or her role in public
life, the ruptures between earlier and later lives fuel contestations of the
iconic image. Parama Roy's treatment of Nargis as an "unstable star text"
monumentalized in Mehboob Khan's film is particularly instructive for
considering the logics of such ruptures. Roy explains how Nargis's iconicity as "Mother India" was premised on a recessed text of Nargis as a
Muslim—an "undead Muslim-ness," writes Roy (1988, 154), that is "neither present not absent, not quite there, but, not quite convincingly
buried, either." This other "life" haunts two de-linked public lives of
Nargis: Nargis the actress and Nargis the politician. Roy describes the
relation between the two Nargis texts as one of *caesura*, one that separates
(and connects), proceeding through indirections, deferrals, and displace-
ments. As ever, repression lends force to resurgences in public memory.

We see such a process at work when competing biographical fragments
focalizing Phoolan Devi cascaded into public view following her murder.
Since above all of the icons treated here she is the one who is most known
in fragments, a brief rehearsal of a well-known story is probably worth
the effort—especially for those familiar with a single avatar of the bandit
queen. Phoolan Devi was born in 1957 into the low caste of Mallahs
residing in Gurha ka Purwa, a remote village in Uttar Pradesh. At eleven
(in 1968), Phoolan was married to an elderly widower with six children,
Puttilal, and sent to live in her husband's village, Maheshpur Ki Mariya.
Within the year, she had left her husband and returned to her father's
house; now in disgrace, she was relegated to the chores of cutting grass
and grazing water buffaloes. We hear of a second (bigamous) marriage to
her cousin Kailash during this decade—nothing more is heard about him
after this. Soon after, Phoolan Devi was arrested on the behest of her
cousin Maiyadin on a charge of robbery that she always claimed was
fraudulent, and she spent a month in police custody, where she was
repeatedly raped and beaten. She was abducted from prison in July 1979
by the Babu Gujar gang, which made her Gujar's "property" until she was
rescued by his deputy, Vikram Mallah. Teamed up with Mallah, the man
Phoolan Devi called "the husband of my heart," she led the gang until
Mallah was betrayed and shot by the police in 1980. The horrifying saga
continued: Phoolan Devi was again abducted, this time by Shri Ram and
Lala Ram, who, betraying the gang, raped her and paraded her naked in
the village of Behmai. After escaping her new imprisonment in February
1981, Phoolan Devi regained control of her gang and returned to Behmai

—the scene of her public humiliation—(allegedly) to kill twenty-two people, an act she always denied. Closely hounded by the police after the Behmai massacre, Phoolan Devi brokered a deal with Rajendra Chaturvedi to serve eight years of prison time in February 1983. Amid bitter police rivalry between the Uttar Pradesh and Madhya Pradesh police, and the resignation of V. P. Singh in Uttar Pradesh over the Behmai and Dastampur killings (Sunder Rajan 2004, 222), Phoolan Devi, fearing the wrath of the Thakurs in her home state of Uttar Pradesh, agreed to surrender in Madhya Pradesh.

Thus far a "law-and-order" problem, Phoolan Devi, through her surrender, was quickly positioned as an "authentic" subaltern whose illegal acts were consequently read as retributive justice against a violent state and an equally violent socioeconomic system. As an expiation rite, if the surrender brought the bandit queen into the "care" of the state, one is tempted to read her post-surrender vicissitudes as a tragic farce. After her much publicized surrender, Phoolan Devi languished in jail for eleven years. In 1991, the authoritative biography of the bandit queen by Mala Sen appeared in print, culled from a series of interviews with Phoolan Devi in jail. This revived public interest in the forgotten icon. Telling the life resurrected the forgotten iconic outlaw who had captivated the nation in 1983. Fortuitously, Mulayam Singh Yadav came to power in Uttar Pradesh in 1994, riding a Muslim and Other Backward Classes backlash vote against the previous Hindu right-wing government. Posing as Phoolan Devi's political "father," Yadav facilitated her release after a series of negotiations with the feminist activist Kamini Jaiswal, who intervened on Phoolan Devi's behalf when her case came before the Supreme Court. The same year, British television's Channel 4 released Shekhar Kapur's film *The Bandit Queen*, generating an uproar in the Indian national press.

When she emerged from jail in 1996 to immediately stand for elections, Phoolan Devi appeared reconstituted as the Dalit citizen-subject: Her life from 1983 to 1996 had been rewritten to foreground the deleterious effects of upper-caste hegemonies. Such a life story has everything to do with changing caste mobilizations of the period between 1983–94 (those electoral vote banks that have been the recourse of minorities within the postcolonial nation-state), as well as the struggle over quotas, the rise of lower-caste leaders in the Thakur-dominated dacoit gangs of Chambal, and the increasing divisions between Other Backward Castes (OBCs) and Most Backward Castes (MBCs) in the post–Mandal Commission years.[43] The bandit queen was reinvented as historical conditions

FIGURE 25
Phoolan Devi
with a picture of
"the bandit
queen," 1997.
AP Photo / Ajit
Kumar.

changed. Given her lack of economic and political agency, Phoolan Devi
readily agreed to a new public image as the empowered representative of
Dalit MBCs, the proof of democratic success as the outlaw faded to gray
(see Phoolan Devi's self-conscious irony in figure 25).

The new public image was an obvious success, just as the biopic was
turning outlaw into sexual victim. In 1996, Phoolan Devi was elected to
Parliament from the Samajwadi Party, winning V. P. Singh's Mirzapur
seat. She inaugurated her new role as Dalit citizen by launching the
Eklavya Sena, a group formed to teach lower-caste men and women the
art of self-defense. Soon Phoolan Devi became the "face" of MBC sub-
castes (the Gadarias, Lohars, Jogis, Dhiwars, Nais, Kumhars, and Mallahs, who occupy the lowest levels of the caste ladder) who were increasingly alienated from the economically mobile OBCs (the Yadavs, Ahirs,
and Kurmis) in Uttar Pradesh. Her overt support for separate MBC quotas

in government made her the locus of MBCs' desires for political represen-tation. In fact, by 2001, several commentators in the Dalit Forum (a watchdog group on Dalit rights) were claiming Phoolan Devi as distinctly MBC, born into the low caste of Mallahs but who had been manipulated for OBC agendas. Hence, it is hardly a jump to think that the murder of the legendary outlaw would provoke a complex response from subaltern MBC populations with nascent but unfulfilled desires for political repre-sentation; hardly a jump to think her death might serve as a reminder of both what the subaltern could achieve and what had remained virtually unchanged in the lives of the Dalit populace she supposedly represented in Parliament. In 1998, Phoolan Devi lost an election, only to regain her seat in 1999. But her tumultuous life was drawing to a close. In 2001, she spent a month in the United States to have a tumor removed. On her return to India, she met her death at the hands of three men outside her residence in New Delhi.

We can plot this disjunctive biograph, with multiple eruptions of pub-lic images in which each partially obscures a previous one, along five flashpoints in which Phoolan Devi "made the news": the reports of the Behmai massacre (1981), the historic surrender (1983), the film contro-versy (1994), the election bid (1996–88), and the murder (2001). Each juncture foregrounds a very different life story that focalizes the bandit queen; each text forgets the one that preceded it. A distinctive central protagonist pitted against overwhelming odds—natural, social, psycho-logical—emerges as the stereotype within each life story. There is the persecuted girl who is equivalent to all victims of physical abuse; the female Dalit who is paradigmatic of all low-caste denizens of the Cham-bal; and there is the criminal masquerading as politician, with so many counterparts in New Delhi, who met a violent end. Each story has a different temporality set in motion by different "origins" that naturalize Phoolan Devi's subsequent actions, imparting an inexorable sense of her "destiny." For instance, at the moment of the Behmai massacre of 1981, the feminist parable (of the Kapur biopic) dominates as the life story, focalizing Phoolan Devi as a primarily sexual victim, especially since her "rape," the most controversial part of the film, was extensively circulated in popular and critical discourse. Here, the "origin" of Phoolan Devi's agency is located either in 1968 (her first sexual molestation at the hands of her husband Puttilal) or in 1979 (the moment of her multiple rapes). The Behmai massacre is clearly the logical end to Phoolan Devi's sexual victimization, the carnage seen as a female virago's bid for retributive justice. By contrast, in the life story of the Dalit icon that emerged in 1994, after Phoolan Devi was released from the Gwalior jail, the "origin" of her political agency is located before her birth, in the region-specific articulations of caste and property at her native Gurha ka Purwa. In this second life story, Phoolan Devi's surrender and the state's acquiescence to her demands forecast the political ascendancy of Dalits. The courageous outlaw opens into a different potentiality from that of the angry female avenger focalized in the feminist biographies. Finally, in the whodunit narratives of Phoolan Devi's death, rife with speculation about the "revenge of the Thakurs," the Behmai massacre is the originary event that sets in motion the cycle of retribution; the bandit queen's violent acts destine her to a violent death. We measure the rise and fall of these avatars based on the diminishing volume of one image against the accumulation of another. And beyond formal measure, the rhetoricity of the performances reveals the affective charge that accrues to the iconic images—a barometer that will be central to our pursuit of the volatile icon in the next chapter.

The endlessly "recessed" texts focalizing multiple public images of the icon bring on an exuberance of significations in the coverage of Phoolan Devi's assassination. No one figuration of the outlaw will stabilize the syntax of the iconic message transmitted by the iconic image; hence, no stereotype can claim centrality in the public imagination. There is no equivalence—only the excess of frantic commoditization and re-singularization. Refutations, ruminations, reflections, declamations, and reconsiderations follow. In the midst of vociferous debate, with the unleashing of affects harnessed by the iconic images, Phoolan Devi becomes the embattled icon we pursued in the iconocrises recounted in chapter 3. In death, narration moves mourners to action we can read as signs of the popular.

I will turn to reading social action when I pursue the volatile icon more fully. Embattled icons point the way: toward confrontations in the social, enabling scrutiny of abiding fractures in a "people," that ever resonant myth that upholds the idea of a democratic polity. A lightning rod for controversy right from her first public avatar as the vengeful virago of Behmai in 1981, Phoolan Devi undoubtedly garners affect from heterogeneous publics and populations who vociferously claim or disown her.[44] The commoditized icon hides what the volatile intimates: a larger text of social antagonisms that divide the hegemonic and the popular. Far from being a sign of democratic possibilities resonant in the rags-to-riches story, the continuing subalternity of the bandit queen reminds us of the failures of the (now global) "democratic project" (signaled by "free and fair elections") as it plays handmaiden to neoliberal regimes.

As sustained performances, narrations incorporate us into the world of the icon so that we may enter into a social relation with this Other who, it turns out, opens into something else. Hence, telling life stories bear a high affective charge that is not easily contained by the reflection these stories demand. No wonder these narrations rarely proceed smoothly. There are interruptions. There are refutations. There are retellings. Untruths are revealed and secrets are disclosed as icons become embattled signs. Narrating the icon becomes combat in the social world, a struggle over one's location in the social through icon consumption. The exorbitance in signification signals latent forces at work in the social—not easily legible, not easily read. Jacques Derrida's emphasis on this structural logic of the supplement intimates that the critic's labor is directed not only at marking irruptions in gaps, elisions, or slips, but also at proposing what lies behind this supplementarity. What historical forces create hot zones around icons? How do we read the constituencies who gather to forge social bonds through them? These are questions to which we shall return in the last segment of the book, to the locations where our bio-icons materialize as technologies of the popular. But we have a sighting before that: of the volatile icon whose iridescence demands meticulous scrutiny.

Iridescence marks the difference of the volatile image from the public "star" image. The public "star" image—distilled, designed, legitimated, and widely distributed—endures (duration), accumulates (volume), and repeats (frequency) over time. The volatile image is short-lived, ephemeral, erupting briefly in mass media. Volatile images do not exhibit one pattern; they appear only in adversarial relation to the star images reassembled in expressive remediations. Hence, they may be considered expressive culture, performative adoration and desecration that re-singularizes highly commoditized signs. Their assault fissures the hard, smooth surfaces of the commodity image; in the fissures we move toward a there still to come.

We have dwelled on the smooth, hard sheen of the commodity image; we have traced its unimpeded flows. Fissures in its surface alert us to periodic eruptions of a heterogeneous volatile image that is re-auratized in embodied acts of consumption. It compels us to look more closely at the embodied citational performances that reassemble public images; it moves us closer to historical actors constituted as the popular through consumption. This chapter pursues such images of our three icons we encounter in the mass media, arguing for the social efficacy of the "volatile icon." It is not that any reassemblage of these intermedial images necessarily produces volatility. Only under certain conditions of possibility—lived experiences of macro-scalar change—this may indeed be the case. To move into the scenes where volatile icons function as magical technologies of the popular, catalyzing forms of collective action, I begin with the notion of volatility that signals instabilities, disturbances, fluctuations, and variabilities.

Volatility describes a heterogeneous image whose significations, once recoded, will not stabilize. It is an image that, intensifying sensations, attracts expressive dissension that can snowball into collective action. We may recall the loss of the icon's epistemological coordinates destabilizes emotional investments, disrupting the organization of pre-experienced perceptions and affections. Those sensations, still harnessed by the image, begin to circulate as pure sensation flowing freely between the territories of subject and object. Volatility signals the dynamism of this encounter; volatility refers to the incoherence of perceptions too slow to organize an onrush of sensations. And beyond the encounter, volatility further captures the instability of an image that can be harnessed both for hegemonic and for popular gain. Of course more often than not, hegemonic institutions undertake the deliberate and controlled labor of re-auratization in mounting statues and memorials or consecrating art, flags, and buildings; these institutional practices are a far cry from the popular sacralization with which we are concerned here. In this regard, volatility signals the indeterminacy of the social effects the reassembled iconic image might produce, the uncertainty of prediction; of gauging how an image will be cited and repurposed in everyday practice or for staged spectacle. Given the dependence of the icon on inductive logic, there is no a priori estimate we can forward of a particular icon's social efficacy, only a reasoned one of its localized effects. Finally, the images that flit through this chapter are volatile in their short-lived circulation in media networks, quite unlike the recursive "star images" distributed through publicity machines or recycled from widely accessible broadcast media databases (e.g., the *Time* magazine, BBC news, or *The Times of India* news databases readily accessible on Google or Yahoo, search engines that algorithmically regulate content on the basis of the volume of traffic). They are never exactly repeated, as we saw in the case of the recursive public image, but they can be tracked as generic variations in a repertoire of performances. Hence, as I consider the auratic flicker of volatile icons, this chapter performs a method for reading popular expressivity as the supplement to the public images of the icon.

If the images in question re-assemble—that is, cut, paste, remix, or embellish—the well-known established minimal graphic inscriptions, they might be considered expressive responses to the influx of mass-mediated signs. Conceptions of popular culture—as artistic practice, as a social economy, as alternative media practice, as contingent performance—offer a broad rubric for unraveling the particularities of the volatile icon. We return to the provocations of the introduction, where expressive popular culture performed in mass-mediated locations forges social bonds through icons. The critical history of divergent theoretical perspectives on social agency that is expressed in popular culture is only too well established, and warrants little elaboration; I simply evoke a very short genealogy here to acknowledge the intellectual formation pertinent to this study. The notion of popular culture gained resonance in contemporary cultural theory in dialogue with the Frankfurt school's dark view of the culture industry (especially the claim of the German émigrés Theodor Adorno and Max Horkheimer that standardized mass products generate false needs that integrate consumers into the logic of capital). Following Antonio Gramsci, the Birmingham school would insist on the possibility of resistance to the hegemon in acts of consumption.[1] Dick Hebdige's oeuvre elaborated the compositional elements of such popular negotiations, while Stuart Hall marked expressive divergences from the dominant codings of the sign. On another front, feminist theorists such as Janice Radway, Constance Penley, and Angela McRobbie, gathering social histories of consumers, argued for pleasure as resistance. Together, these theorists established the political significance of an intermediary realm of cultural activity—the popular—where mass-media flows were daily negotiated, contested, and arrested in their transmission of hegemonic ideologies; a domain where socially minor or politically disenfranchised subjects with little access to elite cultures could articulate their worldviews. This is not to suggest that "popular culture," in this book, is necessarily "resistance"; those wars have long since faded before the ubiquity of mass-mediated quotidian lives. Rather, the term enables us to conceptualize a realm where participation in commodity culture can, on occasion, facilitate a relocation of the subject within networks of global exchange.

It is in this context we see "citations" of mass-mediated signs as expressive culture. In the eruptions of the volatile icon, we witness attempts to renegotiate the social contract mass-mediated messages attempt to privilege and maintain. Familiar questions return: When does an icon turn volatile? How do we read traces of volatility in mass media? And newer ones arise. If it is a repertoire of performances we are concerned with here, we confront the image in situ. We are therefore propelled toward defining localized sites of enunciation. How do we relocate these constantly migrating, plastic signs? What cultural arena best captures their "local" media ecology? And perhaps most important, how do we evaluate their social efficacy?

The chapter engages these questions in three ways. Since performance studies (whose fortunes have changed substantially since the Birmingham school's incitements to popular culture) remains foundational to considering the social efficacy of contingent, embodied citational practices, we begin with the notion of the "repertoire" to assemble the short-lived traces of our global icons. Citation is most central to the specific sign we have been following, since the icon as graphic inscription depends on iteration; generally, recursive circulation is its game, the most stable significations harvested and protected in institutional archives. In this chapter, however, we pursue a specific kind of repetition—a repetition with a difference that signals the recoding of a well-known mystified public image, rendering it historical. The notion of an ephemeral and changeful "repertoire" of images, as opposed to those readily found in institutional archives, is our first order of business, offering an overarching conceptual rubric for the study of the heterogeneous images emergent in acts of reassemblage.

But the mutability of the repertoire, as we follow images recycled, repurposed, and constantly cited, raises the further difficulty of scale and duration. If the volatilized heterogeneous image has a short-lived appearance in mass-media archives (some disappearing from search engines over time), how do we establish their "presence" as auratic objects of veneration? Returning to the methodological question of reading "mass-media archives"—my shorthand for the news media databases that are widely accessible through globally popular search engines—this chapter performs a critical analysis of the "rune," a complex aggregate of correspondences where one finds an image auratized or re-auratized in popular culture. As we shall see, the scholarly excursion across media platforms— from high art paintings to popular murals—inevitably presents the problem of location. Where do we look for the volatile icon? The challenge is to localize the popular consumption of these icons. The second section of the chapter attempts to bring transnational images home to South Asia, where they are re-auratized in popular cultures variously articulated against both elite high cultures and standardized mass cultures.

Finally, if the popular signals "the people," we are further pressed to locate a collective subject whose embodied performances constitute expressive popular culture. Although we delve into such a subject with greater depth in part 3 of the book, here I anticipate such a turn with a consideration of the volatile icon as a "magical" object imbued with agency (to recall Arthur Gell). Keeping faith with the study of material culture as a domain of objects, I close the discussion of popular culture with the "capacity" of the volatile icon to forge social bonds—a term that warns against any idealization of these magical technologies. As we see in one cultural arena, South Asia, collective agency expressed through volatile icons can be quickly harnessed as political capacity. By the close of the chapter, we settle into South Asia, where popular culture remains a robust enterprise and where, in reassemblages of mass-mediated signs, we witness complex responses to global modernity.

THE REPERTOIRE

Perhaps it is best to begin with a potentially disruptive, often emotionally pregnant, occasion: the death of an icon, with its conventional outpouring of accolades, reflections, and debates. Two emergences of our global icons that are both consistently present on varied media platforms well past their physical deaths provide my point of departure. Figures 26 and 27 feature performances of the embodied veneration of Phoolan Devi and Mother Teresa in widely circulating news photographs found in broadcast news media archives.

Both photographic captures, shot by members of the Press Trust of India and the International Associated Press and circulated embedded in news stories from the BBC News or *Time* magazine, record embodied gestures of veneration. I choose these particular images as illustration because they exemplify the two most common genres of photographs that mourn icons: photographs of unidentified "mourners" clutching cheaply made and easily accessible mass-mediated public images of the bio-icon against their bodies (figure 27) and those that capture performances of wild grief (figure 26). Soon after Phoolan Devi's death, several photographs materialized (and then disappeared from the search engines through which one accesses broadcast media) where mourners weep over their slain bandit queen while cradling her portrait. And in the footage of Mother Teresa's funeral, one can see variations of the affective expression shown in figure 26 as the mourner reaches toward her iconic bandit queen. The fact that not all of these photographs are available for reproduction (*Time* magazine actually could not tell me where to find a photograph of Phoolan Devi's mourners that I discuss later) underscores the ephemeral nature of these images. Their disappearance might in part be explained by a dip in their newsworthiness: after all, the volume of traffic for stories on a particular icon's death will inevitably decrease, and so the coverage of the death where we find the volatile signifier might disappear into recessed electronic space.[2] Broken links or images removed by the news media (such as *Time* or BBC News) might further exacerbate our sense of their presence as ephemera. In contrast to these disappeared images, the major public images of the same bio-icons—public because they are made for publicity, and public because they are widely accessible across transnational media networks—are easily retrieved. With variable volatile images we are on the opposite side of the spectrum from the

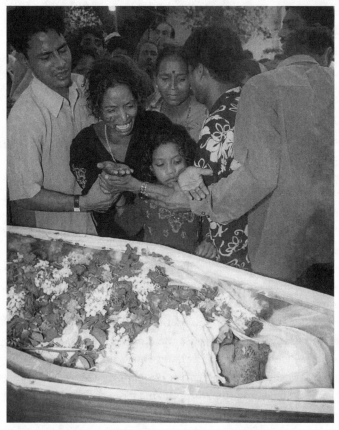

FIGURE 26 Mourners with Phoolan Devi's casket, 2001. AP Photo/Press Trust of India.

FIGURE 27 Monica Besra in Nakore village, December 2002. AP Photo/Rana Chakraborty.

peaking frequencies of public images; we are confronted with loss, elision, and forgetfulness. Hence, the scholar is left to narrate them to complete the picture.

These difficulties notwithstanding, together the images in figures 26 and 27 present a repertoire of expressive mourning in South Asia. Figure 26 snaps a spontaneous outpouring of grief right after news of Phoolan Devi's assassination broke on July 25, 2001. News reports (televisual, digital, and print) were littered with photographs of mourners—short-lived, ephemeral images of collective grief. A woman rushes toward the icon's body, palms upturned in a gesture of helpless incomprehension, even as she is restrained from touching the decorously laid out body of the member of Parliament by several men; behind her, another face records anguish, while still others, anonymous crowds, stretch into the depth of field. That the photographer could not capture the full body of the icon, readily present in mass media at that time, intimates that the collective grief manifest in the rush of bodies toward the icon disrupted an attempt to stage the perfect shot. Such a sensational photograph—recording sensation, and producing sensation through our attachment to the corporeal iconic image—illustrates the momentary presence of an auratic object. The focus in both figures is the performance of touch, held at bay in the first instance but enfolded into the body in the second.

Figure 27, a news photograph of the infamous Monica Besra taken in 2002 at her home in Nakore village as news of the miracle leaked, features a plain, laminated photograph of Mother Teresa as the centerpiece of a beautifully lit and staged composition—note the carefully selected iconography of the village in the rolled up straw mat, the kerosene lantern, and the bamboo scaffolding of the hut. Besra, obviously dressed in her best (a matching dark red sari and blouse) for the photo shoot, glows dimly against the dark background, caught in meditation as the light falls on the object assembled against her heart—the gleaming, white-veiled visage of Mother Teresa. We have a photographic capture of the embodied consumption of a mass commodity image, albeit "arranged" to re-enact Besra's unflinching belief in Mother Teresa's touch cured her abdominal tumor. Besra's veneration appears studied; perhaps she was asked to pose for the news photograph. This is no spontaneous event, and the visual design rather carefully focalizes the icon's animation of her devotee. In other variations of Besra holding the saint against her (other disappeared photographs), she appears with her husband, Seiku Murmu (who refused to believe her story) always cradling a laminated photograph of Mother Teresa (given to her by the Missionaries of Charity) or "caught on camera" in active worship (lighting incense sticks) of the photograph.[3]

We find the enfolding of icons into the body of the devotee in a genre of photographs mourning the bandit queen, as well, but these are often hasty captures of mourners reacting to the news of her assassination. One memorable photograph in my personal collection (but that I could not get permission from *Time* to reproduce) features an unidentified man clasping a cheap photographic reproduction of Phoolan Devi in a damaged photo frame as others gather around it to mourn her.[4] The accompanying caption identifies the mourners collectively as those who flocked to the lawn of Phoolan Devi's residence in New Delhi. The difference in these images—the Phoolan Devi and the Mother Teresa photographs—is telling, despite the formal similarity of the performative gesture. The damaged portrait of Phoolan Devi clutched against the chest of a mourner, with crowds burgeoning beyond the photograph's frame, is starkly different from the carefully centered portrait of Besra. The former is one among many frantic photographic images that followed Phoolan Devi's death; the second, a carefully arranged mise-en-scène supporting Besra's belief in the miracle. The differences present us with a challenge: What do we make of them when our major preoccupation is with the expressive culture of embodied veneration?

Here the elaborations of the "repertoire" developed in contemporary performance studies offer means of unpacking these images: specifically, Diana Taylor's (2003) muddying of the archive (enduring texts, documents, buildings, bones), with all its institutional supports, with a repertoire (ephemeral spoken language, dance, sports, ritual). Taking performance as her subject of study, Taylor invites us to rethink the easy opposition between the (embodied) spoken word and the written one, especially in the age of digital reproduction. For in what Richard Schechner (1989, 39) has named "twice-behaved behavior," Taylor reminds us, performance can be highly mediated: It can store knowledge like a written text; it can reproduce hegemonic political power (e.g., in orchestrated demonstrations); and it can "lose" the body as we see in digital media. A better way to critically parse performance is to consider the shifting relations between the two. Archival memory stores core elements of the performance resistant to change—its "DNA," so to speak. These elements are revitalized in expressive performances that follow. The iterated familiar iconic image, often an intermedial one, lodged in social memory and archived in multiple media formats, can function as the DNA of a repertoire of expressive "citations," each performance altering the value of the iterative sign—hence, the need for a situated understanding of the contingencies that motivate each performance.

In our illustrations, we see embodied performances resuscitating institutionalized mass-mediated photographs of icons, often distributed for publicity. The recessed photograph of the bandit queen clutched by the mourner (in the lost photograph I described earlier), a mass-produced and circulated public image, is obviously not from her violent past. The visual, a common public image of the bandit queen as parliamentarian, captures Phoolan Devi clad in a golden sari in a bucolic setting, complete with an innocent lamb in her arms; its painterly overtones recasts the bandit queen as the bourgeois subject of portraiture, in a willed effort to establish the overtly respectable, kinder-and-gentler image Phoolan Devi fought for when she entered Parliament in 1996. In the photograph, the DNA from the archive (here, broadcast news media databases or institutional image banks[5]) persists, but the expressive gestures catured on camera suggest a re-auratization of the commodity image. To make sense of what drives these performances of grief, we have to relocate to the moment of its capture. We know that, despite the sense that Phoolan Devi had become political pawn, her political ascendancy signaled to many that a modicum of justice had been won by someone who represented the historically disenfranchised Dalits—an electoral constituency in Uttar Pradesh that had gained political leverage in the years Phoolan Devi languished in jail (1983–94). As one Dalit intellectual, Chandrabhan Prasad, noted in response to Phoolan Devi's death: "She was the cause for celebration for many *from her background* who saw her as one of them— not just in caste and class, but also in suffering" (quoted in De Sarkar 2001; my emphasis). Such a response gives us a clue as to who might have rushed to Phoolan Devi's lawn as soon as the news of her death broke. For someone to commandeer a picture of Phoolan Devi, for mourners to burst toward the body of the icon, suggests that the bandit queen was an object of adoration; while the social status of the mourners remains undisclosed, we can surmise from these unrestrained and collective displays of grief, not to mention the social indices of attire, that these are not bourgeois elites accustomed to private mourning. When we consolidate these propositions, the news photograph offers a trace of mass commodity turned a volatile signifier of collective loss, its auratic charge evident in the crush of bodies that converge on it.

Although such photographs capturing outbursts of grief erupted in mass media right after Phoolan Devi's death, few are to be found today. Ephemeral and short-lived in circulation, these traces of the auratic icon are often few and far between. Nor do they readily give up their secrets: Who are the agents here? How can we read their embodied consumption of the public image of bandit queen? This motivates a much closer look at embodied performance, and especially the processes of citationality and expressivity that have long histories in performance studies. Impossible as those conversations are to encapsulate here, clearly a selective discussion is in order to elaborate the creative industry of "reassemblage" as an embodied social act. Speech act theory, following elaborations of the British philosopher J. L. Austin's *How to Do Things with Words* (1962) by Jacques Derrida, Judith Butler, and contemporary queer theory, has long posed identity as a citational practice,[6] and these observations remain critical to the narrations of icons I explore. Another strand focused on gesture, orature, and memory, best represented by Joseph Roach's *Cities of the Dead* (1996) or Elin Diamond's *Unmaking Mimesis* (1997), is equally important to the affective and corporeal enactments that constitute icon consumption. Yet a third trail emerging from anthropology and theater, perhaps best exemplified in Richard Schechner's emphasis on repeated, re-created, and improvised acts, is perhaps most salient to the volatile icon that commands social action. It is the basis of Taylor's splendid *The Archive and the Repertoire* (2003), where the popular as a repertoire of citations emerges as a central category.

Analyzing the *escraches*—acts of public shaming—of the children of the disappeared in Argentina in the chapter "You Are Here" (Taylor 2003), Taylor criticizes Roach's theory of "surrogation" as establishing continuous social memory.[7] In his work on the circum-Atlantic (North Africa, Europe, and the Americas), Roach sees the process of surrogation as an act of substitution for vital but lost historical links. Saying "The King is dead, long live the King" transposes the idea of the "king" to fill the gap between two individuals; such rituals of continuity remain of singular value to cultures experiencing vast dispersion, performative surrogation suturing community (Taylor 2003, 158). Taking her cue from the notion of a surrogate as the linking mechanism between performances, Taylor argues that, in many cases, historical continuity is ensured via the transmission of "DNA," or archived materials resistant to change—something on the order of a stable, culturally familiar iconic sign. There is no substitutive act, as suggested by the notion of surrogation; rather, widely available signs are introduced into the performance as the DNA of social memory. Cut, pasted, remixed, and embellished, these well-known signs carrying material traces of our previous encounters with them, make the new images heterogeneous in signification. In the escraches, for instance, the photographs of the disappeared that once adorned the posters of the Mothers of the Plaza de Mayo are worn on the bodies of demonstrators or reassembled in installation art. These photographs are not substitutions but archival material resuscitated in a repertoire of expressive performances; they are DNA of performance, "coded" genetic materials that are replicated but also recoded to transmit different messages. Taylor's point is that while books fall apart and songs may be forgotten, certain memes remain as raw semiotic material for popular recoding. The widely accessible, symbolically dense, public images of icons available in as recycled broadcast media or in commercial merchandise can readily serve such a function.

In the photographs discussed earlier, mass-produced images of Mother Teresa and Phoolan Devi function as "DNA" revitalized to renegotiate the social contract of the iconic image. Embodied veneration turns the commoditized image of Mother Teresa into a heterogeneous sign. She is obviously beloved saint, but only to one protagonist in the photograph— Monica Besra, an isolated woman abandoned by the one closest to her, her husband. Murmu's disagreement with his wife made every news story that accompanied photographs of Besra and her icon, regardless of whether Murmu was actually in the photographic image. Such underlining of Besra's isolation, quite evident in the stark repose of figure 27, intimates a question that haunts these stories told in image and word: What kind of saint attracts the adulation of a believer like Besra? Hardly a popular one, whispers the induced answer. Here the Vatican's practices of beatification are clearly under suspicion: They lure the gullible soul. By contrast, the mourners are unified in affect expressed as numbing shock to copious weeping in their embrace of Phoolan Devi. Both performances of embodied veneration compel us to rethink any easy recognition of the commoditized image: Mother Teresa is hardly unequivocally the saint; Phoolan Devi, hardly the happy parliamentarian who had transcended her violent past. Both situations turn these performative "reassemblages" into provocative recodings of the public image. As Taylor reminds us, in such citationality the genetic and performative work together as heuristic systems that, in contingencies of the sort she witnessed in Argentina, become articulations of a social demand aimed at a repressive politico-juridical regime. We shall see such social imperatives at work in the consumption of the public images of our three bio-icons: in reassemblages of Arundhati Roy in alternative or DIY media, as well as the expressive consumption of Mother Teresa and Phoolan Devi rife in oral lore (which we find recycled in mass media).

FIGURE 28 Still from *We: The Unauthorised Roy*. Courtesy of Scott Ewing, http://www.weroy
.com.

Citationality is an important feature of the contemporary volatile icon. Expressivity is a necessity. Expressivity signals self-conscious articulation; it signals expression through style, design, and artistry. In classic theories of the popular, expressive culture, even when individually practiced, emerges from a collective location. Acts of consumption that stage "recoding" the icon, often in overtly artistic (orchestrated, rehearsed, designed) performances, express a contingent position. One stellar illustration of such expressive enactment is the musical documentary *We: The Unauthorised Roy*. An artisanal visualization of Roy's "words," the project remixes news footage of wars and corporate greed (mostly news images taped from MSN under the "fair use" provision) with songs and fragments of Roy's many speeches against privatization, militarization, and a compromised corporate media (figure 28). Anonymous and disseminated for free in the blogosphere, the digital audiovisual act is clearly an homage that simultaneously critiques the intermedial televisual Roy, a public image authorizing civil speech as activism.

The frame of the television monitor within the film's frame captures Roy mid-speech, mouthing fragments spliced from her (widely circulated) "Come September" address. In many such disorienting medium and extreme (just her lips or eyes) close-ups, the documentary wears the message—Roy as "voice of the people" caught in mid-speech—on its sleeve, even as the frame-within-a-frame conceit offers a highly stylized expressionist text suturing the consumer to the moving lips. Disorganizing the face, the lips and eyes produce uncontained sensation, as we scramble to assemble body part into public image; simultaneously the kinesthetic force of quick editing waylays such an effort. We are caught in multimodal sensory flux as the coherence of the well-known speaking Roy disintegrates. As the iconic "voice of the people," a global form consolidated through several televised or otherwise audiovisually documented public appearances distributed on multiple media platforms, the "speaking Roy" is the raw archived media content selectively reassembled. With images (moving and stills) and music (whose addressee I focus on later), the documentary functions as one among a repertoire of performative reassemblages of Roy as "voice." Like Taylor's repertoire that stores and enacts embodied memory—the traumatic cathartic shudder, gestures, orality, movement, dance, song, all acts thought to be "live," non-reproducible knowledges—here select fragments of gesture, oration, and words are reassembled, turning stable icon into heterogeneous sign.

Appearing virtually to answer questions posed on MySpace, the (intentionally anonymous) filmmaker characterizes the documentary as a typically "time-based" indie artifact, "free" from media institutions in its recycling of fair-use images: "One thing I love about the information age is that—once something is digitized—then its gone. It's out there, and no control exists anymore over that piece of media. It can be stored and saved and distributed by means other than online, free from censorship and the useless and counter-productive filters of the military press corps and commercial western media."[8] Roy is "consumed" as auratic exemplary and inspirational icon—literally "opening" us to reflect on a world of violence and genocide that implicates us as historical actors—in a creative reassemblage that contests the public image of the civil activist, always decorous before an equally civil, often well-reputed interlocutor (a Howard Zinn or Amy Goodman). The title "We," which the filmmaker intimates comes from one of the musical numbers, gestures toward a networked transnational public constituted, as the MySpace discussion obviously demonstrates, by their participation in certain "cultures of circulation." For as Benjamin Lee and Edward LiPalma (2002) once noted, publics are increasingly self-reflexive about what media they consume and what circuits they inhabit; they are self-perpetuating in their transmission of exactly that which brings them together. Here the contingent nature of digital performances unharnessed by the accumulative logic of capital, doubles as the theme of the documentary—its conceit and its charm. The circulation of the media—which the filmmaker describes as posting on the Internet; burning of CDRs and DVDs; neighborhood disc drops to friends and letterboxes; transfers from laptop to laptop on portable hard drives, iPods, or memory sticks—consolidates a wired public for whom Roy functions as a corporeal aperture, opening the consumer into the social worlds to which they are connected via global financial, military, and political networks.

The collective address "We" further poses the question of the public in a direct manner. Overtly a renegotiation of mass-mediated signs, the documentary bombards us with a plethora of information that replicates the numbing effects of television news. Images of bombs, Iraqi citizens, world maps, newsrooms, Middle Eastern deserts, petrol pumps, cars racing on freeways, armed U.S. Marines forcing brown men out of homes, and other sundry footage sutured together in loose episodic proportion reads, at least generically, like a music video. On few occasions, extreme and disorienting close-ups of Roy's lips and eyes are interspersed between the other randomly connected images, but most often, she is shot on a television screen whose perimeter is clearly visible in the frame. This generates the impression of a handheld digital or video recording. Such editing and framing clearly signals artisanal practice, an "indie" media address that is attractive to certain transnational publics who are deeply suspicious of broadcast news media and infotainment (often targeted as "the mainstream press"). But the most prominent aspect of the documentary, the giveaway cultural address, is the soundtrack. The music is taken from post-punk bands known for industrial or electronic music (Lush, Massive Attack, Faithless, and Boards of Canada play in the background); only sometimes do we sense synchrony between the lyrics and the images, as when Télépopmusik's languid "another day, just for me—I'm used to it by now" plays over the poignant images of Iraqi children in hospital and Iraqi citizens picking up their belongings from bomb-shattered homes and war-torn streets. The music-video genre, the bands, and the admonition that closes the video ("Start reading . . . or we are all screwed") reveals much about the intended audience—most likely young adults who will be familiar with these bands; young adults who are largely disaffected by the war in Iraq. Roy's mass-mediated sign is a recursive trace, de-familiarized, fragmented—an unenclosed graphic mark opening "us," the wired youth (many of whom constituted the Obama vote bank) to a social imaginary where "we" disconnect from rogue governments, rapacious corporations, and a compromised media. Through the homage "we" relocate.

Such an imaginary projection of a collective "we" invites us to consider what this phantasmic virtual public might be and, more important, what it might seek to achieve together. We shall turn to these provocations shortly. One other feature of the heterogeneous image in the repertoire captures our attention: its auratic charge. Aura, the Benjaminian shibboleth, evokes a priceless object, singular in its value and at a distance from the standardized public images we encountered in chapter 4. Each of the three reassemblages considered so far foregrounds a public image, perhaps once commodity or waste, rendered singular in an act of embodied veneration. Looking across the repertoire, how are we to distinguish this popular sacrality as opposed to the auratic purchase of a priceless painting? We know that elite "high" art as well as revalued "folk" art can acquire credentialed singularity via institutional sanction (of governments, museums, artistic institutions). Non-reproducible paintings are supremely auratic objects that attract veneration; it is their mechanical reproduction that cancels aura. So are preserved artisanal everyday objects of vanishing cultures. So is lore archived in folklore archives. How might we differentiate these singular auratic objects from the "volatile" auratic object of popular veneration?

Perhaps a return to the "public image" is in order here. There are religious, star, and political icons whose "aura" is strongly legitimated through reputable media institutions. When we look beyond the most widely prevalent commodity images of our three global icons, we find that they are well represented in "high" art sometimes sanctioned (or funded) by the state. This is true of the most (Mother Teresa) and least (Phoolan Devi) institutionalized of our icons. There are few national accolades for the bandit queen; by contrast, official and semiofficial representations of Mother Teresa abound. Soon after her death, one sculptor complained that he could hardly keep up with the demand for Mother Teresa statues—"white, bare-footed, wrinkle-faced statue with folded hands"—commissioned by state and city organizations, churches, and local parishes.[9] These are classic examples of mass-produced commercial artifacts that may or may not re-sacralized through acts of worship, a call one can only make through site-specific ethnographic study; but ethnography is not the methodological concern of this book, so I will venture into popular sacrality by other means. Paradoxically, elite artworks in which the the nun has been a favorite subject can point the way in their obvious auratic purchase. We see eminently reflective, highly interpretive, visual renditions of Mother Teresa in the hands of famous photographers and painters such as M. F. Husain and the photographer Raghu Rai —cultural giants who have most consistently depicted Mother Teresa over several decades. Both have labored to assemble Mother Teresa for a national public, producing singular works credentialed for their artistic merit: Husain's well-known painting of the seated Mother Teresa holding a child (figure 29), his very first painting of her, and Rai's equally famous photograph of Mother Teresa's face on a half-erased mural in Kolkata (figure 30). Most important for us is that these works of high art lead us to the popular consumption of Mother Teresa as auratic object. But let me elaborate.

Husain, the pioneer of modern Indian art, painted Mother Teresa from 1979 to 1997, his last tribute to her a series painted especially for the beatification. He is the painter who famously drew the ire of the Hindu right for his paintings of Hindu goddesses and has often turned to sages, martyrs, and saints in his exploration of amplified human possibilities.[10] So it is no surprise he would turn to Mother Teresa, the subject who could exemplify incalculable giving in its most excellent form. His oil-on-canvas painting of Mother Teresa features the icon cradling a brown baby while another child tugs at her blue-bordered sari.

Simply titled "Mother," the "portrait" has one striking feature: Where we would find the icon's face, there is only darkness, hinting at the excessive expenditure of the self in the service of the Other (manifest in the poor)—the absorption into the flesh of the loved one gradually eroding the saint's body. In such portraiture, Husain captures the city's sense of Mother Teresa as a popular saint, whose logic of giving was clearly at odds with consumerist impulses toward accumulation. But we can only make such assumptions regarding popular sacrality if we can multiply the example, to consider how this visual inscription variably recurs in other media traces of the global icon. In this case, we do not have to look far— only to the enormous photo archive of Raghu Rai images of Mother Teresa. Shot the same year as Husain's painting, 1979, Rai's photo (figure 30) carries a similar message. We saw his more iconic photographs of Mother Teresa in chapter 4. In this capture, Rai shoots two street children lying on cheap mats in front of a wall with a mural of Mother Teresa painted on it. The mural is half-erased, absorbed by Kolkata's habitually verdant moss, subjected to the jostle of bodies in the street. Rai's placement of the young children in the foreground creates a visual funnel in which they seem contiguous with her form—again, a melting of the saintly face into the bodies of the poor represented in realistic detail.

Both texts underscore Mother Teresa as a living saint, the auratic signifier assembling those in need into the surface of the image, but with one important difference. Rai's photograph captures in "high art" one of

FIGURE 29 M. F.
Husain, *Mother
Teresa*, 1979. Digital
reproduction. Courtesy
of M. F. Husain.

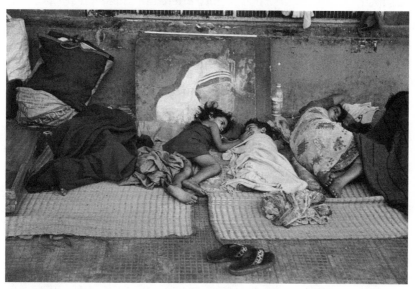

FIGURE 30 Street children sleeping under Mother Teresa's protection, 1979. Raghu Rai,
Magnum Photos.

the most common forms in which Mother Teresa's image circulates in the city: the painted mural or street poster. One stumbles on the famous face all over the city, in unexpected places, such as at football clubs (Mother Teresa and Gandhi are often staple exemplars gracing walls in calendar art[11]) and in more expected venues, such as tourist booths and stores that sell cheap laminated reproductions (alongside postcards, figurines, medallions, and postage stamps). Rai's photograph therefore reassembles a popular mural, presenting not only it as a paradigmatic "location" for the popular saint, but also Mother Teresa as the protector of the indigent—the children who "live" through her benediction.

I argued in chapter 4 that Rai remains complicit in the creation and circulation of the most common commodity images of the missionary. This photograph is no exception. Where it does emerge as a record of the popular consumption of the saint are in the stories, many reported right after her death, that back Rai's interpretation of Mother Teresa's street presence as an auratic object—albeit in different expressive style. My search for a repertoire of images that recoded Mother Teresa as the protector of street dwellers turned out to be simpler than I imagined, despite the voluminous traces of the bio-icon. While looking at Rai's assembling of spatial depth, I was struck by the movement between the face and the bodies of the children. Read in tandem with Husain's visualization of Mother Teresa's unproductive expenditures, I understood Rai's image of the (cited) poster melting into the children to be a complex argument on the material contiguity offered by the popular saint who always intercedes with theocratic or secular authorities on the behalf of "the people." I return to the powerful cultural figuration later in the book, but in looking for corresponding images in mass, DIY, and alternative media, I stumbled across four or five telling stories that recounted the "protection" a cheap poster could offer to street dwellers who appear as illegal squatters to city authorities. Struck by the citation of the poster image (with varying depictions of the bio-icon, I imagine), I began to assemble high-art pieces (the Husain and Rai works) alongside these stories in mass media often sporadically recounted as curiosities, as the occasional amusing news tidbit, to create a complex semiotic aggregate—in fact a "rune" that would require further scholarly divination.

Only one of these stories is still accessible through popular search engines. I recount its "DNA" to illustrate the method of reading I belabor here. A journalist interviewing Kolkata's pavement dwellers after Mother Teresa's death came upon several instances of her protection of the city's homeless poor, whose "right" to occupy a space on the sidewalk is daily threatened. A young rickshawallah, Ram Lakhan Yadav, had bought a cheap poster of Mother Teresa for 25 rupees, a fair amount of change for him, and stuck it on the wall beside his chosen sleeping quarters. When asked what this might achieve, Yadav insisted that the saint might not only "save him" from poverty, but her image would prevent the police from harassing him—he would be "one of hers," under her protection, and therefore beyond the law (Caba 1997). Such a demand against city laws is hardly performed in isolation, even though the story filtered in mainstream media features a lone protagonist. The cheaply available poster hints at the buying, selling, and bartering of the popular saint's commodity image in the social domain that we name public culture. When we can multiply these instances, in the four stories roughly commensurate with Yadav's claim, the auratic purchase of the saintly visage is evident: The object acquires the magical efficacy Arthur Gell (1998) attributed to certain artworks. In these performances, Mother Teresa in the poster is re-located as a popular saint whose task is not to save souls, but to protect the poor against an indifferent state. In its new locations, the re-auratized, cheap, mass-media poster would function as a social hieroglyph of the popular, motivating a story to be told and not found. To attend to popular auratization sans ethnography involves following such correspondences, recording ephemeral traces, and assembling them into a "rune" that enables us to understand the lived sociality of the city from desultory asides in the news.

Clearly, it would be difficult to hypothesize the intent of the young rickshawallah who auratizes the poster. But I am more interested in the suggestion of structural agency in these acts of auratization. One could imagine, on the one hand, that Mother Teresa is indeed an auratic object for Ram Lakhan Yadav and that he is an "illegal" squatter under her protection. On the other, one could also imagine that he cynically gambles on the policeman's "respect" for Mother Teresa, he gambles on her auratic charge for the policeman, to make such a claim. Whatever the intention, Yadav clearly banks on the magical agency of Mother Teresa's image as protector, a social contract visually invoked in Rai's "authentic" street-life photograph. The complex aggregate of icon-devotee variations culled from painting, photo, and story testifies to Mother Teresa's popular sacrality in the city. We are directed to certain segments of the city's population who venerate her as a popular saint across the social striations of caste, religion, and language.

It is also worth looking at the ambiguity of the price placed on the cheap poster. Is Mother Teresa "priceless"? Or were the 25 rupees a worthy investment to earn pavement space from a beguiled policeman (in 1997)? This tells us that the volatile icon exists in mixed economies in which the image is both saleable commodity and gift. The social relations constituted by the image, the recognition of both common knowledge (Mother Teresa as saint) and opposing class interests (police versus urban squatter), are equally mixed, signaling the contingent collectivity that gathers around the icon. Yadav's "citation" articulates a social demand by those who live under the terror of the mega-city to come. After all, the rickshawallah must be kicked off the pavement where he sleeps because Kolkata has embarked on a mission to become a "clean" mega-city attractive to foreign investment; we might say his re-auratization of the saint as popular custodian is motivated by such macro-scalar change. Such historical conditions (that I turn to more substantially in part 3) transform social frictions around iconic images into events. The cultural biography of the commodity image as it is remediated in varied media formats tells the story of global capital through vagaries of mass consumption.

The fortunes of the poster signal its capacity as both gift and saleable commodity. Where Fredric Jameson (1998) has argued that, at the postmodern historical juncture, all cultural activity is subsumed into the logic of capital (the turning economic of the cultural and a turning cultural of the economic), Jean Baudrillard (2003 [1981]) offers a more flexible rubric for understanding the persistence of magical technologies in the world of ubiquitous commodity. Drawing on Marcel Mauss, Georges Bataille, and Thorstein Veblen, Baudrillard argues there are objects of exchange in contemporary consumer societies that remain not transitive but autonomous, opaque, and symbolic—something like a gift or a traditional ritual or artisanal object. A wedding ring, for instance, would constitute such a singular object, its fashion value being negligible to its worth. When "being, cultural trait, ideal, gestural pattern, or language" gains such excessive investment, consuming them defies instrumentality. They "undo" the social order of capital—an excess Bataille (1949) names unproductive expenditure. Hence, even if we stay within the logic of capitalistic exchange as fundamental to our times, Baudrillard (2003 [1981], 255) encourages us to think of a mixed economy in which symbolic objects (looks, objects, dreams, excrement) coexist with saleable commodity in a single transaction. The volatile icon (the re-auratized cheap poster) is precisely such a symbolic object, a point of enunciation for social relations that are not entirely governed by instrumentality. It exists in mass culture and it exists within the logic of capital, but its social economy includes far more than the consumption of reifying commodities.

Not all volatile images in expressive culture will prompt affective re-sponses that are socially transformative, and we shall return to this dif-ferentiation in part 3. Performance as archive and repertoire focuses the critical eye on the network of connected channels through which the iconic image flows. In the case of global icons, it is important not only to track these connections, but also to focus on where they falter, short-circuit, or disconnect, disrupting the unified message. When an icon turned heterogeneous by acts of reassemblage refuses all attempts to stabilize its meaning, and static emerges in lines of connection, we see something volatile, an exorbitant sign that prompts collective action.

PUBLIC CULTURE

If expressive citation of (part or whole) mass-mediated sign constitutes the volatile icon, where do we find its eruptions? If the easily accessible records of mass-mediated images constitute the "archive," how do we track the repertoire in complex media ecologies? Here I return to media ecology as a mechanism for localizing the migration of the sign, an at-tempt that might seem at odds with Matthew Fuller's (2005) conceptual space that is heterogeneous (machine to dance club), multi-scalar (indi-vidual to institutional reception), and multidirectional (moving from re-ception to exhibition and back to distribution). Evidence of the embodied veneration of icons, in the very different expressive performances we have observed, comes in many forms: as reports, ethnographies, recycled media content, and, sometimes, institutionally archived materials. In these forms, we see the volatile icon migrating across media formats and platforms, often repurposed for different publics. The task at hand is to localize a cultural arena where these mass-mediated signs fuction as mag-ical technologies.

Expressive culture guides such localizing, since it signals variation from the "standard"—here, the standardized images of the icon made in publicity. Further, the contingency of expressive culture indexes specific collective subjects who forge social bonds through their embodied perfor-mances. A starting point for such relocation might be the identification of non-standard, or vernacular, forms, conventions, and idioms that "cite" the standardized image, referring us to sites of enunciation where the volatile icon once commanded collective popular veneration. The vernacular is not equivalent to the popular; but vernacular sacrality, lost in the standardizing processes of mass mediation, often returns as a belated trace in acts of re-sacralization. Cultural figurations of oral lore return to fuel new veneration, sometimes expressed in folk idioms (be-

FIGURE 31 Ka Yan Cheung, "The Bandit Queen." Digital art. Courtesy of Ka Yan Cheung.

come culturally recognizable over time). We see this most clearly in the many transcriptions of the bandit queen into "murals," by now a standardized idiom of a once vernacular practice in high cultural "pop art" and in DIY digital and audiovisual media. Always marked as small-scale artisanal productions with limited physical reach, murals now habitually index heterogeneous revolutionary imaginations; their presence expresses contingent social antagonisms, the bio-icon embodying "us" against "them." In the case of Phoolan Devi, numerous contemporary artworks transform the widely available commodity images of the bandit queen into re-auratized objects. For example, in a DIY virtual reassemblage (figure 31), Ka Yan Cheung, inspired by the 2001 edition of Mala Sen's *India's Bandit Queen*, digitally redesigned a news photograph of the frowning Phoolan Devi behind bars after her surrender taken by Pramod Pushkarna in 1983. A robust, magenta-bandanna-clad face appears behind ropes of a ship, an impression enhanced by the brilliant orange sky at sunset and shimmering ocean as backdrop—a romantic fantasy of the bandit queen on the seas.

Posted in a series on the "grrl revolution," the digital "mural" is hardly idiosyncratic. Even superficial digging unearths other, painted murals of the bandit queen turned pedagogic objects for young "girls" found in the physical spaces of urban neighborhoods. Aside from the virtual "murals" we have considered, all of our bio-icons materialize as street art in reflexive formations of translocality. Figure 32 shows a mural with five women, including Phoolan Devi and Mother Teresa, a project enacted by eight young muralists registered in an apprenticeship program with Oasis for Girls in San Francisco.[12] Each woman has her own "weapon" and expresses the excellence of one human quality. "Code-breaking" is Phoolan Devi's attribute, as the mural transcribes her administering a vigorous kick (figure 32a). Mother Teresa flaunts "relentless compassion." The dark figures illuminated against the bright feminized pink link these South Asian icons to Rosa Parks, Emma Goldman, and "Everywoman"— the progressive feminist to come—in this overtly pedagogical project (which is implicit in the title, "Hearts of Gold, Fists of Fury"). Not all of the world is here, but a select few erect a barrier between "us" and "them"; nor is the world here as yet, as Everywoman points us to the liquid social to come. Together, the pantheon imagines a set of linkages between different contexts of action the girls learn about through their creative labor of auratizing these cartographically emplaced icons—linkages that seek to represent not the world but a contingent translocality appropriate to the ever changing ethnic flux of San Francisco's Mission District. In these works, the bio-icons are not local but translocal signifiers marked in social antagonism to destructive globalism. The contiguities between collectively owned translocal vernacular art (the eight girls are the "authors" of the mural) and the individual adoption of a transnational vernacular presents the mixed heterogeneous image volatilized under conditions of possibility.

If we understand volatility in part as the potentialization of human agency, but also as a radical instability of the image, we must include individual cultural productions in the study of the popular. This is not to say that these works of high or DIY art that re-auratize the commodity images are popular culture. Rather, they are important mechanisms for *tracking* popular aura, what is often regarded as the vernacular sacrality of bio-icons. For example, the French artist Amy Marie Daulin's virtual image "Phoolan Devi Icon" (2006), a digitized painting that once circulated widely on the Internet but is not available for reproduction here,

FIGURE 32 The "Hearts of Gold, Fists of Fury" mural in the Mission District of San Francisco, 2004. Courtesy of Oasis for Girls.

FIGURE 32a Inset of Phoolan Devi in the mural, 2004. Courtesy of Oasis for Girls.

traces its lineage to expressive popular culture that marks a distance from the reified commodity focalized in French print media (the narrations encountered in the previous chapter). Daulin "cites" her print DNA in her painting, in which lines cut and pasted from the biographies run vertically behind the visual composition of the bandit queen's bust. But the text is scrambled, recessed, as Phoolan Devi's face—not the iconic inscription of the woman with a gun—looks out at the viewer framed by a golden lotus-leaved halo. Ruby-red blood splatters—highly ornamentalized references to the bandit queen's well-known violent past—mixed with gold flecks are sprinkled on the running text in this expressive recoding. Re-auratizing the bandit queen, the painting "consumes" her public image (the biographical production from established publishing houses), only to transform it into a record of her popular consumption as folk hero. It is a heterogeneous image whose significations are not clear: Is this a criticism of the public image? Is it a re-commoditization via recycled popular culture? It is precisely such indeterminacy that makes this a volatile, unstable text that, under certain conditions of possibility, might provoke debate, anger, irritation, or appreciation. It certainly addresses a wired public who define their social bonds through the consumption of transnational popular heroes, citing "vernacular" culture as expressive of localized "structures of feeling."

Such vernacularism often indexes non-reproducible, collectively owned media marked by variations that are not easily standardized. Among these, oral popular culture is pre-eminent, its traces filtered in print or audiovisual record. For example, regional lore of social bandits finds ample articulation in several mass-culture Hindi-language films, quite self-consciously archiving song cycles faced with loss or erasure. The director of the wildly popular and critically acclaimed Bollywood epic *Omkara* (2006)—also set in Uttar Pradesh (part of the notorious Chambal ravines of bandit-queen lore) and featuring contemporary fictionalized "outlaws" who service politicians — explicitly composed the music for his film based on traditional heroic ballads of social bandits.[13] Bharadwaj noted these were the oral media of his childhood that led to his lifelong fascination with the outlaw, an admission that tells us something about the media ecology of Phoolan Devi lore. The richly melancholic but celebratory melodies of *Omkara* (transnational in its address as an adaptation of *Othello*), with lyrics by the veteran songwriter Gulzar, archive the oral lore on half-caste or low-caste heroes of the region, effectively disseminating these localized media (restricted in its distribution) to national and transnational audiences. We read traces of the vernacular in mass media, but those traces point us to the popular, for if, as

Cesare Casarino argues, the vernacular can be regarded as both common practice and common potential (Casarino and Negri 2008a, 9), then traces of such vernacular sacrality indicates a potentiality yet to be actualized, to be repurposed for either popular or hegemonic gain.

For both Phoolan Devi and Mother Teresa, "lore" dominates the expressive veneration of the icon. We find apocryphal stories of the nun circulating in the popular memory of city denizens, faithfully recorded in her many mass-produced print biographies (many with worldwide distribution through a variety of online vendors). Several of these testify to her commitment to Kolkata's poor. Navin Chawla (2002) proffers one well-known narrative in which Mother Teresa refused to vacate an empty building adjoining the Hindu temple at Kalighat (Kolkata), despite threats from locals, Hindu priests, and the police. Striding in with the intention of removing the recalcitrant nun, one police officer recalls stopping short at the sight of Mother Teresa removing maggots from a patient's face. Moved by her dedication, her indifference to the odor that made everyone else reel, the police officer left the unrelenting nun to her own devices. The memorable account, differently embellished in each telling, situates her as the prototypical saint who incorporates the poor into her corporeal form. Another tale of Mother Teresa's beginnings that establishes her as auratic object across religious communities narrates her care of a Hindu priest ridden with cholera and abandoned by his colleagues in Kalighat. He was to become one of the nun's first patients at Nirmal Hriday (the Home for the Destitute and Dying). The story becomes a recursive one, underscoring Mother Teresa as a radical entrepreneur before her reincorporation into the Roman Catholic church; its reiteration reinscribes her as an exemplary public actor in the city, the face of local humanitarianism. The biopic *In the Name of God's Poor* (1997) dramatizes another occasion on which Mother Teresa sat with a dying woman all day outside the Nilratan Sarkar hospital in Kolkata because the hospital would not give the patient a bed—it considered the dying virtually disposable. Braving a rain-and-hail storm, the petite nun attached herself to the beggar woman until a bed could be found for her. Exasperated by the nun's patience, hospital authorities finally gave in to her demands many hours into the evening. No doubt the oral lore is cleverly repurposed in biography and biopic. Yet when we find the same story (the DNA) repeated within the media ecologies of the icon, we can assume we have stumbled on a repertoire.

The tales are the stuff of hagiography: They testify to the saint's exemplary and extraordinary life, reassembled in retrospect by devotees. As exemplars, if saints are in fact inextricable from their hagiographies (they are "made" by their devotees), so are legendary social bandits whose turn to lives of crime seem historical fait accompli. Phoolan Devi's sister once made the connection inadvertently when she reportedly snapped at a nosy journalist snooping around for a psychological motive for Phoolan Devi's massacre of the Thakurs at Behmai. Instead of providing information tailored to individuate Phoolan Devi, Rukmini Devi remarked: "God never makes dacoits or saints. It is men who make other people into dacoits or saints" ("The Day of Reckoning" 1981, 33). Here, Rukmini Devi quixotically captures the constant "making" (and mutations) of her sister as iconic sign.

Always the enemy of the state, Phoolan Devi is ever animate in oral culture that more often than not celebrates the sentiment echoed by her sister. Her circulation in oral media, before her entry into regional and national print and audiovisual media, highlights a vibrant volatile icon mostly consumed in northern Uttar Pradesh. In fact, both Putlibai (the first bandit queen, who lived in the 1950s) and Phoolan Devi (1963–2001) were locally celebrated in the popular idiom of *nautanki* performances, rural traveling theatrical forms in which heroic stories were told in song. A few recordings of *Phoolan Devi Biraha* (The Sorrow of Phoolan Devi), performed in regional Bhojpuri around Varanasi in 1983–84, remain.[14] In *Phoolan Devi Biraha* we hear of a legendary hero (not a victim) whose unjust fate is collectively and cathartically relived in local venues—perhaps because, as Dalit intellectuals have suggested, her circumstances resonate with the nautanki audiences. Nautanki performances often emphasize the religious and mythic features of the *virangana* (a woman who manifests the qualities of *virya*, or heroism), and we know this was an iconographic compass that Phoolan Devi used to great effect (Hansen 1988). She reputedly assumed the mantle of Durga, one manifestation of Shakti (embodied power), and the guise of the epic heroine Draupadi, whose curse had turned the Chambal into the river of revenge, to foreground the righteousness of her acts. No doubt, she was drawing on the force of her avatars in oral culture—the auratic icon of the adulatory melancholic biraha performances. The mythic virangana was to remain alive among Dalit supporters of Phoolan Devi long after her evolution into mass commodity. In October 2001, for example, Ramdev Deshbandhu, writing in the popular Hindi-language 'zine *Ham Dalit*, chose to title his eulogy to the bandit queen "Virangana Phoolan Devi." More recently, the vernacular song cycles (stored in ethnomusicology archives) have experienced a revival in live performances. Shirish Korde, accompanied by the tabla player Samar Chatterjee and the Da Capo Chamber Music Orchestra, performed a series of songs that received critical acclaim in the *New York Times*, *Boston Globe*, and elsewhere, while the dancer Padma Menon offered her own version of the life and times of Phoolan Devi in "Fireborn," performed for international audiences. (The Canberra Street Theater performance is the most widely discussed one.) Both of these accounts recycle the vernacular sacrality of the legend.

In such expressive performances, Phoolan Devi's genealogical ties, once lost in her transcoding as global outlaw (standardized through equivalence to Bonnie Parker), remain strong. The DNA of the original bandit queen, the one-armed Putlibai (daughter of the famous Muslim "dancing girl" Ashgari of Agra), persists in early oral recollections of Phoolan Devi that remember a tall one-armed bandit (not at all the petite Phoolan Devi of the famous photograph). Jon Bradshaw, who followed Phoolan Devi for *Esquire* in 1984–85, reports a telling eyewitness account: "'She was cruel,' said Muhti. 'She was passionate.' . . . I had never seen her before, and when she returned my heart went to my head. I was dizzy with desire. She was nearly six feet tall, believe me, and her skin was the colour of dried blood. I swear to you, on the head of my son, a night with a woman like that would be like drinking the most delectable poison" (Bradshaw 1985, 73). Long after Phoolan Devi's incarnation as legal citizen and parliamentarian, a commentator on her assassination would acknowledge the undying legend in expressive vernacular performances. Phoolan Devi, declaimed Rajat Bhattacharjee (2001, 8), remains "a character in one of the innumerable legends which folk singers in Northern [Uttar Pradesh] sing in her name."

The vernacular in these in situ performances with limited transmission effectively localizes auratic objects, restricting the geographic scale of popular culture. We find the belated trace of the vernacular volatile icon in mass media, even if we start with the most reifying commodity images of our bio-icons. After all, the mass media distributes iconic images widely, maintains them in the public eye for years, generates symbolic density, and intensifies sensations. Even as Shekar Kapur's *The Bandit Queen* (1994) was a single, anomalous, and therefore singular eruption in transnational mass media, it archived certain popular genealogies of bandit-queen lore. These only become visible when one follows the provocations in the film to other productions, on smaller scale—some of which are no longer in circulation. Once again, the runes of the popular are complex aggregates of image variations the critic consolidates in their brief appearances across media networks and from ethnographic regional scholarship.

A quick look at the aggregative logic of bandit-queen lore illustrates the point. Many who watched Kapur's film remember the character Phoolan Devi going to see the legendary Bombay Hindi-language film *Sholay* (1975), a national hit that ran for more than a year in theaters.[15] Now, several moviegoing publics instantly recognize *Sholay* as the story that popularized the social bandit in mass media, irrevocably focalizing Amitabh Bachchan (playing opposite his equally famous spouse, Jaya Bhaduri) as the moody vigilante who acted for the common man. The movie buff might pursue *Sholay*'s well-publicized production story further, thereby stumbling onto the Chambal Valley as its inspiration. We know that when Amjad Khan signed up to play Gabbar Singh, another unforgettable performance, Jaya Bhaduri made the actor read *Abhishapta Chambal* (The Accursed Chambal; 1958), written by her father, Taroon Bhaduri, as preparation for his role. Here, the plot thickens; the trail takes us to smaller scale: The transnational film *The Bandit Queen* (1994) directs us to the national hit *Sholay* (1975), which propels us inexorably toward the Chambal Valley, where Phoolan Devi arose as vengeful virago during the Behmai massacre of 1981. Taroon Bhaduri was an acclaimed journalist whose book was so popular in Kolkata that Satyajit Ray, no less, encouraged him to write an English version; it, in turn, received even wider circulation—hence, the emergence of one of the first national accounts of Chambal outlaws, *Chambal: The Valley of Terror* (Bhaduri 1972). In both the Bengali- and English-language texts, the bandit queen's genealogies are restored. First circulating among a metropolitan reading public, *Abhishapta Chambal* presented an empathetic account of Putlibai as the bandit queen; Phoolan Devi had not yet arrived. Given that Bhaduri had accompanied Gandhi's disciple Archarya Vinoba Bhave on Bhave's famous but controversial Chambal peace "mission" to "reclaim" the hearts of the *baghis*, or rebels,[16] the publication was considered a "true" eyewitness account. Yet the legends already were undeniably repurposed for the regional public, the bandits capturing the imagination of literate Bengali elites who had long cathected the Chambal as modern metropolitan Kolkata's "heart of darkness."[17]

Despite the commoditization, Bhaduri's text did not isolate an iconic female bandit queen; many illustrious Chambal dacoits and their exploits find their way into *Abishapta Chambal*. The book became a historical record of this hitherto little studied heartland, one that inspired several less-well-known, and now out of circulation, regional films about bandit queens in Bengali and Hindi. Ashok Roy's films on Phoolan Devi, the Bengali-language film *Phoolan Devi* (1984) and its Hindi version, *Kahani Phoolvati Ki* (1985)—preceded by *Putlibai* (1972) and followed by *Daku Hasina* (1987)—were inspired by Bhaduri's reports. Like Taroon Bhaduri, Ashok Roy took on the pedagogic role of speaking for the subaltern: *Phoolan Devi* commences with a voiceover from an omniscient perspective (which never returns in the film text) in which Phoolan Devi's historical plight is translated as a story about "a few helpless humans" persecuted at the hands of "a few ferocious/predatory animals." Not only does the framing transcode a historical subject as a universal helpless human, but the film portrays the young Phoolan Devi as a deeply ordinary girl whose only desire, to live a happy domestic life with her husband (even if he is cruel and rapacious), is constantly thwarted. The gendered logic establishes Phoolan Devi, and other female bandits in the film such as Mira Thakur, as primarily focused on men: There are catfights and competitive dance spectacles aimed at pleasing the male bandit protagonist, the heroic Vikram Mallah. A melodramatic arc ensues in which, as Christine Gledhill (1991) reminds us, not only is social change refracted through lives of individuals, but the bandit's turn to violence is rationalized through building affect from lost dreams that are recognizable to middle-class audiences. Any traumatized young girl with dreams such as ours, so the narration suggests, would resort to heinous crime in such circumstance. Nor are (Bengali middle-class) stereotypes of the bandits' lower caste and class social position really questioned. Phoolan Devi's costumes expose her midriff; the dance sequences are salacious in the extreme; the villagers address each other with the informal "you (*tui*)"; the rural police are bumbling comic figures; and sexual speech about the budding Phoolan Devi is excessively vulgar (one lewd village honcho, licking his lips on see Phoolan Devi, exclaims, "Oh, I crave those ripe mangoes"). In the decorous gaze of the bourgeoisie, these folks from the heartland are unmistakably simple, lowly in speech, comic in buffoonery, and unrestrained in their sexual appetites. But the middle-class representatives of the law, the police officers from the national force, are eminently dignified.

Nevertheless, the film remains a clear critique of the state, a popular parallel to new-wave Indian cinema's engagement with the subaltern in films that began in the mid-1970s.[18] For one, Roy's *Phoolan Devi* is far more historically accurate in its depiction of Phoolan Devi's story: The extended negotiations within bandit groups, presence of other female bandits, and tracking of social relations within the village and beyond

that it portrays betray careful research. So the film produces a commoditized low-caste woman while simultaneously revealing her story as a
collective one, as the events unfolding around the Mira Thakur character
clearly show. The rape sequence is graphic by violent suggestion (blood,
torn clothing) but shot in negative so that the rapist appears beast-like
(his raised head facing the camera); we can hardly see Phoolan Devi, the
character. The murder of the rapist, however, is a long, cathartic shot in
slow motion that is the logical end to the affective momentum garnered
by the narrative. The film becomes a regional indictment of a failed social
system (including legal protections) in which Phoolan Devi's plight is
hardly an isolated instance. As a regional vernacular citation of the lore of
bandit queens (there are at least two in the film, despite the title *Phoolan
Devi*), Roy's film becomes a linking mechanism between the bandit queen
of the *biraha* song cycles and the global fetish in Kapur's *The Bandit
Queen*. Only the careful scholarly tracking across media platforms can
consolidate the complex aggregate constitutive of the non-standard, variable, heterogeneous image that is the volatile icon.

The movement of iconic images across media platforms and networks
encourages us to think the location of the popular in complex ways, signaling a media ecology that disrupts the bounded domains of cultural activity
such as high, folk, and mass cultures. No wonder many critics have chosen
to do away with those distinctions altogether, choosing to locate the constant remediation of a particular mass-mediated sign within a conceptual
zone of cultural bartering, negotiating, wheeling and dealing that is public
culture. Art historians, media scholars, and cultural anthropologists have
led the way in their robust explorations of transmedial forms within complex media ecologies.[19] Investigating the remediation of media content
from the cinema, satellite television, newspapers, magazines, and popular
music business, critics such as Christopher Pinney, for instance, have encouraged us to consider cultural objects (icons among them) as pathways to
more than politics per se; sensual pleasures combined with cognitive grasp
can facilitate the forging of multilevel social bonds (Pinney 2001).[20] Others,
such as Sandra Freitag and Patricia Uberoi, on the trail of magazine romances, calendar art, and Bollywood cinema (Freitag 2001), foreground
the negotiation of mass-mediated signs (plagiarizing, rescripting, and col-
lating [Uberoi 2006]) as crucially productive for identity. If in public cultures we see an enormous capacity to aspire expressed in vertiginous reassemblage, it is the volatile icon—citational, expressive, auratic—that leads
us there.

In public culture, we find multiple efficacies of the auratized icon, its volatility often quickly tamed—recycled and repurposed for hegemonic and popular ends. If as social bandit Phoolan Devi rises from the "fail-ures" of democracy, Arundhati Roy enters mass media at the very opposite end of the spectrum: the best of Indian democracy, a sign of its success. Her efficacy as a technology of the popular is especially mixed for, as a member of the bourgeois elite, Roy, like Bhaduri, is an effective producer of highly reflexive social critique; she galvanizes networked publics whose access to media platforms remain vastly diverse. I look at these publics closely in the next chapter. But here, public culture offers a zone of contestation in which differently constituted collectivities trans-act icons. Here, subjects are in fractal objecthood. Probing the volatile icon yields not a historical subject but a series of subject effects produced (as Gell would have it) by these magical technologies.[21]

COLLECTIVE AGENCY

That the popular invokes collective agency is a commonplace. Our study of material culture encourage us to think about the agency the volatile icon shares with its adorers as a objective condition, a "capacity"; for those invested in social change, this capacity signals the human capacity to aspire, Arjun Appadurai's term for the compromised agency (within a civil-liberal framework) of the disenfranchised. Suggesting fractal per-sonhood as a quotidian condition in globalizing South Asia, Appadurai reminds us that the "wants, preferences, choices, and calculations" (Appadurai 2004, 68) embedded in cultural and social life reveal disenfranchised populations as economic actors adept at navigating a real world of conjectures and refutations, and not simply communities of the past bound by unchanging culture (habit, custom, heritage, tradition). The capacity to aspire therefore signals a sense of acting within civil or demo-cratic constraints, with the resources of mass media; in this sense, the capacity to aspire signals a certain epistemological capture of human agency and, therein, the possible repurposing of agency for hegemonic or popular gain. One particular cultural arena relevant to the study of bio-icons who draw their iconographic charge from star images illustrates such a repurposing of the volatile image, testifying to the radical indeter-minacy of its social efficacies. It is one that has been abundantly the-orized in studies of star reception—especially in the study of the South Indian stars—an interdisciplinary field to which I owe considerable intel-lectual debt. I close the discussions of the location of the popular here with the debates over "cine-politics" to correct for any idealization of agency my reading of the volatile icon might suggest so far.

Capacity does not reside only in historical agents or objective conditions; rather, it encompasses both as the location of socially efficacious mass consumption. Such an insight comes at the tailspin of a long engagement with spectatorship. In the early years, star studies remained fixated on the industrial, technological, and social production of stars; feminist theorists such as Laura Mulvey and Gaylan Studlar, among others, however, effectively dismantled the abstract category of the ideal spectator to reveal a host of spectatorial positions governed by the distinctive social histories of the spectators.[22] One effect of such theory was to produce empirical and ethnographic data on audiences in what is now regarded as reception studies. These conversations have a parallel in scholarship on Indian cinemas, with scrutiny of fan activity in South Indian cinemas (especially Tamil cinema) commanding the lion's share of critical attention (Dickey 1993b; Pandian 1991; Prasad 2004; Sivathamby 1981; Srinivas 1996 and 2009).[23] Many critics writing on Indian cinema describe the vernacular roots of star adoration. The structure of devotion of the *bhakta* (devotee) in the sphere of religious life remains in place in film-viewing practices, especially since many film stars from the three southern states (Andhra Pradesh, Tamil Nadu, and Karnataka) played roles in the so-called mythologicals. Here, theological iconophilia directly affects cinema—or "stars displace God," as Robert Hardgrave (1979) once put it. The bhakta, Madhava Prasad notes, does not see the star as God or think that he or she has unmediated access to God; there is no realist premise here. The star image is artifactual as ever, but, as we have seen, the Hindu relation to the image allows God to be housed even in the material support of a fool. Hence, in Andhra Pradesh, the star commonly known as NTR (the popular shorthand for Nandamuri Taraka Rama Rao) who played Krishna in several films would make an appearance from his bungalow balcony in Hyderabad where crowds gathered for dársan—to see and be seen—every morning (Gandhy and Thomas 1991). In recent years, we have seen the emergence of temples to worship such megastars as Amitabh Bachchan, complete with shrines where fans offer flowers, burn incense, and await dársan.[24] Such embodied veneration has prompted critics to theorize a domain of popular consumption, "cine-politics"— public cultures in which the social efficacies of iconic stars are repurposed for specific political agendas. The story of cine-politics therefore most directly raises questions regarding the collective subject that I turn to at the close of the chapter.

Sara Dickey's meticulous plotting of the political ascendancy of M. G. Ramachandran (known popularly as MGR) in Tamil Nadu demonstrates exactly how party honchos were able to mobilize fan cultures to form an electoral base (Dickey 1993b). Indeed, MGR has auratic charge, but his volatile image is constantly re-territorialized for electoral benefit. It was MGR's star image, coupled with his charismatic personality, that enabled him to form his own party, the Dravidian Munnetra Kazhagam (DMK), in 1972. He was then able to become chief minister in 1977 because of the highly organized political activities of his fan clubs, a pre-existing network of supporters. Of course, MGR's highly eloquent speeches contributed to his rise, Dickey intimates, but his charge as a political aficionado suggests cinema exists as an alternative public sphere constituted by what Miriam Hansen (1991, 94) has called "local conditions and constellations." With wide viewership of MGR films among the poor, vernacular structures of devotion rendered him increasingly intimate, since in Hindu polytheistic worship god-heroes are often regarded as family members (brother, child, mother). This local constellation of spectatorial activity soon incorporated MGR as "elder brother" for many viewers (interviewed by Dickey). Far from regarding MGR's wealth and fame as indexical of successful individualism (as Richard Dyer [1979] has suggested about the Hollywood star), the prevalent myth about MGR circulating among his devotees was the childless star gave profusely and abundantly to the poor—giving being the cultural sign for extraordinary wealth and success worthy of emulation.[25] In such local consumption, we see a movie star as an exemplary icon: MGR sets an example of how to be wealthy, how to deploy political power ethically for the good of all—in fact, how to live in common. The worship of MGR's giving parallels the adoration of Mother Teresa by the indigent who celebrate the incalculable gift at odds with the ubiquitous logic of accumulation.[26]

Arguably, MGR becomes the magical technology through which diverse populations forge social bonds that have found institution in politics. When MGR comes to power, such a popular collective subject assumes the garb of a hegemonic populism; the star image, now re-territorialized by the party, concretizes a public in its circulation. The scene of cine-politics therefore provides one illustration of a vibrant historical arena in contemporary South Asia in which icons are technologies of the popular. But what becomes equally evident is the quick aggrandizement of volatile icons for hegemonic repurposing—a process that complicates social efficacy. For whom are auratic icons efficacious? Who does the capacity to aspire serve? Does the volatile icon, the eruption whose significations will not settle, survive hegemonic repurposing? These questions are not easily answered; they direct us toward the historical conditions of auratization that are the subject of the next chapter. In the events recounted there, we gather seemingly isolated eruptions of sensational actions around our bio-icons to tell a story of human agency in the face of macroscalar change.

On these occasions, the volatile signifier—the blue-bordered sari, the wrinkled face, the arms bearing a rifle, the red bandanna, the colorfully adorned gamine body, the curls and collarbones—drifts free, endures, captivates. We see its luminous spark in the eyes of a rickshawallah comforted by his cheap poster of the watching saint; the body of the "we" sutured to the disorienting lips of Arundhati Roy; and the hands that reach to touch the decorative dead body of the murdered bandit queen.

PART 3

Locations

THE POLITICS OF THE ICON

People waiting for Mother Teresa's funeral cortège, September 13, 1997. AP Photo/Bikas Das.

The biographs we have traced across media platforms and networks alert us to eruptions of the volatile icon, a socially efficacious image whose contingent enunciation "opens" us into the social world that animates it. Such an opening anchors the drift of this ever mobile image to a specific historical context, one where the icon locates the consumer within globalized social relations. In popular consumption, Coca-Cola appears to refresh the bodies of others, the Christian missionary tallies good deeds for a market in souls, and both embody transnational institutions with scant local accountability. On these occasions, icons are locative technologies that situate us in relation to the "global" through a mythic image turned historical. The underlying cartography of universal aspiration returns with vengeance: Coca-Cola becomes America, or the Roman Catholic missionary becomes the Vatican's lackey. When these frictions are newsworthy, appearing sporadically in mass-media archives, when the significations of global icons are contested, we begin to ask: Who venerates (adores or desecrates) the volatile icon at this juncture? How might we conceive of the collectivities that forge social bonds through the icon? And when they do, what social demands—goals, platforms, agendas—seek institution in politics?

In this move into the social, I return to the icon as a technology of the popular. Embodied veneration allows the subject to move through a corporeal aperture toward other subjects, the logic of incorporation integral to encounters with icons. So far we have presumed a historical collective subject whose aspiration finds articulation through the icon, moving on to theorize aspiration (affect, desire, or fantasy) as a "capacity" of collectivities—an objective indicator of agency. Such a turn follows the lead of Madhav Prasad (2004) when he describes a process whereby (cinematic) identifications are objectified in politics: If the stars have their objective correlative in the world of governance, icons emerge as exemplary actors who signal a possible social. Such objectification recognizes both the danger and the possibility of magical technologies that "manage" dreams, technologies that are as capable of consolidating the hegemonic as they are of forging an anti-hegemonic popular.

As in the case of the stars, the embodied veneration of icons certainly makes them ripe for manipulation; Prasad alerts us to cases in which adoration can quickly create a vote bank. In such cases, the magical agency of icons enters the calculus of capacity. Capacity captures aspiration as a potentiality that is easily harnessed to fossilize political power but also to effect socially transformation. To consider how potentiality is actualized as capacity, we are directed to the locations of agency: to particular historical situations, but also to the collective subject who acts through the popular consumption of icons. In this chapter, I focus on the lineaments of the collective subject that makes up the popular. I begin with conceptions of such a subject most relevant to the mass consumption of global icon before moving to particular historical constituencies for whom our bio-icons operate as socially efficacious technologies.

But history signals contingency, those conditions of possibility that potentialize an icon. How do we approach the "conditions" of the icon's potentialization? Here again, the conversation on cine-politics is instructive in attending to the processes of subjectification that facilitates the transport of stars into politics. This transfer ensues in situations where, Prasad notes, the question of political representation—who speaks for me?—remains unsettled.[1] Hence, Bachchan as the angry young man speaks for the lumpen proletariat even when he has amassed great wealth; the South Indian stars MGR and NTR represent specific linguistic communities of the southern states where viewers dis-identify with Hindi-language actors. In the elections of 2004, parties and political organizations tried to harness the force of these unmet aspirations, playing to the uncertainty about political representation in the Indian democracy. In this chapter, I focus on specific historical situations where the three bio-icons are potentialized in the face of escalating uncertainty: the effect of neoliberal restructuring in South Asia. Macro-scalar changes—the emergence of mega-cities, the reorganization of mass protest as civil speech, and the fossilization of electoral democracy—bring our global icons to epistemological crises, releasing them as volatile signifiers.

These "conditions," the changing rules of the game, bring us back to the human agency expressed in the embodied veneration of volatile icons. If the body is constantly taking form or becoming, its dynamism occurs in historical situations that actualize its field of emergence. The rules of a field of emergence, Brian Massumi (2002, 73) suggests in an evocative visualization of a ballgame, produce conditions; the rules structure the play, but not completely, for the romance with the ball as the catalyst for movement is limitless. We can conceptualize the movement of players as potential pathways that can be re-territorialized, redirected into calculable goals (Massumi 2002, 9). Massumi's "game" frames the operation of affect in the field of social relations. If we conceptualize macro-scalar change as a sudden shift in the rules governing play, then these conditions of uncertainty can catalyze the pursuit of new pathways, directions, and connections. Culturally familiar icons, mundane mass-mediated signs readily accessible in the quotidian media environment, can become the cultural mechanisms for channelizing new redirected desires, since these are distinctively sensuous forms. Their corporeal dynamism harnesses the agency of the body, a privileged site where the subject lives its networked materiality. In this line of thinking, even when harnessed to calculable goals the body retains an open-ended sociality, a surplus "living in common" that is never fully captured.

Throughout part 2, "Biographs," I argued that the sensuous icon incorporates the body of the historical actor who struggles against hegemonic institutions. The consequent event of becoming icon discloses a producing, laboring, attending body as the field of power. As a source of both critique and capture, as feminist materialism has taught us, such a pre-individual body—a body constantly interacting with what appears as Other in its field of emergence—expresses its force through the magical capacities of icons.[2] In other words, the potentiality of the icon includes the potentialities of the subject-become-icon. Human agency (the underlying concern of Marxist feminist materialism) vested in the body effects historical change through the processes of becoming social explored in the next chapter. The icon provides a ready technology, in its intensification of sensations, for such expression. When the sensations released by the icon cannot be bound to one common goal, but instead remain disruptive to the hegemonic capture of the icon, we witness the volatile icon, the catalyst for change. In its shadow, we intuit the magical agency of embodied veneration. We move from capacity back to potentiality *qua* potentiality, a living in common that is the popular.[3] Such "living" requires embodied knowledge beyond the rational cognition of goals and tasks, activated in encounters with icons as sensuous media. Toward the close of the chapter, I return to the significance of this corporeal potentiality in our bio-political modernity.

THE COLLECTIVE SUBJECT

As magical technologies of the popular, volatile icons are necessarily anti-establishmentarian. Their significance will not stabilize; they cannot represent only one aspiration. But they remain open to capture, as we see everywhere in the locations on which we alight in this chapter. Hegemonic religious social elites, for one, can quickly mobilize unmoored political affect or aspiration generated in practices of popular consumption; we see this most clearly in the rise of religious nationalism in South Asia mobilized through mass demonstrations, religious gatherings, training in politics in mosques, and spectacular *rath yatras* (mass pilgrimages). These function as associational practices for those who historically have been outside the domain of civil society but who have a stake in state power. In the case of Hindu right-wing organizing in India in the late 1980s and early 1990s, several scholars have investigated how cheap technologies (audiocassettes, pamphlets, calendar art) with limited circulation and mass-media networks (airing television shows such as *The Ramayana* [see Mankekar 1999]) constituted religious publics who articulated themselves as a hegemonic collective "we" in a carefully calculated move to exclude lower-caste Hindus, Muslims, and other religious minorities. Much like the Indian People's Theatre Association at the other end of the political spectrum, who deployed local cultural forms such as *jatra* in Bengal, *tamasha* in Maharashtra, and *burrakatha* in Andhra Pradesh to mobilize support for a Marxist future, the Rashtriya Swayamsevak Samiti, the parent body of the Hindu right, also harnessed local social and cultural rituals to garner consensus for a Hindu India (Bhandari 2006, 10). Public culture was where the war over signs—Husain's paintings of Hindu goddesses, Shilpa Shetty's being kissed by Richard Gere—emerged in orchestrated media spectacles that attempted to harness nascent political aspiration. In fact, the secular intelligentsia's alienation from popular religiosity, its privileging of secular over devotional reason (as Kajri Jain

[2007] has amply shown), led to their stupefied response to the rise of a militant Hindu political movement. And auratic icons—the virile Ram, the valorous Shivaji, the learned Vivekanada—became the apertures through which the social demand for a Hindu nation was placed. No wonder icons became embattled signs in the culture wars of the period.

While volatile icons are easily re-territorialized, they can also open viewers into a liquid social that is not yet territorialized. In this regard, they are potentialities, unstable in their promise. In these situations, the volatile signifier yokes aspirations of "a people" to come, a phantasmic projection that recalls Laclau's important differentiations of this term. The "people," Laclau (2005) explains, is, after all, a hegemonic signifier that seeks to embody a totality; it produces a horizon for the community whose totality demands representation. This may be a "nation" as the imagined community, a distinct "people" against whom others must be differentiated. Those who do not belong are crucial ex-corporated objects for such hegemonic articulations of the people. In the case of the popular, however, the "people" are perceived to be *less than the totality* of a community. Therefore, populism is the surrender of particularity to expanding equivalences among social demands. But such surrender can take various paths, giving rise to the hegemonic and the popular. Sometimes we see the rise of the popular in search of hegemony, possibly seeking institution in a state. One social element can borrow the "people," now a fungible commodity, to assemble all differences into its field. We see this happen when the Hindu right expands its legitimacy by harnessing all social demands into an equivalential logic. Such populism in pursuit of hegemony (especially with the Hindu right's call for a Hindu Raj) will often introduce a necessary rupture in the equivalential logic at some point. In this instance, the Muslim emerges as the Other, the ex-corporated object internal to the national community. Potent Hindu icons facilitate such a fracture in "the people" the secular nation once took as the subject of history.

But this populism that seeks rupture is not the populism of ever expanding equivalences, where there is a sense of something that exceeds all social demands. Both hegemonic and popular articulations mobilize a name. Empty, vague, imprecise, it is a placeholder for the social. In the case of hegemonic populism that has found institution in politics, such a name bears the burden of representing all social totality. It closes the gap, the impossibility of social totality, through a phantasmic object. There is no "us" and "them"—just a reified common "all." Such a strain on the name demands strong legitimation—repetition, condensation, and standardization by institutions. By contrast, the name that harnesses a heterogeneous common, the popular *qua* popular, is far more volatile, because heterogeneous significations attach and detach from it. It provokes high affect without the legitimization (of its aura) from institutions, states, or corporations; it seems to be caught in ongoing epistemological crises. The name that cannot speak totality, that is historically limited but forwards a possible social, and that erects an internal frontier of social antagonism between "us" and "them" is a phantasmic placeholder for linking heterogeneous demands. The icon, once territorialized, drifts, adored or desecrated in multiple and contingent performances. Its undisclosed auratic itinerary, the affective intensity it garners, leads the critic to the particular populations or publics who adore or revile it.

Here one enters the thorny subject of collective expressivity. Where do we find it? What are its locations, theoretical and historical? Since we are looking at the articulation of the popular, the public constituted through social communication would be the logical starting point, but there is the rub for populations beyond traditional publics who forge social bonds against hegemonies through volatile icons. Publics and populations are historical designations for the open-ended sociality icons can activate, two very different kinds of collective subject. What frame brings publics (marked as speaking subjects) and populations (marked as objects of study) into contact with each other? Public culture, I have argued, is one capacious frame, but it is time now to impart some depth to heterogeneous inhabitants of this domain. If we begin with publics, the brilliant exegesis in Michael Warner's *Publics and Counterpublics* (2002) offers a way into the conversation. A "public" is a relation between strangers, Warner argues, a fiction that takes on real life. But this is hardly just an expansive dialogue among strangers. Publics are autolelic, in Warner's view, and membership is always negotiable, never guaranteed. Moving away from the positivity of an identifiable sum of people, Warner insists on the public "we" as a special imaginary reference that comes into being at the moment of enunciation in a given rhetorical context: "Publics do not exist apart from the discourse that addresses them" (Warner 2002, 72). Such a conception is particularly valuable to considering how different publics claim and disclaim embattled icons, especially in their global forms. Clashes over speech acts often arise from serious misunderstandings of discursive rules from a rhetorical context that are unknown in other public spheres where the act makes an appearance. We know this from the many reflections on affair surrounding Salman Rusdie's *The Satanic Verses*, whose spectral presence we witnessed in the controversies over cartoons in Denmark in 2006.[4] In controversies over our global icons, we witness the clash of multiple and competing publics—non-bourgeois counter-publics that include national publics; elite women's publics; working-class publics; and now, increasingly, Islamic, Hindu, Christian, and other religiously constituted publics.

One might consider the reading constituencies proficient in particular Indian languages as local (Bengali-language readers in Kolkata or Dhaka; cities with small-press publishing in Bengali) or translocal (Bengali-language readers in Kolkata, Dhaka, and London; cities yoked together through the distribution infrastructures of Bengali print media) reading publics who sometimes position themselves as counter-publics against English-language readers. Arvind Rajagopal's (2001) investigation of differences between Hindi- and English-language news media on a single event has effectively demonstrated how "structured misunderstandings" emerge in their awareness of each other. Counter-publics are often constituted in opposition to a larger public as a point of reference; counter-publics often have their own creative idioms that are markedly different from the larger public to which they refer. Even when we do not have a reflexive articulation as a counter-public, the notion invites us to carefully consider idiomatic differences between different publics in consuming global icons. For example, even if we limit ourselves to one localized site of consumption—print media consumed in Kolkata—we see that significant differences emerge in Bengali- and English-language reflections on Mother Teresa's value. While the English-language biographies—Navin Chawla's authorized and reasoned *Mother Teresa* (2002) or Aroup Chatterjee's polemical *Mother Teresa: The Final Verdict* (2002) —participate in a well-modulated debate over the value of Mother Teresa's life, the Bengali-language biographies are idiomatically hagiographic. Within these small-press Bengali-language hagiographies with limited circulation, Mother Teresa is a highly auratic object who is impossible to rationalize but always revered.

One such worshipful text,[5] the cheaply produced Bengali-language hagiography *Biswajanani Mother Teresa* (Mother of the World, Mother Teresa [Kumar 1997]), for example, positions Mother Teresa as a "foreign" woman who, like Sister Nivedita, the Scottish devotee of the widely revered nineteenth-century Bengali mystic Ramakrishna,[6] and Sri Sri Ma at Pondicherry, a mixed-race French citizen who joined the Hindu religious leader Sri Aurobindo's order, became "our" mother in Kolkata. A familiar dyad of the male political subject and Mother India looms over these declarations, with Kumar re-territorializing Mother Teresa by placing her within an iconographic compass of Hinduized maternal religious leaders known for their revolutionary or anomalous charge. Yet beyond the preface, the life story fades into highly adulatory, dreamlike prose, evoking sensations and erecting an image of veneration for local readers in Kolkata who are able to lay their hands on the limited number of copies of the slim volume. And this is not an anomaly. Such Bengali-language hagiographies of the saint routinely appear, remaining in circulation for only two or three years.[7]

Global icons with contested global forms (such as Mother Teresa) are made by multiple and competing publics. Such publics contribute to lively public culture in which participation in consumption involves sharing social imaginaries. But it would be limiting indeed to consider the social efficacy of these icons primarily through their "publics," for the conversation on publics has long noted the privilege implicit in articulating a "we." To read a book, to see a play, to know a popular song, to possess calendar art may express a will to collectivity, only this is easier for bourgeois elites with access to media, who can effectively engage in the abstraction of a disembodied "we." The musical documentary "We Roy," for instance, reflexively works toward consolidating a transnationally networked "society" that links users in the wired world (accustomed to the luxuries of personal computing) to the disenfranchised against whom states and corporations wage wars. In the political message of the documentary—knowledge is a weapon—the public is abstracted into a countervailing force that is civil society. Yet even those imbricated in transnational activist networks have emphasized the difficulties of forging such a "global civil society." Neera Chandhoke (2002), for instance, catalogued some of the debates around the neoliberal moral vision promulgated by certain groups based in the global North that contest the notion of a global civil society. By 1995, when 35,000 actors (NGOs, advocacy groups, social organizations of all colors) descended on Beijing for the Fourth World Conference on Women, the fault lines between North and South on the question of a global civil society had already increased (Chandhoke 2002). Such accounts warn against universalizing paradigms that appear to work for all, the drive toward social totality formalized through icons in their global form.

"We," then, is to be approached with trepidation, as several theorists of civil society have taken pains to emphasize. In his elaboration of civil society, Geoffrey Eley (2002) notes, while the public sphere is always an arena of contestation where opposing publics maneuver for space, civil society emerges as the gradual abstraction; in civil society, publics become the formal counterpart to the state. Here, in the process of abstraction, again we are reminded of Anna Tsing's warnings against universal dreams and schemes that do not benefit all (Tsing 2004). Like Michael Warner and Nancy Fraser, among others, Eley remains attentive to the restricted membership of this domain, which is largely perceived as the institutional vehicle for transforming political domination.[8] Congeries of voluntary associations that make up civil society historically have extended limited membership to mostly bourgeois men who participated in public talk as full citizens or would-be citizens; a vast number of groups were left out of this equation in the European examples that Eley pursues.[9] What Eley identifies in the European example is calibrated slightly differently in Partha Chatterjee's seminal conception of "political society" as the logical "outside" to the narrow reach of civil society in the post-colonies (Chatterjee 2002).

With the emergence of nation, in Chatterjee's view, there is the concomitant development of a realm of social activity that we can name a public sphere; this realm evolves into the "modern associational forms based on equality, autonomy, freedom of exit and entry, contract, deliberative procedures of decision-making, recognition of rights and duties" we think of as civil society (Chatterjee 2002, 165). But participation in these forms is restricted to a small section of citizens, a mark of non-Western modernity in which the bourgeoisie and landed elites engage in a pedagogical mission of making a modern liberal democracy. Outside the fold lie the "rest," often described as "populations," who nevertheless have a will to political power. They express this will, they aspire through a series of strategic maneuvers and negotiations that exert popular demands on the state, creating a domain of temporary institutions and activities (political parties, movements, non-party formations) that Chatterjee characterizes as a "political society." We see this in those pavement dwellers who live under the protection of the local saint; we see this in those Dalit mourners who express their grief in outpourings of violence.

These conversations about political societies direct us to those who might not necessarily articulate a reflexive "we"—actors central to the potentiality of the icon to be an agent of social change. Populations often mobilize in violation of the law, as we see in the case of the social demands rickshaw pullers or squatter organizations in Kolkata place on state (Chatterjee 2002, 177), often through their actions ("committing nuisance," the polite term for urinating in public, or refusing to remove temporary pavement shops) registering as recalcitrance to civility in mass media. The horizon of popular politics remains vibrant in this expanded sense of the public, which Warner (2002, 62–63) marks as "active participation rather than ascriptive belonging." Indeed, a common term for populations who inhabit public space in India is the *"am janata,"* understood as avowedly non-elite "regular folk." Of course, Laclau's entire project in *On Populist Reason* claims political legitimacy for these masses who express their demands as the popular. Laclau notes that, while crowds intimate the dissolution of the differentiation proper to the rational organization of society, the popular stems from differentiations held together in a chain of equivalences at contingent moments through signifying practice. When those bonds become expressive as specific ones on multiple platforms we have the emergence of popular politics. The expanded notion of public culture—a zone of contestation—in Appadurai and Breckenridge (1995) accommodates the possibility of such social and political aspiration. No wonder they claim public culture to be an ally of subaltern studies, particularly since subaltern cultures combat hegemony through the use of signs ("code-switching" mechanisms, in Ranajit Guha's [1983] terms).[10]

But such observations are best borne out now with a focused look at who the historical actors haunting this book really are. When do they erupt in mass media? How are we to read their actions as articulations of "common" aspiration? In their historical lineaments, we see a complex public culture, an interlocking of publics and populations who consume icons.

SCENES OF THE POPULAR

In Phoolan Devi we see a volatile icon with auratic charge among Dalits (and other heterogeneous, politically disenfranchised populations), who might not belong to her Samajwadi Party. If we advance Guha's optic to read the events motivated by her death, to most they would seem isolated, causally unrelated outbreaks of violence and grief that erupted between her murder and the last rites. On the day of her assassination, sporadic violence erupted all over Delhi as anonymous "crowds" disrupted traffic, smashed police windshields, and overturned cars even as political parties in opposition to the BJP-led government turned tragedy into media spectacle (figure 33).[11]

Nor were her last rites easily completed. Against her mother's wishes, the Samajwadi Party flew Phoolan Devi's body to Mirzapur, the town in Uttar Pradesh where she won her electoral seat, for cremation on July 26, 2001. To a certain degree, the pitched personal battles over who "owned" her last rites entered a collective arena as virtuoso political theater. Her

FIGURE 33 Protests after Phoolan Devi's assassination, 2001.
AP Photo / John McConnico.

coffin was carried by Mulayam Singh Yadav in a canny pitch for credit in
the next elections, while other politicians lined up to pay homage. As a
commemorative gesture, the Samajwadi Party organized a spontaneous
twelve-hour *bandh* (general strike), hoping to cash in the Phoolan Devi
dividend with their MBC voters. Not only did Phoolan Devi come from the
MBC caste stratum (the impoverished Mallahs) but, they argued, she had
supported the MBC agitation for special reservations. But such orchestrated rituals were disrupted by sporadic bursts of violence and protests
in Varanasi, Mirzapur, and Bhadoi (one dead and twenty-seven injured)
against no particular enemy ("Phoolan Supporters Come to Blows" 2001).
Motley marauding crowds attacked the police, the BJP headquarters, and
the railways, creating traffic snarls, road blockages, and train delays.
Police jeeps, a power substation, and a police outpost were burned. These

outbursts were reported in a scattered manner through the days following Phoolan Devi's death and funeral; no one connected any of the incidents, and no one asked why this death might provoke such intensity.
With a cynicism that comes from watching quotidian political antics, the
Mirzapur episodes—and several other, seemingly unrelated outbreaks of
violence over either the police handling of the case or the cremation—
were summarily dismissed in the press, with some commentators offering weak readings of collective loss.[12]

But if we were to gather together all of these unreasonable and excessive incidents, we might understand them as political affect. These were
not party henchmen on a lark for a media event, and short of a police-log
entry or two on disorderly conduct, their social location (age, gender,
caste or class) cannot be determined. Rather, they signal a heterogeneous
social held together as a popular in their embodied veneration; grief-
stricken, they wreaked havoc on the machinery (a police or power station)
of the state. As in many such cases, such disaffected actors—Prasad's
spectators who live through the stars—often communicate through burning buses, derailing trains, attacking policemen. From this history, we can
assume that many of the actors who led the incidents were not middle
class, and they probably did not have access to lines of civil communication.[13] In this case, Phoolan Devi's death proved the catalyst, indicating
her powerful presence as volatile icon. While such actions do not bring
about large-scale social transformations, they indicate the everyday work
of icons as technologies for the expression of discontentment against the
hegemon—here, embodied in the state. After all, before her election to
Parliament, Phoolan Devi was legendary for outwitting the law. As early
as 1981, a reporter had recounted how Phoolan Devi, the subject of
conversation in tea stalls and streetside restaurants, was often "spotted"
in the neighborhood, just before—always before—the incompetent police
arrived ("The Day of Reckoning" 1981, 32). The same writer, fascinated
by the rural lore of the bandit queen, recalled how locals laughed at the
police closing down a movie theater in Lucknow where the bandit queen
was purported to have been watching Sholay.

Such auratic purchase has proved handy for more cynical use. Most
notably, Seema Parihar has adroitly manipulated Phoolan Devi's public
image to legitimize her request for bail. Recent reports on the Chambal
relate a spike in female dacoits, many of whom either lead their own gangs
or act as financial managers of other gangs; one disgruntled former dacoit,
cooling his heels in the Tihar jail, grumbles that these new dacoits all want
to become Phoolan Devi.[14] Parihar is therefore hardly an exception (unlike

Phoolan Devi), but she, above all others, has most been most savvy in harnessing Phoolan Devi's auratic force among Dalit supporters. The famous iconic photograph of Phoolan Devi (see figure 1) most recently accompanied a news item recounting the stardom of this other "bandit queen," who agreed to stand for elections from the very same Mirzapur parliamentary seat that Phoolan Devi had occupied.[15] Despite her protests against comparisons to Phoolan Devi, Parihar drew heavily on Phoolan Devi's electoral base, strengthened as it was by a sense of lost aspiration at Phoolan Devi's tragic death. Phoolan Devi's capacity to aspire was Parihar's windfall. We see once more the persistence of an objective correlative in the world of governance, actualizing the prototypical outlaw who would effectively commandeer state resources to her advantage. The Indian Justice Party, which hosted Parihar as a candidate against the only other famous Dalit female leader—Mayawati of the Bahujan Samaj Party, who once served as chief minister of Uttar Pradesh—gauged Phoolan Devi's capacity to channel aspirations quite correctly when it strenuously marked the similarities between the lives of the two figures with great deliberation. Like Phoolan Devi, Parihar, ran the party's publicized "life story," came from the Chambal; like Phoolan Devi, she was abducted at thirteen and joined the life of crime as a last resort. No wonder the mantle of the bandit queen fit Parihar well, the originary exemplary iconic image sanctioning her surrender with twenty-nine cases pending against her.

Most important, Parihar turned to film to make her case before the public, quickly accepting Krishna Mishra's offer to make a "realistic" biopic in which she would star as herself.[16] The move to a faux realism— the use of non-actors and the actual settings where the story takes place —was no doubt a well-planned strategy to spark public interest, if only to compare Mishra's revisionist bandit queen to the one in Kapur's melodrama. Mishra's chief ambition was to make a film not to sensationalize the life of a Chambal dacoit but to reveal it in its fragility and violent despair. Parihar, too, contested the iconic message of Kapur's portrait— the bandit queen as a wronged woman whose life, actions, and beliefs were largely motivated by originary sexual violence—agreeing to make the film only if it would repudiate the earlier text. She would not appear as a victim and certainly not in the nude, Parihar insisted, reiterating the common misrecognition of the Kapur text and recoiling in studied horror at what has been "done" to Phoolan Devi in mass media. "Usme Phoolan Deviko nanga dikhaya" (They showed her nude [my translation]), exclaimed the next-generation bandit queen, marking her distance from the iconic figure whose auratic value gave her the political credence to roam free on bail. Predictably, like Kapur's *The Bandit Queen*, Mishra's film about Parihar, *Wounded* (2007), languished for a year as the Indian Censor Board debated its ethical value. In the meantime, Parihar, acquitted of fifteen charges but still facing fourteen others, remained on bail. Not only did Mishra pay her bail, but he also took his plea for her release to the Supreme Court, emphasizing public sentiment in which social bandits appeared as wronged heroes who deserved clemency. Nor was this an isolated appeal. *Pakkad*, starring Kusuma Nain, was already planned as the second film in Mishra's trilogy on contemporary bandits. The mixing of cinema with politics in the case of Seema Parihar proves Prasad's hypothesis of a realm of cine-politics, where political imaginings outside the regular business of the state remain vibrant. In this sense, Phoolan Devi's purchase reaches beyond the specific MBC communities who claim her to the heterogeneous politically disenfranchised for whom she remains the eternal outlaw. When we combine the events that followed Phoolan Devi's funeral with these continuing legacies, we see the ongoing potentiality of the iconic image as a technology of the popular.

A similar continuity of aspiration is evident among devotional constituencies for Mother Teresa in incidents reported in mass media as isolated curiosities. Occasionally, when the Little Sisters of the Poor come under scrutiny, reporters reflect on Mother Teresa's legacy among the city's famous indigent. Unlike Phoolan Devi's devotees, who are marked by lower-caste and lower-class social disenfranchisement, Mother Teresa's adorers more often than not are patently economically impoverished. After Mother Teresa's death, Rupali Ghosh (1999) remarked that her "life divine" continued to inspire the poor. Her illustration comes in the guise of an indigent mother, Ameenabai, who had brought her four daughters to pay respects to "Ma Teresa" on a day Ghosh visited the Mother House on Lower Circular Road in Kolkata (Ghosh 1999, 1). The force of Ghosh's commentary reaches toward proving that Mother Teresa still exists as auratic object, and across boundaries of religion, for although the carefully chosen Ameenabai is Muslim, she still regards the missionary as a mother,[17] still partakes in the embodied veneration of the icon. More telling is Ghosh's juxtapositioning of Ameenabai's adoring gaze with the commoditizing one of a group of an economically plush, laughing, photosnapping Koreans who dotted the courtyard the same morning.

One could multiply such reports that still trickle in. They can be read as traces of popular veneration when we link them to a media event, Mother Teresa's funeral, a dreary day when the indigent turned out in force to mourn their saint. The frontispiece to this section, part 3, captures the crowds pushing forward for a glimpse of nun as the funeral cortège made its stately way through the city. Funerals as social rituals are well covered in mass media, so they are meaty events for traces of expressive veneration—especially veneration from those who are not easily visible as publics that engage in debates over the heterogeneous image, those with little media access, those whose social communication "reads," as Guha argues, as disruptive. By most accounts, the crowds would interrupt the decorum of the staged procession.

We know that the funeral was a resplendent affair. Once the cortège wound its way into the huge Netaji Indoor Stadium, the re-territorializing rituals began: wreaths laid for forty-five minutes by dignitaries who ranged from Bill Clinton to General Suharto; goose-stepping military guards carrying wreaths of white flowers; sumptuous red drapery; the ceremonial swish of saffron, white, and green of the Indian tricolor; the somber speech by Cardinal Angelo Soldano, the Vatican's secretary of state, once more celebrating the nun's commitment to "the defenseless unborn"; Sister Nirmala's thanks for the state funeral, which Mother Teresa would have only accepted in the name of the poor; eulogies from religious leaders of other faiths; and the arrival of Jyoti Basu, then chief minister of West Bengal, who entered after the religious ceremony to claim Mother Teresa for a secular polity.

Reports on the formal spectacle only heighten the force of uncontained popular mourning whose traces we find in desultory and sporadic accounts of "incidents" that took place as Mother Teresa's body lay in state at St. Thomas Church. Together, the isolated fragments present a cogent picture of those who felt barred from mourning their beloved "mother." One account recalled a motley crew surging toward the body during the funeral march shouting, "Mother is ours; We will not harm her" (quoted in "Tears Mingle with Pain" 1997). Another correspondent ran a piece titled "Mother's People Find No Place in Funeral March," which was critical of the sidelining of the "masses" in the pomp of mourning.[18] A third reported a huge crowd all over the city, some walking for hours to get to the streets where the carriage was to pass. A beggar following the cortège scrawled a message of love on his face; a coterie of young Muslim boys held up handmade postcards that read, "Long Live the Goddess of Humanity, Mother Teresa." Other mourners hurried off sidewalks and crowded public transportation clutching hastily assembled bouquets and garlands. Journalists attentive to these heterogeneous Others underscored the indeterminacy of the crowd, often emphasizing mourners from all religions. "She was a poor man's God. She gave them clothes, food, medicines," said one report on

Mohammed Wasim, a Muslim tailor (Cooper 1997). Another reporter described a Muslim man following the cortège with blue and white strips painted on his face as a curiosity, and several others highlighted Hindus bringing white (the color of mourning) wreaths to St. Thomas Church. But most often, mass-media coverage focused on the poor.[19] Sometimes they were visible in their disregard for rules, sneaking past the police to view the body lying in state after the 7 p.m. curfew; such "behavior" would lead one senior priest to wonder whether "they" might turn violent ("People Sneak Past Police" 1997). Sometimes they were marked by awkward expressions of desire: "The uncared for and the unwanted stood huddled together at the street corner leading to the St. Thomas Church not knowing how to pay their respects to Mother Teresa who gave them a reason to live for," ran one sentimental story, going on to surmise perhaps this crowd feared disrespect toward the "well-dressed sahibs" ("When the Rich and Poor United" 1997).

As the cortège wound its way to the stadium gates, the febrile crowds refused the elaborate choreography of the media spectacle,[20] their affective intensity intimating the presence of a volatile icon. But if the spectacle is not, as the performance theorist Diana Taylor reminds us, following Guy Debord, simply a "collection of images" but "a social relation among people mediated by images,"[21] then we can assume that the officially estimated crowd of 150,000 were held together as a popular for the moment when they glimpsed the decomposing, eighty-seven-year-old flesh in the carriage. This collective mourning was quite distinct from the dignitary-filled televised service that beamed the famous global face of charity to transnational audiences.[22] These traces give us a fair idea of a large number of the city's economically indigent who mourned the saint, claiming her as their own. They also relate practices of embodied veneration—the touching of the body, the surging crowd, the press against the carriage, the physical exertions of walking miles to pay one's last respects —that could not be contained by the spectacular event intended to produce a decorous, reflective mourner, the bourgeois subject of colonial modernity. Here we see the manifest corporeality of the crowd as it flows toward and into the icon, evidence of the shared potentiality of subject and object I present throughout the book.

If the subaltern/outlaw exerts a regulative logic against the state, the saint embodies the logic of giving. I argue that the populations whose traces we have witnessed so far forge their bonds against political and financial institutions in their embodied veneration of these two highly auratic volatile icons. What we witness in the popular mourning of Phoolan Devi and Mother Teresa directs us to other such appearances in mass media if we follow the temporal logic of the popular. Mother Teresa's mourners are continuous with Ameenabai; Phoolan Devi's, with those would continue to recount the lore of the defiant outlaw. But it is much more challenging to consider the articulation of the popular through an icon who has never inspired social disruption, never set in motion collective action. Arundhati Roy, whose heterogeneous image is consumed by transnational publics, therefore presents a rather different kind of popular from Phoolan Devi and Mother Teresa. But this is precisely why she is important to this book, which seeks to extend the geo-physically bound locations of the popular.

If the main critique of Roy's alliance with the Narmada Bachao Andolan (NBA) has been that she does not seem to be deeply immersed in that struggle alone, that her targets are diffuse, that her facts merge into fiction, then one might be tempted to ask what social to come, if any, Roy harnesses in her auratic appeal to transnational audiences. Certainly, she is not as volatile as Phoolan Devi; she does not provoke the burning of buses or the smashing of windshields. But she does seem to act as catalyst for transnational collaborations on environmental advocacy, among other initiatives such as antiwar/peace mobilization. We may think of Roy's collaborators as translocal publics in the sense that they seek to intervene in particular, often discrete, local struggles—that is, when they raise funds, lobby governments or institutions, and archive conflicts or abuses for a specific struggle, they become local collaborators acting through her image widely available in transnational networks. In some of the artworks on Roy, we see such aspiration for a world to come—our world that will undo the existing one we inhabit. "Translocal" signals reflexivity about local engagement, a situated activism rather than action taken on the behalf of transnational organizations or network cultures. Roy's social efficacy lies in how her iconic image is often the corporeal aperture through which transnational publics localize their actions to express solidarity with those situated in specific affected sites. To be incorporated into the banks of the Narmada through Roy's manifest corporeality (after all, she is one of the most photographed icons of the NBA) is to form contingent linkages that are not inclusive of all social totality. And through this image, the sensations released by the lustrous icon would be reorganized into affections directed toward those who do not "speak," the "populations" surrounding Roy in innumerable photographs. Together, articulate public and silent populations would become anonymous crowd, transporting transnational (often bourgeois) publics into a liquid social peopled by unfamiliar others who stretch beyond the frame. As activist, the icon would express its agency as her own quality—her excellence as a political actor who reaches beyond the sanctions of civil action.

This is a process that worries Roy, who is deeply cognizant of the power of her own celebrity. With the publication of *The God of Small Things*, a highly literary, self-reflexive intervention that foregrounds the social other of the Indian bourgeoisie—the low-caste, aspiring Dalit subject Velutha[23]—Roy was quickly territorialized after she won the Booker Prize as the "face" of globalizing India: the articulate, educated, and successful professional. Troubled, she turned to nonfiction to contest her star image as the glamorous "multicultural" or "postcolonial" writer par exemplar, refusing the luxuries of "subtlety, ambiguity, complexity" to ask "in ordinary language, the public question and to demand, in ordinary language, the public answer" (Roy 2002a, 24). Hence, she would repurpose her public image to highlight those subalterns whose "voice" she had become in her commoditization. For instance, in 2005 Roy dramatically turned down India's prestigious Sahitya Akademi Award (for *The Algebra of Infinite Justice* [2002b], a collection of essays written between 1998 and 2001) in a well-publicized media event. Even though the award came from an autonomous body sympathetic to Roy's political platforms, the Sahitya Akademi sought to recognize Roy as a litterateur, sanctioning her nonfiction through technologies of recognition, just as the Booker Prize had anointed *The God of Small Things*.[24] But Roy refused such official legitimization, using the glare of publicity to make a symbolic gesture of protest against the Indian government's policies of targeting the disenfranchised:

> In the last few months, apart from the growing numbers of farmers' suicides (now running into tens of thousands) and the forcible eviction of people from their lands and livelihoods (in the hundreds of thousands), we have witnessed the police brutalization of industrial workers in Gurgaon, the killing of a dozen people protesting against a dam in Manipur, and the killing of another dozen people protesting their displacement by a steel plant in Orissa. Even as we call ourselves a democracy, Indian security forces control and administer Kashmir, Manipur and Nagaland—and the numbers of the dead and disappeared continue to mount.[25]

Such enumeration is typical of Roy's strategy, which turns multiple corporealized bodies palpable, immediate, and intimate for the transnational audiences who religiously follow her untiring lecture circuit in the global North, on television and radio, in print, and over the Internet as the chronicler of local struggles.

In time, such image manipulation on Roy's part would affect the social efficacy of her public image. Mass-media institutions increasingly would photograph her "in a crowd," responding to her performance as activist, the singular iconic image always harnessed to its social others. Obviously, this does not mean that Roy occupies the structural location of those who encounter the violence of techno-scientific development (manifest in the building of dams for the NBA, car plants in Singur, or steel plants in Orissa). But her reconstitution as activist has indeed changed the efficacy of her public image, now a technology for articulating translocal solidarity. When we catalogue the many photographic captures of Roy since she burst on the scene in 1997, her emergence as an activist is often visually signaled by framing her within a crowd. Shortly after Roy entered her alliance with the NBA, a genre of photographs in digital and print news media showed her always in relief against the backdrop of a crowd that exceeded the photograph's frame. Though still the body that counts, Roy is visually linked to actors with little or no press exposure; though the photographs zoom in on Roy, they inevitably render the "crowd" meaningful by hitching the indistinguishable many to a familiar, recognizable, and symbolically loaded star body.

Figure 34 is a still from Aradhana Seth's *DAM/Age: A Film with Arundhati Roy* (2002). Roy is the star in the center, a participant in a rally against the Narmada River Valley project; others in the struggle recede into the depth of the photograph. By contrast, a shot of Roy taken by Hari Katragadda (figure 35) at another rally for the same movement and posted on the NBA's website focalizes the two icons, Medha Patkar (far right) and Roy (left center), along with other activists: Devika Jain (right corner) and Dedlibai, one of the activists affected by the dam (center). We begin to see changes in the carefully arraigned star body; we witness an activist whose body gains auratic charge from its incorporation into a collectivity. The historical actors who constitute such are collectivity are many, as we saw in chapter 3,[26] diverse groups held together in their articulation of specific social demands—here, literally the demand for common resources. Such incorporation of the crowd into the activist icon continued unabated in the photographs that followed, the crowd becoming central to the increasingly minimal traces of Roy. By 2001, in several photographs of the NBA mobilization, Roy had become one among many, sometimes almost cut out of the frame by other activists. Pushed, pressed, obscured, and drowned in the bodies of many, the boundaries of the activ-

FIGURE 34 Still from Aradhana Seth's *DAM/Age*, 2002. Aradhana Seth.

FIGURE 35 Arundhati Roy at the "Rally for the Valley," 1999. Photo. Courtesy of Hari Katragadda.

ist's body become permeable; the potentiality of the crowd staked its claim, even in a mass media obsessed with individuated celebrity. The *dupatta* (or scarf) slips off the shoulder; the face is not angled for a photo shoot. The star's romance with the camera is over.

This corporeal assemblage invites transnational publics to become virtual translocal crowds, yoking their social demands for environmental justice with other, often diverse, demands in discrete locales through the technology of the global icon. Obviously, this is a very differently situated icon from the low-caste, violated Phoolan Devi. Roy is a bourgeois subject who mobilizes like-minded transnational publics in contingent political collaborations. The oral legends, lore, songs, and tales of the Narmada, for instance, do not collect in sites where Roy is consumed as icon—even when she is a highly auratic figure. Rather, the visual image of her star body effectively renders the unfamiliar disenfranchised as legible subjects, opening transnational consumers into a highly mass-mediated social, but, because of the heterogeneity of actors who descended on that locale (especially in the case of mobilizations of the NBA), the photographs orient viewers toward a liquid social that is unrepresentable as a totality. Through the corporeal aperture, transnational publics, the imaginary "we" harnessed by the icon, move toward undisclosed others defined by their location of social action (on the banks of the river, on the streets of Mumbai, outside the Supreme Court). The image forges a transnational social bond. Here, subaltern "speech" (expressed in anger or grief) jostles the public image of the icon shot by famous photographers.[27]

In these traces of the collective subject we see the surge of common aspirations beyond the obvious re-territorializing imperatives that engage with universal dreams and schemes through the star image. Some of these arise from social networks we call publics; some emerge as disruptive forces at work in less visible, more fraught ways. Without idealizing the aberrant or the supplementary, my effort in the next chapter is to comprehend what appears as illogical, affective, or violent as a logical challenge to hegemonic ideologies (e.g., selling democracy or consumerism). That is, if the body's open-ended sociality also has logic (and Massumi encourages us to think of the *logic* of affect), how do we characterize it? I return to these logics, to a populist reason sometimes seeking institution as politics, in the next chapter

But here I conclude with the question of potentiality with which we began: the potentiality of the anonymous crowd manifest in the corporeality of the historical actors assembled here. Certainly, in these "becomings" reviewed as historical events, I have suggested that we look beyond epistemological crises to the underlying dynamism signification curtails. The body of the unmannerly crowd, where actors materialize as undifferentiated and sometimes threatening, illuminates the corporeal dynamism I proposed earlier as sheer potentiality.

CORPOREAL POTENTIALITY

All three bio-icons, incorporating the crowd into their image—mourned in Kolkata, rousing passion in northern India, laboring for a commons on the banks of the Narmada—are immensely corporeal in their historical manifestations as socially shared cultural figurations of the saint, outlaw, and activist. Within the sensation-provoking accounts gathered here, we witness the embodied veneration of highly corporeal icons. These traces in mass-media archives remind us that these bio-icons have always been subject to biopolitical capture. If in the oversexed female outlaw we find extreme pathologization of manifest corporeality, in the saint, sanctioned by global institutions, we find corporeality actualized as a movement toward the divine. Given these variations, these corporeal traces are worth a closer look if we are to pursue the historical potentiality of these bio-icons.

Since the outlaw provokes the law, she is subject to bio-political capture by the state as all *homo sacer* are. In the Indian case, feminist theorists such as Rajeswari Sunder Rajan (2004) and Nivedita Menon (2000) have underscored sexual difference as one important marker of disposability. Explaining the "hysterectomies scandal" of 1994, in which eleven female inmates in a home for the mentally ill at Shirur had their wombs removed at Sassoon General Hospital (in the nearby city of Pune), Sunder Rajan criticizes the postcolonial state's propensity to abandon women or to banish them to a state of exception to the law. The mentally challenged appear as exceptional cases, not yet adults, and therefore "a category of political beings who do not have full equivalence to citizenship" (Sunder Rajan 2004, 80). These thanatopolitics of the Indian state exemplified in the hysterectomies scandal have particular resonance for Phoolan Devi, since the bandit queen once occupied exactly such a liminal position as those sexed subjects of biopolitical capture whose sexuality and reproductive capacities were brought under the authority of the state. During her tenure at the Gwalior jail, Phoolan Devi's womb was removed without her consent while doctors operated on a bleeding cyst. One doctor's nonchalant remark pithily summarized the horrifying power of the state over

this bare life: "We don't want Phoolan Devi breeding more Phoolan Devis
—or Phoolan Devi's *son* for that matter" (Sen 1991, 51).[28]

Such biopolitical capture can be attributed in part to Phoolan Devi's
structural position as a subaltern Dalit, the unmarked bodies of Dalit
female subjects bearing the historical inscription of a sexually penetrable
body. "The bodies of women," writes Anupama Rao (1988, 105), are "seen
as collectively mute, and capable of bearing penetration and other modes
of marking upper-caste hegemony without the intervention of a discourse of desire and/or sexuality because of the over-determination of
this violence as caste privilege." When sexual promiscuity or deviance is
attributed to these historical bodies, they become vulnerable to charges of
solicitation in cases of sexual violation. Phoolan Devi provides a paradigmatic instance of this sexually penetrable body, and beyond this specific
historical inscription, one might expand the centrality of corporeality to
anyone who occupies the position of the subaltern. The body remains a
key social hieroglyphic for signaling a subaltern social position via para-
linguistic codes: bodily markings (posture, gesture, insignia, clothing and
headgear), movements in space and time, and nonverbal and visual
signs.[29] Such corporealization would remain central to the image of the
bandit queen throughout her life, so much so that she would habitually
address it, distancing herself from sexualized capture. Thus, toward the
end of her life, Phoolan Devi expressed a desire to "die a *sadhavi*," a saint
who had renounced all pleasure.[30] Perhaps it is this violent cultural, social,
and juridical aggrandizing of the bandit queen's body that provokes an
equally violent corporeal reaction to the bandit queen's mortality if we
remember the events succeeding her death. One may argue, following
Foucault, the most repressive bio-political apparatuses provoke embodied expressions of agency against the state; only a sensory history of the
popular can attend to such embodied acts as anti-hegemonic emergences.

By contrast, the saint's corporeality is often celebrated as sublime.
Corporeality is matter in divine guise, the saint's iconic image evoking the
possibility of material continuity with others. Devotees habitually consume the saint for her continuity with the divine, to paraphrase Bataille
(1949), overcoming their discontinuity through a corporeal exchange.[31]
To venerate a popular saint is to enter a fictive material contiguity with
the divine, a sensation we find in several devotional accounts of Mother
Teresa that are constantly, and quixotically, focused on her corporeal
presence—the emaciated, stooped, tiny form; wrinkled face; clasped
hands or outstretched arms. A moment of visionary encounter, a moment

of communication with the divine, recounted by the Kolkata journalist and art critic Jug Suraiya exemplifies these celebrations in the mass media. At an ekphrastic moment in an interview with Mother Teresa, Suraiya recollects the saint, who was known to give interviews while doing her rounds, stooping to pick up a "huddled figure" who was so "impossibly emaciated" and "covered with sores" that he or she seemed to have no identity at all. But upon Mother Teresa's touch, "it" was revived: "The gaunt skull appeared to clear and shine momentarily with a peace and lucid understanding" (Suraiya 1997). Suraiya's encounter foregrounds the saint's corporeal touch, the passing of substance from the saint's body to the dying man through an energy discharge; in such narration, he unconsciously foregrounds the quintessential corporeality of the saint.[32]

Despite such poetic evocations of the saint's corporeality in organized religious discourse, the saint's popular potentiality erupts in the Raniganj miracle affair in which Mother Teresa's touch acquired the aura widely found in popular saints of lore. Popular practices of saint worship continued to believe that relics—fingers, foreskins, or embryos—were embodiments of saints, the flesh remaining infused with the saint's spirit; hence, the bodies of the saints were considered incorruptible, not subject to ordinary decay. As ample scholarship on popular saints reveals, religious institutions have always sought to contain these excessive attachments to materiality.[33] But in popular lore, the perception of the saint's touch of the divine, restoring ordinary corruptible flesh and healing sickness and wounds alike, remains vibrant. Such a sense of corporeality persists in accounts of miracles forged by touch. Monica Besra believed that she was cured by Mother Teresa's incorrupt touch, which was "alive" in the medallion she had given to one of the sisters of her order. Rita Mascharenus, too, depended on Mother Teresa's living touch in a piece of cloth. While critics in mass media dismiss such desires for material contiguity as "superstition," in these corporealized portraits we have evidence of a movement toward the divine and the dissolution of the sovereign territory of the subject.

In both of these instances, corporeality signals the body of the adorer as a field of power. As ever, its force is expressive as a quality *of* the icon, pathologized or celebrated in outlaw and saint. While these two cultural figurations, always deeply corporeal, have long genealogies in popular culture, our last figure, the activist, is a more contemporary corporeal icon whose body incorporates us into risky ventures. The environmental activist in particular, engaged in battles over the biosphere, mirrors the corporeal violence of resource extraction in the political theater of her body; she is most relevant to the new bio-political extraction and accumulation of bio-resources and of planetary space. If our bodies literally ingest the violence perpetrated against air, water, or trees, the activist's situated, and often exemplary, risk-taking actions (hunger strikes, standing in water for hours, hugging trees as they are under the ax) express agency against such planned capital appropriations. Devoid of protection in its staged illegality, nakedly subject to discipline and punishment, the activist's body often stands in danger of experiencing the corporeal violence against which it protests. Sometimes such risk extracts a high price, as in the case of Chico Mendes and Ken Saro-Wiwa, for whom it took a death to grab global attention. Such corporeal politics turns the body of the activist icon into a "soft body" whose boundaries exceed individual boundaries to assemble in its perceptual field the scars of others and the violation of the biosphere.[34] Here we might recall Elizabeth Grosz's (1994, 116) conception of the body's social materiality, its existence as "a series of linkages (or possibly activities) which form superficial or provisional connections with other objects and processes." If we understand Arundhati Roy's audiovisual image in this sense, she appears alongside the saint and outlaw as a highly corporeal object who incorporates her public into material contiguities of planetary space. Her "green" activism draws its auratic charge from a long history of struggle against resource extraction on the subcontinent, best known in Gandhian corporeal idioms of the body deployed against the colonial state. For the contemporary activist in India, these idioms would provide a recognizable vocabulary sanctioned by the historic freedom struggle that forecloses possibilities of violent response to these actions from the state. In times to come, many of these idioms—the sit-in demonstrations, tree hugging, and hunger strike—would enter global vocabularies of protest.[35]

   If activism as struggle meant that the body of the activist was under physical duress, the female body was quixotically poised as both a penetrable body (the "soft body" culturally positioned as needing patriarchal protection) and the symbolic embodiment of generative shakti, or power (a body endowed with rage and endurance). Such corporeality of the female body has become inextricable from women as political actors, as militants and as sataygrahis. The contradictory corporeal significations volatilize the female activist's corporeality, for the female political actor's body is at once invincible (passing into legend) and violable (scorned as weak).[36] Hence, in the popular consumption of Roy, we see contradictory responses to her corporeal actions. On the one hand, she is blamed for her "weak" body, her inability to "suffer" adequately for the causes she espouses (or that are espoused in her name); on the other, her corporeal image located in sites of risky action, incorporating the crowd and the biosphere into its form, expresses aspirations to renegotiate coming changes. By incorporating the present (or future) loss of substance into her body, Roy makes visible the unproductive expenditure of flesh in service of a common.

When the iconic outlaw, saint, and activist are volatilized, we can surmise embattled responses to flesh under threat, either as expropriated labor or as the disposable subject of the sovereign power at hand. A corporeal politics suggests that flesh might also provide the means of folding back the stranglehold on bodies. Theorists of biopolitical modernity intimate that such a politics of flesh enacted in new social movements such as Act Up are indeed revolutionary; the revolution now articulates as a series of dispersed and ongoing struggles against an equally dispersed system of power. Corporeal icons embody such a politics, signaling the force of flesh, at once a target and a field of power. They alert us to challenges posed against universal hegemonic abstractions (science, capitalism, democracy). In their eruptions, we witness "frictions" that recalibrate intensified contemporary global interconnections.

If the volatile icon enables a corporeal politics made possible by embodied veneration, it treads lightly in the mass media. We are alerted to its presence when deep media events erupt, bringing heated words and images in their wake. Among articulate publics, we hear heated debates on the successful "slumdog," the "face of charity," or the "voice of the voiceless," but forms of communication beyond civil speech rarely emerge as the well-told story. Rather, it is left to critical divination in search of populist reason to tell those "other" stories from the life worlds affected by the contemporary restructuring of late capital. We are back to the old question, with a new twist: How do we read the runes of the popular in the mass media? And when we find these runes, how do we narrate them as history? The critical labors of reflexively connecting the sometimes voluminous (when its global form is contested) and sometimes obscure, sporadic, and ephemeral (when it volatizes) traces of the icon throughout this book presents general propositions to scholars of the popular who are not ethnographers. In this chapter, I complete the methodological promises of the opening chapters, recasting the adoration of icons as historical becoming.

To read events stemming from the adoration of volatilized icons as embattled responses to global capital, as it morphs and reorganizes, one must press the question of human agency further. How do we know whether the sporadic outbursts that turn volatile signifiers into social phenomena are not just social aberrations? When do we read them as chapters in the long buildup to social transformation? In other words, we are still left wondering whether collective aspirations expressed through icons can be considered accumulating social demands for large-scale structural changes, even if they are precipitated by a sudden event such as the death of an icon; we still wonder if the controversies that launched our tour of the fabulous biography of our three icons are indeed far-reaching deep historical events, creative in their consequences. One point of entry into these questions is to methodically unpack the social processes of icon veneration as a reasonable pitch for a sociality apposite to that engendered by the neoliberal ethos. I argue that the events of icon adoration we explored in the previous chapter are indeed creative events, for they disclose desires for "living in common," a reconstituted open-ended sociality that does not celebrate personal choice as evidence of human agency at its best. Rather, the logics that underlie these modes of living in common guide us to a populist reason moving against new empires. We find reason in sweat and tears, sociality in the anonymity of the crowd, agency in highly charged acts of adoration and desecration. These are indicators of a prize beyond the concrete demands of compensation for land, for court orders against dam building or closing a factory, for making a home on the pavement. They index a social to come that is unrealized but possible. In such a turn, the potentiality inherent in the body, its futurity, is oriented toward a lived sociality emerging as possibility.

What desire for a change in social relations underlies these concrete agendas? If we follow the argument on human agency I made earlier, we know the bio-icon expresses as her quality the sensations shared between subject and object. For example, if an icon embodies selfless generosity, this quality is an abstraction of a sociality shared between icon and devotee; only, in the labor of worship, the social logic of giving is re-located to the icon. Human agency as sensible (sensory and affective) social relations appears as the magical force of the icon that can inspire great deeds in ordinary persons. The icon's quality signals lived social logics under threat when the rules of the game change. Selfless generosity, for instance, is once more celebrated in the cultural figure of the popular saint, jolting historical habits of vernacular sacrality, when the social logic of the incalculable gift is threatened, when it is confronted by the market rationality of consumer choice. In turn the desires for a rejuvenated sociality materialize into specific initiatives, agendas, and programs. The aim of this chapter is to look closely at these inarticulate desires, "structures of feeling" moving toward new pathways, and to read them as episodes in the push for social change. In the critic's gaze, "reviewable" and "writable" becoming (Massumi 2002, 77) arrives as history; amid the changing conditions of media consumption, something "untimely," to borrow Amit Rai's (2009) phrase, something that will not follow the "progress" sold in neoliberal mantras, unfolds. The corporeal dynamism of the icon as it activates ontological becoming now reveals a story still to be told: the contestations of a single logic of global modernity vibrant in public cultures today.

The exuberance of chaos, expressed in the body of the subject, persists in the unthinkable excellence of the icon. As saint, Mother Teresa embodies endless giving; as outlaw, Phoolan Devi embodies unfettered courage and defiance; and as activist, Arundhati Roy embodies daring, risky action. Here, widely shared cultural figurations, often deployed to standardize these figures, also appear in their anti-institutional guises celebrated in popular lore. One might say they are reactivated to intuit a collective sociality still to be actualized. Is Phoolan Devi the righteous virangana (female hero) or the criminal *daku* (social bandit)? Does Arundhati Roy play safe as satyagrahi (nonviolent protestor)? Is Mother Teresa our sant (saint) or theirs? If we probe the multiple fictions swirling around each bio-icon, we witness the expression of a potentiality against the mantras of personal choice (the vote, individual compensation, or consumer choice), even a blueprint for living in common.

If this book were a taxonomic work, the epistemological compass of these cultural figurations—traditional to iconographic analysis—would merit a closer look. I would elaborate a pantheon of cultural figurations as they provide a "common understanding that makes possible common practices and a widely shared sense of legitimacy," the bases of a social imaginary (Taylor 2004, 21).[1] But my focus lies elsewhere: in the corporeal dynamism of icon consumption as a social process that reorders existing social relations in the name of the popular. In what follows, each cultural figuration is important only insofar as it functions as an analytic category for understanding a desire for social change in a contemporary world still dominated by the neoliberal ethos. If the saint enacts incalculable giving because she is selflessly generous, or the outlaw wins justice

from the duplicitous state because she is courageous, each quality expresses a potentiality for opposing existing social relations, human
agency as the social logic of living in common. By living such potentiality
through embodied veneration, subjects express their collective aspirations for a social to come, unrealized but possible. As we shall see, each
figuration aligned here highlights the potentiality of the body in enacting
social change. This chapter pursues the reorientation into the social
through these three cultural figurations, each equally significant to our
historical relocations in contemporary global modernity, each in constant mutation in our vast image cultures—in the indomitable underdog
(fashionably, the "slumdog"), the sexualized victim, the protestor who
risks her life, the indigenous owner of the commons, the anti-capitalist
living in voluntary simplicity, and so on.

It must be apparent that I see the popular as a form of human agency
against new empires and, therefore, as the site for any analysis of historical change to come. In this regard, this book is deeply informed by
critical enterprises such as subaltern studies that have developed formidable methodologies for investigating the structural agency of those
whose stories do not appear in commodity form as the success of personal achievement. The subject is a collective one but opened by the
analytic of the subaltern to grasp the force of anti-hegemonic insurgency
as precursor to revolutionary change. The first generation of subaltern
studies scholars, who were deeply influenced by the poststructuralist
turn to semiotics, offered different models for relating the untold story,
and these endeavors remain central to the historical arc of the book. The
embodied veneration of bio-icons not only presents evidence of exuberant social imaginations, but it also guides us to the underlying logics of
social relations in the face of macro-scalar change. In turn, the logics
highlight the populist reason of the anonymous crowds whose agency we
pursued in the previous chapter. In pursuit of historical becoming, I
follow this lead through the categories of the outlaw, the saint, and the
activist, analytics that open us to human agency expressed as a demand
for changed social relations.

If the critical task at hand is to unearth populist reason, then Ranajit
Guha's invitation to apprehend what may not be readily visible, readily
accessible, easily divulged, is a viable point of entry—and especially for
the bandit queen, who was clearly subaltern in her early years, before her
co-optation as democracy's success story. As I have argued elsewhere, his
arguments plainly foreground the stakes of the critical method he deploys
to read social history. As insurgent, Guha (1983, 37) argues, the subaltern

exerts pressure on semiotic codes necessary for the maintenance of established political and moral hierarchies—systems "waxed fat on signs" codifying authority. If relations of dominance and subordination are regulated by basic codes of language, gesture, or habit, the subaltern's code
switching, the *"real* turning of things upside down" (Guha 1983, 36)
radically subverts existing codification. The level meeting of eyes before a
feudal landlord or the loud singing that disrupts British colonial ceremonies, when repeated, might appear to pose a permanent threat to such
established hierarchies. To read the subaltern, Guha suggests, the critic
also must participate in sustained code switching, reading seemingly
sporadic and unrelated acts of violence—which appear as "crime" to a
local landlord or British colonial official (or to modern legal institutions in
the case of Phoolan Devi)—as justifiable retribution for a peasant, a
message with class content. In fact, Guha focuses on the "crimes" of social
banditry such as looting, arson, and murder as his chosen illustration.
These diverse illegal acts, tellingly directed against a particular objects
(moneylender, landlord, or British officer), repeated (a necessary redun-
dancy), and increasingly communal, are precursors to rebellion, Guha
intimates, even though their status as rebellion is considerably ambiguous. Where the records of the colonial state remain uncertain about how
to read the "criminal" subaltern (are these "dacoits" or "rebels"?[2]), regional folklore codifies these violent acts as rites of passage to rebellion
undergone by lone, self-sacrificing heroes.[3]

   In the lore of their legendary commitment to the poor, social bandits,
as outlaws, often act for us against the politico-juridical order (embodied
in the law), articulating social demands for justice beyond legal redress.
Guha highlights, among others, the case of Sultana, a legendary dacoit of
the Chambal Valley from the colonial era whose record "was remembered
no longer as one of offences against the law but that of valour and humanity" (Guha 1983, 79). We see a similar turn in popular appropriations
of Phoolan Devi re-codified as Draupadi, a postcolonial avatar of the
dacoits in Guha's analysis. Crime, in other words, might come to signify
"an integral part of a comprehensive system of defiance, a *parole* in a new
langue" (Guha 1983, 93) only when one "reads" signs of insurgency
against the grain of a logic that transcribes them as criminal, sporadic,
and unrelated. Obviously, Guha's insurgent subaltern as a sign for collective aspiration is most borne out in the case of Phoolan Devi; in her, the
analytic category materializes as the outlaw. Of our bio-icons, she is the
one most directly politically efficacious in all kinds of ways, while Mother
Teresa remains the most obscure in her role in forging social bonds. But,

as I have noted on several occasions, the popular is always an impure category, working with the logic of capital to dream of a social to come. Like subaltern insurgencies, expressions of popular agency do not bring about large-scale social transformations, but they may be precursors *to* revolutions. While I do not have the comforts of history for accurate prediction, in the stories I craft here I pose the possibility of historical becoming through bio-icons—a becoming that can potentially disrupt existing hegemonies in transformative ways.

DEMOCRACY'S OTHER: THE OUTLAW/SUBALTERN

The category of the subaltern here is particularly useful in its regulative role against the limits of the state.[4] Subalterns demand recognition of historical differences in power, a blind spot for the state that treats all of its citizens as equal in its juridical sphere. In our case, the female Dalit is rather differently positioned within socioeconomic systems, a difference that the Indian state fails to recognize in its juridical operations—hence, the legal aporia at the moment of Phoolan Devi's death. Hegemonic nationalist consumption of Phoolan Devi, the reformed citizen signaling the triumph of electoral democracy, produces her political ascendance as indexical of structural changes in the lives of female Dalit citizens.[5] The rags-to-riches story imagined by bourgeois national (and transnational) publics places a social demand for a neoliberal democracy through the bandit queen.[6] In her embodiment as the quintessential disenfranchised —the social Other who is absolutely necessary for the neoliberal mantra of individual rights and freedoms—Phoolan Devi becomes evidence of a successful electoral democracy, the great support of the free market at its unregulated best. Rising above adversity, she is the caste Other who is currently replaced by the indomitable slumdog of the vast shadow cities,[7] a heroic figuration (and fetishized avatar) of the subaltern. Through this historical Other, the reformed outlaw, we see the hegemonic aspiration to vote as the standardized measure of success for a political system. One standard establishes the credibility of one common horizon for all. There are no uneven, diverse demands in this version of Phoolan Devi as the heroic disenfranchised. Her transition to member of Parliament unequivocally signals the coming of democracy to the India heartland, closing the fractures in the Indian polity feared by the middle classes. To be a member of Parliament meant that the outlaw had been brought into the fold of the law, administered by a juridical system where all citizens are equal. To be brought into the fold meant justice had been won.

Yet, of course, the persistence of Phoolan Devi as outlaw alerts us to the fact that her transformation into citizen was never complete, that justice remained only an aspiration that was irreducible to the generality of a common measure. Being a citizen, in other words, does not enable the right to justice promised by the agency of the vote. The category of the subaltern, articulated in the enduring figurations of the outlaw, is extremely productive in highlighting the failure of the political support of capitalist development. If the right to political representation (expressed in "free and fair elections") has become the universal mantra for democracy, then eruptions of volatile "subaltern icons" bring friction to that democratic calculus. Hence, until the very end of her life Phoolan Devi remained a conundrum for Indian middle classes wedded to liberal conceptions of democracy.

The subaltern, Gayatri Spivak (1988) reminds us, remains singular and incapable of absorption into generality. Indeed, it was Phoolan Devi's singular experiences—rape, abduction, and physical violence—that initially presented a rationale for moral forgiveness and redemption, if not legal absolution, for the historic laying down of arms in 1983. If the law had failed to protect its most disenfranchised citizens, the argument ran, surely a moral appeal for justice could make amends for the violated bandit queen—if only by exception. If we follow contemporary thought on the state of exception, then the singularity of Phoolan Devi as sexed female Dalit subject stands at a reasoned distance from Phoolan Devi the legal citizen. The one problem that constantly resurfaces in mourning Phoolan Devi is her tenuous legal status: Given the cases pending against her, was the bandit queen just a criminal? Indeed, if she were just so—a criminal gunned down by other criminals—the case would be closed. But in that case, what kind of state allows such an illegal subject to make its laws? Such inquiries lead us unerringly to an original fracture in the law that returns to trouble its reach in Phoolan Devi's last rites, a fracture that has been widely discussed in political theory by feminist scholars (such as Rajeswari Sunder Rajan) and legal theorists (such as Upendra Baxi). Their investigations of Phoolan Devi's jerky transformation from a state of exception to norm intimate the play of heterogeneous singularities that, as Laclau (2005) has argued, disrupt a hegemony that depends on one social element gaining consent to speak for all.

As subaltern, Phoolan Devi is the icon under scrutiny most wedded to the state—and, of course, historically the subaltern is a figure whose fortunes are inextricable from the modern state. Sunder Rajan's and Baxi's commentaries on the Chambal peace missions highlight this particular surrender, foregrounding the general failures of the postcolonial state. For our purposes, I focus primarily on the social efficacy of the outlaw as heroic figuration that pits legal justice against social justice. Phoolan Devi indexes other social demands that question the capacity of the state to administer justice and, therefore, to fulfill the aspirations of a historically disenfranchised citizenry. The social demand for justice challenges state-sponsored aspirations for equality (expressed through individual rights) administered within a civil-legal framework. The outlaw, along with the saint and the activist, is a cultural figuration celebrated for acting against regimes, systems, and institutions. She embodies disruptive forces that pose living in common against institutionalized power. Hence, the outlaw, acting for a heterogeneous common, is a phantasmic projection that directs us to the possibility of a just community, a social to come.

But let us return to the surrender for a closer look at this outlaw whose presence marks an antagonistic frontier within the social totality. The surrender marked Phoolan Devi's "baptism" into citizenship, her instant transition from wolf boy to citizen-subject. Orchestrated at the behest of Indira Gandhi, the "moral redemption" of the Chambal outlaws—Phoolan Devi among them—gained its authority from the moral stature of the Gandhian stalwarts who, in agreement with the government and party leadership (at Gandhi's behest), bypassed the Indian Penal Code to negotiate "voluntary surrenders." Appealing to the moral conscience of the nation, Jayaprakash Narayan explained, that within this matrix of "trusteeship," every human heart was redeemable, capable of "repentance and introspection."[8] Not surprisingly, K. K. Rustamji, then the inspector-general of police for Madhya Pradesh, pointed out that these proceedings not only violated the law of the land, but they confused the entire police force (Bhaduri 1972, 25). Taroon Bhaduri, a self-described "hard-boiled journalist" who accompanied Vinoba Bhave on his *padyatra* (mission on foot) to India's Chambal Valley in 1958, initially voiced his concerns about the peace mission in no uncertain terms. "Wasn't law and order, the Indian Penal Code, Criminal Procedure Code and the constitution being thrown out of the nearest window?," Bhaduri recounts. "Would not such a mission undermine people's faith in the rule of law that prevailed in the country?" (Bhaduri 1972, 114). Bhaduri was not the only cynic. When Narayan revived the redemptive strike in 1972, bringing about the surrender of 180 dacoits with a total of 4.91 lakh rupees on their heads,[9] major opposition came from P. C. Sethi, chief minister of Madhya Pradesh, who welcomed the surrenders but could not look past the atrocities committed by the dacoits. Special courts inside the Gwalior jail held trials for these dacoits in secret deals made away from the public eye. By contrast, Phoolan Devi surrendered alone in 1983, yet her renunciation of arms inevitably joined this long tradition of "morally" circumventing the rule of law.

Such circumvention seemed rational to a middle class anxious to bring its heart of darkness into the fold of modernity. The Chambal, as we have seen, had always been the still-to-be-developed hinterland in the national imaginary. Phoolan Devi's troubles simply confirmed this notion. A rugged, inhospitable terrain including the five northern districts of the Indian state of Madhya Pradesh, the area surrounding the Chambal River —the forbidding "Chambal Valley"—was ever an administrative problem.[10] Dacoits organized in earlier centuries in resistance to foreigners (e.g., the opposition to Marathas in Ujjain and Gwalior). Their practices became a "law-and-order" problem only later, in the eyes of the colonial state (Colonel Sleeman's reputed report on Thugee in 1915), after the massive restructuring of land-revenue systems in the area. Social banditry reappeared in earnest with the transition to agrarian capitalism in the nineteenth century, when local and regional structures of power (land ownership, certainly, but also kinship linkages, legal adjudication of disputes, and local market patronage) were increasingly replaced by the abstract power of the state and the market.[11]

With pervasive landlessness, industrial backwardness, and persistent feudalism (including entrenched caste loyalties), the Chambal Valley had emerged by independence as the lawless Indian "interior" in the national social imaginary, the forest within the *polis*. Phoolan Devi, affixed to the Chambal, exemplified the singular subject who should be brought into the generality of citizenship, as had other social bandits before her. Such efforts had released a silent reign of terror on the Chambal. In 1953, three years before the birth of Madhya Pradesh as a separate state, the governments of several states consolidated a Joint Anti-Dacoity Police Command, bringing about the death of the formidable Man Singh in 1955; a few years later, local lore reported the death of Putlibai, the one-armed reigning bandit queen who died with the Qur'an in one hand and a bottle of rum on the other. In the fifteen-year purge that followed, the lives of social bandits (Giorgio Agamben's *hominus sacri*) were often exterminated without the commission to homicide in (what became widely known as) "encounters." In 1956, Madhya Pradesh came into being amid a bloody string of atrocities committed by the dacoits aimed at destroying the police pogroms, and into that bloodbath Vinoba Bhave arrived pleading for a "change of heart" with or without a surrender of arms.[12]

Given such a history, it is no coincidence that Phoolan Devi often underscored her father's loss of property (and the Mallahs' loss of their jobs as ferrymen with the coming of steamboats) as the root cause of her oppression. In her many disagreements with the "press-wallahs" and "film-wallahs," Phoolan Devi proffered a more nuanced critique of sexual, physical, and economic violence. She understood "rape" as the articulation of class and caste privilege, remaining resistant to liberal feminist readings that sought to produce her as the universally persecuted female subject of sexual violence. When questioned once again on her multiple rapes by Mary Ann Weaver (1996, 2), Phoolan Devi hissed: "You can call it rape in your fancy language. . . . What you call rape, that kind of thing happens to poor women in the villages every day. It is assumed that the daughters of the poor are for the use of the rich. They assume that we're their property. . . . We can't cut grass without being accosted by them." This allusion to "cutting grass" surfaces on many occasions in Phoolan Devi's effort to focus on a complex corporeal violence—being owned and losing ownership—as the key to her "destiny." Socioeconomic injustice, in Phoolan Devi's view, governed the lives of those on the lowest rungs of the caste and class ladder.

Sunder Rajan's meticulous investigation of Phoolan Devi's surrender links this corporeal violence perpetrated on the Dalit subject to the question of sexual difference.[13] In her study of political citizenship, Sunder Rajan (2004) argues that the surrender was a crisis in legal systems instructive for feminists invested in realignments between women as citizen-subjects and the post-independence Indian nation-state. If we look carefully at the complex orchestration by multiple players of the historic surrender, it becomes clear that the operations of the postcolonial state are never unitary or monolithic. In fact, the state often contradicts its own institutions, its provenance, and its abstractions, as the overlapping negotiations around the surrender reveal. Interstate rivalry leading to power bids, political-party showdowns, police department crises, and, sometimes, the symbolic cachet of a figure such as Rajendra Chaturvedi, all played a role in orchestrating the event. Of course, Sunder Rajan's investigation of the behind-the-scenes bartering indicates that "moral redemption" was hardly the point; in fact, the surrender fulfilled multiple agendas for the key players. Nevertheless, for a moment it seemed as if Phoolan Devi had the upper hand in her elaborate deal with the state.

Sunder Rajan's attention to the singularity of this event—the one-time, symmetrical encounter between the outlaw and the officials of the

state that brings about a crisis in legal systems—is perhaps most significant for the line of argument I have been developing here.[14] At the moment of her surrender, Phoolan Devi is neither a local criminal nor a
victim who commands forgiveness. Rather, she is a formidable external
adversary, a singular subject who confronts the official representative of
the state *if only for a moment*, as Sunder Rajan argues persuasively. In the
years to come, the state would either treat her within its own logics as
entirely legal or entirely criminal, often compelling Phoolan Devi to
speak of suicide—to quench her bare life, to remove it from the state's
reach—or return to the "free" Chambal, now nostalgically juxtaposed to
the constraints of political life in Delhi. As we have seen, at her death the
legendary outlaw returned in full measure, a constant reminder of the
exceptional, the singular, subaltern subject.

Upendra Baxi (1982) historicizes this singular face-to-face encounter
between the law and its dangerous supplement as a legal "crisis" for the
postcolonial Indian nation-state.[15] A legal theorist known for his ongoing
analyses of Indian legal systems, courts, human rights, and concepts of
justice, Baxi offers a historical analysis of legal liberalism in modern India
where parallel legal systems coexist: "one for the rich and resourceful,
and those who wield political power and influence, and the other for
small men without resources and capabilities to obtain justice or fight
injustice" (Baxi 1982, 4). The ensuing "low commitment to legalism," in
Baxi's view, generates different modalities of crises in the Indian legal
system that are mostly fueled by the "exceptional" deployment of political power outside the law. Baxi offers the dacoit missions by Vinoba
Bhave and J. P. Narayan as spectacular instances of such crises, which, in
the larger scheme of things, he sees as productive. The logic of the law is
called into question, he argues, in the name of a radically different logic
that, if we follow the scene recounted earlier, disconnects morality from
the law (Baxi 1982, 25).[16]

Seen against such a philosophical and historical canvas, Phoolan Devi's
surrender presents a spectacular instance of exception. Frozen in an iconic photograph, the moment encapsulates an originary image in national
memory—the prototypical, powerful outlaw, an imaginary projection of
the "force of the people" that democracy signifies but more often than
not fails to recognize through political representation. Here the outlaw
icon embodies everything for those who saw themselves as divorced from
the Indian democracy; vague, imprecise, and phantasmic, the icon quilts
the aspirations of all who are cognizant of historical disenfranchisement.
There is no common agenda here—no vote, no policy, no legal right.

Rather, in this manifestation as outlaw, the icon holds together an opposition to the existing state. A frontier between "us" and "them" appears constituted by differing notions of justice. The iconic image is
unforgettable: the bandit queen turning away from Arjun Singh, the chief
minister of Madhya Pradesh to whom she hands her rifle, to greet with
folded palms the roaring crowds. Fixed forever as the exorbitant subject
of the law, the memory of the indefatigable outlaw is consistently superimposed on the decorous member of Parliament lying in state so many
years later.

Far from the legendary social bandit living in permanent revolution,
Phoolan Devi in the whodunit narrative of her murder is unreservedly a
criminal with several cases pending against her, who invites the violence
she once inflicted on others. But if we look carefully at accounts of Phoolan Devi's murder that speak of criminality and lawlessness, the forest
returns to haunt the city, and the liminality of the outlaw seems unassailable. Constituting Phoolan Devi as criminal certainly contains her transgressions through legal inscription; yet such inscription will not stabilize.
For one, no motive seemed readily available for the crime; Sher Singh
Rana could not be easily tied to Behmai, despite all efforts to revive the
"revenge theory." So the bandit queen's death had to be a symptom of
something deeper, more worrisome. Hence, the demands for police inquiries, autopsies, and the legal adjudication of assets were strongly laced
with spiraling fear and anxiety. Some decried the Chambal "infection" of
New Delhi, raising a hue and cry about the lack of security against common criminals ("Chambal Infected" 2001). Legislators, they contended,
were increasingly exposed to violence in the general lawlessness and
availability of small arms in the capital. This reading of a general condition was just as anxiously accompanied by attempts to isolate Phoolan
Devi as criminal anomaly. "Those who live by the gun have reason to fear
death by the gun," argue many, ungenerously implying the bandit queen
could have very well got what she deserved (Bhattacharjee 2001). The
two responses contradicted each other. If Phoolan Devi's violent death
was indeed simply a "natural culmination of events," an act of retribution
by her victims, why should any other law-abiding parliamentarian fear a
similar end? Obviously, the anxiety ran deeper, stemming from those
subterranean links between politicians and the criminal underworld—
Baxi's parallel legal system of debts and credits—that habitually throws
the law into confusion. The persistence of the outlaw once more foregrounds the "common understanding" (or social imaginary, as Taylor
[2004] defines it) of a system of justice that does not work for all even as

it "sees" all as equally enfranchised. Such a fallen world mandates the rise of the outlaw.

The memory of the outlaw questions the democratic state's promise of social progress through political representation; it interrogates civil society's inability to bring the disenfranchised into the fold of modernity. As we have seen, most efforts to re-auratize the bandit queen return to the "uncivil" outlaw who speaks with the bullet. The corporeal body of the bandit queen, bearing witness to her lived physical and material experiences, reminds the nation of its deepest fractures that have neither healed nor disappeared. No wonder it draws devotees into the body of the icon. The exorbitant logic of the outlaw explains why Phoolan Devi volatilized in 2001, despite her publicized departure from a life of crime. Her death reactivated the cultural figuration of the outlaw, living a reverse temporality to the rags-to-riches slumdog millionaire that troubles the subaltern in its commodity form (democracy's success) and brings the public image of Phoolan Devi to epistemological crisis. The persistence of the outlaw as legend signals the bandit queen's efficacy in forging a popular that will not buy into the promises of the neoliberal state. Hence, C. Rammanohar Reddy (2001) stumbles upon an honest admission when he notes that "we"—the members of civil society—might never really know the answer to, "Who killed Phoolan Devi?," and surmises, "Indian society probably killed her when it got her married at 10." Reddy, pointing a finger at socioeconomic inequities that makes the exercise of legal liberalism particularly violent in its exclusions, goes on to underscore why the bandit queen's life and death continues to be an enigma even when all legal cases against her are closed: "The truth is we [presumably speaking for the national, middle-class, English-speaking public] were never quite comfortable with Phoolan Devi, not once but twice, becoming a Member of Parliament" and never quite got past the fact that a "low-caste farmer dacoit could sit in Lok Sabha" (Reddy 2001). This is a telling indictment— one that once more superimposes the memory of the outlaw firmly on the visage of the dead citizen or the criminal who got her just desserts.

BEYOND ACCUMULATION: THE SAINT

I have suggested that icon study contributes to our sense of how modernity—with democracy as one of its most enduring projects—is daily negotiated in local contexts all over the world. The category of the saint adds another dimension to this story. As a materialization of the divine prototype, the imaginal exemplar toward which the subject reaches, saints have long harnessed a sense of collective belonging. Certainly, we can see this from the crowds mourning Mother Teresa in their own ways quite apart from the funeral spectacle in Kolkata. But heavily sanctioned by states, religious institutions, and civil society (Mother Teresa is the subject of the nation's foremost bourgeois artists, after all), saints are also trademark commodities for global institutions. In her unequivocal legitimization as the embodiment of charity, Mother Teresa operates on the other side of the spectrum from Phoolan Devi. She can hardly be seen to mobilize a concrete social demand such as that for the political institution of justice. Yet if we look beyond the hegemonic guise—the face of charity, the missionary, or the mother—the category of the saint prepares us for Mother Teresa's efficacy in catalyzing a demand for social relations unfettered by economic calculation, for the saint opens the indigent into a horizon where incalculable gift produces incalculable fellowship.

As a global icon, Mother Teresa quilts social demands across communities in the city she made her home, her translocal appeal stretching beyond her territorialization as a beatified Roman Catholic saint. Hence, significations that attempt to territorialize her, to harness her for hegemonic agendas such as regulated bankable charitable actions, are often met with refutation. The controversies that hound her therefore signal her volatility as popular auratic object, quilting diverse demands held together at contingent moments of articulation such as the funeral. But what kind of social bond is effected through such a popular saint? A social bond across heterogeneous social groups, differentiated by religions, caste, or creed in their worship of religious figures, I would argue, among those who face escalating economic disenfranchisement in the face of a growing consumerist economy. There is no common aspiration here that seeks institution in politics—nothing like Hindu territory to be won in the name of a Hindu nation that has absorbed all difference. But the saint as a cultural figuration in popular lore—and not in the guise of a Roman Catholic or Hindu saint legitimated by institutions—is a phantasmic object who intercedes for the common, across differences in wealth or social status, health or illness. Immensely corporeal technologies of the popular, saints relocate collectivities. As a popular saint embodying the social logic of the gift antithetical to (the logics of) accumulation confronting the indigent every day, Mother Teresa lives a rich social life as a highly auratic icon in contemporary Kolkata. If economic exchange is an inescapable aspect of contemporary life, a closer look at the saint offers us a sense of a mixed economy where exchange need not always be harnessed to the logic of accumulation. Just as the re-territorialized Phoolan Devi (the sign of a successful democracy) could never eclipse the outlaw, so Mother Teresa's capture as bankable star (for the Vatican's financial and symbolic profit) or local saint (selling the mega-city to corporations solicited for direct investment), I submit, never quite eliminated the popular sense of the radical revolutionary who embodied the exorbitant logic of the incalculable gift.

For any Marxist critic, Mother Teresa at first glance is just a bankable star. Her status as liturgical icon certainly derives from the massive institutional support she received from the Vatican. The message she beams conceals the hegemonic schemes of religious expansionism. I have little quarrel with such materialist critique; indeed, as we shall see, I gather evidence for some of these allegations. Yet to dismiss Mother Teresa's auratic value as simple-mindedness ensures a certain loss of imagination I am at pains to recuperate here. As so many scholars of multiple modernities have argued, enchanted objects remain robust in our seemingly disenchanted modern world;[17] their social efficacy as magical technologies mandates a consideration of devotional reason for scholars of the popular.

Despite their traditional lineaments, saints persist in multiple guises in popular culture. Feminist debates on medieval and early modern saints, the many female mystics who strayed from the church but also remained (or were later contained) in its confines, are particularly instructive to comprehending an economy of faith that is not easily perceptible to a scholar, like me, wedded to atheism and secularism. They lead twentieth-century thinkers who have actively struggled toward a materialist conception of mysticism to explain the role of the affective in public life—the affective often heralding social change, even revolution. They turn to intellectuals such as Georges Bataille, whose (often discredited) base materialism provides a remarkably flexible frame for grasping the mystic's potentiality for living an economic logic exorbitant to the logic of accumulation—a logic that connects her to the economically disenfranchised so that she appears to "act" on their behalf. If the saint expresses discontentment with accumulation, we can surmise she embodies the possibility of another lived sociality in a city on the brink of reinvention through high rises, gated communities, leisure facilities, and glitzy shopping malls. In the mega-city, the force of consumption as consumerism is ubiquitous. Even the child in a slum in Kolkata is surrounded by hoardings selling household appliances, air travel, and insurance; even an unregistered Bangladeshi migrant worker who daily crosses the border into Kolkata puts something by for a *pukka* (concrete) house to replace a temporary dwelling. Hence, Bataille's elaboration of consumption beyond consumerism offers a compelling schema for grasping negotiations of the lure of accumulation through the potentialities of the popular saint.

Focusing squarely on consumption, Bataille (1994 [1945]) projects the human subject as a field of unbound energies whose expenditure constitutes the very act of living.[18] In this "base materialism," he joins a lineage of thinkers who posit human flesh as a field of power. In Bataille's account, exuberant energies are constantly and consistently bound by the homogenous social order, a restricted economy where expenditures are calculated for appropriate returns.[19] But what exactly is being spent? How does Bataille's hydraulics of human subjectivity elucidate the logic of the gift? Eschewing religious divisions of body and soul, Bataille perceives the subject as matter or mortal substance energized by forces that course through the universe. Such a subject shares an experiential continuum with the material substance of the universe, but this heterologic is continually contained by a social order that produces the discontinuous individual marked by separation and self-interest; full dissolution, after all, would imply fragmentation, dissolution, and the death of the subject. The experiential continuum is, of course, continually experienced in the excesses of eroticism, carnality, torture, or mystical ecstasy, where the discontinuous individual dissolves into the Other—the spoor of the Other ever resonant in the face of the beloved or the divine (Bataille 1988 [1943]). While this base materialism—one that places carnal love, war, and carnival alongside mystical excesses—does not seem a far cry from psychoanalysis, the relevance of Bataille's formulations to the saint lies in his daring articulation of a collective force field.[20]

If one important form of dissolution is eroticism, or the tearing or opening into the other, another is incalculable fellowship, an expenditure religions sanction as sacrifice but fear when taken to extremes. The popular saint offers such incalculable fellowship, quilting social bonds among those who venerate her—a fellowship Bataille aligns with the unproductive expenditure of the gift. If saints more often than not are insubordinate figures (and this is certainly true of Mother Teresa) who are only later aggrandized by institutions or states, then they clearly lean toward an excess that puts pressure on established norms and codes of religious conduct. Not drawn to production (the banking of finances, lands, souls, cultural capital, political power), the saint enacts a corporeal expenditure, a consuming of her corporeal substance in her excessive love for the other. This is exactly the expenditure that Raghu Rai and M. F. Husain capture in their evocations of Mother Teresa's popular sainthood.

Bataille enables us to read religious fervor as a mode of consumption, the saint's sumptuary expenditure providing the devotee with a brief glimpse of material continuity. Such a desire explains the sacrificial logics of primitive and modern human societies, the witnessing of the other's suffering bringing the subject closer to the alterity within. In Christian discourse, of course, the general social Other (the poor, the destitute, the dying) is formalized into the figure of Christ, whose form Mother Teresa saw everywhere: "In the slums, I see Christ in the distressing disguise of the poor—in the broken bodies, in the children, in the dying" (Chawla 2002, 263). In a double movement, the saint sees her flesh fragmented to the point of dissolution like Christ's lacerated flesh, her body incorporating fragments of his, while also "seeing" in Christ's suffering the denuded substance of the poor, which she must replenish through expending her own flesh. Bataille sees unleashed human potentialities in the unproductive expenditures of Christian agonistic orgies, but organized forms of the religion inevitably limit such excess through a series of procedures, taboos, prohibitions, and rules of conduct. Organized religion cuts off our relation to the scared from its transgressive root in desire and violent expenditure. Yet the popular saint presses for an ethics beyond sanctioned moral codes to enact a "morality beyond morality." The sumptuary expenditures of sainthood exist ever in tenuous balance with the restricted economy of churches, religious institutions, and organizations.

The scholarship on saints allows us a point of entry into interpreting Mother Teresa's "sacrifice" as a rich movement toward the Other that incites adoration from the public, even as the flow is always curtailed by the homogeneous order of the Roman Catholic church she never fully abandoned.[21] To think of sacred encounters as the giving of substance brings it into the same operational field as labor, the body's life potential that is transformed into time and money in systems of capitalist exchange. Here, corporeality as bodily phenomena materialized in specific ways imagines the role of the body in relations of exchange: when the body's substance is sumptuously expended, we are in the domain of the gift, while controlled expenditure that produces surplus value is charity (of our times). After winning the Nobel Peace Prize, Mother Teresa was increasingly subjected to restriction as she garnered social capital for her unproductive expenditures, becoming Vatican II's most productive emissary. The gift, the great capacity for unproductive social expenditure, was to appear as "charity," a measured act of giving in our times that sometimes enables tax write-offs. In her gradual restriction, Mother Teresa's untiring work would be bound in its commodified representation as "the Work."

Here Scott Shershow's (2005) extension of Bataille via Mauss is illuminating, for he investigates what happens to "work"—the unproductive expenditure Bataille privileged—at the moment in which affective labor is increasingly instrumentalized. In a complex sleight of hand, Shershow argues that when self-fulfilling work outside the calculus of returns appears as a gift (something one receives for something performed), the work becomes measurable, it meets restriction. Its name is "charity."[22] Historically in the domain of the gift (always collective, always immeasurable), charity in our times has shifted into an economic mode where giving is a private act with private (and immediate) returns, financial or otherwise. Such privatization is commensurate with individualized rights, property, and ownership of resources within neoliberal regimes. In the privatized regime of "charity" that has replaced state-sponsored welfare, and in the new philanthropies of present-day globalization, "suffering with the poor" becomes restricted within systems of mutual exchange and obligation.[23] In other words, charity is hardly simply generous giving, let alone unproductive expenditure; the regimes of charity and philanthropy "really conceal a prohibition or refusal of the gift" (Shershow 2005, 133). The release of work into an investment was made most clear in 2000 when, at the end of the holiday season, President Bill Clinton released a "report" boasting a "record increase in charitable giving"—a tabulation that is clearly at odds with the very notion of the incalculable gift.

Most materialist criticism of Mother Teresa has focused primarily on her links to global capital flows—on the restriction of the saintly icon. Such a focus is in part fueled by economists who have been preoccupied, at least from the mid-1990s, with the flows of religious capital engendering infrastructural changes in global religious networks that are straining to keep up with competing regimes of global governance.[24] Profits take the form of successful evangelization, well-attended church worship, donations, public prestige and recognition, and moral influence. Holding up the example of aggressively evangelical religious institutions, economists have drawn our attention to exchanges modeled on notions of rational production that seemingly are incommensurable with spiritual life. In such discussions, heterogeneous elements of the traditional Catholic rubric—the poverty, suffering, and asceticism celebrated by Mother

Teresa, for instance—are not just holy manifestations of self-sacrifice but a well-conceived policy that ensures a benefit. Such a logic explains why Mother Teresa was parsimonious in making enemies in her fight against poverty, offering troubling injunctions to forgive infraction and tolerate great pain with joy. In the aftermath of the Bhopal gas leak, she once infamously said, "Forgive, forgive, forgive." Moreover, Mother Teresa's international network was notable in its evangelical activities. By 1995, her order included 4,000 nuns and monks, with as many as 40,000–300,000 laypeople employed by the Missionaries of Charity. The social work of the Missionaries of Charity had ubiquitous coverage in mass media, but little was heard of another powerful branch of the order, the Sisters of the World, an evangelical branch whose monies were explicitly to be spent not on social work but on evangelism (the running of contemplative houses).

Several transnational networks contributed to Mother Teresa's gradual incorporation into a restricted economy. Social capital garnered by her mass-mediated commodity image clearly increased donations to the church, as well as to its moral influence and public prestige. Shershow would probably read the increasing restriction on the logic of expenditure as a general sign of the times, and Mother Teresa's insertion into the Vatican's global makeover bears out his hypothesis. It is not that her order was singular in its interpenetration by economic logic. Her incorporation was simply one of the many effects of globalizing capital on religious life, practices, and institutions. The Roman Catholic church had significantly expanded its political, social, and financial networks, effectively streamlining church policy from the early 1990s.[25] The fast track to sainthood developed by Pope John Paul II reflects such a model of efficiency, a canny pitch to increase Roman Catholic membership by canonizing local saints more alive in public memories than esoteric figures from centuries past.[26] And with the availability of mass media, the Second Vatican Council could become a full political partner with other hegemons in the spread of Christian democracy. If the Roman Catholic church was to become a transnational enterprise, it had to stabilize an international "charity" regime to manifest good faith. The social capital of Mother Teresa was invaluable to this makeover, her readymade mass-mediated commodity image easily mobilized by the church as its twentieth-century "multicultural" avatar. Mother Teresa "sold" Christianity like a brand, offering pithy media-savvy slogans—"Works of love are works of peace"—for transnational circulation.[27]

But at home in Kolkata, as we have seen, Mother Teresa's re-absorption into church hierarchies was *the* global form that became highly contested in the public mourning rituals. One of the most interesting commentaries reflecting on the Vatican's attempt to legitimize Mother Teresa emerged from Achin Vanaik right after Mother Teresa's death in a polemic appropriately titled "No Sense of Proportion" (1997). In the middle of outpourings of grief, adulation, and criticism, Vanaik pointed out one could mourn Mother Teresa's passing without seeing her as the greatest embodiment of institutionalized charity in its most self-sacrificing form, for certainly there were others who deserved such praise within Roman Catholic orders. Mother Teresa seemed exemplary partly because her work was sanctioned as the acceptable path in the Christian commitment to the poor. Other journeys met with direct disapproval from the Vatican: the path of those Roman Catholic priests who fought for distributive justice, took sides with the poor against the rich, and attacked the causes rather than the effects of poverty—the most famous among them the assassinated Archbishop Oscar Romero of El Salvador. Many Latin American priests have not forgiven the Vatican for turning its back on Romero when he asked for support before his death. Mother Teresa's de-politicized compassion—her inclination to teach the poor to bear their burden stoically—prompted a form of institutionalized charity that is less problematic for the Vatican to credential than Romero's liberation theology. In fact, Mother Teresa quite publicly toed the Vatican's political line on this line of work with the poor, flatly declaring, "I say to all priests: You have not become priests to be social workers" (quoted in Chatterjee 2002, 262). The fact that Mother Teresa was not received very well in Latin America was a well-kept secret. One biographer mentions that the Missionaries of Charity Fathers, a wing of her order that taught the gospel and worked among the poor, met with little success in Brazil and was told to "move on" by local priests; others record her obsessive zeal for opening contemplative houses in post-socialist countries after 1989, once more as the Vatican's emissary.

One may argue that Mother Teresa's authority came directly from God—this was her greatest gain, after all, in being exclaustrated—so these could be considered positions of disinterest, actions motivated by compassion. Yet the historical timing of Mother Teresa's entries into particular debates—timed at particular historical junctures when the Roman Catholic church's regime of humanitarianism could maximize their benefits—intimates the deeply political bent of such articulations. On such occasions, the unproductive expenditure of the saint enters a different hydraulic flow: contained, banked, and bound rather than released. Certainly, Mother Teresa's unproductive expenditures have often been recycled into restricted economies with hordes of tourists signing up for "charity" while on vacation in India.[28] But one wonders if such representation cancels out her consumptive practices of love, for where she circulates as a commoditized sign in mass media accumulating social capital for the Vatican, she also erupts constantly as "our Mother"— unmoored to any religion but anchored to the poor in local hagiography. Bataille's notion of expenditure invites us to look at both the exorbitant and the bound, a double articulation of the saint capable of harnessing either the hegemonic or the popular.

While Bataille's schema establishes expenditure to be the general logic of living, with India's fervent embrace of consumerism spending has become not only ubiquitous but a highly reflexive activity. Consumer identity now garners social capital. As we have seen, even self-denying figures such as Gandhi have been re-territorialized to sell consumer goods, the social demand to be a good consumer placed through the famous icon at his spinning wheel. Recent scholarship on the middle class foregrounds consumerist activity—at the department store, engaging in global fashion or recreational cultures—as key to India's post-1991 de-regulated public cultures, with middle-class households (the very rich, the consuming class, and the climbers) at 87.8 million by 1996, just before Mother Teresa's death (see Fernandes 2006; Jaffrelot and van der Veer 2008; Rao and Natarajan 1996). The visual culture of consumerism is everywhere in new malls, hoardings choking metropolitan skylines, electric displays casting their shadow on the pavements where the eco-nomically disenfranchised continue to eke out traditional livings (e.g., by pulling rickshaws, selling goods, managing tea or food stalls) or newer forms of living (as cheap cell phones make underground and imitation economies in goods possible). Within these historical conditions, the saint embodies a quality—"giving"—that eschews accumulation and privileges living in common. The shared resources and spaces of the city "belong" to the poor, who express their social demands for these in the lengthening shadows of the coming mega-city.

Since spending has become an aspect of daily life even for the indigent urban poor, its supplementary logic—giving or unproductive expendi-ture—gains affective charge. Hence, the saintly icon that embodies incal-culable giving, despite her binding as bankable star, incorporates de-votees into a liquid social that is incommensurable with the logic of accumulation. She expresses a sociality obscured in the rush to aggran-dize property and to protect it from others. So it is no surprise that

Mother Teresa garners such affect; no surprise that she becomes a contested sign. Hence, in spite of Mother Teresa's later efforts to suppress memories of her early radicalism (reports of her loss of faith would appear posthumously [see Kolodiejchuk 2007]), idealizing, even worshipful, accounts of her unsanctioned expenditure remain vibrant and consistent, provoking adoration and desecration. Speculations on Mother Teresa's strange sacrifices perform the desire for a living in common, with common resources and common spaces. They register the collective sense of the saint's excessive giving, her corporeal expenditure expressing a structure of feeling not yet articulated as a concrete social demand of the sort we see placed through Phoolan Devi or Arundhati Roy. Rather, the popular saint continues to forge social bonds among those who live with the rising uncertainties of a changing city.

PUNCTUATING GREEN: THE ACTIVIST

In my perusal of the local negotiations of democracy and capitalist exchange, the emphasis has fallen on a supplementary logic, one that challenges unimpeded flows of abstract ideologies only to a degree. While friction slows traffic, as Anna Tsing's (2004) evocative metaphor of roads emphasizes, they also facilitate flows. In the balance of this chapter, I turn to negotiations that not only question, arrest, or contest unimpeded flows but that also seek to redirect them substantially in collaborative transnational praxes based on well-considered local platforms. If "global green"—our test cast here—seems to sell a neoliberal environmental agenda that is inattentive to the distribution of planetary resources, local environmental struggles seek to recalibrate the power of green for funds, advocacy, and media coverage rather than wholly resist such "global" ideologies. These negotiations do not take states to be their primary target; they aim at global civic organizations to build translocal alliances. The actors involved are hardly invisible; they are, rather, self-reflexively constituted publics who place demands through iconic images of famous activists—a Noam Chomsky, a Ken Saro-Wiwa, or an Arundhati Roy.

Here, many, and often sharply differentiated, social demands are held together in coalitional equivalence through the iconic figure of the activist. The activist icon forges a social bond aimed at global interconnections that are not governed by what hegemonic techno-scientific aspirations tell us—the building of dams, the invention of seeds, the cloning of sheep. The heterogeneous icon illuminates a field of heterogeneous singularities where environmental disaster is unequally experienced and therefore cannot be yoked to a single claim or agenda: Social demands cannot be instituted in politics, despite the seeming universal platform of global green. The environmental activist is that vague, imprecise icon that continuously opens into the ground of a transnational social totality composed of incommensurable demands, for while the activist is clearly a linking mechanism that holds an ever receding horizon in her image, the varied "actions" she embodies, once more the subject of creative speculation, signal heterogeneous singularities within environmental struggles.

The universal mantra of science for the equal benefit of all, a techno-scientific demand that promulgates neoliberal development, is our primary concern. It has spawned a strong response from transnational organizations and movements who pitch redistribution as their agenda. Pollution, waste, big pharmaceutical companies' testing of experimental drugs, deforestation—the abuse of techno-scientific schemes are immeasurable. Among a litany of responses to them, environmentalism has emerged as the strong antagonist of technological advancement for a privileged few. Posing "nature" (sometimes in reified terms, as Bruno Latour [2004] has noted[29]) as belonging to all, global green has come to symbolize the other side of globalization: a transnational movement that cobbles together common concerns from local platforms. But this is not as utopian as it may first appear. It is often the case that, saving "nature" (embodied in an endangered species, for example) appears opposed to the interests of the poor, who need redistributed resources. We shall return substantially to the struggle between the two, between (neo)liberal and redistributive "green" ideologies. But whatever the shortcomings, global green has managed to project an alternative image of planetary space as an antidote to schemes that extract, divide, and control resources. Global green is a contemporary call to expand the horizon of the "local" to a vision of networked locales that are always reflexively attentive to everyday, concrete life worlds. Global icons such as Arundhati Roy, Chico Mendes, Ken Saro-Wiwa, and Wangari Maathai are linking cultural mechanisms that enable such a transnational social imaginary.

How might we understand the social icon's efficacy in forging these translocal bonds? The category of the activist is the relevant one here, evoking an intermediary who renders local struggles legible to (transnationally) networked publics who often constitute themselves as an emergent global civil society. The commodity image of the the activist gains its purchase from the demands for a "global civil society" (Kaldor 2003) that emerged with the spread of democratization processes, communications technologies, and deregulated markets promoting "free" trade in the 1990s—a general intensification of global interconnections. Environmental advocacy has been one of the central platforms of such a venture; human rights has been another. In many environmental justice struggles, both concerns are equally relevant. And activists have been critical to the translation of local concerns that enable processes of deliberative democracy in global governance. Roy therefore joins a grand roster of intermediaries linking particular constellations of environmental struggle to a self-reflexively constituted global civil society—that is, audiences who see themselves as working in cahoots with local actors. As an activist, Roy enables, on the one hand, a transnational social imaginary in which her acts (parleyed into civil-legal demands for rights, redress, and compensation) legitimate the actions of others against virulent corporations and states, and, on the other, translocal solidarities in which singular demands from local contingency are articulated provisionally through her image. Together, both manifestations of the activist provoke speculation about this icon's embodiment of an efficacious blueprint for living in common.

Unlike those of popular saints and outlaws of yore, the social logics that pertain to the activist, a relatively newer cultural figuration, are yet to stabilize. The instability of the "global green" the activist unifies in his or her public image, for instance, was once more apparent in the fractured solidarity we saw at the United Nations Conference on Climate Change in Copenhagen in 2009. The debates cast doubt on the social demands expressed through activist icons. Therefore, logical opposition to neoliberalism is less clear in the case of bio-icons that are habitually deployed to garner consensus for a global civil society. In chapter 3, we saw how the global legibility of the Narmada Bachao Andolan (NBA) has been a subject of controversy, putting pressure on the global form of the "green activist." Like the saint, the iconic activist is easily appropriated by liberal agendas inattentive to syncopated differences in the common. We can obviously understand why the NBA might still desire such legibility for purely strategic reasons.[30] In fact, if we look beyond local platforms of environmental movements to transnational advocacy networks we can see how they become crucial to local struggles over common bio-resources. But this legibility, partially enabled by the "green activist" as a linking cultural mechanism, is often viewed with suspicion. If global legibility is a political project powered by media networks, alliances between urban activists, nongovernmental agencies, local protestors, and those directly dispossessed by dam building, it has many detractors who worry about the transformations in modes of protest and organization. Much opposition to transnational collaboration has come from a traditional left that is also invested in redistribution, but with the state as its target.

Despite these frictions, it would be simplistic to dismiss the social efficacies of the activist icon altogether, to say that the impulse to global legibility completely hijacks the deep environmentalism embodied in the situated activist in favor of a neoliberal consensus over global green. Environmental struggles worldwide strive to gain global legibility because a collaborative praxis aimed at the redistribution of resources—not just the unifying imposition of global governance—is now possible. The targets of these collaborations are foreign governments, institutions of global governance, aid agencies, NGOs, and other institutions; collaborators speak the civil tongue of these institutions to wrest compromises. Such collaborations fit Tsing's notion of environmental advocacy as a global cultural form that results from unpredictable encounters across difference. The strange conjunction of local forest peoples' joining corporations to destroy Indonesian forests, for instance, provoked strong response from multiple fronts in the 1980s, leading to the emergence of a democratic movement by the 1990s. Tsing's examples tell us that the story of compromise has complex potentiality, for even the most compromised collaborations generate unpredictable global connections, bringing "awkward" and "unstable" frictions in their wake. The liberal dream of a reconfigured globality shatters in the face of incommensurable demands, agendas, and initiatives. Hence, global social totality can only be conceived as contingent translocal alliances. The situated environmental activist once more forges a transnational social imaginary, but it is one in which the "global" is an impossible social totality. It appears as the fragmented space of translocalities that rise and disappear as struggles for the logic of dwelling in an interconnected system wax and wane. I return to the underlying logic of the environmental activist shortly, a logic that is most explicit in signaling a concrete common. But since the activist is a rather recent figuration in the South Asian context, and one that has not quite stabilized to signify either the satyagrahi (nonviolent protester) or the *virodhi* (militant), it requires a closer look.

The story begins elsewhere, since the activist has "arrived" only lately in South Asia. In general, the activist can be tracked to the near past, with the beginnings of second-wave environmentalism in the 1960s. With the publication of Rachel Carson's *Silent Spring* (1962), the social historian Ramachandra Guha (2000) argues, environmentalism emerged as an intellectual framework that gave shape and force to the first responses to industrialization that were largely heterogeneous, uncoordinated on national or global scale, and mostly local in imagination and practice.[31] With the second wave of environmentalism, participants in a transnational environmental "movement" worked strenuously to bring media coverage to local struggles, lobbying funding organizations such as the World Bank to withdraw from pernicious projects and raising money for demonstrations, strikes, and protests on multiple fronts. The heft of environmentalism as a transnational popular movement was clear on the streets of Seattle during the World Trade Organization meeting of 2000; no center was readily discernible, but a network of participants acting in concert managed to disrupt the global conglomerate. Green was legible everywhere, and the environment emerged as a global commons under attack from private and state interests. Hence, radical deep ecologists joined hands with anti-globalization critics who are more concerned with global governance and justice than the biosphere. What had become visible in transnational mass media networks was the "environmentalism of the poor" vibrant in the global South, where countries such as India, Brazil, Thailand, and Kenya shared concerns about deforestation, dam building, pollution, and biodiversity. With such a historical turn, we witness the rise of the iconic activist whose capacious image indexes worlds that are unfamiliar to transnational audiences.

In South Asia, the environmental activist inhabits a complex compass, given the historical backcloth of the freedom struggle as it reframes second-wave environmentalism. The second wave goes as far back as Chipko, a movement launched in Garhwal in April 1973, that spawned the now commonplace tactics of "tree hugging." The initial protest against logging based on agricultural and household concerns, like many local movements, later evolved into an articulation of broader ecological concerns, an intellectual consolidation that is "environmentalism" as we understand it today. In the interlinking of social demands, we would see a concrete common, a project with specific agendas. But it was the struggle against Karnataka Pulpwoods Limited's appropriation of public land in 1987 that generated the first environmental movement in India to stabilize a vocabulary of protest drawn from the freedom struggle, stabilizing the Indian variant of environmental activism. A close alliance of peasants, pastoralists, intellectuals, and fishing folk in the Kithiko-Hachiko (Pluck a Plant), satyagraha finally succeeded in closing down Karnataka Pulpwoods by September 1990. The scene was to be repeated in several consequent struggles between antagonists Guha (1983) describes as "ecosystems people" (communities that rely heavily on the natural resources of their locality) in perpetual conflict against "omnivores" (industrialists, professionals, politicians, government officials, corporate representatives). The NBA joined the fray in the mid-1980s, the first stirrings of active struggle in 1978. It would turn into a palpable social movement in 1985 with the arrival of the charismatic Medha Patkar, a social scientist from Tata Institute of Studies in Bombay who mobilized the first acts of opposition against submergence zones in the villages of Maharashtra. Patkar's urban contacts drew media attention first, then the participation of city-based NGOs, which began disseminating news of the struggle in briefings, newsletters, and films, lobbying legislators, collecting funds, and organizing solidarity events to keep the NBA in the news. The efforts on the part of NGOs based in the North to pressure international funding agencies to withdraw aid met with substantial success in 1992, when the World Bank instigated an independent review.[32] This produced a well-known and highly detailed report that led the World Bank to withdraw its support for the building of the Sardar Sarovar dam in 1993. International recognition for Patkar followed through established technologies of recognition: She was awarded the Right to Livelihood Award by Sweden in 1991 and the Goldman Prize in the United States in 1992. A local grassroots mobilization was now legible to a global civil society invested in creating modes of global governance that could combat the more rapacious effects of globalization.

If we understand the activist to be a linking mechanism for diverse, unequally located actors engaged in translocal struggles, the environmental activist is currently the most familiar manifestation of this cultural figuration. Her situated protest—refusing to move as waters rise, melding into barks as logging commences—expresses the logic of dwelling in a biosphere that is a shared commons. We shall see how the environmental activist (much like the saint and the outlaw) is a highly corporealized figure whose image provokes ontological becoming; she embodies the quality of unwavering commitment to a "cause," which in this case would be to both economic justice and the redistribution of planetary resources. She is the intermediary par excellence between human and non-human worlds, and through her political theater we open into a planetary common. In the contemporary Indian context, three female icons have commanded global attention in environmental movements: Patkar, the leader of the NBA, in her battle against the Indian state's technological hubris; Vandana Shiva, the face of the bio-piracy initiatives that attempt to wrest common ownership of knowledge and plants from rapacious corporations backed by legal institutions based in the North; and Roy, the glamorous "artist and global citizen" at war against privatization and militarization (see Prasad 2003).[33] These three figures have not only garnered considerable social capital through their speech acts and actions, but they have further consolidated a vocabulary of protest globally recognized as "activism," much as Gandhi did with civil disobedience more than a century ago.[34] Of course, the legitimacy of the new female activist as icon gains its charge from a long line of predecessors—a history impossible to rehearse here at length. What is new is the centrality of Patkar, Shiva, and Roy to global perceptions of Indian environmentalism, which is strikingly at odds with the lighter visibility of female leaders as icons in the freedom struggle, despite widespread participation of women in collective action. After all a Sarojini Naidu, Matangini Hazra, or Durgabhai Deshmukh crops up only periodically beside the towering figure of Gandhi.

Furthermore, unlike the female freedom fighter of yore who was always a national icon, the environmental activist is avowedly a global one who quilts demands of heterogeneous transnational publics and populations even as her image makes worlds through its affixation to particular locations of action in South Asia.[35] While South Asian women were active as public figures in the early reformist and cultural nationalist movements of the late nineteenth century and early twentieth century, it was really with Gandhi's mass mobilization of satyagraha that women entered the nationalist movement in large numbers, throwing into relief their iconic representatives.[36] By the 1970s, the female environmental activist had already made a spectacular appearance on the national stage. The primal scene of the Chipko movement against deforestation in the 1970s, for instance—the confrontation between sixty men (contracted to cut trees) and twenty-seven women led by the legendary Gauri Devi—was popularly remembered in oral lore as the Reni forest encounter. In years to come, the head contractor of the encounter sang of Gauri Devi's prowess, rendering her iconic in popular memory. Such female iconicity became common fare in the post-independence years, no doubt legitimized by the institutional presence of Indira Gandhi. Women's activism spawned several female-dominated movements, such as the Shahada anti-alcohol agitation and, later, the urban-based mobilizations in solidarity with Shah Bano and against dowry deaths that gave Indian feminism a distinctive character. Into this mix came second-wave environmentalism, with its vast array of activists become icons—mediators of local situated "actions" for transnational publics. Activism signifies intentional action—disruption, boycott, performative protest, demonstrations, guerrilla tactics, persuasive or critical speech acts—to bring about social and political change; by the late 1970s and 1980s, "activism" had become an industry comprising individuals or organizations who were professionally involved in action to bring about social change.[37] Back in South Asia, women had come into the national eye by the 1980s as lobbyists, journalists, and media spokespeople, and the contemporary meaning of the female "activist" began to stabilize.[38]

By the time a new social movement such as the NBA would articulate its heterogeneous demands through its icons, the "activist" would evoke a situated actor, an intermediary or translator who would embody unthinkable risk on the behalf of others, an innovator who would not restrict herself to sanctioned civil speech or action. Like the other cultural figurations, the activist could be invoked for hegemonic gain (pitching universalizing green agendas), as well as to place diverse popular demands. For the popular in question here, the tireless leader of the NBA has been its most iconic activist. As an aperture that expresses aspirations for common bio-resources, Medha Patkar is consistently mobilized for a will to not move (from the banks of the Narmada) in an ever more mobile world; such a will to immobility is one response to the ongoing privatization of bio-resources that accompanies the restructuring of global capital. If the activist "acts" with her body, Patkar continues a long tradition of corporeal activism in which the body has always been vibrant political theater. Habitually putting her body at risk, Patkar has used a rich vocabulary of protest that has met with corporeal punishment to great effect.[39] Patkar's body not only mirrors the violence of the state in a classically Gandhian fashion, but the state's care of that body exemplifies the kind of restrained response these established and legible idioms of protest—made visible in this highly legitimate activist body—elicits from a state also known to eradicate activists in police custody.[40]

But Roy is a somewhat different activist whose body and speech "act" against techno-scientific development. Hence, her efficacy can be understood within a spectrum inhabited by Patkar on one end and Vandana Shiva, the cerebral activist who speaks in civil tongue, on the other. Shiva, an intellectual force, is well known in India as a physicist and as an eco-feminist. She emerged as an environmental activist when she became involved in the Indian government's case against W. R. Grace, the transnational American corporation that tried to patent the neem tree's pesticidal and fungicidal properties, then sued the European Union for its legal institutional support of such patent regimes. Shiva soon gained international recognition as an intellectual who consolidated a framework for transnational collaborations on the movement against global bio-piracy.[41] A recognizable warrior for the global South, she is the guru of environmental knowledge rather than activism.[42] Unlike Roy or Patkar, who are often visually captured at local sites of protests and demonstrations, Shiva is better known in rooms where negotiations take shape. If we place these three figures in a continuum, Roy inhabits a place somewhere in between the corporeal activism of Medha Patkar, who continually puts her body at risk, and the cerebral activism of Vandana Shiva. Like Patkar, Roy's star body also harnesses local actors to "global green" alliances; we have seen such yoking through visual images in mass media delivered through multiple technologies. But like that of Shiva, an eminently *audio*visual icon, Roy's speech is inextricable from her image. Her "speech" signifies as action (as Judith Butler [1997] might argue[43]) beyond the event of representation. Like both Patkar and Shiva, Roy "worlds" the locations she evokes as situated in the global South, with its particular environmental platforms and agendas.

In Roy's speeches, amorphous "masses" appear as corporeal singularities occupying the same space as the more privileged listeners who constitute her publics. I have considered Roy's enumerative idiom elsewhere; here I will briefly highlight Roy's ability to turn statistics into a singular body.[44] For example, in her Sydney Peace Prize lecture in 2004, Roy characteristically offered a statistic—"An estimated 100,000 Iraqis have lost their lives since the 2003 invasion"—and then placed those bodies close to the bodies and hearts of her audience. "That's one hundred halls full of people—*like this one*. That's one hundred halls full of friends, parents, siblings, colleagues, lovers, *like you*."[45] The repetition, the colloquial ordinary prose, the tactile image of bodies pressed against one's skin translate a distant "they" into the known parent, lover, colleague, or sibling. If the icon is at once sonorous, visual, and tactile, Roy's widely distributed speech (on DVDs and audiotapes; in audio files and podcasts), invoking intense sensation, incorporates the corporeal other into "our" space. Quixotically, the political work of such speech acts, including Roy's alleged delocalization of historical actors, precisely prompts desecrations of Roy's image.

The veneration (adoration and desecration) of Roy—both in linking translocal environmental agendas and in attacking neoliberal platforms through her image—shores up a globality in which the demand for *oikos* (or dwelling) has become a fundamental one. The environmental activist becomes an aperture for such social "ecologics," highlighting situated habitation and translating local idioms of redistributive justice into the common parlance of global green.[46] The exceptional activist indexes a "movement," indexes the ordinary logic of living in common, generating considerable social capital for the movement with which she is most directly connected. Often distant from the local struggles she translates, as her critics relentlessly point out, Roy surfaces episodically in such a guise, the sheen of her star image yoking desires of distant audiences to aspirations on the banks of the Narmada.

Roy's "star image" and virtuoso public performances exemplify a new kind of figure called forth by new configurations of global power: a mediator, a translator, a media-savvy actor equally invested in local action and global change—in short, the activist whose scale of imagination is necessary for the scale on which power operates. Moreover, if we look at bio-power as a dominant form of power in our bio-political modernity, the activist has a historically contingent role to play, for the body and its significations are inextricable from the idea of the activist. The activist is a body in motion, a body that acts by physical intervention (putting her body at risk), and, more often than not, a body that "screens" the violence of political regimes. Obviously, such a body would become a weapon for those who are engaged in bio-political wars over bodies, natural resources, and planetary space. Hence, the prototypical activist who moves consumers to act with those at risk enables a translocal popular; the visual, tactile, and sonorous traces of activist icons in mass media assemble consumers into the force field of bodies at risk, forging social bonds across distant locales.

The populist reason underlying these cultural figurations illuminates the processes relevant to historical becoming in the face of macro-scalar change. The saint and the activist broaden my dalliance with the outlaw; if the outlaw is inevitably harnessed to the state, the saint and the (environmental) activist disclose other aspirations against consumerism and techno-scientific development. In every case, the icon materializes in hegemonic guise but also to constitute social bonds that break with universal schemes, mobilizing a horizon that is both unachievable and possible.

This is why I argue that the study of icons constitutes a historical intervention into rethinking global modernity as it touches on life worlds. Not only is this an "other" story of global modernity; it is also one that encompasses various scales of political action—local and translocal, personal and collective—eschewing critical orthodoxies that relegate micro-scalar change to a "weak" politics. Such a scalar shift between the tiny fragment and an expanding horizon captures the perceptual field of the icon: the innocuous Google Earth, shimmering at the corners of our computer screens, that, when we click on it, can propel us into the recesses of planetary space.

The ontological plunge motivates the renewed materialism of this book as it "matters" the glittering forms we approach as icons in their fabulous proliferation. My insistence on corporeality, as it disinters the subject into matter, foregrounds the dynamism of the body. For a critic invested in social transformation, the story of potentialization is retold as story of historical becoming as we gather mass-media traces of volatile icons. Amid changing rules, new conditions sold as calculable dream in the neoliberal ethos co-opt the body in new ways. But in these upheavals, the body continues to disorganize its own capture, an unmannerly force moving in unpredictable directions; its open futurity undoes the rigor of progress. As lives, bodies, labor, resources, homes, and land are newly appropriated, mundane everyday objects regain their force as magical technologies that express human agency. Through these lustrous corporeal apertures we are once more aware of the body as a field of power— active, bristling, and energetic on the long road to social transformation.

INTRODUCTION: ICON MATTERS

1. The recycling of the photograph taken by Sondeep Sarkar (rivaled only by Pramod Pushkarna's photographs) will receive greater attention in chapter 4, where I look at the best-known public images of the bandit queen.

2. "Dalit" is the term of self-determination taken on by those communities in post-independence India who belong on the lowest rungs of the caste ladder; after the four major castes, there are the untouchables, a historically underprivileged group officially designated the Scheduled Castes—an affirmative-action category mobilized to reserve seats in educational institutions and jobs. At the present juncture, Dalits in India number about 250 million, or 25 percent of the population.

3. At "Iconoclash: The Struggle for Religious Identity," a conference held at Utrecht University in 2005 that elaborated on a prior Karlsruhe exhibit of artworks (May 4–August 4, 2002), historians sought to distinguish iconoclasm (the use of images) and iconoclash (a more technical term for the "destruction of or suspicion against the physical representation of the divine, the sacred, the transcendent"): see Van Asselt et al. 2007, 4. *Global Icons* takes a series of iconoclashes as points of departure for examining the use of images.

4. In her recent Deleuzian reading of Australian art, the feminist philosopher Elizabeth Grosz (2008) argues that art and philosophy both territorialize chaos even as they retain the potential of opening us again into "shards of chaos" framed within a work. Her evocation of the "frame" as a plane of composition that turns

chaos into territory is especially important for the icon, a sign always grasped as an epistemology. See also Deleuze 2003, a work with which Grosz converses.

5. This aphoristic capture of the icon is widely quoted, most emphatically in Bruno Latour's introduction to the exhibit "Iconoclash" (Latour and Weibel 2002).

6. Karl Marx (1867) reads technologies as commodities with enigmatic appearance. See the discussion of this conception of technology in McQuire 2006, 253.

7. Most famously, Heidegger (1977 [1949]) has revitalized the notion of techné. Heidegger, of course, speaks of technology as "enframing" nature as calculable force. As a "stance" toward the world, technology is a mode of revealing, a summoning to action I ascribe to the icon.

8. Daniel Miller's long engagement with materiality is useful here in situating the different disciplinary traditions consolidated in *Global Icons*. Eschewing a vulgar theory of artifacts, Miller (2005) explains that materiality has been theorized in three ways: as a theory of objects, the purview of material culture, where the appearances of the world around us are objectified; as a theory of matter, in philosophy, aesthetics, and theology, where we become the world as it acts on us; and as a theory of agency (in the work of Bruno Latour and Arthur Gell), where human and non-human actors are invested with power. Miller's point is that a plural conception of materiality has broad implications for the study of power, a proposition *Global Icons* shares in its preoccupation with the popular.

9. As Pheng Cheah (1996) notes, Grosz's and Butler's work exemplify this post-Cartesian move, with Butler (following Plato, Hegel, Freud, and Lacan) developing a notion of agency as the force of negativity and Grosz (following Spinoza, Nietzsche, Foucault, and Deleuze) proposing a positive dynamism.

10. I consciously do not adopt a Deleuzian vocabulary (dominant in theories of affect) in *Global Icons* to keep faith with the established terminologies of icon study. But Deleuze's emphasis on sensation, as affects and precepts (extracting affection and perception), and his elaboration of Henri Bergson's notion of perception (the tension between pure sensation and cognition) is of considerable salience to the cognitive, sensuous, and affective intensities of icon veneration. In chapter 2, I return to this genealogy as I unpack "sensation" in greater depth to take into account the phenomenology of the iconic encounter. My primary investment in the question comes from my location in Marxist, feminist, and queer critiques that have re-evaluated "perception" as including embodied responses and affect. See also the elaboration of the relation between affect and sensation in Massumi 2002.

11. *The World Factbook* registers India as the fourth largest nation in broadcast television stations (see https://www.cia.gov/library/publications/the-world-factbook), while Internet use has skyrocketed to a reported seventy-one million users, see "Indian Internet Users Grew to 71 Million: IMRB," *The Economic Times*, March 20, 2010.

12. I will elaborate on strategies for reading mass media more substantially in chapter 3, but here it suffices to say I am drawing on Walter Benjamin's propositions in the unfinished *Arcades* project (Benjamin 1927–40) to forward a thesis on social hieroglyphics.

13. This could be a name such as Arundhati Roy or Phoolan Devi or a title such as Mother Teresa, the Bandit Queen, or the Tank Man.

14. Immanuel Wallerstein, "2008: The Demise of Neoliberal Globalization," *Monthly Review*, January 2, 2008, available online at http://www.monthlyreview.org/mrzine/wallerstein010208.html.

15. The Washington consensus is so widely discussed that it is hardly necessary to belabor the point. For elaborations on the mantra of deregulation and privatization, see Stiglitz 2005. For elaboration of the underlying economic theory to military efforts of the Bush era, see Kalb 2000.

16. Here I am invoking the elaboration of static in Larkin 2008.

17. Giovanni Arrighi underscores the constant and dynamic restructuring of financial capital as it gradually incorporates large swathes of the world, drawing insightful comparisons between four long systemic financial cycles (starting with the medieval Genoese financial expansion). These cycles, in Arrighi's (following Braudel's) view explains the "cycle" underlying the long twentieth century and gestures to what lies ahead: see Arrighi 1994. Arrighi's work has influenced Harvey's critique of the effects of flexible accumulation.

18. See, e.g., early diagnoses of localism in opposition to global flows in contributions to Dissanayake and Wilson 1998, esp. Michael Featherstone, "Localism, Globalism, and Cultural Identity," 46–77. See also the "Alternative Localities" section in Jameson and Miyoshi 1998.

19. In this sense, I would liken my efforts to the saturated sense of the "present" in Mazzarella 2003, a deeply historical juncture that does not necessarily demand a historicist reading of the region.

20. See Henry Jenkins's (2005) argument on participatory culture, posed against older notions of passive spectatorship, where media producers and consumers both participate in generating media content according to an evolving set of still ill-defined rules. Jenkins is careful to note he is not suggesting that the partnership is an *equal* one, just that consumers have greater cultural power in defining media content.

21. Such a "liquid conception of the social," as Antonio Negri recently put it to Cesare Casarino when Casarino pressed him on Negri's silence about Gramsci, certainly offended scholastic Italian Marxists such as Asor Rosa, who attacked Gramsci precisely for not attaching people to class: Casarino and Negri 2008b, 162. Hence, Gramsci has had a beleaguered place in Italian, and other, Marxisms.

22. Despite Guha's frequent evocations of "the people," the popular would remain under-theorized in his work, perhaps because of historians' insistence on written records of popular mobilization. Where the subaltern could remain a pure analytic category, the popular, participating in social communication, signaled compromise, and this sense of co-optation in popular culture, where subalterns cut deals, make compromises, or enter dubious contracts with their enemies, possibly dictates why scholars of the enterprise have largely skirted extensive analyses of this domain. The unresolved question of the popular has prompted a group of younger scholars to pursue the entanglements of the subaltern and the popular, a project in which I have participated for the last four years. For a manifesto on the elision of the popular in Ranajit Guha, see, among others, Chattopadhyay and Sarkar 2005.

23. Culture, in this strain of thinking, persists in the anthropological sense of a domain of practices organic to specific communities; the expressive rituals of re-assembling mass-produced commodities elaborated in the Birmingham school's Gramscian interventions (particularly in Stuart Hall and Dick Hebdige) were rarely, if at all, present in the work of most subaltern studies scholars.

24. If we take the local actors, often working in loose coalitions, as paradigmatic of the collective, it is one quite different from the sharply demarcated, closely coor-dinated, socially antagonistic *bricoleur* communities in Dick Hebdige's famous *Subculture* (1979). The "nontraditional" effervescent popular culture I gesture toward here often gains its value quite directly from its collusions with mass media. It depends on the news to spotlight symbolic performances; in such com-promise with mass culture, we see incorporated agents who seek institution in politics as soon as they are "heard."

25. Laclau's earlier work on radical democracy with Chantal Mouffe, *Hegemony and Socialist Strategy* (1985), evoked suspicion from Marxists of all stripes, with An-tonio Negri christening the book a "saccharine sweet concept of interclass collab-oration" (Casarino and Negri 2008b, 163). Certainly, the notion of the "common" that Laclau and Mouffe forward works from within the logic of capital; it is a compromised "common" that does not move toward a revolutionary event. De-spite such "failings," I argue that Laclau's *On Populist Reason* (2005) has much to offer scholars of transnational mass media, for his "popular" provides a flexible rubric for thinking the popular as contingent linkages between heterogeneous actors dispersed over geographically distant locales.

26. For both Laclau and Mouffe, Gramsci's reorientation to the political moment of articulation as the contingent war of position, away from the structural deter-minism of class, proved fertile ground for thinking antagonism within the social fragmentation of late capitalist societies. Laclau 2005 extends the notion of signification developed in Laclau and Mouffe 1985—the suggestion that we can only glimpse the social in the articulation of social demands.

27. See "Thirst Knows No Season," 1935, available in the online press kit at http://www.thecoca-colacompany.com, 1935 U.S. advertisement.

28. The Spencerian script (a style prevalent in the United States from 1850 to 1925) originated with the invention of Coca-Cola, written by the inventor John Pem-berton's bookkeeper Frank Robinson.

29. See Bhaskar Sarkar's (2010) argument on "plasticity" as the descriptor for the constant mutability and mutuality of forms, in the contemporary mediascapes of globalization.

30. This image is from the Geocities portal on Roy, http://www.geocities.com/jporta _99/aroy.html (accessed November 2008), but it circulated widely on several other sites, such as http://people.famouswhy.com/arundhati_roy, http://www .sawnet.org, and http://www.wmich.edu/dialogues/texts/godofsmallthings .html.

31. While leaders can become iconic, I am less concerned here with the qualities (or circumstances) that draw crowds to a leader, the subject of charisma theory based on Max Weber's oeuvre, than on the graphic inscription instrumentally har-nessed to function as a symbol of the popular. For paradigmatic discussions of charisma and populism, see Allahar 2001; Robinson 2000.

32. Max Weber's underscoring of the conditions of possibility that enable the rise of charismatic leaders, however, has some salience to our bio-icons: Mass-mediated star icons become politically efficacious media under particular historical conditions I explore throughout the book. For a lengthier discussion of different types of charisma, some pertinent to the narrations of our bio-icons, see Schweitzer 1984.

33. Hence, media theorists of this period return to the theorists of space for human geographies of globalization; the work of Marxist geographers such as Henri Lefebvre, Edward Soja, David Harvey, and Fredric Jameson are most pertinent to *Global Icons*, with its emphasis on laboring bodies whose agency erupts in expressive popular culture.

34. "The waiting room of history" refers to the analysis "Two Histories of Capital," in Chakrabarty 2000; see the elaboration in Sarkar 2008.

35. By the "periphery" I mean those locations from where surplus value (both resources and labor) is extracted for accumulation at global financial centers (consolidated through the Dutch-led banking system and maintained by colonialism), mainly in the global North. Here I rely on the elaboration of the world system as shifting core–periphery relations as global capital restructures and reorganizes in Arrighi 1994.

36. In his self-reflexive acceptance of the Nobel Peace Prize on December 10, 2009, on the eve of a troop surge to Afghanistan, President Barack Obama gave a classic American rationale (as Michael Bechloss put it) for the considered use of force. While inspired by Martin Luther King Jr., Obama would remind the world (again) that Hitler's armies could not be stopped without military intervention. All over the news media, the speech was instantly read as shades of John F. Kennedy and Franklin D. Roosevelt.

37. See *Newsweek*, March 1, 2006; *Time*, July 26, 2006.

38. The figure of Indira Gandhi, a highly public image eliciting strong interest in her private life, is central to any discussion of female iconicity in South Asia. Gandhi, after all, consciously drew on the iconographic charge of Mother India—"Indira is India"—for her political efficacy. But female leaders (Benazir Bhutto, Khaleda Zia, Sirimavo Bandaranaike, Hasina Wajed in South Asia) working directly in the domain of politics function in different ways from the genre of bio-icons I am tracking: "ordinary" citizens who erupt as stars in mass media, whose iconicity *later* turns them into apertures for political mobilization. For discussions of Indira Gandhi, see Sunder Rajan 1993; see also Everett 1993.

39. See, e.g., essays in Jeffery and Basu 1998 and in Bacchetta and Power 2002.

40. These can be readily found in Google images from all over the world. The Adams inscription in particular is quoted vertiginously, from multiple websites to statues: see, e.g., the one sponsored by the Knights of Columbus, North Carolina, posted on a pro-life Flickr album at http://www.flickr.com/photos/ted_abbott/164415359 (accessed July 2005).

41. An excerpt from Hitchens (1997) was recently posted on the blog Neverwasanarrow.blogspot.com, from which the image of the stained-glass window (The Transfiguration of Our Lord Parish, Archdiocese of Toronto) was taken, provoking a heated discussion more than a decade after the publication of the piece; hence, it has periodically revived reflections on Mother Teresa.

CHAPTER ONE: MOVING TECHNOLOGIES

1. For a current estimate of a continent-by-continent assessment of digital access, see Tharoor 2005. While the Indian government has launched a massive e-governance initiative, administered by the Department of Information Technology, access to mainframe computing is largely restricted to matters relating to land rights (automated land records), farming (questions regarding crops), card registration (for voting capacity), and other such interactions with the state. As R. Chandra-shekar and S. R. Das (2006), working with capacity building, note in their white paper, even these facilities remain poorly distributed across the states with the Indian federation. We are far indeed from the luxury of personal computing.

2. In her reputed call for the materiality of information, N. Katherine Hayles attempts to constrain celebrations of the post-human's informational immaterial structure (with new models of subjectivity emerging from cognitive science and artificial life), which supposes that all humans are systems that can be downloaded. While proponents of cyborg culture, like feminists and postcolonial theorists, have launched an attack on the liberal humanist subject in the name of collective distributed intelligence, the price has been to downplay embodiment—the specificity of material constraint that disallows frictionless transfers of information: see Hayles 1993, 1997.

3. For a historical approach to Peirce's life and works, see Misak 2004. See Freadman 2004 and relevant essays on the icon in Peirce 1992 (1867–93), 1996.

4. But why return to these all-too-familiar arguments after computer-generated images? Barthes certainly provides a point of departure for developing a grammar appropriate to the icon's complex operations, where already existing signs function as raw material for the iconic message; such a move is critical for grasping how icons are resignified. Perhaps more important, when one reflects on Barthes's fascination with indexicality, one is struck by his congruence with the Peircean insistence on the icon as "natural" or "degenerate" sign. Both intimate that the index imparts an "aperture-like" function to the icon, and given their radically different critical genealogies, this becomes a function worth pursuing.

5. The essay builds on Barthes's earlier diagnosis of modern myths as central to the identity of a community. For example, the Eiffel Tower or French wine function as guarantors of French identity. For a longer discussion of Barthes's meditations on the image, see Olin 2002.

6. *Tank Man*, a documentary directed by Katerina Monemvassitis and Brent E. Huffman that aired in 2006 on the news program *Frontline*, uses the iconic photograph to reflect on the pro-democracy demonstrations of June 1989. Charles Cole recalls how he smuggled the footage out of China. Jeff Widener of the Associated Press took the most widely circulated version of the photograph, but Stuart Franklin of Magnum Photos won an award for a similar capture. Even in the case of such rare footage, one point of origin is hard to stabilize. Several of the "original" photographs were taken from a hotel overlooking the Cháng Ān Dà Jiē (长安大街), or Great Avenue of Chang'an. The so-called Tank Man blocked a column of tanks heading east of Beijing's Chang'an Boulevard (Avenue of Eternal Peace) near Tiananmen Square during the student uprising. For further details, see http://www.pbs.org/wgbh/pages/frontline/tankman/view.

7. The drama of getting this coveted shot is eloquently narrated in the documentary, where Charles Cole narrates hiding the film roll in the toilet to salvage it during a raid by the Chinese authorities (agents from the Public Security Bureau who crashed through the hotel door), auratizing the surviving roll.

8. In a conference on style (World Picture: Style, Oklahoma, October 23–24, 2009), Rosalind Galt, presenting on Derek Jarman, spoke about the "decorative eye" as a key historical sense. Her emerging work on synaesthesia (and especially design) makes an important contribution to my arguments on the tactile, sonorous, and visual dimensions of the icon: see Galt 2009.

9. The Swiss Pirate Party became the main server after EveryDNC (a hosting company in Manchester, New Hapshire) stopped accepting traffic from Wikileaks, bowing to pressure from the government. Other large corporate entities such as Amazon followed suit, refusing to host the Wikileaks website. It may be too early to diagnose what might happen in this case, but the Wikileaks episode illuminates the constraints on media networks in an age of celebrated information flows.

10. Shu-mei Shih's (2004) analysis of how the Cultural Revolution circulates in the West to reinforce the value of democratic humanism, a predetermined signifier for the sign, presents a parallel case. Her reading is instructive in pausing, once more, on the worlding capacities of allegory.

11. In their recent commemoration of fifty years of the World Press Photo Foundation, Hans Pool and Maaik Krijgsman catalogued four photographs—including the one of the Tank Man—that have become iconic at certain points of enunciation. Their film elucidates circulation and consumption practices as central to the formation of the icon: see Hans Pool and Maaik Krijgsman, dirs., *Looking for an Icon*, Icarus Films, 2005.

12. In the episode, the menopausal Selma involves Marge and Homer in her scheme to adopt a Chinese baby, asking Homer to pose as her husband for the adoption agency. Mockingly titled "Goo Goo Gai Pan" (a mix of baby talk and the Americanized version of a Cantonese dish), the episode pokes fun at numerous stereotypes of China, including that of Chairman Mao (Madame Wu watches Homer, Selma, and Marge through the "eyes" of a portrait of Chairman Mao hanging on a wall, much like Norman Bates in Alfred Hitchcock's film *Psycho*). For details, see the website at http://www.tv.com/the-simpsons/goo-goo-gai-pan.

13. See the analysis of the Coca-Cola campaign in Mazzarella 2003, 215–49. Before 1977, under Indira Gandhi's regime, Coca-Cola held 100 percent of its equity share in India, a de facto privilege rescinded by the government led by the Bharatiya Janata Party that invoked the Foreign Regulations Act of 1973 (instructing non-Indian corporations to limit their equity share to 40 percent). Coca-Cola saw such insistence as an act of aggression, arguing that giving up equity would mandate sharing the "secret formula." This led to Coca-Cola's departure from Indian markets in 1977 and the emergence of Indian colas such as Thums Up and Limca, which remained popular even after Coca-Cola returned (Mazzarella 2003, 221–25). Coca-Cola returned to India in 1997 after being granted approval to set up subsidiary holding companies (such as Hindustan Coca-Cola Holdings and Bharat Coca-Cola Holdings), having first bought up the thriving local competition in colas for the paltry sum of $60 million.

14. For a history of Coca-Cola in India, especially the cola wars, see Amit Srivastava's articles on the India Resource Center website at http://www.indiaresource.org.

15. See Amit Srivastava, "Coca-Cola Destroys Indian Villages, despite Warning by Coca-Cola Study," March 9, 2009, available online at http://www.indiaresource .org/campaigns/coke/2009/cokedestroysvillages.html.

16. A word on the specificity of Kerala within the India polity: Along with West Bengal in eastern India, Kerala has been governed by the Communist Party since 1957 (with a few interim governments led by the Congress Party) and sports high literacy rates (the 90 percent literacy rates among rural women in Kerala is higher than the 88 percent literacy rate among urban men in the rest of India), high life expectancy, and a strong economy (the state has the highest gross income per net cropped area). Political initiatives, often arising from local popular demands, historically have found civil-legal expression in state policy (e.g., *Ezhava* demands for policy on caste discrimination). The quiet vigil in Plachimada was therefore quite quickly channeled into the recognizable political idioms of *dharnas* (sit-ins) and *yatras* (marches) with the entrance of statewide organizations and all-India watchdog groups.

17. For more on Haksar's oeuvre, see http://www.sharadhaksar.com. Besides, it was not as if Haksar had singled out Coca-Cola for witty repartee on the contradictions of mass consumerism. His photographs of a boy urinating on the iconic Nike flourish (embellished with the words "Just Do It") and of bony hands cradling a tin cup sporting a MasterCard sticker had passed unnoticed: see discussion of Haksar's work in Ghosh 2010.

18. The newspaper remained unfazed, with its managing director, Virendra Kumar (who is also a member of Parliament), asserting that since the paper does not accept ads for Coke, Pepsi, or Palm Oil, it is free to campaign on issues of its choice.

19. The Taj hotels are an elite chain managed by the Oberoi Group (Mumbai's Taj was a site of tragedy on November 26, 2008), attracting the wealthy with rooms that range in price from $400 to $1,000 a night. Locally, such elite hotels draw metropolitan diners who can afford the high-end cuisine; shoppers for their boutique-lined shopping arcades; and curious grazers out for a stroll, a date, or an outing.

20. Here I use the useful elaboration of the "rune" developed in the introduction in Sarkar 2009a.

21. See the widely circulated, "Coke Loses Fizz over Photographer," available online at http://www.rediff.com; "Cola behind Empty Pots?" 2008; and a multitude of blogs and websites, the most important of which is the website of the India Resource Center (http://www.indiaresource.org), a nonprofit organization based in California that has archived much of the visual data.

22. In aligning adoration and desecration within the same psychic structure, I follow the provocations in Taussig 1999, in which Michael Taussig argues that defacing images intimates enchantment: One defaces the thing (with magical powers) one fears or hates.

23. Claude Markovits (2004, 17) presents Gandhi's global legacy "outside India," starting with Romain Rolland's famous essay published in 1923 to the current

moment. For a discussion of Gandhi's iconicity, see Hardiman 2004; Markovits 2004.

24. Even though Markovits marks *Gandhi* as *the* screen consecration, Gandhi had entered Indian regional cinemas as early as 1966. Indian "art cinema" directors have taken up various fragments of the biograph. Shyam Benegal's *The Making of the Mahatma* (1996) focused on Gandhi's stay in South Africa, for example, while Feroz Abbas Khan's *Gandhi, My Father* (2007) traced the life of Gandhi's eldest, prodigal son, Harilal.

25. See also the Apple Collection images of Mahatma Ghandi online: http://www .theapplecollection.com/various/Celebrity/ghandi.html.

26. "The premise is that people who use Apple computers are different and that we make computers for those creative people who believe that one person can change the world," said Allen Olivio, senior director of worldwide marketing communications at Apple in Cupertino, California. To clarify the politics of own-ing Apple products, he added: "The ads are for people who don't care what the computer does but care about what they can do with the computer." Stuart Elliot (1998) explains that the campaign has featured more than forty so-called crazy ones, historical and contemporary figures who have included Bob Dylan, Albert Einstein, Ted Turner, Pablo Picasso, John Lennon and Yoko Ono, Thomas Edison, Muhammad Ali, Alfred Hitchcock, Miles Davis, Lucille Ball and Desi Arnaz, the Reverend Martin Luther King Jr., Amelia Earhart, Jim Henson, Rosa Parks, Frank Lloyd Wright, and Jerry Seinfeld. More are on the way.

27. The term "*satyagraha*" is a combination of "*satya* (truth-love)" and "*agraha* (firm-ness or force)." As Gandhi explains, it is the "the vindication of truth not by infliction of suffering on the opponent but on one's self." Satyagraha is peaceful; opponents must be converted by a demonstration of purity, humility, and hon-esty. See the discussion of satyagraha in Gandhi 1993 (1925–28), esp. 434–40.

28. Zubir Ahmed, "Gandhi-style Farmers Protest," BBC Bombay, October 12, 2006.

29. Sharat Pradhan, "Lucknow Citizens Go Gandhian on Liquor Merchant," Septem-ber 9, 2006, available online at http://www.rediff.com (accessed April 25, 2007).

30. Christopher offers certain Peircean shibboleths of such reality testing, such as if a "proposition is true" for Peirce, then anyone inquiring about the nature of reality will be destined to believe in it. Hence, reality comes about through belief but also through verifiable truths: Hookaway 2004, 130.

31. See the discussion of his entire oeuvre in Short 2004. For a different reading, see Silverman 1984.

32. See, e.g., the otherwise useful pursuit of Peirce's diagrammatic and pictorial draw-ings as he moves toward the logical method in Leja 2000, 100.

33. This later Peirce is considerably undervalued, as many of his contemporaries— most notably, the Russian linguist Roman Jakobsen—have pointed out. "The iconic and the indexical constituents of verbal symbols have too often remained underestimated or even disregarded; on the other hand, the predominantly sym-bolic character of language and its constituent cardinal difference from the other, chiefly indexical or iconic, sets of signs likewise awaits due consideration in modern linguistic methodology" (quoted in Freadman 2004, 97).

34. This is Peirce's scheme of "intentions": The "first intention" is a pre-semiotic

awareness of the object; the second intention of signs is semiotic in that it registers the object as a representamen that is like, but also different from, the object. The third intention is achieved when the representamen (an impression, a word, an image) is interpreted or framed by general (universal) laws. When it is put to use, or circulation, it becomes a sign: Bruss 1978.

35. Perhaps the point that has received the most attention in recent scholarship on visuality and visual culture is the simultaneous danger and promise of indexical and iconic capacities: see, e.g., Evans 1999. Peirce's account of the index's causal and physical link to its object is pertinent to the photographic image. As Barthes reminds us, despite its aesthetic coding, the photographic image operates as an index pointing to a corresponding ontological (inferred) object. Hence, it promises a fullness of presence that captivates the spectator. A further inference of the correspondence of the experiential space of the photograph with an inferred "real" place renders the world of the image more immediate than ever.

36. In his later work, Peirce complicates not just the icon. The index also appears as complex and heterogeneous.

37. It follows that the icon can tell us nothing about the ontology of its objects. It cannot differentiate, for example, between a fictional object (the centaur) and an ideal object (diagram).

CHAPTER TWO: CORPOREAL APERTURES

1. Taussig (1991) develops tactility as a peripheral sense unleashed by the vigor of modern life, drawing on Benjamin's notion of "tactile optics"—an apperceptive mode that accompanies cognition in everyday life. Here again, the senses enable dispersion.

2. In "Notes on Societies of Control" (1990), Gilles Deleuze draws a distinction between disciplinary societies (where threats are sought to be limited, restricted, even eradicated) and "societies of control" (where threats are regulated, mobilized, facilitated, and reconfigured). Societies of control operate through "the apparatus of security" that approaches life as multiplicity; security does not kill but lets things be. Such a description—in which bodies, populations, biological resources, goods, and information are in constant mutation—is increasingly forwarded to capture bio-political modernity: see, e.g., Thacker 2008. Thacker's transcription is significant here insofar as I situate the contemporary relevance of corporeal bio-politics as contingent action against regimes of bio-security that aggrandize all biological existence.

3. See the discussion of the Talmudic scholar Moses Maimonides's capture of this reading, in which icon worship is regarded as idolatrous, in Mitchell 1986, 32–33.

4. Carefully navigating the differences between visual and verbal sign types, materials of representation, and institutional traditions, Mitchell (1986) examines the switching between the verbal and the visual (e.g., in ekphrasis or visual description in verbal texts) that proliferates in what he describes as the "pictorial turn" in the twentieth century.

5. Mondzain's work is one of the volumes in the Cultural Memory in the Present, edited by Mieke Bal, that revitalizes theoretical genealogies that are recessive in current critical theory. The Byzantine doctrine of the icon is one of the least understood theories that the series brings back into critical conversation.

6. See, e.g., the chapter "Idolatary and Iconoclasm" in Freedberg (1989).

7. Annabel Wharton (2003) argues that all of these emblems capture the identity of the divine, the icon being the most accredited sign demanding veneration. Her essay is one of several excellent explorations of the icon in the collection, which also includes Anthony Eastmond's complicating of the icon–idol relation in Eastmond 2003. These essays are studies presented to Robin Cormack, one of the foremost art historians who inaugurated serious analyses of Byzantine art in the 1980s, in his famous *Writing in Gold*.

8. James Kearney (2002) explains, in a virtuoso reading of William Pietz's influential work, that "fetish" was a term used to develop a theory of witchcraft in the medieval period (see 436–37).

9. Jain is interested in the fetish as one of the few categories that speaks to the power of circulating images.

10. Mondzain notes that the young Nikephoros was probably motivated to make such a turn as a response to his father's fate. His father had famously lost his job and had gone into exile following his defense of icons during the first iconoclastic crisis.

11. The editor explains that the French word "imaginal" better captures the sense of a projection on the imaginary (the usual psychoanalytic usage) as a social practice than an individual psychic one.

12. In *The Ground of the Image* (2005), Jean-Luc Nancy argues that the sacred is what is cut off, separate, inaccessible; it is the ground of the image that tries to mark it in distinctive trait. Religious and political regimes bind the scared through the image—hence, the danger to the immense potentiality of the image.

13. Embodied visuality has long preoccupied philosophers who have rethought the distancing effects of a visible object encountered by a disembodied, incorporeal look. Among these, Jean-Luc Nancy's "logic" of touch, as Derrida names it in *Corpus* (2005), is most relevant to *Global Icons* here because Nancy revises metaphysics to address the sociality of the look. To put it bluntly, to look or establish contact with the infinite, for Nancy, is at once to make contact with community, a plurality of beings. In the perception of a distant object, we sense another eye (the cornea, the lash, the pupil), even as the gaze that meets our own senses us. As we touch, we are touched; looking is also self-touching in this schematic. In Nancy's elaboration, to look for the origin is not to miss it. "To touch upon origin is not to miss it," Nancy argues in *Être singulier pluriel* (2000, 62), because it is not another thing (*aliud*) that can be missed or appropriated. It does not belong to this logic— "to touch upon origin is to be exposed to it," to be opened to it, just as one looks through the aperture into the infinite. Lest we think such a merging is ecstatic dissolution into the origin, Nancy reminds us that the becoming-haptic optical experience establishes distance even as it we intuit beings / Being all around us. Far from immediacy, touching is quixotically a sense of apartness or spacing from others. Others are held as singularities who are linked in one plurality: "bodies laid out, shoulder to shoulder, edge to edge," in "common" humanity—not by immanence (there is no intrinsic quality that makes us human) or by transcendence (we do not move toward a common project), but by a sense of syncopated differences. Beyond community, such a phenomenological turn extends our bodies into the world. Nancy maintains that we inhabit a body ecotechnics where

techné marshals the body's separateness from other phenomena, one which that can be critically approached by the imagination: an ecotopia that we perceive even as we are held apart from it, providing a philosophical basis for ecological criticality. If we follow Nancy's sense of dislocated touching—a touching that shores up plurality but marks each partitioned self as singular—then we are compelled to think of community as a negative space marked by difference, a view of the social congruent with Laclau's popular (the articulation of diverse social demands).

14. Jonathan Crary's work focuses on the perceptual fields activated by optical technologies where the body emerges as the physiological apparatus for making the world sensible. See *Techniques of the Observer* (1991) and *Suspensions of Perception* (2001), both of critical significance to icon consumption as embodied perception.

15. "Sensuous scholarship" is Paul Stoller's term for these scholarly works, many of which draw on Merleau-Ponty 1962. Jennifer Barker (2009) poses the cinematic body as the "lived body" that participates in intentional acts of perception. The viewer and the film share sensing and grasping the world in a continuum of blood, tissue, light, and celluloid, remarks Barker (2009, 4–5), in another configuration of the material contiguities explored here. See also Marks 2000; Sobchack 2004 (to whom Barker explicitly marks her debt). Merleau-Ponty (1962) in fact develops "incorporating practice" as an action encoded in bodily memory by repeated performances until habitual. See *The Phenomenology of Perception* (1962).

16. The material image came to be, the story ran, after the artist dreamed of the Virgin—a classic example of imaginary projection: see Belting 1994, esp. 146–55.

17. Religious studies scholarship on the subject is vast, but I focus on Davis 1997 and Eck 1988 to cull a corresponding sense of the icon in India because these works are widely influential in media studies.

18. In common parlance, *bhakti* means devotion or veneration. But since loving God as one's beloved is the highest form of bhakti, the term can also mean "love."

19. See the elaboration of the reconstructed historical memory, focusing on the Somanatha temple as paradigmatic example, in Thapar 2004. Thapar reminds us that the great temple of Somanatha was raided several times by Hindu rulers before Mahmud of Ghazni raided it in the eleventh century. This historical iconoclasm was fetishized by the Hindu right in India in the 1990s to mobilize Hindus into a majoritarian electorate against the Muslim invaders, which led to the destruction of the fifteenth-century Babri Masjid in December 1992. As we know, in ancient and medieval India temples and their idols were centers of combined political and spiritual power. So it might be useful to remember that the endowment and destruction of temples (though not necessarily of the icons/idols installed in them) was a fairly unremarkable part of the history of the region indulged in by Hindu and Muslim rulers alike.

20. "Veneration," which entered the English language in the early fifteenth century via the Middle French *veneration*, hails from the Latin *venerationem* (nom. *veneratio*), capaciously signifying "reverence" (from *venerari*); the root *venus* (gen. *veneris*) further connotes "beauty, love, desire," all important qualities and sensations for the icon.

    In many ways, Morgan's "popular Christianity" highlights only some of philosophers of deconstructive Christianity (such as Jean-Luc Nancy and George

Bataille) whose work underlie the book's emphasis on flesh as the conduit to the divine.

21. Bhakti (in Sanskrit) simply means devotion, but it is also understood as a devotional practice that privileges the intimate private relations between the devotee and divinity free of religious authority. Such a practice was critical to a large social movement (replete with leaders, poets, singers, and writers) that spanned several centuries (800–1700) and moved from the south to the northern parts of the subcontinent. Deeply syncretic and inclusive of lower castes, the poor, and Muslims, bhakti is often regarded as a popular social movement that spawned great cultural expressions.

22. Pinney (2004) notes how a popular film such as *Jai Santoshi Maa* (Hail Santoshi Ma, 1975) revitalized the worship of a less well-known goddess, with mass production creating a field of *filmi* gods. His ethnographic work takes place in Bhatisuda, Madhya Pradesh, a state often regarded as the Indian heartland.

23. Panofsky's seminal paper "Iconography and Iconology: An Introduction to the Study of Renaissance Art" (1939) was reprinted in *Meaning in the Visual Arts* (1955); all references here are to the reprinted version.

24. Dadasaheb Phalke is generally considered the filmmaker who produced India's first feature film in 1913; hence, his *Lanka Dahan* would have been quite popular. When the film played in theaters, audiences prostrated themselves before the images of divinity, popular practices of devotion that were extended to the dream screen: Barnouw and Kishnaswamy 1980 (1963), 15.

25. Here I am following the incitement to place the "eye of belief" within media ecology in Morgan. The use of devotional *Shyamasangeet* (associated with the bhakti movement in Bengal) erects the structure of veneration, where the image as manifestation of the divine comes under critique.

26. Bal and Bryson (1991) note that critics such as Alois Riegel and T. J. Clark undertook such a social history in the past. See also Bryson 1981.

27. Hence, she highlights—in the spirit of Derrida and Nelson Goodman—those details that do not fit, those that are exorbitant to the text. Derrida will be a constant presence in this book in too many ways to characterize here, but I will mention Nelson Goodman, whose work I do not pursue at greater length in this chapter, where it would belong. For his analysis of life-like representations relevant to the iconic sign, a theory indebted to Wittgenstein, see Goodman 1976.

28. See Pinney 2001. Pinney pays homage to Gell's provocations; the title of the work was inspired by Gell 1992.

29. Pursuing Islamic traditions, Woodman Taylor elucidates the aural dimension a little differently, drawing our attention to the ways in which the songs in Bombay cinema direct the organization of looks on screen—a "poetics of sight" situated in Islamic courtly poetry, where *nazaar*, or the gaze, is the conveyor of love.

30. We see this particularly in the ways in which popular music from Indian films creates imagined communities everywhere, even establishing sociality between the hijackers and passengers on an Indian Airlines jet in 2000, as one famous story went.

31. Such political usage of images, Pinney (2004) argues, can be traced back to India's nationalist period. The cow, for instance, became infused with the divine when a chromolithograph of eighty-four gods residing in the cow's body, with a group of

devotees kneeling to worship it at the udders, appeared during the Cow Protection agitation of 1891, a rural campaign that mobilized the power of images well before Gandhi entered the nationalist struggle. Compositional variance—the tractor, the gun, or the bomb—harnesses the graphic inscription to convey an altered message by placing the image in relation to other images. The god's relation to the gun re-encodes the icon; it acquires a different syntactical meaning within a signifying chain.

32. See the elaboration of "biocapital" for those who can afford lifestyle-enhancing drugs at the cost of those who are subject to risky drug trials administered by big pharmaceutical companies in Sunder Rajan 2006.

33. Recent theorists of bio-political modernity, such as Cesare Casarino, pose a potentiality *qua* potentiality that, reappropriated again and again as social demands for various commons (media, bio-resources, political programs), remains foundational to the social—a radical "surplus common" that underlies all desire for being-in-common: Casarino (2008, 22). For Casarino, we "live" the surplus common through the body; it enables both personal and collective incorporation into the social. Therefore, "love" can be one experience of the absent common; burning trains to communicate rage or grief can be another. With Casarino, we are in bio-political times when capital expropriations of our bodies have intensified to yield "biocapital." Giorgio Agamben's oeuvre has received the most critical attention, in his engagements with Carl Schmidtt. Indeed, for our purposes, Agamben's figuration of bare life is immediately relevant to the social bandit. But more important, Agamben refocuses us on "bio-politics" as a governing mode of power within modern democracies, marking a turn in political theory developed further in the work of Michael Hardt, Antonio Negri, and Cesare Casarino. With bio-politics, a corporeal politics becomes historical contingency.

34. We can see this "capacity" in the state of play between becoming body and its arrested image, as the former's power rivals those that determine our structural conditions. Such "play," as limitless as the "field" (with its rules and goalposts) is limited, poses an open system, since the connections and pathways toward which the body moves remain unpredictable.

35. For Grosz (1994), corporeality provides a middle ground for debates in feminist theory, positioning the body as an interface where physical materiality and psychic materiality etch their traces. The latency model of the conscious and the unconscious, Grosz argues, and the corresponding devaluation of the body in the Cartesian tradition, offer little recompense for subjects that are often reduced to the body and marked by sexual difference. Although Grosz focuses on sexual difference, one could extend her observations to others who are socially (de)valued in terms of bodily significations. The laborer, the subaltern, the racially marked subject, are some other protagonists one might bring into the conversation.

36. On the other hand, we have the influential refusal to think the body outside of discourse that finds its most significant expression in Butler 1993. For Butler, the body may have a materiality beyond signification, but any effort to conceptualize such pre-discursivity is a deeply discursive project: We experience "matter" through signification, not as a release from it. Putting a phenomenological spin on "social construction," Butler (1993) insists that the body is "a process of materialization that stabilizes over time to produce the effect of boundary, fixity,

and a surface we call matter." Instead of seeing these positions as opposing each other, one might ask: What are the stakes for posing the events of the body that slip the fixity of representation so that we might (discursively) give it another name? If no single event can fully determine the status of the body, how do we name its negotiations of pleasure, pain, other bodies, other objects, or the space it inhabits?

37. Unwilling to jettison the feminist shibboleths of the body as always a concrete, specific thing and inevitably marked by sexual difference, Grosz (1994) poses the inevitable question: If bodies more often than not are marked by sexual differ-ence, how does one use the body to dislocate the regulatory powers of such social inscription? With the critique of Western metaphysics in Irigaray leading the charge, feminist philosophers have embarked on a project to rethink "the body as other than the negation of thought" (and therefore to rethink Cartesian dual-ism), since the body is crucial to gender constitution: see the long summary of the philosophical positions in the debate in Bray and Colebrook 1999. Grosz's attack on somatophobia participates in this debate, where a strong emphasis on cor-poreality evokes the "material remainder to the economy of representation" and indicates that the body has potential beyond its status as "man's deficient other": Diprose 2002, 79. This potential, which is always appropriated and reappropri-ated in representation, foregrounds the many "becomings, connections, events, and activities" of the body, as Deleuze (1990, 40) has argued, a schema in which there can be no single theory of the body's materialization. There is not a body, but only bodies in their concrete specificity; hence, the need for a range of discur-sive materializations of the body in theory. In some important respects, my suturing together of heterogeneously located theories of corporeality is attentive to such caution. Given the different dimensions of bodily experience that icons harness—ethical, legal, and ecological in this volume—there cannot be a single theory of corporeality to impart discursive materiality to those experiences.

CHAPTER THREE: MEDIA FRICTIONS

1. By "reception" here I am referring to a constellation of the social (practices, knowledges, discourses), institutional (media organizations of a fairly complex sort), industrial (financing, tariffs, regulations), and technological (physical in-frastructure of transmission, exhibition, and delivery) practices. For a discussion of such constellations in mass communication, see Grossberg et al. 1998.

2. See Arundhati Roy, "When the Saints Go Marching Out," in Roy 2004a. The excerpt was first heard in a talk for BBC Radio 4 and was later republished in essay form. Roy directly addressed the dangerous process of iconization in an interview with Sonali Kolhatkar for ZNet on August 31, 2004: "This process of iconization is also a political one. That it is a way of making real political resistance very brittle."

3. Both Theodor Adorno (1972) and Walter Benjamin (1927–40) return to the notion of the hieroglyph, but to different ends. For Adorno, mass cultural inscrip-tions (fixed, repetitive images) represent the "will of those in charge," luring spectators to dream-like regression, but Benjamin suggests that the hieroglyphic further embodies a dream of collectivity: see Hansen 1992.

4. For a longer discussion of Benjamin's reading of Marx's notion of the social hieroglyph, see Buck-Morss 1999, 181–85.

5. See Pierre Centlivres's discussion of the proliferation of Buddhas in Latour and Weibel 2002, 75–77.

6. For a rundown of the *Celebrity Big Brother* controversy, see http://en.wikipedia .org/wiki/Celebrity Big_Brother_2007_(UK) (accessed May 15, 2007).

7. There is much speculation that Roy has embarked on her second novel (she supposedly announced it in 2007), but there is no word on its content: Ramesh 2007.

8. To quote Antony Spaeth, Roy "gained renown overnight": Antony Spaeth, "Arundhati Roy," *Time*, April 21,1997, 76.

9. This is a transcription of Roy's speech in Aradhana Seth, dir., *DAM/Age: A Film with Arundhati Roy*, Icarus Films, 2002.

10. The word *adi* means the earliest of times, and *vasi* means resident. The adivasis therefore are the indigenous peoples of the subcontinent in 400 communities that represent 7 percent of the population. In colonial times, they were referred to as "tribals," but the category has no equivalent in the Indian languages. "Jati" is sometimes used as a substitute, since it means both caste and tribe, but "adivasi" is still the best term because it relates to a particular historical development —the subjugation of a wide variety of communities in the nineteenth century that had remained relatively free from control by outside states: see Hardiman 1987, 13–15.

11. The SSP is the second largest dam of the Narmada Valley Project in terms of both area and the anticipated displacement of populations. The project began as early as 1961 under India's first head of state, Jawaharlal Nehru, who was famous for his commitment to industrial and technological growth and is remembered for his aphorism, "Dams are the modern temples of India."

12. Much of the media attention has focused on the loss of adivasi livelihoods and land, leading to a romanticization that Amita Baviskar (2004) strains to correct. She demonstrates how not only low-caste Hindus, but also the Patidars, stand to lose their land in the SSP project, creating alliances across castes in the NBA.

13. For instance, Roy's essay on India's nuclear tests in Pokhran, "The End of the Imagination," was first published in the Indian weeklies *Outlook* (July 15, 1998) and *Frontline* (August 1–14, 1998) right after the Indian nuclear tests of May 10, 1998. The essay was republished for a wider transnational audience in *The Nation* (September 28, 1998) and *The Guardian* (August 1, 1998). In 1999, the essay appeared in a tract that also included Roy's first essay on the NBA, "The Greater Common Good" (which had appeared in *Outlook* [April 1999] and *Frontline* [June 4, 1999]): see Roy 1999a.

14. One of the proponents of industrialization, Gail Omvedt, wrote a widely circulated letter to Roy, "An Open Letter to Arundhati Roy," posted on the Friends of the River Narmada website for the anti–dam building mobilization (www.narmada.org). In an overt reference to Roy's nonfiction, Omvedt followed the letter with the two-part article "Dams and Bombs," published in *The Hindu* on two pieces published in *The Hindu* on August 4–5, 1999. She wrote:

> Do you really think the *adivasis*, *dalits* and *shudra* or Rajput farmers of the Narmada valley want to keep that? Are you so convinced that the thousands of dams built since independence have been an unmitigated evil? Or that the

goal should not be to restructure and improve them rather than abandon them? Or that the struggle should not be to unite all the rural people aspiring to a life of prosperity and achievement in the modern world, drought afflicted and dam afflicted, rather than to just take up the cause of the opposition to change? Development to so many people in India means getting out of traditional traps of caste hierarchy and of being held in a birth-determined play. It is not simply economic progress, but the capacity to participate in a society in which knowledge, grain and songs will be available in full measure to everyone. When you so romantically imply that such development is not possible, when you give all publicity and support to anti-development organizations, are you not yourself helping to close such doors?" (1998, available online on at http://www.narmada.org [accessed July 2005])

15. *The Hindu* started publication in 1878 as a weekly and became a daily in 1889. Since then it has been steadily growing. It has a current circulation of about 11.8 million copies and a readership of about 4.05 million. It is classic mass media produced by a complex institution with several news outlets across media channels (print and digital). The newspaper is printed in twelve centers, including the "Main Edition" at Chennai (Madras), where the corporate office is based. The printing centers at Coimbatore, Bangalore, Madurai, Hyderabad, New Delhi, Vizag, Thiruvanathapuram, Kochi, Vijayawada, Mangalore, and Tiruchirapalli are connected with high-speed data lines for news transmission across the country. The Indian Readership Survey of 2008 estimated that *The Hindu* had 5.2 million (English-literate) readers.

16. For a longer discussion of Guha's views on Roy, see Anita Nair, "Ramachandra Guha—History's Footman," available online at http://www.anitanair.net (accessed September 2007). Guha has certainly been Roy's strongest critic, prompting others to question Guha's politics. Writing in *The Hindu* of December 23, 2000, Chittaroopa Palit remarked that it was "disconcerting to see Ramachandra Guha conferring upon himself the role of elder statesman and presuming to decree who should be allowed to be in the larger environmental movement and who not." She casts doubt on Guha's position vis-à-vis the NBA citing an open letter he wrote to Medha Patkar on the eve of President Bill Clinton's visit to India in which Guha advised Patkar against participating in or organizing protests during the visit. Taking a somewhat narrow view of the movement's articulation, Guha expressed in the letter his inability to understand why the NBA should protest on this occasion.

17. Baxi, the lawyer for the NBA, is well respected in the movement as a scholar who has written extensively on the functioning of the Supreme Court and the legal system in India.

18. "Legible," in the strictest lexical sense, denotes a composition "plain enough to read." To be legible means to exist in common parlance, but we might remember that the term is also etymologically related to the "legitimate" (lawful and conforming to recognized principles or accepted standards) and "intelligible" (that which is apprehended and enunciated).

19. See, e.g., the critique of dependency in Roy 2004b, 43.

20. NGOs have internal "constitutions," a distinct patterning of leadership, decision

making, and arrangements of accountability that replicate that of government agencies: Baxi 2005, 62.

21. Clifford Bob (2005, 4) explains how effective loose groupings of NGOs, transnational advocacy networks, activists, journalists, and bureaucrats have been working toward the goal of global governance by first raising international awareness through media coverage, then lobbying parties involved in financial deals, effectively transforming particular local struggles to match agendas of distant audiences.

22. Armstrong's film was available only as a highly priced documentary through small-scale outlets (e.g., Spanner, Bullfrog, and Icarus) for quite a while before it became available on Amazon.com.

23. In representing the blasts as attacks on a citizenry, one could argue that Amitav Ghosh's essay published at the same time is more attentive to the repercussions of nuclear tests on populations than the impassioned tract in which Roy remains the major protagonist: see Ghosh 1999.

24. Of "The End of the Imagination," Ramachandra Guha says disparagingly, "The essay is also self-contradictory, a jeremiad against the market and globalisation by one who is placed in the heart of the global market for celebrity-hood": Guha 2000a, 1.

25. See my discussion of criticism of Roy's nonfiction in Ghosh 2007.

26. See the image archives at http://www.narmada.org.

27. The speech, delivered at Riverside Church in New York City on October 24, 2003, during the international tour in which Roy spoke against the war in Iraq, has been reprinted many times.

28. Neera Chandhoke is an activist with the NBA. She wrote "The Conceits of Representation" in defense of Roy.

29. I use the term "translation" deliberately to evoke the lack of channels available to many of the indigenous peoples of the NBA to voice their protest and to claim redress. Gayatri Spivak's notion of the subaltern not as one who is without speech but whom we cannot "hear" because he or she is cut off from all lines of communication is relevant to the issue of Roy's voicing "their" losses.

30. In chapter 8, I flesh out the constitution of communities affected by the dam. The indigenous communities will come into sharper focus in that discussion.

31. Arundhati Roy, "Peace and the New Corporate Liberation Theology," Sydney Peace Prize lecture, November 3, 2004, Seymour Centre, Sydney, available online at http://www.abc.net.au/rn/bigideas/stories (accessed July 2005).

32. Kolkata is the vernacularized name for the colonial capital city, Calcutta, founded by Job Charnock in 1690. The name is the modern Bengali rendition of "Calcutta," but the official change was made to signal the making of a brighter, cleaner new city that would attract foreign investors. Throughout the chapter, I have tried to remain as historical as possible, using Calcutta only in contexts where the cultural resonance of the name has salience.

33. The festival of lights celebrated in late fall every year marks the return of Lord Ram home from his exile in the forest. Hindu believers light oil lamps or *diyas* to provide the light to guide him back to the city (Ayodhya, in the epic, *Ramayana*).

34. More recently, the Hindu right has renewed its assault against Christians and, particularly, the Missionaries of Charity, who were harassed for reportedly "con-

verting" the sick at a hospital in Hyderabad on June 25, 2006. The year 2008 saw renewed violence against Christians in Orissa, many incidents instigated by the Hindu right (specifically, by the Vishwa Hindu Parishad).

35. Such powers of intercession have always been key to sainthood. Brown (1981) traces the gradual theological legitimation that the local worship of saints underwent from late antiquity and notes that the lure of the saint lay precisely in her perceived ability to intercede with God on behalf of the individual. Before their entry into scholastic debates, saints were always one's most intimate "invisible companion," almost an upward extension of the self into an other in whose care one could readily cast one's fortunes (Brown 1981, 51). Such a notion of intimacy—the hagiographic reassemblage of the saint as a part of the self—is essential to Mother Teresa's lure. Always cognizant of the arteries of faith, the Roman Catholic church finally brought saint making into church echelons in 1588, when Pope Sixtus V formed the Congregation for the Causes of the Saints, a body charged with bringing vox populi miracles of Latin Christianity into scholastic practice. The local worship of saints was acknowledged in the process of beatification, whose first phase took the form of a diocesan tribunal. The tribunal was explicitly charged with the task of consolidating local accounts of miracles and testaments of the saint's exemplary life drawn from the saint's local place or places of residence. This was followed by a second investigation in Rome, this time by the Congregation for the Causes of Saints, a body that would examine the diocesan report and make a recommendation to the pope. The pope would proceed to beatify the saint in formal ceremonies either as a "blessed" or as a fully canonized saint.

36. The Vatican's definition of the miracles is extensively cited in an article on the beatification. See Tracy Wilkinson, "Confirming Miracles Is Art and Science," published in the *Los Angeles Times*, October 14, 2003.

37. Scheduled Tribes are the historically disadvantaged indigenous communities that, much like the Scheduled Castes, are given special status in the Indian Constitution. The "Scheduled Tribes" and "Scheduled Castes" categories are taken from existing rubrics of the colonial state formulated in the 1930s. The communities in question historically were excluded from the *chaturvarna* system, the social superstructure of Hindu society for some thousands of years. In contemporary India, the Scheduled Castes are the Dalits, and the Scheduled Tribes are the Adivasis. In the 2001 census, 24 percent of India's population qualified for this special status (Scheduled Castes, 16 percent; Scheduled Tribes, 8 percent).

38. The Humanist wing of the Rationalist Association provides marriage counseling, legal help, and school administration among low-caste communities but clearly does not get the kind of coverage Mother Teresa has—perhaps one of the reasons for its antipathy toward the missionary.

39. Cortesini quoted in Wilkinson, "Confirming Miracles Is Art and Science," *Los Angeles Times*, October 14, 2003.

40. Payal Mohanka is journalist who worked for BBC World and CNBC India. Before the homage to Mother Teresa, she betrayed her interest in tracking Christian missionary establishments by making the documentary *Little France on the Hooghly* about the former French colony Chandanagore.

41. Lately, there has been an explosion of protests against land redistribution, the

most famous case being Singur until riots and police violence brought things to a head in Nandigram. After the strikes and demonstrations against the Left Front's land distribution to private corporations came the Nandigram clash, in which fourteen protesting farmers and activists died (March 14, 2007) in a police shooting, bringing the government's development plans to a halt: see http://www.tribuneindia.com/2007/20070107/spectrum/main1.htm.

42. The struggle over the biggest land grab in West Bengal since the Permanent Settlement (under Lord Cornwallis) came to a head when the police killed fourteen farmers in Nandigram who were protesting the government takeover of their land in 2007 (this is the event that sparked the Nandigram clash). In 2008, mobilization against government land requisitioning in Singur created a month-long impasse. As a result, the industrial giant Tata Industries moved its business out of West Bengal. Nandigram and Singur signal a popular mobilized against government takeovers, a re-terriorialization that began with harnessing Mother Teresa's cachet.

43. Contrary to the common belief that Phoolan Devi was *the* Indian bandit queen, the moniker previously belonged to the illustrious one-armed female bandit Putlibai in the 1950s and is still extended to female outlaws in India.

44. For the changing electoral caste landscape of the 1990s and its impact on Phoolan Devi's career, see Pai 2001.

45. Proclaiming that "the jury would always be out on Phoolan Devi," Atiq Khan (2001) caught the national pulse in posing the conundrum that was Phoolan Devi.

46. Both the Other Backward Castes and the Most Backward Castes are politico-juridical designations in post-independence India designed to protect the historically disadvantaged by reserving seats in jobs and educational institutions, much as affirmative action once protected minorities in the United States.

47. In the confusing account of the assassination, it appeared that Singh Rana was actually Pankaj Kakra; he took the name Rana to hide his *thakur* background, then faked his own abduction. In these initial stories, he seemed to have no link to Behmai, but this remains fairly uncertain. More important, the drama of the assassination reads like an involved whodunit replete with getaway cars, a hit-and-run accident, a stolen scooter, a maverick auto-rickshaw, untraceable cars, mobile phones, and SMS or pre-paid phone cards. Eleven people were finally arrested and charged on November 20, 2001, but the prime suspect escaped from the Tihar jail. When he turned himself in, he accused the jailers of trying to poison him. With such a twists and turns, Phoolan Devi's death remained in the news for a few years after 2001.

48. One lakh of rupees is equivalent to $100,000.

49. "Didi" is a common term meaning elder sister. Here it refers to Phoolan Devi as the elder in the Samajwadi Party.

50. Mala Sen insists that Phoolan Devi was legally innocent of murder, though not of other of the fifty-five charges brought against her, including twenty-two counts for murder. She actually shot the men she is accused of killing in the knees while interrogating them: Sen 2001, 54. The story was reaffirmed by Dhruv Kumar, a filmmaker who interviewed Devi extensively on this issue. The bandit queen reported that she headed to the river after she heard shots fired; moreover,

Kumar maintains that Phoolan Devi was in pursuit of Shri Ram and Lala Ram and was *not* at the Behmai massacre. Hence, she never broke the law. In the dispute over Kapur's film, Dhruv Kumar won Devi's trust when he filed a case on her behalf through the NGO Nagrik Seva Morcha and won her the settlement of her house in Chittaranjan Park (a posh neighborhood in Delhi).

51. As Umed Singh embarked on a hunger strike for investigation, Phoolan Devi's mother and sister bitterly opposed him. Others alleged that Uma and Vijay Kay-shap, political workers whom Rana had befriended, gained proximity to Phoolan Devi to plot her death. And, of course, there were those who saw a past never fully dealt with coming back to take its revenge: "Phoolan Case" 2001, 1.

52. Madhu Kishwar (2001) argues the real story of Phoolan Devi is of "child rape, abduction, and abuse," while the image of the vengeful goddess is a "romantic fantasy." For a similar opinion, see "The Phoolan Phenomenon" 2001.

CHAPTER FOUR: PUBLIC IMAGE LTD.

1. Here "networks" refers to technological, industrial, and institutional linkages that reach "the masses," Often broadcast media (e.g., CNN's transnational distributors and local conglomerates) have the widest reach. Broadcast media networks are distinctly opposite to "interpersonal media networks" (the one-to-one link of postal mail or e-mail).

2. Unlike the earlier photographs, this inscription is widely accessible today. The physical archive for Adams's photographs is domiciled at the University of Texas Briscoe Center, Austin; but this image is available for reproduction through image databases like Getty Images.

3. In recent years, efforts to transnationalize "star studies" not only have focused on the "flow" of a star (such as Jackie Chan or Sylvester Stallone) in transnational media networks; they have also been attentive to how star systems operate differently in various localized contexts of consumption. Such turns emerge out of a self-reflexive moment in star studies. As Fischer and Landy (2004, 3) argue, if the movies "invented" stardom, then we must ask: "How has film studies 'invented' its analysis?" Has Hollywood-based star analysis "invented" the legibility of the transnational star in limited ways? And if it has, how might we reinvent star studies through looking at other film industries and their technologies of stardom? Their provocation prompts scholars to move beyond an additive model, in which another Jackie Chan or Sharukh Khan is tagged on to a growing roster of stars, to investigations that substantially recalibrate the models of stargazing. In other words, as transnational stars move across cinemas as translocated signs, they encourage us to consider the very structures of stardom that render them legible to differently situated audiences.

4. Here I am following Matthew Fuller's lead in designating "standard objects" whose equivalence can only be grasped within larger media ecology (Fuller 2005, 95–96).

5. From the 1910s to the 1940s, however, stars were focalized through fan perspectives. Self-reflexive collections sometimes perform this history by incorporating this (continuing) hagiographic aspect of star discourse. Most recently, a double issue of *Camera Obscura* on divas invited "diva appreciations" alongside critical commentary on the phenomena.

6. See selections in Willis 2004 and single monographs on stars such as those in Curry 1996.

7. I deliberately choose "affordances," a term originally introduced by the psychologist James J. Gibson (1977), to think about multiple "action possibilities" in the greater technological and industrial ecology of the star. This is also far more pertinent to design in the post-digital age.

8. In his acknowledgments in *Mother Teresa: A Life of Dedication* (2005), a collection published posthumously, for instance, Rai thanked the Missionaries of Charity for their help in consolidating the book. This is fairly typical of many biographies, documentaries, and coffee-table books on Mother Teresa.

9. See Sunanda Datta-Ray, "Driven by Self-Interest" (first published in *The Australian*, September 11, 1997) accessible on Atanu Dey's blog (http://www.deeshaa .org/906/).

10. The essay on Phoolan Devi surfaced on the Internet after Roy's Booker win ("Shady Girl, Blazing Guns and the Political Fast Lane," *Sunday*, August 28– September 3, 1994. See http://www.telegraphindia.com/1010726/editoria.htm #head3). Beyond the news, Roy also acted in a film, *Massey Sahib* (1985, directed by Pradip Krishen), a visual trace that made a brief reappearance in magazine spreads recognizing her Booker win (for example, in *India Today*, October 27, 1997).

11. Pablo Bartholomew, who is best known for his photographs of the Bhopal tragedy, continues to document current events: see http://www.netphotgraph.com. The photograph referred to here was prohibitively expensive to reproduce (priced higher than the famed photographs by Raghu Rai); hence, the verbal description. See also http://www.india50.com/arundhati.html.

12. See, e.g., the photo spreads on Roy published from July to November 1997 in publications with large circulations, such as *India Today*, *Frontline*, and *Outlook*.

13. The news stories on Roy in 1997 rode a commercial wave in which India, South Asian women, and Indian writing in English had become vaunted consumer exports on the global cosmopolitan stage. As I recount in *When Borne Across* (Ghosh 2004), in post-liberalized India, few trade tariffs and a privatized television industry not only saw a deluge of consumer goods entering India, but it also saw the rising prominence of a professional, largely urban, middle class who dominated the cultural sphere—a class ready to turn the "ancient India" into "indo-chic," as the *New York Times* termed it in 1997.

14. Available online at http://www.india-today.com/intoday/27101997/cov.html (accessed July 2005).

15. The bandit queen's perceived gender transgressions habitually give rise to accounts that masculinize her. One policeman interviewed about his patrol, which almost captured Phoolan Devi, recalled her challenge to his masculinity as her high, metallic voice echoed in the ravines of the Chambal Valley: "Himat na tho chudiya le jao. Goliyan na tho goliyan le jao" (If you don't have guts, take my bangles. If you don't have balls, take my bullets).

16. My emphasis. Another, similar translation is enacted by *Outlawed*, a television show hosted in Canberra, Australia, by the well-known television personality Scott McGregor. The show accompanied the "Representing Outlaws" exhibition

at the Canberra National Museum of Australia in 2004, which aimed at celebrating the folk tradition of outlaws.

17. Other representative works can be found online at http://moochasgracias .blogspot .com and http://www.kodakgallery.com.

18. Perhaps the most institutionalizing among these are "Leading the Way: Twentieth Century Women," a triptych by the New York artist Mireille Miller that was commissioned for an exhibition at the fiftieth session of the Commission on the Status of Women at the United Nations in 2006. For details, see the website at http://www.mireillemiller.com/pdf/Leadingwomen.pdf.

19. The mural-like paintings are by Erin Currier and are from the exhibition "From Vietnam to Venezuela," at the Parks Gallery in Taos, New Mexico.

20. See the website at http://www.saintsgallery.com/products.html (accessed May 1, 2007).

21. Rai is a highly credentialed photographer who joined the prestigious cooperative Magnum Photos in the 1970s and World Press Photo in the 1990s. He has won several awards, including Photographer of the Year in the United States in 1993. He met Mother Teresa in the fall of 1970 and has often recounted how she allowed him to photograph her after much protestation; she granted permission only when he suggested that his photographs were a form of prayer. The story of Mother Teresa's acquiescence serves to ratify *Mother Teresa: A Life of Dedication*.

22. Rai, who is also famous for his collection on Calcutta, has published several volumes on Mother Teresa: see, e.g., Rai 1996, 2005.

23. Panjiar 2004 is introduced by the nationally known journalist Khuswant Singh.

24. Roy chose the photograph from several shots of the river on whose banks the central events of the novel unfold; the photograph was later titled "Water Lilies": see Saith's commentary on it in Panjiar 2004, 128.

25. Focusing primarily on Hong Kong television, Curtin (2003) maintains that we need to think beyond a conception of the present globalization as marked by unilateral media flows. Instead, he illustrates how media content is "switched" in local, metropolitan centers such as Laos, Mumbai, or Hong Kong. Such "switching" is governed not simply by industrial, financial, and technological particularity but also by social and cultural norms.

26. What Curtin suggests with regard to local television, Amit Rai (2009) poses with regard to Bollywood, a media assemblage constituted by a cluster of technological, industrial, social, and physical processes.

27. I am following the lead of Vivian Sobchack's (2004) lead here, in *Carnal Thoughts*, when in which she she suggests that, despite the audience's knowledge of the documentary's "constructed-ness," the footage in these films carry a phenomenological charge of the real.

28. IndiaWorld.com, diversified into several Internet sites, generated 95 percent of its traffic outside India, according to the search engine at http://khoj.com.

29. For a detailed empirical account of changes in media institutions, see Kohli-Khandekar 2003.

30. Language was always the key to local and regional identities, but this was further solidified in 1956 when the different states in India formalized their borders along linguistic lines. Such political carvings resulted in language riots.

31. See also Jeffrey 1997. Jeffrey notes the Indian newspapers took their cue initially from Gandhi's weeklies, seeing their role as primarily pedagogic, but they remained resonant when they began to address local identities, since in India these were often the borders of the public.

32. Forty million newspapers are being printed each day in India's twelve major languages, nearly half of them in the national language, Hindi.

33. Antara Dev Sen, editor of the *Little Magazine*, wrote against this control in Dev Sen 2003.

34. Jeffrey (1997, 81) lists the K. M. Matthew (Kandathil) family of *Malayala Manorama* in Kerala, the Sarkars of *Ananda Bazaar Patrika* in Calcutta, and Ramoji Rao of *Eenadu* in Hyderabad.

35. Sometimes conflicts lead to what Arvind Rajagopal (2001) has called "structured misunderstandings" between news in the Indian languages and news in English on a single event.

36. In this case, these surrender photographs are the first visual traces of Phoolan Devi, who appears in a few isolated articles in transnational news print media in 1981, just after the Behmai massacre.

37. For Srivatsan, the personal anecdote exemplifies a social ritual of viewing news photographs in India. It is a ritual that seeks to bring geographical zones of instability under a national gaze that organizes the event.

38. In fact, early depictions of Phoolan Devi underscored her unruly androgyny, as well. M. J. Akbar (1981, 22), the editor of the weekly *Sunday* magazine, famously and ekphrastically captured the sexualized subaltern this way: "She wears jeans. She carries a sten gun, which she can use with great accuracy and without mercy. . . . She became a dacoit after she was spurned by her husband and spat upon by society. Today she is the most powerful dacoit in Uttar Pradesh. And she will have her revenge on both the [Thakurs] and society."

39. Anupama Chopra's recent *The King of Bollywood* (2007), a study of Shah Rukh Khan, marks one attempt to move beyond regional and national circulations of the stars of Indian cinema.

40. Such as *Cinema Sansar*, *Rangbhoomi*, *The Cinema*, and *Chitrapat*.

41. The Cow Protection movement, which targeted British authorities, demanded the end of cow slaughter in an early articulation of Hindu nationalism. For a extensive discussion, see van der Veer 1994, 83–88.

42. I will not rehash Partha Chatterjee's famous argument on the division between home and the world, which is most extensively elaborated in Chatterjee 1990.

43. Female stars have always needed to overcome conservative proscriptions of shame relating to the public display of the female body (Gandhy and Thomas 1991, 109). Even in present-day Indian politics, Sara Dickey describes MGR's (M. G. Ramachandran, the megastar who became the chief minister of Tamil Nadu in 1977) female successor Jayalitha's contorted negotiations of politics and her deployment of MGR's star image to legitimize her move from the performing arts to politics.

44. For a discussion of Nargis as icon, see Majumdar (2009); Roy 1988. For a discussion of the film, see Dasgupta 1991; Schulze 1995.

45. See http://www.stanford.edu/group/ivfaculty/Essays/mtkio.jpg (accessed May 1, 2007).

46. See, e.g., http://www.thehypertexts.com/Mysterious_Ways/Images.

47. See http://www.alternativetentacles.com and http://weblog.liberatormagazine
.com (accessed December 30, 2009).

48. The intertextual star texts consolidated primarily through biographies are a key
dimension of producing the icon, as are extratextual sources (legal cases, import
tariffs, state policy, building designs, censorship boards), especially because the
icons in question are heavily contested political figures: see White and Corrigan
2004, 463. We see this most sharply in the response of the Indian Censor Board to
Kapur's *The Bandit Queen*, the censorship fueling the sexualized appeal of Phoolan Devi's screen portrait.

49. Gandhy and Thomas (1991) demonstrate such a turn to icon in a few cases
historically set apart from each other, notably fearless Nadia, the Australian-born
B-movie action hero of the 1930s, whose whiteness rendered her inscrutable to
Indian audiences, who flashed on Indian screens first in *Hunterwali* (1934), and
Smita Patil, the feminist icon from a lower-middle-class socialist family whose
roles positioned her as an advocate for social change. These figures commanded
veneration; their screen roles, public performances (speech acts and actions in
the public sphere), and hagiographies condensed symbolic meanings drawn from
iconographic traditions.

50. New Indian cinema was a highly self-reflexive cinema prevalent from the mid-
1970s that featured auteurs such as Mani Ratnam, Govind Nihalini, and Shyam
Benegal.

51. Part of this singling out of the female bandit arises from the historical fact that
female social bandits were less common than their male counterparts, at least
until the last decades of the twentieth century: Hobsbawm 1965. Encouraged by
the popular acclaim his account received, Bhaduri went on to publish an English-
language version in 1972.

52. This is worth noting because Jaya Bachchan is also Amitabh Bachchan's wife, and
the couple reportedly read *Chambal: A Valley of Terror* before starring in *Sholay*.

53. In a strange confluence (of the palette of bio-icons here), Arundhati Roy famously
wrote a controversial piece in defense of Phoolan Devi's refutation of Kapur's film
before she rose to fame as a Booker Prize winner in 1997: Arundhati Roy, "The
Great Indian Rape-Trick I and II," 1994, available online at http://www.sawnet
.org/books/writing/roy_bq1.html.

54. Fernandes sees the autobiographies as far more successful in disrupting a hegemonic frame of reference through the rhetorical strategies. For example, Puttilal's taking Phoolan Devi away from her home before she was an adult clearly
violates customary practice. But this is a position I would not agree with, as my
analysis makes clear.

55. Zee Cinema reaches 75 percent of cable-connected households in India, in addition
to large transnational audiences in the United States and the United Kingdom.

56. The colonial fantasy of "white men saving brown women from brown men"
follows from Gayatri Spivak's (1988) famous thesis on the female subaltern, in
which *sati* exemplifies the structural location of the female subject.

57. For analysis of Jackie Chan, see also Gallagher 2004.

58. One might argue such a sense of demarcation moves beyond Britain to its colo-
nies, where an Anglicized elite model themselves as a striated society. It is in this
stratum one would find other publics for British films.

59. National stars therefore become icons at certain moments of enunciation (for Gledhill, Britain in the 1920s) when such a collective horizon seems especially important to demarcate against hegemonizing forces. Sophia Loren, for example, became an icon for the Italian public long after her most famous roles, her association with Vittorio De Sica lending her a residual density. Loren exemplifies a star who endured as an icon. As late as 1989, millions of Italians voted for "Italy's national idol (*mito nationale*)," as she became known, and when Loren erred (as in 1979, when she was arrested in Rome's airport for non-payment of taxes and other financial irregularities), the Italian public expressed outrage, anger, and sorrow that clearly suggested a loss of collective self-esteem. Like that of other stars of her ilk, Loren's accretive image gave her a symbolic density that has enabled her to remain an icon through upheavals, uncertainty, and changes. Even as her fortunes have changed, the public's memory of an original image persists in the icon: Gundle 2004.

60. Drawing on John Ellis, Christine Gledhill (1991, 217) notes how the circulation of the star image in studios' promotional media, television talk shows, film criticism, fan magazines, and so forth gives rise to gossip and speculation, even as these media disperse the meanings, values, and styles of the star. Hence, stars are always ripe for controversy in this repeated reassembling of their image. Historical contingency mandates the condensation of certain values around a star, especially, Gledhill argues, when those values are deeply contested. The star therefore emerges as sites of ideological struggle for different social groups.

61. While slavery might provide the most extreme instance, Kopytoff notes similar commoditization of humans that are also under way in adoption practices, as well as the buying of ova, organs, and blood.

62. Despite the differences between the star, the icon, and the celebrity, Chris Rojek (2004) notes that celebrities often command reliquaries that imitate religio-mystical practices. The collection on Marilyn Monroe also concludes with a Monroe reliquary: Rojek 2004, 208–14.

63. It was stolen from the Vevey cemetery in Switzerland for a ransom of 600,000 Swiss francs: Rojek 2004, 61.

64. Warner advances an argument that Lauren Berlant (1991) makes with regard to binding fantasies of nation.

65. Prompting taxonomies, such debates have arisen out of a turn in star studies that is attentive to star crossings: Not only were film stars crossing into other media (television, fashion, politics, sports, entertainment, or infotainment), but other media now had their own "stars" in an expansion of the cultural concept. The musical star Paul Robeson crossed into cinema (poignantly circumscribed as Sambo, as Dyer [1987, 134] explains); Jennifer Lopez or Barbra Streisand enacted a reverse crossing. Movies had their Tom Cruises and Meryl Streeps; basketball had its Magic Johnsons and Michael Jordans. Such transmedial movement pushed critics to formulate more expansive typologies of stardom, sometimes sharpening the lines around the movie star as a distinctive phenomenon. Where the celebrity's fame rests primarily on his or her lifestyle, the professional's star cache depends on his or her public roles (regular soap opera or situation comedy stars best fit this category). Hence, when action figures such as Stallone or Jean-Claude Van Damme try to move into other roles, audiences seem disinclined to

view the transition favorably, the seamlessness between the role and the "real" figure rendering the switch difficult, though not impossible. In contrast to these extremes, some stars are regarded as performers, bringing to film or television the high cultural values of theatrical performance. Here the emphasis is on skill and technique; a distinct sense of the star in a film as inhabiting a role is extremely clear. Since film stardom exploits the star image across entertainment formats—the star may appear as celebrity on Ellen DeGeneres's talk show or Oprah Winfrey's, for example—contemporary audiences bring very different kinds of knowledge to consuming star texts. See Gledhill and Williams 2000, 183–201.

66. Schickel (1985) provides a long list of celebrity stalkers, such as John Hinckley (who stalked Ronald Reagan), who saw themselves as intimately connected to the mass-mediatized sign.

67. In his sharply argued *Understanding Celebrity* (2004), Graeme Turner hints at the turn to the icon, even though he never uses the term, in his recollection of the confusion Lady Diana's death engendered among cultural critics. If celebrity denuded our social relations, then how might we explain the collective onslaught of grief felt all over the world? Why would minority populations within the United Kingdom (people of color, gay communities) unthinkingly mourn the social establishment (with Diana as the representative of a kinder, gentler royalty)? Turner suggests that Diana's death was an unpredictable event that should prod scholars of celebrity to think beyond the para-sociality of celebrity consumption.

CHAPTER FIVE: THOSE LIVES LESS ORDINARY

1. Gita Rajan (1992) notes that Indira Gandhi's revelations were carefully orchestrated political ploys, given the harsh measures she took against unauthorized exposés. Most famously she banned the Hindi-language film *Andhi* (Tempest) during the Emergency (1975–77) because it was a *roman à clef* of her failed marriage with Feroze Gandhi.

2. We know that such corporeal politics was rather effective in rallying support for the suffragettes who finally won the political status for which they had fought. For a discussion of the corporeal politics of the suffragettes, see Phillips 2003.

3. One finds a range of responses to what constitutes autobiographical disclosure, especially in anthologies: see, e.g., Brodzki and Schenck 1988.

4. See, e.g., Sidonie Smith and Julie Watson, "Introduction," in Smith and Watson 1992.

5. John Beverley (1992) explains that these are usually produced in books or pamphlets.

6. See also Sommer 1988. For a discussion of the Menchu controversy, see Arias 2001.

7. They are likewise distinct in their ethical temper, in their demand for justice from readers who are socially more privileged than the speaking subject, from the "autobiography of conscience" to autobiographical fiction, diary, or memoir, where a personal tale is metaphorically posed as paradigmatic: Varner Gunn 1992.

8. Sen 1991 (with reprints in 1993, 1995, and 2001); Cuny and Rambali 1992; Shears and Gidley 1984; Frain 1992.

9. These biographies remained immensely popular in global public spheres, some of them appearing in new editions after Devi's death. Cuny and Rambali's *I, Phoolan Devi*, for instance, first came out in 1996, with a second edition, retitled *The Bandit Queen of India: An Indian Woman's Amazing Journey from Peasant to International Legend*, published on the heels of Phoolan Devi's death in 2003. Similarly, Frain's fictionalization was reprinted in English translation in 1994.

10. See Srilata Ravi's (1999) genealogical account of the French fascination with the divine feminine force. Devi became a marketable signifier of sacred violence because this was a staple stereotype for India in the French imagination, fed on accounts of Thugee (with Thugs worshiping the goddess Kali) from the nineteenth century. The fascination with the bandit queen began with Michel De Grèce's (1984) valorization of the Rani of Jhansi. But the earliest account of Devi in French was a largely unnoticed realist piece by the journalist Pierre Joffroy, who recorded the exploits of Kusum Devi (modeled on Phoolan Devi) in *Le Chaval Chauve* (1976).

11. By contrast, the critical testimonial pays close attention to the ethnographic project of recording a life. For example, Josiane Racine and Jean-Luc Racine complement their publication of *Une vie paria* (published in Tamil and French and translated into English as *Viramma: The Life of an Untouchable* [1997]) with a critical essay explaining the politics of collaboratively producing the Dalit Tamil female life. Racine and Racine (2004) situate Viramma's life story within a tradition of Dalit life-story writing in Tamil, represented by Bama's *Karukku* and Laxman Mané's *Oupra* (1987), the latter winning a Sahitya Akademi Award. They thank Jean Malauri for his help with the process of ordering, selecting, and editing the life of Viramma, an illiterate Tamil-speaking agricultural worker and midwife from Pondicherry. While careful of their collaborative effort, they nevertheless position Viramma as more authentic in her immersion in her local life world, unlike other Dalit writers, such as Madhau Kondvilker, who, upon becoming a teacher and producing his own life story, found himself entirely alienated from the collectivity whose lives he sought to illuminate through his own. The telling of the life story can therefore position the icon as a controversial subject.

12. Ghosh's biography can be characterized as local tribute pitched to a national public proficient in the English language, which is evident in his introduction of Mother Teresa as the "third *among Indians* to get the Nobel Prize" (Ghosh 2002, 1; emphasis added). Other biographies with larger international circulation, such as Edward Le Joly's *We Do It for Jesus* (1977), also fall into the devotional category— enough, at least, to qualify as hagiographic in the religious sense. We might further include the aforementioned BBC biopics *Something Beautiful for God* (1969) and *Mother Teresa: A Life of Devotion* (1997) in this hagiographic category.

13. Encouraged by Tariq Ali of Bandung Productions, the film starred a series of witnesses who corroborated Hitchens's critique, such as the journalist Mihir Bose and Mary Loudon, a nun who had left the order. The documentary was recently dropped from a film festival on Mother Teresa hosted on October 19, 2003, to celebrate her beatification. It seems to have become a lost text that finds no willing exhibitor.

14. Sunanda K. Datta, for example, once the editor of the respected Calcutta daily *The Statesman*, follows the money trail, questioning why the large donations Mother

Teresa received after 1979 did not manifest themselves in better care facilities. Like Chatterjee and Hitchens, he shows surprise at Mother Teresa's acceptance of donations from the likes of Charles Keating, a California banker who was jailed for swindling $252 million from the public. Keating gave Mother Teresa $1.25 million; in appreciation, Mother Teresa wrote a letter to the judge on his behalf when Keating was brought to trial.

15. The money trail glimmers in Chatterjee's account, when he tries to track Mother Teresa's banking methods. The Missionaries of Charity's main bank was the Vatican bank, Chatterjee points out, which had been investigated for its dubious connections to the Mafia in 1981—an audit that included the accounts of the Missionaries of Charity (Chatterjee 2002, 246). Both Chatterjee and Hitchens are recognized as valid researchers of the icon, since both were invited as witnesses in the diocesan inquiry into Mother Teresa's life that preceded her beatification.

16. Dodging charges of making profit off Mother Teresa, Lapierre further insisted that he was donating the entire amount Hallmark paid him for the script to a leprosy clinic in Calcutta: "Lapierre Blames Order Members for Teresa Film Controversy" 1997.

17. Still others showed irritation at historical inaccuracies that abound in the biopic —for example, a convent choir that sings the evangelical song "Majesty" from 1970 at a flag-raising ceremony set in 1947 (Chandran 1997). More movies on the diminutive nun are on the way. A French and Indian production directed by Gautam Das, *The Beatification of Mother Teresa*, proudly locates itself in 30,000 pages of research material provided by the Vatican while adding Bollywood flavor with the inclusion of song sequences. Another animated film, *Mother Teresa of Calcutta*, part of the "Saints and Angels" series for children, is an overly sentimentalized display of Mother Teresa that is readily available through online vendors trading in pedagogical resources for religious instruction.

18. For Hollywood biopics, see Custen 1992. In more self-conscious biopics, the star might refuse the specularization of her image, as Lucy Fischer shows in her discussion of Maxmillian Schiller's *Marlene*: Fischer 2000.

19. Focusing on her early life in Skopje, Gëzim Alpion (2007) is one of the few to offer such a psychosexual biography, delicately suggested rather than heavily underscored.

20. She did not take the name from the famous Teresa of Avila (as it is widely assumed), whose devotion to Jesus, expounded in *The Story of the Soul* (1899), inspired the young Bojaxhiu.

21. Hagiographies are widely defined as idealizing biographies; sacred hagiographies attempt to demonstrate not just an exemplary life but also someone who intercedes with God on the behalf of ordinary people.

22. John Stratton Hawley (1987) illustrates his hypothesis by analyzing the Bhaktamal (Garland of Devotees), a text that assembles the lives of sixteenth-century and seventeenth-century Hindu saints: the saint's unconventional life; the saint's departure from religious, social, and political orders; the saint's revision of the moral codes (in this case, codes from the Laws of Manu written two millennia ago) from the ground of personal ethics underscores his or her appeal to devotees.

23. Hawley lists the *tsaddiqin* of the Hasidic Jewry, the lives of Christian saints, the Hindu recounting of bhakti sants, the Buddhist *avadānas* and *jātaka* tales, and the

hadith that supplements the Qur'an, as well the Islamic tales of *walîs*, *shaykhs*, *sûfis, and pîrs*, as parallel hagiographic efforts.

24. Navin Chawla, an election commissioner of India and a former Indian Administrative Service officer, met Mother Teresa in 1975. He is the author of *Mother Teresa: The Authorized Biography*, first published in 1992 and available in fourteen languages around the world.

25. For an explanation of the difference between the two see, http://universalindult .org.

26. Alpion makes this argument in his long meditation on what actually occurred in this pivotal juncture in Mother Teresa's life.

27. The new collection of Mother Teresa's writings includes a letter from the archbishop that attempt to tame her impetuousness. The reprinted letters reveal an obedient Sister Teresa who read the archbishop's advice and took it to heart (there are long, heavily underlined passages on his cautions to her) (Kolodiejchuk 2007, 112).

28. Kolodiejchuk (2007, 108) tells us that Mother Teresa herself insisted on secularization, inciting a debate within the Roman Catholic clergy as to the nature and source of her call.

29. Chawla presents the most sympathetic portrait of the archbishop of Calcutta by suggesting that the change may have occurred because of the comments he had included in his letter accompanying the request to Delhi. But this does not explain the archbishop's insistence on secularization twice before in assembling the request.

30. Such a request had been given 300 years earlier to Mary Ward, another recalcitrant nun, whose Institute of the Blessed Virgin Mary, the base organization for the Loreto Order, had to wage a long and arduous struggle against the Vatican to find its feet. When Ward asked to leave the cloister to found her institute—made possible by the indent of exclaustration—she had been granted permission, at least initially, according to laws governing nuns' conduct in the church. But shortly thereafter, the Vatican suppressed the institute's activities, reimposing the rule of enclosure so that, in 1630, Ward found herself a prisoner in a convent in Munich. It would take seventy long years for her institute to be ratified, the Irish branch merging in 1821, and the Indian one in 1841. Not estranged from the church, the Loreto Order was nevertheless an unusual congregation, an early example of a female clergy living in faith (with the Virgin Mary as their guide) but with their own organizational hierarchies. Of course, the male clergy were still their superiors—for instance, Sister Teresa's request had to be channeled through the archbishops of Calcutta and Delhi, even though she received direct permission from her direct superior, the Mother General at Rathfarman. The comparison between Mother Teresa and the rebellious Mary Ward is worth making because it frames the singularity of Mother Teresa's request—the strength of a faith that propelled her outside the walls of the cloister, her unfailing determination in the face of institutional resistance.

31. In 2007, Kolodiejchuk, the postulator for the cause of Mother Teresa's canonization, published a collection of her writings appropriately subtitled "The Revealing Private Writings of the Nobel Prize Winner." The collection attempts to put to rest speculation on Mother Teresa's rupture from the Loreto Order, but it does not inductively focalize the saint as the biographies, so I pilfer the contents of the

volume quite cursorily. Possibly the most relevant revision of the saint that emerges in the collection, with its heavy parataxis, is Mother Teresa's lifelong struggle with doubt: "In my heart there is no faith—no love—no trust—there is so much pain—the pain of longing, the pain of not being wanted" (Kolodiejchuk 2007, 193). Kolodiejchuk interprets these difficulties with finding Jesus as the dark night of the soul, the necessary passion of a deep faith. Yet these frank discussions—splayed tabloid-style all over the newspapers when first published—convey Mother Teresa's deep investment in the social rather than the divine. Her work never stopped even as her sense of divine sanction faltered (this letter is dated as early as 1959), rich evidence of incalculable giving that is often recognized in popular veneration of the nun.

32. Certainly Chawla intimates that Mother Teresa actually asked Father Van Exem to return her correspondence with him once she had settled into her own congregation, but the priest refused to return it, arguing that the letters belonged to church archives (Chawla 2002, 213–15). Katherine Spink, Mother Teresa's friend and biographer, recalls that Father Van Exem had in his possession two boxes of documentation relevant to the matter of Mother Teresa's departure from the Loreto Order, which he refused to part with. In Spink's view, this prompted the only quarrel between Mother Teresa and the mentor who had been her first believer and intermediary.

33. Sister Cyril's Rainbow Program is a present enterprise for slum children, while her Barefoot Teachers Training Program (serving remote rural areas) began in 1985. Unlike Mother Teresa, Sister Cyril has remained within the Loreto Order, which seems to have relaxed its rules governing the conduct of nuns. Perhaps this is indeed Mother Teresa's legacy.

34. Her former students joined her first, making up an order of twelve by 1950.

35. Alpion, for one, recounts hearsay from students at the Loreto Entally (Convent School) who witnessed Sister Teresa's departure, leading him to surmise that Mother Teresa's leaving must have caused the order some embarrassment. Some students at the Loreto Entally, where Mother Teresa taught, recall a scrawl on the blackboard while Sister Teresa was negotiating her departure that read: "Do not criticize. Do not praise. Pray." Whispers in the school testify to the fact that Sister Teresa, the geography teacher, was considered an aberration in the regimented echelons of Loreto, even a "freak" (Alpion 2007, 201).

36. Where Chawla hesitates, other texts forward well-formed hypotheses. The narrative of *In the Name of God's Poor*, which dramatizes Sister Teresa's life at the Loreto Entally, suggests that her request hardly had a sympathetic reception in the order. One scene portrays the then head of the Calcutta Loreto order, rolling her eyes in her discussion of Sister Teresa's vision—an interpretation that no doubt contributed to the famously secretive Mother Teresa's refusal to endorse the film as a realistic portrait.

37. Bharati Mukherjee recalls students who thought Mother Teresa was a "freak" (quoted in Alpion 2007, 198), while in her book on Mother Teresa, Charlotte Gray mentions, "We [the students] thought she was cracked!" (quoted in Alpion 2007, 199).

38. Muggeridge's book alone sold more than 300,000 copies. It has been reprinted twenty times and translated into thirteen languages. The decade following Mug-

geridge's homage saw other accolades. As early as 1971, Mother Teresa received recognition for her contributions to international relations—the Jawaharlal Nehru Award for International Understanding—from her home nation. In 1978, Pope John Paul II, a fellow Eastern European, came to head the Vatican, and Mother Teresa's international credentialing gathered momentum. With lobbying from conservatives such as Robert McNamara and Muggeridge, Mother Teresa received the Nobel Peace Prize in 1979, the British Order of Merit in 1983, and the American Presidential Medal of Freedom in 1985.

39. Hester Goodenough Gelber (1987, 15–35) examines Saint Francis of Assisi's flamboyant asceticism—parading naked and self-flagellation for having eaten a little meat while he was ill—as something regarded with ambivalence in some of his hagiographies.

40. Jinnah's last words, "Pakistan was the biggest mistake of my life," have been hotly debated in the Indian press, given the history between the two countries. The mainstream English-language press treated the statement as something of a secret that would revise the common perception that Jinnah's dream material-ized in Pakistan: see, e.g., Aiyar 2009.

41. Katherine Verdery (2003) makes such an argument, drawing on post-socialist transformations as her cases in point.

42. Jacques Derrida (1988) in fact claims that "legacy" is a line of credit the famous owe to their critics, a life gained through consumption.

43. The Mandal Commission in India was established in 1979 by the Janata Party government under Prime Minister Morarji Desai with a mandate to "identify the socially or educationally backward." In 1980, the commission's report affirmed the affirmative-action practice under Indian law whereby members of lower castes (known as Other Backward Classes and Scheduled Castes and Tribes) were given exclusive access to a certain portion of government jobs and slots in public universities; it also recommended changes to these quotas, increasing them by 27 percent, to 49.5 percent: Ramiah 1992. But anti-reservationist protests against the commission's recommendation exploded in 1990, ranging from road closures to self-immolation and bringing to the surface tensions around political enumer-ation along religious and caste lines.

44. The battles over owning Phoolan Devi are rather obvious in the coverage of her death recounted in the paper. But as the historian Gautam Bhadra once reminded me, we must also remember those who actively disown her. Those who lost rela-tives in Behmai, not to mention other bandits who saw her surrender as a be-trayal, disown Devi with some vigor. For some of these claims, see Saxena 1996.

CHAPTER SIX: VOLATILE ICONS

1. Stuart Hall (1977) argued for a double movement of popular culture: capitulation but also resistance to mass cultural products at sites of consumption. In his many works on subcultures (mods, rockers, punk), Dick Hebdige has argued that con-sumers habitually and self-consciously position themselves against the main-stream through consumption.

2. Different search engines have varying algorithms for regulating what content is easily accessed in the first ten to twenty pages: some simply regulate by sheer volume of traffic, such as Yahoo; others, such as Google, have more complex

mechanisms, including financial incentives to keep content alive and among the first links. What is striking is action on the part of news media institutions that remove images judged no longer newsworthy; short of a scholarly sojourn to the physical and digital news media databases, these images are no longer "public" as accessed transnationally.

3. The photograph was once found at http://www.traditioninaction.com (accessed October 2007).

4. The photograph was once found at http://news.bbc.co.uk/2/hi/south_asia/1458152.stm (accessed May 2008).

5. Magnum Photos, the image banks of the Associated Press, the Hindu, the BBC, as well as Getty Images house most of the now-famous public images that are considered the most representative inscriptions of these public figures. These databases are accessed through a variety of user-friendly image search engines such as Google images, Altavista / Yahoo, Picsearch, Visoo, and so forth. These banks and search tools have become increasingly crucial to the recursions of iconic inscriptions; while one might imagine they would enable the proliferation of non-standard, or singular images, in fact web art practitioners and bloggers often return to the same iconic image coteries I have characterized as "public images" as their intermedial templates.

6. For a thorough discussion of this strand of performance studies, see Parker and Sedgwick 1995.

7. Taylor's " 'You Are Here': The DNA of Performance" appeared in *Drama Review* 46, no. 1 (Spring 2002): 149–69, before it was incorporated as a chapter in Taylor 2003.

8. Scott Ewing is the anonymous author of the piece, but I relegate the artist's name to a footnote because he explicitly refuses the luxury of individually owned ideas. For the full documentary, see http://We/Arundhati/Roy/Filmmaker/20Interview.webarchive.

9. "Mother Teresa Statues in Great Demand," n.d., available online at www.mercatornet.com/articles/trashing_the_icon_of_altruism (accessed July 7, 2007).

10. In September 1996, *Vichar Mimansa*, a Hindi journal from Madhya Pradesh, published an article by Om Nagpal that asked whether Husain was "an artist or a butcher." The article pointed to a "painting" that *Vichar Mimansa*'s editor, V. S. Vajpayee, had come across while reading a book on the artist. The "painting" showed a "nude" Saraswati—in fact, a highly stylized sketch in which only contours, not detailed physical features, were evident. Nagpal's article made its way to Pramod Navalkar, the minister for culture in Maharashtra and leader of (the Hindu right-wing political party) the Shiv Sena. The Mumbai Police, with extraordinary vigor, took the complaint by Navalkar and filed criminal charges against Husain for promoting enmity between different groups of people on the grounds of religion and acting to insult religious feelings and beliefs. Three days after the complaint was filed, Bajrang Dal (another Hindu right-wing political party) activists stormed the Husain Doshi Gufa gallery in Ahmedabad, damaging tapestries and paintings valued at more than 1.5 crores rupees (ca. $222,346), including representations of the Buddha, Hanuman, and Ganesh.

11. For analyses of this media practice and for illustrations of Gandhi, see Jain 2007; Pinney 2004.

12. "Hearts of Gold, Fists of Fury," a mural in Clarion Alley, was painted in 2004 by eight teen muralists of the Oasis for Girls Paid Arts Apprenticeship Program: Sierra Bloomer, Micaiah Caplong, Su Mei Mai, Sunum Mobin, Nancy Salcedo, Amber Sanchez, Jennifer Tse, and Lily Zhen, with artist-trainer Marisa Jahn. The mural features Mother Teresa, Emma Goldman, Rosa Parks, Phoolan Devi, and Everywoman, each wielding her own secret weapon.

13. Bharadwaj's father is a noted lyricist at whose knee the director claims to have learned the lore, compositions, and techniques of vernacular ballads: see "Extras," *Omkara*, DVD, dist. Eros International.

14. The ethnomusicologist Scott Marcus has some of these recordings in his collection of viraha performances.

15. *Sholay* grossed more than $50 million (in equivalent rupee amount) at the box office when it first opened.

16. An early Bengali-language film based on this report, *Abhishapta Chambal* (1967), was made by Manju Dey, but a copy has been impossible to locate.

17. The Chambal is inhospitable terrain of phenomenal soil erosion (the cultivatable area has been reduced from 52.8 percent to 36.7 percent in the past seventy years) spanning 17,000 square miles and including the five northern districts of the Indian state of Madhya Pradesh. The area surrounding the Chambal River—the forbidding "Chambal Valley"—was always an administrative problem, the lawless Indian "interior" in the national imaginary (see elaboration in chapter 8).

18. Shyam Benegal's *Ankur* (1974) was one of the first films to articulate the dilemma of the subaltern female protagonist.

19. Those focused on South Asia argued that this is a region where vast numbers of the middle class, but also significant sections of small-town and rural populations, negotiate mass-media flows in ways that are quite distinct from those of bourgeois elite "high" cultures or traditional "folk cultures" (the two customary opposing cultural coteries officially sanctioned by national institutions such as the Sahitya Akademi and the Lalit Kala Akademi in India).

20. Pinney (2004) presents an extended analysis of political icons such as Gandhi, Khudiram, and Bhagat Singh; interestingly, the militant aestheticism of Bhagat Singh did not travel as easily as the "passive" form of Gandhi. Jain (2007), as we have seen, directly addresses icons when he pursues the images of cult leaders such as Balaji, Vaishno, Srimathji, and Sai Baba to unmask the political potentiality of mass-produced icons.

21. The case in point in Appadurai (2004) is Shackdwellers International in Africa and Asia (but also in Japan, Latin America, and the United Kingdom). We are not necessarily concerned with an economic calculus; rather, I have been arguing that expressive reassemblages of mass-mediated icons turn these signs into socially efficacious technologies for forging social bonds. On one end of the spectrum, one could imagine the popular as the locus of insurgency; on the other, the popular could be a loose coalition articulating social demands that only mildly question existing civil-legal institutions. These are different "capacities" that directly affect the volatility of the icon.

22. Others, such as Constance Penley and Jackie Stacey, further elaborated on collective viewing practices (fan clubs and subcultures) that demonstrated how consumption could be an active production of identity; Henry Jenkins (2005) would

further explicate exactly how viewers poached or re-scripted film stories at sites of reception in cultures of distraction or resistance. Still others returned to lost genealogies of mass culture to rethink the equation of consumption with a passive acceptance of the logic of capital or consumerism. Returning to Ernst Bloch, Jane Gaines (2000), for example, insisted on the strong utopianism of the dream factory, a world-improving dream or a hope consciousness. Even the most reified products could motivate yearning for something we have never known or might never know; capitalism, in fact, could motivate a dream of socialism.

23. See also S. V. Srinivas, "Is There a Public in the Cinema Hall?," 2000, available online at http://www.frameworkonline.com/42svs.htm (accessed August 2008); his insights here are now elaborated in a larger work, *Megastars* (2009).

24. In the blogosphere, such devotional activity consolidates a public who characterize themselves as the "Bollywood bhakts" (Bollywood devotees), posting their worshipful commentaries or digital art on musical and movie stars. See the report on the Bollywood bhakts, in "Amitabh Bachchan" 2006.

25. Richard Dyer (1979) reads the personhood of stars we garner from star images as indicative of successful individualism, including the possession of wealth and property (the excessive wealth of stars is a source of fascination). Dyer harnesses the study of popular biographies in which Leo Lowenthal (1944) argues that stars have become models of consumption—fashions copied, sports emulated, hobbies pursued. I would argue that personhood can mean something very different for disenfranchised subjects who speak their politics through consuming icons. The icon therefore has a greater reach than the star in terms of the personhood it might embody; when stars become icons, they have a heft among heterogeneous populations that is often confusing to critics who pursue stars as commodities that reify (rather than stimulate) social relations.

26. Tuned in to the electoral clout of movie stars, we witnessed efforts in the 2004 elections to harness structures of feeling vibrant in this alternative public sphere. Hence, star-politicians entered the business of standardizing and stylizing their commodity images, coached and groomed by hired technicians. In the bustle of the election, journalists reported the mad rush from Bollywood, with the Congress Party and BJP, the major parties, vying with each other to turn fan bases into electoral vote banks. The BJP enlisted Jitendra, Suresh Oberoi, Manoj Kumar, Hema Malini, Vinod Khanna, among others, while Congress roped in Asrani, Shakti Kapoor, Zeenat Aman, and Om Puri, to name a few. For their part, stars accompany party leaders at functions mouthing a few well-rehearsed speeches and sometimes memorized film dialogue; in three northern Indian states, for instance, the BJP's "Dream Girl," Hema Malini, campaigned for the party by mouthing dialogue from her blockbuster *Sholay* (1975).

CHAPTER SEVEN: IN THE NAME OF THE POPULAR

1. These crossings intimate that we must think beyond Weberian notions of charisma in which a person is invested with natural magical qualities by his supporters or devotees, a vestigial trace of the religio-mystical in modern disenchanted spheres. Charismatic leaders rise, in Weber's view, in conditions of instability because they operate outside of traditional kinship and economic organization: see selections by Weber in Gerth and Mills 1946. But the uneven reach of moder-

nity in South Asia presents a very different possibility for the existence of highly public figures that attract such adulation. The structure of veneration we ascribe to icon formation—the enchantment the icon demands—explains the rise of star politicians far better than sociological theories of charismatic leadership.

2. I am indebted to one of the external reviewers of the manuscript for highlighting this body that persists throughout the book in his or her underscoring of the book's renewed materialism. As I noted in the introduction, Grosz's development of the positivity of this body is the materiality on which my argument depends. In addition to the genealogy of philosophers who speak to the abundance of matter, it is worth noting, as the reviewer pointed out, that theorists of affectivity (Brian Massumi and Steven Shaviro, among others) have been highly influential in highlighting an embodied ontology that is critical of social constructivism.

3. In the thoughtful introduction to his conversations with Negri, Casarino theorizes a "surplus common," a living in the social with a sense of a shared social that no reappropriation of the common—common goals, aspirations, agendas—can harness, that is pertinent to the open-ended sociality of the body that is vibrant in theories of affect. In difference from the "common *project*" in Hardt and Negri's oeuvre (2000; 2004), Casarino insists on a more radical potentiality (*qua* potentiality) to the common, a living as surplus that discloses the difference between capital and the common: Casarino 2008, 23; emphasis added.

4. The *Satanic Verses* controversy that broke in early 1989, popularly known as "The Rushdie Affair," began with British Muslims burning Salman Rushdie's magical realism account of the migration of Islam into the profane world on grounds of blasphemy against the Prophet Muhammed; the Iranian theocracy followed with a death threat (a *fatwa*) against Rushdie that sent the writer into hiding and spurring a decade-long debate on free speech, secularism, and civil rights. The Danish cartoon controversy is much more recent: another fight over freedom of speech erupting after Islamic publics reacted strongly against a cartoon contest hosted by the *Jyllands-Posten* newspaper.

5. I have collected several such local publications from the famous bookstores of College Street in Kolkata (surrounding the equally famous Coffee House Dipesh Charabarty wrote about in his description of *adda*). These are one-time publications from small press runs, but Mother Teresa remains a staple subject for the Bengali-speaking metropolitan and small-town readers who haunt these stores.

6. For an analysis of Sister Nivedita's absorption into Indian culture, see the discussion of this figure in Parama Roy 1998.

7. During my annual research trips to Kolkata, I visit a couple of well-known bookstores on College Street, a famous neighborhood for books as well as the street in which Presidency College, Medical College, and Calcutta University are located. After 1997, I collected at least four such slim hagiographic volumes, which generally are out of print within two or three years. Biswa-da, a veteran bookseller, however, proudly assures me this is because Mother Teresa's life story is still a bestseller.

8. As Fraser (1996, 110–11) intimates, Jürgen Habermas saw the public sphere as "a theater in modern societies in which political participation is enacted through the medium of talk"—a sphere of life distinct from the state and critical of it, distinct from the arena of market relations but also a stage for debating on buying or

selling that is indispensable to democratic political practice. Fraser's explorations of the post-liberal public sphere that emerged in the context of the United States in the 1960s demonstrates that feminists made "private" matters, domestic or sexual, a public matter, the politics of gender dissolving older distinctions between public and private. Warner (2002) underscores the counter-public making of new worlds of culture and social relations, prompting the articulation of new subjectivities—one can be homosexual in isolation, for example, but "queer" elaborates a world together.

9. Such a divide in which the will to political power could be the purview of few, on the one hand, inevitably gave rise to an ethos of distinction—ways to define the emergent elite from older aristrocratic elites from the various plebian and popular it sought to rule (Eley 2002, 114). On the other, it gave rise to vibrant political cultures in which public life could be lived through riot, revelry, or music.

10. See the discussion of public culture with subaltern studies in Bhandari 2006.

11. In part, such protest signaled the widely held conception that the micro-elites who spearheaded the Hindu right's Sangh Parivar coalition were in cahoots with upper castes in Uttar Pradesh for electoral gain. Hence, when Devi's body was to be flown to Mirzapur, anonymous crowds (not belonging to a particular political party) smashed the windows at the Chief Minister Rajnath Singh's residence in Delhi, chanting, "Phoolan Devi Amar Rahen" (May Phoolan Devi remain immortal): see Onkar Singh and Tara Shanker Sahay, "Phoolan Devi's Supporters Turn Violent," July 26, 2001, available online at www.rediff.com.

12. In "Canonising Crime" (2001), Visa Ravindran, for example, cursorily noted that Devi had obviously "captured the imagination of different segments of our society" but dismissed reports of violence as unimportant to the task of understanding her.

13. Here I depend on the long conversation on social violence as communication that has followed riots, genocide, and social suffering: see, e.g., Das et al. 2000.

14. "Sochet hai main bhi Phoolan Devi banoongni" (They think, I, too, will become Phoolan Devi), remarked Malkan Singh, a contemporary of Devi's. For more details on the social phenomenon of women's banditry, see Menon 1999.

15. "Bandit Queen Set for Uttar Pradesh Ballot," n.d., available online at http://www.ibnonline.com (accessed June 10, 2007).

16. This was hardly surprising, since Phoolan Devi's "cine-luster" was no anomaly. Veerappan, the notorious legendary outlaw of the south (at the border of Tamil Nadu and Karnataka) who was active in the 1990s, drew his symbolic cachet from the fictional Gabbar Singh, the fearsome bandit of Sholay. Parihar (and the twenty to twenty-five other female bandits still working in the Chambal) had Phoolan Devi, ever volatile in inspiring a search for justice beyond the law. Hence, the dreaded Kusuma Nain, another contemporary female bandit who faced eighty-four murder charges, anointed herself "dasyu sundari" (the beautiful bandit queen), jogging memories of another who had borne the appellation two decades earlier.

17. The lack of prohibitions of icon worship in Hindu cultures no doubt facilitates the worship of secular figures. Even in the case of Islamic cultures in South Asia, scholars such as Pnina Werbner effectively demonstrate the easing of proscriptions against image worship in syncretic Muslim traditions: Werbner and Basu 1998.

18. "Mother's People Find No Place in Funeral March" was *The Statesman*'s cover story on September 7, 1997.

19. Many of these cases were collected on my visit to the Mother Teresa Museum at the Little Sisters of the Poor in Kolkata, where two large scrapbooks hold all news coverage of her death, funeral, and legacy.

20. For a full account, see "The Undertaking," *Frontline*, October 3, 1997, available online at http://www.pbs.org/wgbh/pages/frontline/undertaking/talk.

21. In "Dancing with Diana: A Study in Hauntology," Diana Taylor compares Mother Teresa to Lady Diana. The article originally appeared in *Drama Review* 43, no. 1 (Spring 1999): 59–78, and was revised and reprinted in Taylor 2003.

22. In her "hauntology," Taylor temporalizes the unfolding of controversies involving Lady Diana along Victor Turner's model of social drama in an effort to explain the sense of resolution funeral spectacles might bring. Explaining public consumption of the famous dead, Taylor reads the reintegration of the dead into the social order as a last stage in a longer drama in which publics participate in the unfolding of the famous life. Attempting a typology based on Turner's paradigm, Taylor's exposition puts the first stage of such a drama at a breach with social norms that marks the famous person as "one of us"—Diana's divorce, her feud with the Windsors, and her affair with Dodi Al-Fayed. Mother Teresa's exclaustration and founding of a separate order also constitute such a breach. This is followed by a crisis—such as a death—in which the one who is like us passes into singularity ("She has left us") within a tragic frame. The funeral is the redressive act where the tragic figure is given recompense, becoming legend. Citationality and theatricality are key elements: Lady Diana's joining Marilyn Monroe through Elton John's "Candle in the Wind"; Mother Teresa's joining Gandhi and Nehru, a pantheon of national leaders, as well as Catholic saints evoked in the service. Finally, the closing chapter is a reintegrative stage in which the dust over the contested meanings of these lives finally settles. This is not to say there are no ongoing refutations of the final image produced by the icon's reintegration into the social; rather, Taylor indicates the often ceremonial claiming of the exceptional dead by a regime or institution of which they were once a part, but from which they subsequently departed.

23. The Kerala chapter of the Dalit Sahitya Akademi subsidized a Malayalam edition of *The God of Small Things* and held a reception in Roy's honor in 1999. In *The God of Small Things*, Roy engages in the corporeal speech that was to become her hallmark in her nonfiction, foregrounding the singular body of Velutha, abandoned, abused, and destroyed by the violent Indian postcolonial state, and its legal representatives, brutalized by their "inchoate, unacknowledged fear" of the subaltern other. "Boot on bone. On teeth. The muffled grunt when a stomach is kicked in. The muted crunch of skull on cement. The gurgle of a man's breath when his lung is torn by the jagged end of a broken rib": Roy 1996, 308.

24. See Shu-mei Shih's (2004) exploration of prizes as technologies of recognition that impart cultural purchase to writers of global literature.

25. Excerpt from Roy's letter to the Sahitya Akademi, January 13, 2006, available online at http://www.southendpress.org/news/news4 (accessed July 2007).

26. For a longer discussion of the various actors in the NBA, see Ghosh 2009.

27. The shot of Roy at "The Rally for the Valley," for instance, was taken by Hari

Katragadda, a well-established photojournalist who periodically has worked for media institutions such as *Business Today*, *Stern*, *Geo*, Amnesty International, *Frontline*, *Internazionale*, and *Missio Aktuel*: see http://www.lightstalkers.org/harikatragadda (accessed July 2005).

28. The bio-politics of such sexual coding is evident everywhere in Devi's case, since her treatment in jail—her treatment by the state—was largely informed by fantasies of nymphomania in the yellow press. A prison doctor, Manoj Marthur, exemplified the state's prejudice when he was interviewed by a Bombay tabloid: "The officers are helpless and have to concede her each and every demand, including her desire to have sex. Under the *Jail Manual*, male and female prisoners cannot be kept together, nor can they be in touch with each other. But Phoolan, who is a known nymphomaniac and has an insatiable urge for sex, insists that she be kept with her fellow [male] dacoits. This has put jail officials in a quandary": quoted in *Blitz*, March 1983. Such sensationalism exposes the moral criteria that governs the operation of state power. No wonder jailers would labor to prevent Devi from breeding more Phoolan Devis! One might say that Devi was rarely the legal subject before law but always the object virulently judged by normative heteropatriarchal criteria—criteria that, as Flavia Agnes (1990, 86) suggests, promoted a "negative view of women's sexuality" so that sexual violence perpetrated against certain sexual subjects could be rationalized as the result of the subject's sexual promiscuity. Historical scholarship on specific cases in which sexuality emerges as a problem in the Indian context underscore the heteropatriarchal basis of codes that come into play where things sexual—acts or bodies—appear before the law. Feminist legal theorists such as Agnes and Nivedita Menon, commenting on the long battle by Indian feminists, from 1980 to 1989, to bring about the legal recognition of sex and sexuality, underscore how deeply the symbolic order "inscribes a body as a body, and separate from other bodies": Menon 2000, 42.

29. Following Pierre Bourdieu, Ranajit Guha (1983, 55) notes that the body plays a particularly critical role in codifying and storing cultural values in abbreviated and mnemonic form.

30. As expressed to Dhruv Kumar, who interviewed Devi for the half-hour documentary *Phoolan: The First Rebel*, co-produced and directed for the Italian network Rai International.

31. The strong identification between the saint's body and the devotee's is once more apparent in Sister Marie Simone-Pierre's claim that she was cured of Parkinson's disease by Pope John Paul II, who suffered from the same disease.

32. Such reports proliferate. Raghu Rai, responsible for so many of the saint's public images, reiterated the "touch" of the icon in his paean to Mother Teresa in *Mother Teresa: A Life of Devotion* (2005), which begins with an epigraph: "Those hands with which you held other hands as you held mine, every time you restored me to myself." The "Saint Mother," in this evocative pronouncement, links the individual to the social body through her flesh, the iconic aperture a conduit for dispersion into the social.

33. If corporeal exchange has always been an unsanctioned, but wildly popular, interchange with saints, religious institutions have always scrambled to bring such interchanges into their control. In her tome on debates over the body's material

continuity in the twelfth century and thirteenth century, Caroline Bynum (1992), for instance, explains that theological discourse eventually came around to providing a scholastic rationale for popular beliefs that would not disappear. She is referring to scholastic arguments that the body was simply matter without personhood once the soul had left it; debates on the resurrection of the body centered on the identity or personhood of body parts (fingernails, foreskins, embryos) and the relation between those parts and the body as a whole. Bynum argues that scholastic debates finally made room for popular beliefs in continuity between the body part and the soul of the saint so that the relic—a finger, a hair—would indeed carry the spirit of the saint. Bynum's argument therefore establishes the unassailable corporeality of the saint's body in the mind of the devotee.

34. In recent years, such corporeal activism has won important battles. For example, one Supreme Court ruling (an interpretation of Article 21 of the Indian Constitution) recognized violence on the biosphere as moral violation perpetrated on citizens and non-citizens. Justice Krishna Iyer wrote: "The right to life means the right to livelihood, to dignity in existence. The right to health, to drinking water, to a pollution-free environment, to a biosphere where people can live, is all a part of the right to life": quoted in Sharan 2002, 31.

35. The female body has a particular symbolic charge in this history—one that significantly affects contemporary women's activism in India. As early as the late nineteenth century, the Bengali-language novelist Bankim Chandra Chattopadhyay famously portrayed the physical training of a poor, kidnapped, and molested widow—the iconic helpless woman who was to become the nationalists' "project" —as transformative, turning Chaudhurani into the leader (and muse) of anti-British "thugs": Chattopadhyay 1884. "Devi Chaudhurani" became the chosen title for Sarala Devi, an early nationalist who became involved in women's education (including physical training). For recent scholarship on Sarala Devi (1875–1945) of the Tagore family, see Roy 2002.

36. Yet the corporeality of the female body in the field of political action cannot be considered in isolation from male actors whose corporeal strategies were absolutely seminal to the freedom movement. I am speaking, of course, of Gandhi's harnessing of the spectacle of the suffering body as a moral weapon, a political strategy that has been extensively analyzed in recent works: see, e.g., Alter 2000. Gandhi's essentialist construction of women as better suited to satyagraha because of their greater capacity for self-sacrifice not only feminized the male satyagrahi's body but rendered the corporeal performance of suffering—hunger strikes, enduring torture or physical punishment, or putting one's body at risk in sit-in demonstrations or activities like standing in chest-deep water for hours—legitimate, moral, and authoritative.

CHAPTER EIGHT: BECOMING SOCIAL

1. For a discussion of social imaginaries, see Taylor 2004. See also Gaonkar 2002.

2. See the discussion of David Arnold's study of the Madras presidency, in which Arnold cites the inspector-general's report on crime, in Guha 1983, 87.

3. See the elaboration of global examples of "crimes of indigence" that are precursors to rebellion in Guha 1983, 93.

4. The subaltern as a figure of disenfranchisement (extrapolated from Gramsci) in

South Asian contexts, which is modulated quite differently in Ranajit Guha's and Gayatri Spivak's formulations, first emerged in the subaltern studies critiques of colonialism and nationalism. In subsequent conversations, however, the pitfalls of cursorily evoking the subaltern became very clear. Too often, the subaltern becomes abstract trope: a metaphor for any form of disempowerment, a free-floating signifier for consuming victimization. Spivak (1996) herself rigorously insisted on retaining the specificity of the analytic category, applying it to those people cut off from all lines of mobility (therefore, the subaltern cannot "speak") and "sighted" at points of their insurgency. The subaltern marked a power differential, a demographic difference, and is best understood as a subtraction in a defined field of social relations. This means that, depending on the demographic field in question, small-town elites could be subaltern with respect to national elites, or displaced Indian indigenous peoples could be subaltern to peasants farming settled land (peasants are the subaltern in Guha's oeuvre): see Guha 1983; Spivak 1988.

5. Hence, her iconic value—as Rajeswari Sunder Rajan warns in her recent assessment of the bandit queen's surrender—is hardly the measure of agency. "Our understanding of the politics of surrender," she writes of Phoolan Devi's case, "must be informed, then, by both the *exceptionalism* and the *paradoxical representativeness* of Phoolan Devi's career": Sunder Rajan 2004, 214; emphasis added. She suggests that women's militant agency (exceptionalism) does not necessarily count as progressive feminist politics, as scholars grappling with the phenomena of Hindu right-wing militant icons in India have long argued.

6. For a sustained theorization of such a rapidly changing middle class, see Fernandes 2006.

7. I borrow the term from Robert Neuwirth (2005) to designate the translocal new urbanism of slums.

8. Vinoba Bhave, the first individual satyagrahi chosen by Gandhi, was known for his Bhoodan pilgrimage, in which he wandered all over India on foot asking citizens to grant him land so he might redistribute it among the landless poor.

9. One lakh equals $100,000.

10. Social banditry in the region can be traced back to the age of Sher Shah Suri and Prithviraj Chauhan. While it is tempting to follow Eric Hobsbawm's (1965) hypotheses on social banditry emerging at an evolutionary phase from pre-capitalist feudalism to agrarian capitalism, the "dacoit problem" in the Chambal, Bhadhuri notes in his appendices, can be traced as far back as the sixteenth century.

11. Hobsbawm records the rise of Kalhua, the brigand chief of the local Gujars (a minority population in Saharanpur) who captured the local imagination and led a rebellion against the state, as having taken place only eleven years after the great land-estate breakdown of 1813.

12. At the time of the Vinoba Bhave mission, there were five hundred known bandits in the Chambal Valley.

13. In Anupama Rao's analysis, Dalit women are not universal subjects of humanism, not universal subjects before law. They are subjects marked violently as sexually different, with gendered and sexed differences overly determined by their location in caste hierarchies. Yet the law turns a blind eye to the specificity of these bodies, even as their corporeality renders them distinct from others: Rao 1998.

14. The singular encounter is arguably the most radically ethical one, because it cannot be subsumed into generality. In a lengthy reading of Walter Benjamin's ruminations on divine violence in "Force of the Law," Derrida reiterates the link between justice and force, posing the question: How does one differentiate just use of violence, the force of the law, from violence deemed unjust? A radical notion of justice, Derrida maintains, would mean a Levinasian (ethical) opening to radical alterity, an addressing of oneself to the Other in the language of the Other, a singular moment that is not iterative and therefore is unrepresentable (Cheah and Grosz 1996, 17). Yet justice in the politico-juridical realm requires a translation of the singular into the general, an act of interpretive/performative violence foundational to the law. The concept of violence, for Derrida, belongs to the spheres of law, politics, and morals (1992, 31); the law tends to prohibit violence (e.g., the taking of bare life) to monopolize the exercise of violence or force. Hence, it habitually performs violence against those who do not recognize this monopoly, as in the case of the brigand or outlaw (Derrida 1992, 40). These figures who challenge the state's monopoly on force must be positioned as "criminal," even dispensable, for the law to retain its reach and power.

15. Where Derrida establishes the violence of generality in metaphysical terms (though illustrated by example), Agamben historicizes the legal use of force, especially when "necessity" (such as a national emergency) makes it possible for "a single specific case of transgression by means of an exception" to be released from the norm: Agamben 2004, 25. Modern Western states, in their encroachment on the bare life of human beings, seem in perpetual crisis; hence, the proliferation of states of exception.

16. The long postcolonial history of opposition to the (colonial) state no doubt brings more suspicion to operations of the law in the postcolonial state than in Western democracies, where legal liberal ideology and practice seem deceptively stable. The Gandhian legacy of moral redress against the force of the law, the demand for distributive justice, now confounds the politico-juridical order of the decolonized state. Upendra Baxi lists neo-Gandhian modes of direct action—satyagraha, processions, hunger strikes, general strikes, *gherao* (the direct action of surrounding authorities, thereby stalling all work), and sit-ins—as expressions of a "countervailing power" that seriously weakens the logic of legalism: Baxi 1982, 9.

17. For South Asia, one of the most important contributions to the modernity debate is Chakrabarty 2000, followed by Chakrabarty 2002, a collection of essays illustrating specific admixtures of the (bourgeois) modern with the "non-modern" in this specific articulation of modernity.

18. An energetics in which Nietzsche is clearly the inspiration is elaborated in Bataille 1994 (1945).

19. While Bataille readily acknowledges that a certain degree of energy consumption is required to produce the subject (within the homogeneous social order), the subject has a plethora of energy to be expended unproductively, excessively, and with seeming unreason.

20. The subject's intimacies mobilize an economy that is as faithful to the revelations of mystics as it is to those of Marx, Freud, and Nietzsche. In bringing religious and secular objects within the same economy, this book aligns the metaphysics of the icon with scholars who have deconstructed Christianity (as Derrida names it)—

the work of Jean-Luc Nancy, certainly, but also the base materialism of Georges Bataille. Far from an advocate of the spiritual—remember that Bataille left the Catholic seminary and "lost" his faith in 1922—Bataille is able to read the untrammeled power of the spiritual through a materialist lens. Most important for Bataille: It is the body that joins the religious and the economic in a single focus; it is the material substance that links the subject to the world, a substance expended in sacrifice or banked in accumulation of capital. Hence, he is one of the major theorists of flesh central to my consolidation of a counter-history of the body in which corporeal exchange can be theorized as the basis for political action. For a perusal of Bataille's formation and development as an intellectual, see Botting and Wilson 1998. For a full discussion of Jean-Paul Sartre's opposition to Bataille, see Hollywood 2002. Bataille's notion of unproductive expenditure—spending one's matter against the postulates of a social order that admonishes us to be productive—hypothesizes a collective force field (a common humanity) that arises from our deepest encounter with the Other; our "touching," as Nancy (2005) would have it, mobilizes us in a collective economy. It is only in recent years that some of Bataille's theories have been recuperated, most notably by Jacques Derrida, who points to Bataille's critique of Hegel: Bataille's economies, for Derrida (1978), present exchanges outside the rational domain while working from within a Hegelian perspective, a reworking of the master–slave dialectics of labor. Bataille's notion of unproductive expenditure is critical to understanding the potentialities of disposable peoples who are positioned outside relations of production, Derrida argues—disposable peoples who proliferate in our times in the guise of the multitude, the *homo sacer*, the refugee, the camp dweller, and the asylum seeker. It is from the deeply abject that revolution comes; military, religious, and fascist organizations can often partially contain it, but never completely. Bataille's value, Derrida argues, lies in marking a possibility that Bataille neither celebrates nor denigrates. One can see how such a conception of an open potentiality is highly salient to the volatile icon, an auratic object that opens to the possibility of social change but might just as easily be yoked to hegemonic aspirations.

21. Arguing in a Bataillean vein in her phenomenology of saintly exorbitance, Edith Wyschogood (1990) reads the saint's altruism as inherently excessive, the sumptuary expenditure of a discontinuous individual undoing her own substance. Her reading of the consumptive sainthood finds gendered explication in Hollywood (2002), which hypothesizes the lure of flesh as the draw of the female mystic: both the particularity of the body transcended through the senses and masochistic self-shattering as ethical practice beyond the restriction of politics are directly modeled on the meditative practices of late medieval mystics.

22. Attentive to the discursive capture of sacrificial logics, Shershow (2005) insists that the representation of work as "Gift" (garnering obligation), or the incalculable gift that appears as a great "Work" (garnering social capital), in late capital, marks a historical shift in which, in the mutual imbrication of the general and restricted economies, the latter is constantly privileged.

23. The term was popularized by Marvin Olasky, the adviser to George Bush, but initially coined by Doug Wead in 1977; see Olasky, *Renewing American Compassion* (1996).

24. For relevant details, see the carefully researched chapter on Mother Teresa's

accounts in Chatterjee 2002. These explorations of rational instrumentality are key to comprehending the nature of restriction that compromises Mother Teresa's selfless sacrifice. Laurence Iannaccone (1995), for one, reminds us that religious markets prompt policies that maximize profits that are not only monetary (although these are considerable in Mother Teresa's case, as several commentators have noted). Other rational-choice theorists attempt to bring religious affiliation and participation into the realm of rational production: see, e.g., Kwilecki and Wilson 1998.

25. In her rumination on Roman Catholicism's newly calibrated transnationalism (since this has always been a transnational religion), Danièle Hervieu-Léger (1997) notes that a shift in Vatican II was perceptible in the re-homogenization and standardization of appropriate Catholic conduct, on the one hand, and a greater ecclesiastical tolerance of cultural diversity (incense fumes and saris, in our account), on the other. These changes were supplemented with an overhaul of the vertical organizational hierarchies and bureaucracies of church governance, now deregulated to function like NGOs through ecumenical and fundamentalist networks.

26. Scholars such as José Casanova (1997) see such transformation as a return of the church's global ambitions. Transnational religious organizations such as the Roman Catholic church, Casanova insists, were never really at home in the Westphalian system of territorially sovereign states; hence, with the weakening of nation-states' borders in our times, Pope John Paul II slipped easily into his new role as "the high priest of a new universal civil religion of humanity."

27. Mother Teresa's commodity image as the face of charity is reiterated every day. Alpion (2007, 229), for example, closes his biography by foregrounding the encyclical letter of 2005 in which Pope Benedict XVI makes as many as three references to Mother Teresa as the "model of charity" before emphasizing charity as the most important feature of Christianity in general and of Roman Catholicism in particular.

28. See the account of Clinton's visit in June 1995 in Hitchens 1994, 9. Some artists have mocked such a reification of charity in their works. The British playwright Helen Edmundsen's play "Mother Teresa Is Dead," for example, is a critique of white privilege that is enacted by deploying the nun as a signifier for self-evident selfless charity.

29. In *Politics of Nature* (2004), Latour begins by suggesting that political ecology has to let go of "nature" as a reified category.

30. See my discussion of legibility in Ghosh 2009.

31. It is within the second wave that activism morphed into legitimate political action. Guha (1983) describes the watershed moment as having come at a seminar on natural history at the University of Copenhagen in 1969, when a group of students locked in Denmark's foremost scientists, cut off ventilation, and sprayed water from polluted lakes to jump start political action on environmental degradation. Their performance of social action inaugurated the new scene of environmental activism whose modes of protest crystallized over the next decade in the global North. In South Asia, the first attacks critiqued the colonial state's project of scientific forestry, which was inaugurated by the Indian Forest Act of 1878. Guha catalogues early intellectual responses from Jyotiba Phule and, later, Gan-

dhi, whose famous axiom linked consumerism to environmental devastation: "The world has enough for everybody's need, but not enough for one person's greed." But Phule's and Gandhi's "environmentalism" was primarily a social critique of the colonial state and a moral protest against the appropriation of commons. The Gandhian prescription for the reconstruction of an ideal village economy was promoted by a slew of Gandhian industrialists, including J. C. Kumarrappa and Mira Behn (Madeline Slade), early activists who constituted the first wave of environmentalism on the subcontinent.

32. In his work on international law, Balakrishnan Rajagopal (2003, 122) notes that the quasi-independent inspection panel that wrote the report was the first such institutional body created to allow individuals to bring legal actions against an international institution.

33. Prasad quotes Patrick Lannan, president of the Lannan Foundation, which offered Roy the Lannan Prize for Cultural Freedom.

34. Where the enemy is no longer a single colonizing nation-state but a networked conglomerate, different modes of political action are necessary—all of which can be consolidated under the rubric of activism.

35. Radha Kumar's *The History of Doing* (1993), a historical account of women's activism and the Indian feminist movement, provides a vast catalogue of female actors that ranges from early militants such as Sarala Devi Ghoshal to contemporary activist icons turned politicians such as Brinda Karat. Devoted to describing collective action, Kumar highlights female icons as signs that are classically materialized in visual formats (reproductions of sketches to photographs).

36. These women included Sarojini Naidu, a well-known poet and the first woman to be arrested at the Salt March of 1930, as well as Kamala Nehru, Lado Ran Zutshi, Kamala Chattopadhyay, and other such political luminaries. On the other side of the spectrum (of nonviolent agitation), radicals such as Preetilata Wadekar and Bina Das shot to sensational fame for their participation in armed resistance of the 1930s.

37. The term "activism" was used first in 1916 in connection with the Belgian Flamingant movement, but it picked up its contemporary modes in the protest and dissent of the social movements of the 1960s. It has become so professionalized that activism is now a job classification. Activist organizations are primarily nonprofits and rarely manufacture goods.

38. I am indebted to Madhava Prasad for encouraging me to track the iconic purchase of the activist to the freedom struggle that overwrites this cultural figuration.

39. In past twenty years, Patkar has fasted for more than 320 days at various points of time seeking justice for people displaced by the construction of big dams over the Narmada River, reports Sheela Bhatt ("Medha Patkar: The Struggle Prolongs," available online at http://www.rediff.com [accessed April 17, 2006]). Hence, her body is repeatedly visualized in mass media, often in scenes of protest against dams in the Narmada Valley (standing firm as waters rise, avoiding police batons) or when engaged in hunger strikes. In her most recent twenty-day hunger strike in March–April 2006 (launched by Patkar and Jamsing Nargave and Bhagwatibai Jatpuria, two other participants from affected villages in Madhya Pradesh), in response to an apex court decision to allow the dam's height to be raised, not only did Patkar dominate every headline, but so did her body. Many of the

accounts began by describing her "frail" body, then moved on to present detailed accounts of her suffering body and its (forced) care in a Delhi hospital. "Today she risks damaging her kidneys permanently due to fluctuating ketone (product of fat metabolism) level due to constant fasting," Bhatt reported in terms couched in anatomico-medical jargon pitched at a health-obsessed national middle class. "Her left leg is wrapped in bandage. She suffers from a painful skin disease called Psoriasis": ibid. Another report characteristically commenced with the "frail-looking Ms. Patkar": "Medha Patkar Ends Fast" 2001.

40. See Amita Baviskar's (2001) analysis of the Indian state's handling of two incidents, varied responses that depended on the global legibility of the social movements (the Narmada Bachao Andolan and the Adivasi Mukti Sangathan) in question.

41. Biopiracy is a term that describes the "misappropriation of indigenous people's knowledge and resources through intellectual property mechanisms": Mgbeoji 2006, 12.

42. For example, *Biopiracy* (Shiva 1997) was published by South End in Boston, which not only brought out some of Roy's nonfiction works but also published the "Open Democracy" pamphlet series that featured such luminaries as Tariq Ali and Noam Chomsky. In *Biopiracy*, Shiva explains that the resources of the global South (plants, air, water, and knowledge) have been subjected to direct attacks by corporations (such as Enron and Bechtel) that, operating under the intellectual-property regimes of the global North, attempt to patent medicinal plants such as neem trees, spices such as turmeric, and rice strains such as basmati. Shiva is the exemplary citizen of a global civil society, a philosopher of heft and legible as an intellectual on par with Chomsky. She is largely known through the biographies transmitted in blurbs and articles that feature her, as well as through a formidable technology of prizes (much like Roy). A recent article in *India Currents* magazine, sporting a smiling, gray-haired Shiva on its glossy cover, positions her as the arbiter/translator of the age-old knowledge of farmers. "Vandana Shiva knows what most farmers do about our food: that it is good to save seed for next season, it is good to diversify the genetic base of your crop so you get a sturdy harvest and more defenses against pests and the local climate": Primlane 2000, 8.

43. In *Excitable Speech* (1997), Butler argues that hate speech produces an event beyond the body, as illustration of the force fields of speech acts.

44. For an elaboration of Roy's speeches, see Ghosh, "Tallying Bodies."

45. Arundhati Roy, "Peace and the New Corporate Liberation Theology," Sydney Peace Prize lecture, November 3, 2004, Seymour Centre, Sydney, available online at http://www.abc.net.au/rn/bigideas/stories; emphasis added.

46. Activism not only signals new modes of action (such as the circulation of petitions over the Internet) but also expansively incorporates older notions of "struggle" (the Marxist notation of objective relations) and "resistance" (the poststructuralist capture of the subjective aspects of protest). Activism also modulates the temporality and spatiality of struggles in flexible ways. Activism can be situated, brief, or long and fierce and not as part of a larger social movement; it equally can be episodic and distant from the locality of struggle: Baxi 2005, 66. The activist can function as the leader of a struggle and as an intermediary who connects the local struggles to national and transnational networks.

Adorno, Theodor W. 1953. "Prologue to Television." *Critical Models: Interventions and Catchwords*, trans. Henry W. Pickford, 49–58. Columbia University Press, 1999.

——. 1981. "The Schema of Mass Culture." *The Culture Industry: Selected Essays on Mass Culture*, trans. Nicholas Walker, ed. Jay M. Bernstein, 54–83. Routledge, 1991.

Agamben, Giorgio. 1998. *Homo Sacer: Sovereign Power and Bare Life*. Stanford: Stanford University Press.

——. 2004. *State of Exception*. Chicago: University of Chicago Press.

Agnes, Flavia. 1990. *Journey to Justice*. Bombay: Majlis.

Agnivesh, Swami, and Valson Thampu. 2001. "The Parable of Phoolan Devi." *The Hindu*, August 10, 4.

Aiyar, Shankkar. 2009. "Jinnah and a Mistake Called Pakistan." *India Today*, March 9, 18–19.

Akbar, M. J. 1981. "Phoolan Devi: Queen of Dacoits." *Sunday*, March 15, 22.

Allahar, Anton. 2001. *Caribbean Charisma: Reflections on Leadership, Legitimacy and Populist Politic*. Boulder: Lynne Rienner.

Alpion, Gëzim. 2007. *Mother Teresa: Saint or Celebrity?* New York: Routledge.

Alter, Joseph S. 2000. *Gandhi's Body: Sex, Diet, and the Politics of Nationalism*. Philadelphia: University of Pennsylvania Press.

Amin, Shahid. 1984. "Gandhi as Mahatma: Gorakhpur District, Eastern UP, 1921–2." *Subaltern Studies III*, ed. Ranajit Guha. New Delhi: Oxford University Press India.

"Amitabh Bachchan: Man and Myth." 2006. *Little India*, May, 27–33.

Appadurai, Arjun. 2004. "The Capacity to Aspire: Culture and the

Terms of Recognition." *Culture and Public Action*, ed. Vijayendra Rao and Michael Walton, 59–84. Stanford: Stanford University Press.

Appadurai, Arjun, and Carol Breckenridge. 1995. "Public Modernity in India." *Consuming Modernity: Public Culture in a South Asian World*, ed. Arjun Appadurai and Carol Breckenridge, 122. Minneapolis: University of Minnesota Press.

Arias, Arturo. 2001. "Authorizing Ethnicized Subjects: Rigoberta Menchú and the Performative Production of the Subaltern." *PMLA* 116, no. 1: 75–88.

Arnold, David, and Stuart Blackburn. 2005. "Introduction: Life Histories in India." *Telling Lives in India: Biography, Autobiography, and Life History*, ed. David Arnold and Stuart Blackburn, 1–28. Bloomington: Indiana University Press.

Arrighi, Giovanni. 1994. *The Long Twentieth Century: Money, Power, and the Origins of Our Times.* London: Verso.

Austin, J. L. 1962. *How to Do Things with Words,* 2d ed. Harvard University Press, 1975.

Babb, Lawrence A. 1981. "Glancing: A Visual Interaction in Hinduism." *Journal of Anthropological Research* 37, no. 1: 387–401.

Bacchetta, Paola, and Margaret Power, eds. 2002. *Right-Wing Women: From Conservatives to Extremists around the World.* New York: Routledge.

Bal, Mieke. 2001. *Looking In: The Art of Viewing.* London: G&B Arts International.

Bal, Mieke, and Norman Bryson. 1991. "Semiotics and Art History. *Art Bulletin* 73, no. 2: 174–208.

Balázs, Bela. 1970 [1949]. *Theory of the Film: Character and Growth of a New Art,* trans. Edith Bone. New York: Dover.

Banerjea, J. N. 1974. *The Development of Hindu Iconography.* New Delhi: Munshiram Manharlal.

Banerjee, Santanu. 1997. "Mother House in the Throes of Controversy." *Indian Express,* September 17, 1.

Barker, Jennifer. 2009. *The Tactile Eye: Touch and the Cinematic Experience.* Berkeley: University of California Press.

Barnouw, Eric, and S. Kishnaswamy. 1980 [1963]. *Indian Film,* 2d ed. New York: Oxford University Press.

Barthes, Roland. 1964. "The Rhetoric of the Image." *Image–Music–Text,* trans. Stephen Heath, 32–51. New York: Hill and Wang. 1977.

———. 1968. *Elements of Semiology,* trans. Annette Lavers and C. Smith. New York: Hill and Wang.

———. 1957. *Mythologies,* trans. Ann Lavers. New York: Hill and Wang, 1972.

Bataille, Georges. 1988 (1943). *The Inner Experience,* trans. Leslie Ann Boldt. Albany: State University of New York Press.

———. 1991 (1949). *The Accursed Share,* trans. Robert Hurley. New York: Zone.

———. 1994 (1945). *On Nietszche,* trans. Bruce Boone. New York: Paragon House.

Baudrillard, Jean. 2003 (1981). "The Ideological Genesis of Needs." *The Consumption Reader,* ed. David B. Clarke, Marcus A. Doel, and Kate M. L. Housiaux, 254–58. New York: Routledge.

Baviskar, Amita. 1995. *In the Belly of the River: Tribal Conflicts over Development in the Narmada Valley.* New York: Oxford University Press.

———. 2001. "Written on the Body, Written on the Land: Violence and Environmental Struggles in Central India." *Violent Environments,* ed. Nancy Peluso and Michael Watts. Ithaca: Cornell University Press.

Baxi, Upendra. 1982. *The Crisis of the Indian Legal System*. New Delhi: Vikas Press.
——. 2005. *The Future of Human Rights*. London: Oxford University Press.
Bazin, André. 1967. "The Ontology of the Photographic Image." *What Is Cinema?*, vol. 1, trans. Hugh Gray. Berkeley: University of California Press.
Belting, Hans. 1994. *Likeness and Presence: A History of the Image before the Era of Art*. Chicago: University of Chicago Press.
Benjamin, Walter. 1999 (1927–40). *The Arcades Project*, ed. Roy Tiedemann, trans. Howard Eiland and Kevin McLaughlin. Cambridge: Harvard University Press.
Berlant, Lauren. 1991. *The Anatomy of National Fantasy: Hawthorne, Utopia, and Everyday Life*. Chicago: University of Chicago Press.
Beverley, John. 1991. "'Through All Things Modern: Second Thoughts on *Testimonio*." *boundary 2* 18, no. 2: 1–21.
——. 1992. "The Margin at the Center: On *Testimonio* (Testimonial Narrative)." *De/Colonizing the Subject: The Politics of Gender in Women's Autobiography*, ed. Sidonie Smith and Julie Watson, 91–114. Minneapolis: University of Minnesota Press.
Bhaduri, Taroon. 1972. *Chambal: The Valley of Terror*. Delhi: Vikas Publishing House.
Bhandari, Vivek. 2006. "Civil Society and the Predicament of Multiple Publics." *Comparative Studies of South Asia and the Middle East* 26, no. 1: 36–50.
Bhatta, S. D. 1962. *And They Gave up Dacoity*. Delhi: Akhil Bharat Sarva Seva Sangh.
Bhattacharjee, Rajat S. 2001. "Guns Cast a Shadow over Bandit Queen's Life." *The Statesman*, July 28.
Bhattacharya, Chandrima. 2008. "Cola behind Empty Pots? Coke Thirsts for a Fight—No Water, No Problem?" *The Telegraph*, July 18.
Bhaumik, Saba Naqvi. 2003. "Saint Teresa: The Vatican Gets an Indian Flavor." *Outlook*, November 3, 25–26.
Bob, Clifford. 2005. *The Marketing of Rebellion: Insurgents, Media, and International Activism*. Cambridge: Cambridge University Press.
Bose, Brinda, ed. 2000. *Translating Desire: The Politics of Gender and Culture in India*. New Delhi: Katha.
Bose, Purnima. 2003. *Organizing Empire: Individualism, Collective Agency, and India*. Durham: Duke University Press.
Botting, Fred, and Scott Wilson. 1998. "Introduction." *Bataille: A Critical Reader*, 1–23. Oxford: Blackwell.
Boyce Davis, Carol. 1992. "Collaboration and the Ordering Imperative in Life Story Production." *De/Colonizing the Subject: The Politics of Gender in Women's Autobiography*, ed. Sidonie Smith and Julie Watson, 3–19. Minneapolis: University of Minnesota Press.
Bradiotti, Rosi. 1994. *Nomadic Subjects: Embodiment and Sexual Difference in Contemporary Feminist Theory*. New York: Columbia University Press.
Bradshaw, Jon. 1985. "The Bandit Queen." *Esquire*, October, 73.
Braudy, Leo. 2001. *Frenzy and Renown: Fame and Its History*. New York: Replica Books.
Bray, Abigail, and Claire Colebrook. 1999. "Haunted Flesh: Corporeal Feminism and the Politics of (Dis)Embodiment." *Signs* 24, no. 1: 35–67.
Brenkman. John. 1979. "Introduction to Bataille." *New German Critique* 16: 59–63.
Brodzki, Bella, and Celeste Schenck, eds. 1988. *Life/Lines: Theorizing Women's Autobiography*. Ithaca: Cornell University Press.

Brown, Peter. 1981. *The Cult of Saints: Its Rise and Function in Latin Christianity.* Chicago: University of Chicago Press.

Brown, Wendy. 1997. "The Time of the Political." *Theory and Event* 1, no. 1.

Bruss, Elizabeth W. 1978. "Peirce and Jakobsen on the Nature of the Sign." *The Sign: Semiotics around the World*, ed. Richard W. Bailey, Ladislav Matjeka, and P. Steiner, 81–98. Ann Arbor: University of Michigan Press.

Bryson, Norman. 1981. *Word and Image.* Cambridge: Cambridge University Press.

Buck-Morss, Susan. 1992. "Aesthetics and Anesthetics: Walter Benjamin's Artwork Essay Reconsidered," *October* 62 (fall): 3–41.

——. 1999. *The Dialectics of Seeing: Walter Benjamin and the Arcades Project.* Boston: MIT Press.

Burgin, Victor. 1982. "Looking at Photographs." *Thinking Photography*, ed. Victor Burgin, 142–53. New York: Macmillan.

Burgin, Victor, ed. 1982. *Thinking Photography.* New York: Macmillan.

Butler, Judith. 1993. *Bodies That Matter: On the Discursive Limits of Sex.* New York: Routledge.

——. 1997. *Excitable Speech: The Politics of the Performative.* New York: Routledge.

Bynum, Caroline Walker. 1992. *Fragmentation and Redemption: Essays on Gender and the Human Body in Medieval Religion.* Zone Books.

Caba, Susan. 1997. "Pomp, Prayers for Mother Teresa." *Houston Chronicle*, September 13, 1.

Caldwell, John. 2008. *Production Culture: Industrial Reflexivity and Critical Practice in Film and Television.* Durham: Duke University Press.

Calhoun, Craig, ed. 1993. *Habermas and the Public Sphere.* Cambridge: MIT Press.

Cartwright, Lisa, and Marita Sturken, eds. 2003. *Practices of Looking: An Introduction to Visual Culture.* New York: Oxford University Press.

Casanova, José. 1997. "Globalizing Catholicism and the Return to a 'Universal' Church." *Transnational Religion and Fading States*, Susanne Rudolph and James Piscatori. 120–43. Boulder: Westview.

Casarino, Cesare. 2008. "Surplus Common: A Preface." *In Praise of the Common: A Conversation on Philosophy and Politics*, ed. Cesare Casarino and Antonio Negri, 1–40. Minneapolis: University of Minnesota Press.

Casarino, Cesare, and Antonio Negri, eds. 2008a. *In Praise of the Common: A Conversation on Philosophy and Politics.* Minneapolis: University of Minnesota Press.

——. 2008b. "Vicissitudes of Constituent Thought." *In Praise of the Common: A Conversation on Philosophy and Politics*, ed. Cesare Casarino and Antonio Negri, 134–92. Minneapolis: University of Minnesota Press.

Centlivres, Pierre. 2002. "Life, Death, and the Eternity of the Buddhas in Afghanistan," trans. Liz Libbrecht. *Iconoclash: Beyond the Image Wars in Science, Religion, and Art*, ed. Bruno Latour and Peter Weibel, 75–77. Cambridge: MIT Press.

Chakrabarty, Dipesh. 2000. *Provincializing Europe: Postcolonial Thought and Historical Difference.* Princeton: Princeton University Press.

——. 2002. *Habitations of Modernity: Essays in the Wake of Subaltern Studies.* Chicago: University of Chicago Press.

"The Chambal Infected Delhi." 2001. *The Statesman*, July 31, 8.

Chandhoke, Neera. 2001. "The Conceits of Representation." *The Hindu*, February 7.

———. 2002. "Civil Society Hijacked." *The Hindu*, January 16.

Chandran, Ramesh. 1997. "Mother Teresa." *Times of India*, October 7.

Chandrashekar, R. and S. R. Das. 2006. "Capacity Building for E-Governance in India." Asia Pacific Development Information Programme.

Chatterjee, Aroup. 2002. *Mother Teresa: The Final Verdict*. Calcutta: Meteor Books.

Chatterjee, Partha. 1990. "The Nationalist Resolution of the Woman Question." *Recasting Women: Essays in Colonial History*, ed. Kumkum Sangari and Suresh Vaid, 233–53. New Brunswick: Rutgers University Press.

———. 2002. "Sovereign Bodies and the Domain of the Political." *Sovereign Bodies: Citizens, Migrants, and States in the Postcolonial World*, ed. Thomas Blom Hansen and Finn Stepputat, 82–102. Princeton: Princeton University Press.

———. 2008. "Critique of Popular Culture." *Public Culture* 20.2: 321–44.

Chattopadhyay, Swati, and Bhaskar Sarkar. 2005. "Introduction: The Subaltern and the Popular." *Postcolonial Studies* 8, no. 4 (November): 357–63.

Chawla, Navin. 2002. *Mother Teresa: The Authorized Biography*. New Delhi: Penguin.

Cheah, Pheng. 1996. "Mattering." *Diacritics* 26, no. 1 (spring 1996): 108–39.

Cheah, Pheng, and Elizabeth Grosz. 1996. "The Body of the Law: Notes Towards a Theory of Corporeal Justice." *Thinking through the Body of the Law*, ed. Pheng Cheah, David Fraser and Judith Grbich, 3–25. London: Allen and Unwin.

Chopra, Anupama. 2007. *The King of Bollywood: Shah Rukh Khan and the Seductive World of Indian Cinema*. New York: Warner Books.

Cooper, Kenneth J. 1997. "Calcutta Mourners Its Mother: Hindus, Muslims, and Christians Gather at the Mission to Pray for Beloved Mother Teresa." *Washington Post*, September 1.

Cooper, Melinda. 2008. *Life as Surplus: Biotechnology and Capitalism in the Neoliberal Era*. Seattle: University of Washington Press.

Corrigan, Timothy and Patricia White. 2004. *The Film Experience: An Introduction*. Boston: Bedford/St.Martin's Press.

Crary, Jonathan. 1991. *Techniques of the Observer*. Cambridge: MIT Press.

Cuny, Marie-Thérèse, and Paul Rambali. 1992. *I, Phoolan Devi: The Autobiography of India's Bandit Queen*. London: Little, Brown.

Curry, Ramona. 1996. *Too Much of a Good Thing: Mae West as a Cultural Icon*. Minneapolis: University of Minnesota Press.

Curtin, Michael. 2003. "Media Capitals: Cultural Geographies of Global TV." *The Persistence of Television: Critical Approaches to Television Studies*, ed. Jan Olsson and Lynn Spigel. Durham: Duke University Press.

Custen, George. 1992. *Bio/Pics: How Hollywood Constructed Public History*. New Brunswick: Rutgers University Press.

Das, Veena, Arthur Kleinman, Mamphela Ramphele, and Pamela Reynolds, eds. 2000. *Violence and Subjectivity*. Berkeley: University of California Press.

Dasgupta, Chidananda. 1991. "The Iconic Mother." *The Painted Face: Studies in India's Popular Cinema*, 106–25. New Delhi: Roli Books.

Davis, Richard H. 1997. *The Lives of Images*. Princeton: Princeton University Press.

"The Day of Reckoning." 1981. *India Today*, March 1–15, 30–33.

Dean, Jodi. 2002. *Publicity's Secret: How Technoculture Capitalizes on Democracy*. Ithaca: Cornell University Press.

de Certeau, Michel. 1979. *Heterologies: The Discourse of the Other*, trans. Brian Massumi. Minneapolis: University of Minnesota Press.

——. 1984. *The Practice of Everyday Life*, trans. Steven F. Rendall. Berkeley: University of California Press.

——. 2001. *Picture Personalities: The Emergence of the Star System in America*. Champaign: University of Illinois Press.

De Grèce, Michel. 1984. *La Femme-Sacrée*. Paris: Olivier Orban.

Deleuze, Gilles. 1990. "Notes on Societies of Control." *L'Autre* 1 (May 1990): 1–4.

——. 1990. *The Logic of Sense*. New York: Columbia University Press.

——. 2003. *Francis Bacon: The Logic of Sensation*, trans. Daniel W. Smith. Minneapolis: University of Minnesota Press.

De Sarkar, Bishaka. 2001. "Phoolan Devi: The Untold Story." *The Telegraph*, July 25.

Derrida, Jacques. 1974 (1967). *Of Grammatology*, trans. Gayatri Chakravorty Spivak. Baltimore: Johns Hopkins University Press.

——. 1978. "From Restricted to General Economy: A Hegelianism without Reserve." *Writing and Difference*, trans. Alan Bass, 251–77. Chicago: University of Chicago Press.

——. 1988. "Otobiographies: The Teaching of Nietzsche and the Politics of the Proper Name." *The Ear of the Other: Otobiography, Transference, Translation*, trans. Christie McDonald. Lincoln: University of Nebraska Press.

——. 1992. "Force of Law: 'The Mystical Foundation of Authority.'" *Deconstruction and the Possibility of Justice*, eds. Drucilla Cornell and Michael Rosenfeld. New York: Routledge.

——. 1994. *The Specters of Marx: The State of Debt, the Work of Mourning, and the New International*. New York: Routledge.

——. 2005. *On Touching—Jean-Luc Nancy*, trans. Christine Irizarry. Stanford: Stanford University Press.

Dev Sen, Antara. 2003. "NewsWatch: In Search of a National Culture." *India: National Culture?*, ed. Geeti Sen. New Delhi: Sage.

Diamond, Elin. 1997. *Unmaking Mimesis: Essays on Feminism and Theater*. New York: Routledge.

Dickey, Sara. 1993a. *Cinema and the Urban Poor in South India*. Cambridge: Cambridge University Press.

——. 1993b. "The Politics of Adulation: Cinema and the Production of Politicians in South India." *Journal of Asian Studies* 52, no. 2: 340–72.

Diprose, Rosalyn. 2002. *Corporeal Generosity: On Giving with Nietzsche, Merleau-Ponty, and Levinas*. Albany: State University of New York Press.

Dissanayake, Wimal, and Rob Wilson, eds. 1996. *Global/Local: Cultural Production and the Transnational Imaginary*. Durham: Duke University Press.

Dwyer, Rachel, and Christopher Pinney. 2001. "Introduction: Public, Popular, and Other Cultures." *Pleasure and the Nation: History, Politics, and the Consumption of Public Culture in India*, ed. Rachel Dwyer and Christopher Pinney, 1–34. London: Oxford University Press.

Dyer, Richard. 1979. *Stars*. London: British Film Institute.

——. 1987. *Heavenly Bodies: Film Stars and Society*. New York: Routledge.

Eastmond, Anthony. 2003. "Between Icon and Idol: The Uncertainty of Imperial Images." *The Icon and the Word: The Power of Images in Byzantium*, ed. Anthony Eastmond and Elizabeth James, 73–85. Burlington, Vt.: Ashgate.

Eck, Diana L. 1988. *Dársan: Seeing the Divine Image in India*. New York: Columbia University Press.

Egan, Eileen. 1986. *Such a Vision of the Street: Mother Teresa—The Spirit and the Work*. New York: Doubleday.

Eley, Geoffrey. 2002. "Politics, Culture, and the Public Sphere." *Positions: East Asia Cultures Critique* 10, no. 1: 219–36.

Elliot, Stuart. 1998. "Behind 'Think Different': The People behind Apple's 'Think Different' Campaign." *New York Times*, August 3.

Evans, Jessica. 1999. "Introduction." *Visual Culture: The Reader*, ed. Jessica Evans and Stuart Hall, 11–20. London: Sage.

Everett, Jane. 1993. "Indira Gandhi and the Exercise of Power." *Women as National Leaders*, ed. Michael A. Genovese, 103–94. London: Sage.

Fernandes, Leela. 1999. "Reading India's Bandit Queen: A Transnational Feminist Perspective on Discrepancies in Representation." *Signs* 25, no. 1: 123–53.

——. 2006. *India's New Middle Class: Democratic Politics in an Era of Economic Reform*. Minneapolis: University of Minnesota Press.

Fischer, Lucy. 2000. "*Marlene*, Morality, and the Biopic." *Biography* 23, no. 1: 193–211.

Fischer, Lucy, and Marcia Landy, eds. 2004. "General Introduction: Back Story." *Stars, the Film Reader*, ed. Lucy Fischer and Marcia Landy, 1–10. New York: Routledge.

Foucault, Michael. 2003 (1975–76). "Society Must Be Defended." *Lectures at the Collége de France 1975–1976*. New York: Picador Books.

——. 1977. *Discipline and Punish: The Birth of the Prison*. New York: Village Books.

Frain, Irene. 1992. *Devi*. Paris: Fayard Lattès.

Fraser, Nancy. 1996. "Rethinking the Public Sphere: A Contribution to the Critique of Actually Existing Democracy." *Habermas and the Public Sphere*, ed. Craig Calhoun, 109–42. Cambridge: MIT Press.

Freadman, Anne. 2004. *The Machinery Talk: Charles Peirce and the Sign Hypothesis*. Stanford: Stanford University Press.

Freedberg, David. 1989. *The Power of Images: Studies in the History and Theory of Response*. Chicago: University of Chicago Press.

Freitag, Sandra. 2001. "Visions of Nation: Theorizing the Nexus between Creation, Consumption, and Participation in the Public Sphere." *Pleasure and the Nation: History, Politics, and the Consumption of Public Culture in India*, 35–75. New York: Oxford University Press.

——. 2003. "The Realm of the Visual: Agency and Modern Civil Society." *Beyond Appearances?: Visual Practices and Ideologies in Modern India*, ed. Sumathi Ramaswamy, 365–97. New Delhi: Sage Publications.

Fuller, Matthew. 2005. *Media Ecologies: Materialist Energies in Art and Technoculture*. Cambridge: MIT Press.

Gallagher, Mark. 2004. "Rumble in the USA: Jackie Chan in Translation." *Film Stars: Hollywood and Beyond*, ed. Andy Willis, 113–39. Manchester: Manchester University Press.

Gaines, Jane. 2000. "Dream/Factory." *Reinventing Film Studies*, ed. Christine Gledhill and Linda Williams, 106–9. London: Edward Arnold.

Galt, Rosalind. 2009. "Pretty: Film Theory, Aesthetics and the History of the Troublesome Image." *Camera Obscura* 24 (summer): 1–41.

Gandhi, Mohandas Karamchand. 1993 (1925–28). *Autobiography: The Story of My Experiments with Truth*, trans. Mahadev Desai. Massachusetts: Beacon.

Gandhy, Behroze, and Rosie Thomas. 1991. "Three Indian Film Stars." *Stardom: Industry of Desire*, ed. Christine Gledhill, 107–31. Berkeley: University of California Press.

Gaonkar, Dilip. 2002. "New Social Imaginaries." *Public Culture* 14, no. 1 (winter): 1–19.

Gatens, Moira. 1996. *Imaginary Bodies: Ethics, Power, and Corporeality*. New York: Routledge.

Gelber, Hester Goodenough. 1987. "The Exemplary World of St. Francis of Assisi." *Saints and Virtues*, ed. John Stratton Hawley, 15–35. Berkeley: University of California Press.

Gell, Arthur. 1992. "The Technology of Enchantment and the Enchantment of Technology." *Anthropology, Art, and Aesthetics*, ed. Jeremy Coote and Anthony Shelton, 40–63. Oxford: Clarendon Press.

——. 1998. *Art and Agency*. Oxford: Clarendon Press.

Genovese, Michael A., ed. 1993. *Women as National Leaders*. New Delhi: Sage Publications.

Gerth, H. H., and C. Wright Mills, eds. 1946. *From Max Weber: Essays in Sociology*. New York: Oxford University Press.

Gherladini, Paolo. 1997. *Mother Teresa: The Missionary of the Impossible*. Milan: Gruppo editoriale.

Ghosh, Amitav. 1999. *Countdown*. Delhi: Ravi Dayal.

Ghosh, Bishnupriya. 2004. *When Borne Across: Literary Cosmopolitics in the Contemporary Indian Novel in English*. New Brunswick: Rutgers University Press.

——. 2007. "Tallying Bodies: Arundhati Roy's Moral Math." *Arundhati Roy: Critical Perspectives*, ed. Murari Prasad, 126–56. New Delhi: Pencraft International.

——. 2009a. "'We Shall Drown but We Shall Not Move': Ecological Testimonies in NBA Documentaries." *Documentary Testimonies: Archives of Suffering*, ed. Bhaskar Sarkar and Janet Walker, 59–82. New York: Routledge.

——. 2009b. "The Bigamous Body of the Bandit Queen: Corporeality and the Arithmetic of the Law." *States of Trauma: Gender and Violence in South Asia*, ed. Manali Desai, Piya Chatterjee, and Parama Roy, 23–50. Delhi: Zubaan.

——. 2010. "Looking through Coca-Cola: Global Icons and the Popular." *Public Culture* 22, no. 2 (spring): 333–68.

Ghosh, Gautam. 2002. *Mother Teresa: The Apostle of Love*. Kolkata: Rupa.

Ghosh, Rupali. 1999. "A Life Divine." *The Telegraph*, November 16.

Gitelman, Lisa. 2006. *Always Already New: Media, History and the Data of Culture*. Cambridge: MIT Press.

Gledhill, Christine. 1991. "Signs of Melodrama." *Stardom: Industry of Desire*. Christine Gledhill, ed., 207–32. New York: Routledge.

——. 2003. *Reframing British Cinema, 1918–1928: Between Restraint and Passion*. Berkeley: University of California Press.

Gledhill, Christine, and Linda Williams. 2000. "Re-examining Stardom: Questions of Texts, Bodies, and Performance." *Rethinking Film Studies*, ed. Christine Gledhill and Linda Williams. London: Edward Arnold.

Gombrich, Ernst H. 1956. *Art and Illusion: A Study in the Psychology of Pictorial Perception*. Princeton: Princeton University Press, 2001.

———. 1972. *Symbolic Images: Studies in the Art of the Renaissance*. London: Phaidon.

———. 1981. "Image and Code: Scope and Limits of Conventionalism in Pictorial Representation." *Image and Code*, ed. Wendy Steiner. Ann Arbor: University of Michigan Press.

Goodman, Nelson. 1968. *The Languages of Art: An Approach to the Theory of Symbols*. Indianapolis: Bobbs-Merrill.

Gordon, Avery. 1996. *Ghostly Matters: Haunting and the Sociological Imagination*. Minneapolis: University of Minnesota Press.

Grossberg, Lawrence, Ellen Wartella, and D. Charles Whitney. 1998. *Media Making: Mass Media in Popular Culture*. New Delhi: Sage.

Grosz, Elizabeth. 1994. *Volatile Bodies: Toward a Corporeal Feminism*. Minneapolis: University of Minnesota Press.

———. 2008. *Chaos, Territory, Art: Deleuze and the Framing of the Earth (The Wellek Lectures)*. New York: Columbia University Press.

Guha, Ramachandra. 1997. "The Environmentalism of the Poor." *Varieties of Environmentalism: Essays North and South*, ed. Ramachandra Guha and Juan Martinez-Alier, 1–22. London: Earthscan.

———. 1999. *Environmentalism: A Global History*. New York: Longman.

———. 2000. "The Arun Shourie of the Left." *The Hindu*, November 26.

Guha, Ranajit. 1983. *The Elementary Aspects of Peasant Insurgency*. New York: Oxford University Press.

Gundle, Stephen. 2004. "Sophia Loren, Italian Icon." *Stars: The Film Reader*, ed. Lucy Fischer and Marcia Landy, 77–96. New York: Routledge.

Hall, Stuart. 1977. *Culture, Media, Language: Working Papers in Cultural Studies 1972–79*. London: Unwin Hyman, 1980.

Hansen, Kathryn. 1988. "The Virangana in North Indian History: Myth and Popular Culture." *Economic and Political Weekly of India*, April 30, 25–33.

Hansen, Mark B. N. 2006. *Bodies in Code: Interfaces with Digital Media*. New York: Routledge.

Hansen, Miriam. 1991. *Babel and Babylon: Spectatorship in American Silent Cinema*. Cambridge: Harvard University Press.

———. 1992. "Mass Culture as Hieroglyphic Writing: Adorno, Derrida, Kracauer." *New German Critique* 56 (special issue on Theodor W. Adorno) (spring–summer): 43–73.

Hardgrave, Robert. 1979. "When Stars Displace the Gods: Folk Culture of Cinema in Tamil Nadu." *Essays in the Political Sociology of South India*, 33–78. Delhi: Usha.

Hardiman, David. 1987. *The Coming of the Devi: Adivasi Assertion in Western India*. Delhi: Oxford University Press.

———. 2004. *Gandhi in His Time and the Global Legacy of His Ideas*. New York: Columbia University Press.

Hardt, Michael, and Antonio Negri. 2000. *Empire*. Cambridge: Harvard University Press.

———. 2004. *Multitude: War and Democracy in the Age of Empire*. New York: Penguin.

Harvey, David. 1989. *The Condition of Postmodernity: An Enquiry into the Origins of Cultural Change*. Oxford: Blackwell, 1991.

———. 2005. *A Brief History of Neoliberalism*. New York: Oxford University Press.

Hawley, John Stratton. 1987. "Morality beyond Morality in the Lives of Three

Hindu Saints." *Saints and Virtues*, ed. John Hawley, 52–72. Berkeley: University of California Press.

Hayles, N. Katherine. 1993. "The Materiality of Informatics." *Configurations* 1, no. 1: 147–70.

———. 1997. "The Posthuman Body: Inscription and Incorporation in *Galatea 2.2* and *Snow Crash*." *Configurations* 5, no. 2: 241–66.

Hebdige, Dick. 1979. *Subculture: The Meaning of Style*. London: Routledge.

———. 1987. *Cut n' Mix: Culture, Identity and Caribbean Music*. London: Routledge.

Heidegger, Martin. 1977 (1949). *The Question Concerning Technology and Other Essays*, trans. W. Louitt. New York: Harper and Row.

Held, David, and Henrietta Moore. 2009. "Introduction: Cultural Futures." *Cultural Politics in a Global Age*, 1–15. Oxford: One World Publishers.

Hervieu-Léger, Danièle. 1997. "The Face of Catholic Transnationalism: In and beyond France." *Transnational Religion: Fading States*, ed. Susan Hoeber Rudolph and James Piscatori, trans. Roger Gleason, 104–18. West Hartford: Westview.

Hitchens, Christopher. 1995. *The Missionary Position: Mother Teresa in Theory and Practice*. London: Verso.

Hobsbawm, Eric. 1965. *Primitive Rebels: Studies in Archaic Forms of Social Movement in the 19th and 20th Centuries*. Boston: W. W. Norton.

———. 2000 (1969). *Bandits*. New York: New Press.

Hollywood, Amy. 2002. *Sensible Ecstasy: Mysticism, Sexual Difference, and the Demands of History*. Chicago: University of Chicago Press.

Hookway, Christopher. 2004. "Truth, Reality and Convergence." *The Cambridge Companion to Peirce*, ed. Cheryl Misak, 127–49. Cambridge: Cambridge University Press.

Iannaccone, Lawrence. 1995. "Voodoo Economics?: Reviewing the Rational Choice Approach to Religion." *Journal for the Scientific Study of Religion* 34: 76–89.

"Image India." 2005. *Times of India*, October 10, 4.

Iyer, Pico. 1989. "The Unknown Rebel." *Time*, June 19.

Jaffrelot, Christopher, and Peter van der Veer. 2008. "Introduction." *Patterns of Middle Class Consumption in India and China*, 11–34. Delhi: Sage.

Jain, Kajri. 2007. *Gods in the Bazaar: The Economies of Indian Calendar Art*. Durham: Duke University Press.

Jameson, Fredric. 1988. "Cognitive Mapping." *Marxism and the Interpretation of Culture*, ed. Cary Nelson and Lawrence Grossberg, 347–60. Champaign: University of Illinois Press.

———. 1991. *Postmodernism, or, The Cultural Logic of Late Capital*. London: Verso.

———. 1998. "Notes on Globalization as a Philosophical Issue." *The Cultures of Globalization*, ed. Fredric Jameson and Masao Miyoshi, 54–81. Durham: Duke University Press.

———. 2002. *A Singular Modernity: Essay on the Ontology of the Present*. London: Verso.

Jameson, Frederic, and Masao Miyoshi, eds. 1998. *The Cultures of Globalization*. Durham: Duke University Press.

Jeffery, Patricia, and Amrita Basu, eds. 1998. *Appropriating Gender: Women's Activism and Politicized Religion in South Asia*. New York: Routledge.

Jeffrey, Robin. 1997. "Advertising and Indian-Language Newspapers: How

Capitalism Supports (Certain) Cultures and (Some) States." *Pacific Affairs* 70, no. 1: 57–84

———. 2000. *India's Newspaper Revolution*. Delhi: C. Hurst.

Jenkins, Henry. 2005. *Convergence Culture: Where Old and New Media Collide*. New York: New York University Press.

Johnson, Emma. 2003. *Mother Teresa (20thC History Makers)*. London: Heinemann Library.

Kak, Sanjay. 2004. "Politics in the Picture: Witnessing Environmental Crises in the Media." *Sarai Reader 04: Crisis/Media*, ed. Shuddhabrata Sengupta et al., 327–28. Delhi: Center for the Study of Developing Societies.

Kakaria, Bachi. 2001. "The Queen Could Not Call This Final Shot." *The Telegraph*, July 29.

Kalb, Don. 2000. *The Ends of Globalization*. Lanham: Rowman and Littlefield.

Kaldor, Mary. 2003. *Global Civil Society: Answer to War*. New York: Polity.

Kaplan, Caren. 1992. "Resisting Autobiography: Out-Law Genres and Transnational Feminist Subjects." *De/Colonizing the Subject: The Politics of Gender in Women's Autobiography*, ed. Sidonie Smith and Julie Watson, 115–38. Minneapolis: University of Minnesota Press, 1992.

Kapur, Geeta. 1993. "Revelation and Doubt: *Sant Tukaram* and *Devi*." *Interrogating Modernity: Colonialism and Culture in India*, ed. Tejaswini Niranjana, Vivek Dhareshwar, and P. Sudhir, 1–23. Calcutta: Seagull.

Kaviraj, Sudipta. 2004. "The Invention of a Private Life: A Reading of Sibnath Sastri's *Autobiography*." *Telling Lives in India: Biography, Autobiography, and Life History*, ed. David Arnold and Stuart Blackburn, 83–115. Bloomington: Indiana University Press, 2005.

Kearney, James. 2002. "The Book and the Fetish: The Materiality of Prospero's Text." *Journal of Medieval and Early Modern Studies* 32, no. 3: 433–68.

Kelly, Michael. 2003. *Iconoclasm in Aesthetics*. Cambridge: Cambridge University Press.

Khan, Atiq. 2001. "A Life Less Ordinary: 'Bandit Queen' or Plain Old Bandit?" *Indian Express*, July 27, 5.

Kishwar, Madhu. 2001. "Murder as Warning." *Indian Express*, August 21, 1.

Kittler, Friedrich. 2010. *Optical Media*. Polity Books.

Klein, Naomi. 2000. *No Logo: Taking Aim at Brand Bullies*. Toronto: Knopf.

Koerner, Joseph. 2002. "The Icon as Iconoclash." *Iconoclash: Beyond the Image Wars in Science, Religion, and Art*, ed. Bruno Latour and Peter Weibel, 164–213. Cambridge: MIT Press.

Kohli-Khandekar, Vanita. 2003. *The Indian Media Business*. Delhi: Sage.

Kolodiejchuk, Brian, ed. 2007. *Mother Teresa: Come Be My Light*. London: Rider.

Kopytoff, Igor. 1986. "The Cultural Biography of Things: Commoditization as Process." *The Social Life of Things: Commodities in Cultural Perspective*, ed. Arjun Appadurai, 64–91. Cambridge: Cambridge University Press.

Krishnan, G. V. 1983. "The Bandit Queen." *Times of India*, September 6, 1.

Kumar, Radha. 1993. *The History of Doing: An Illustrated Account of Movements for Women's Rights and Feminism in India, 1800–1990*. London: Verso.

Kumar, Sukanta. 1997. *Biswajanani Mother Teresa*. Calcutta: Shaityam.

Kwilecki, Susan, and Loretta S. Wilson. 1998. "Was Mother Teresa Maximizing Her Utility? An Idiographic Application of Rational Choice Theory." *Journal for the Scientific Study of Religion* 37, no. 2: 205–21.

Laclau, Ernesto. 2005. *On Populist Reason*. London: Verso.

Laclau, Ernesto, and Chantal Mouffe. 1985. *Hegemony and Socialist Strategy*. London: Verso.

"Lapierre Blames Order Members for Teresa Film Controversy." 1997. *Times of India*, October 10.

Laqueur, Thomas. 1996. "Names, Bodies, and the Anxiety of Erasure." *The Social and Political Body*, ed. Theodore R. Schatzki and Wolgang Natter, 123–44. New York: Guilford Press.

Larkin, Brian. 2008. *Signal and Noise: Media, Infrastructure, and Urban Culture in Nigeria*. Durham: Duke University Press.

Latour, Bruno. 2004. *Politics of Nature: How to Bring the Sciences into Democracy*, trans. Catherine Porter. Cambridge: Harvard University Press.

Latour, Bruno, and Peter Weibel. 2002. "What Is Iconoclash? Or Is There a World beyond the Image Wars?," *Iconoclash: Beyond the Image Wars in Science, Religion, and Art*, ed. Bruno Latour and Peter Weibel, 1–41. Cambridge: MIT Press.

Lee, Benjamin, and Edward Di Plama. 2002. "Cultures of Circulation: The Imaginations of Modernity." *Public Culture* 14, no. 1: 191–213.

Leja, Michael. 2000. "Peirce, Visuality, and Art." *Representations* 72: 97–122.

Le Joly, Edward. 1985. *Mother Teresa of Calcutta: A Biography*. New York: Harper Collins.

Lloyd, Genevieve. 1994. *Part of Nature: Self-Knowledge in Spinoza's Ethics*. Ithaca: Cornell University Press.

Lo, Kwai-Cheung. 2004. "Muscles and Subjectivity: A Short History of the Masculine Body in Hong Kong Popular Culture." *Stars: The Film Reader*, ed. Lucy Fischer and Marcia Landy, 116–26. New York: Routledge.

Longfellow, Brenda. 2002. "Rape and Translation in *Bandit Queen*." *Translating Desire*, ed. Brinda Bose, 238–55. New Delhi: Katha Press.

Lowenthal, Leo. 1944. *Literature, Popular Culture, and Society*. Englewood Cliffs: Prentice Hall, 1961.

Majumdar, Neepa. 2009. *Wanted Cultured Ladies Only! Female Stardom and Cinema in India, 1930s to 1950s*. Champaign: University of Illinois Press.

Mankekar, Purnima. 1999. *Screening Culture, Viewing Politics*. Durham: Duke University Press.

Markovits, Claude. 2004. *The UnGandhian Gandhi: The Life and Afterlife of the Mahatma*. London: Anthem.

Marks, Laura. 2000. *The Skin of Film: Intercultural Cinema, Embodiment, and the Senses*. Durham: Duke University Press.

Massumi, Brian. 2002. *Parables of the Virtual: Movement, Affect, Sensation*. Durham: Duke University Press.

Marx, Karl. 1867. *Capital*, vol. 1, trans. E. Paul and S. Paul. London: Dent and Sons.

Mazzarella, William. 2003. *Shoveling Smoke: Advertising and Globalization in Contemporary India*. Durham: Duke University Press.

McQuire, Scott. 2006. "Technology." *Theory, Culture, Society* 23, nos. 2–3: 253–69.

"Medha Patkar Ends Fast." 2001. *The Hindu*, September 28, 5.

Menon, Nivedita. 2000. "Embodying the Self: Feminism, Sexual Violence, and the Law." *Translating Desire*, ed. Brinda Bose, 200–37. New Delhi: Katha Press.

Menon, Vijay. 1999. "Women Break the Chambal Dacoits Glass Ceiling." *Indian Express*, December 18, 4.

Merleau-Ponty, Maurice. 1962. *The Phenomenology of Perception*, trans. Colin Smith. London: Routledge.

Mgbeoji, Ikech. 2006. *Global Biopiracy: Patents, Plants, and Indigenous Knowledge*. Ithaca: Cornell University Press.

Miller, Daniel. 1997. *Material Culture and Mass Consumerism*. Boston: Wiley-Blackwell.

——. 2005. "Materiality: An Introduction." *Materiality*. Durham: Duke University Press.

Misak, Cheryl. 2004. "Charles Peirce (1839–1914)." *The Cambridge Companion to Peirce*, ed. Cheryl Misak, 1–26. Cambridge: Cambridge University Press.

Mitchell, Timothy. 2000. "The Stage of Modernity." *Questions of Modernity*, 1–34. Minneapolis: University of Minnesota Press.

Mitchell. W. J. T. 1986. *Iconology: Image, Text, Ideology*. Chicago: University of Chicago Press.

——. 1994. *Picture Theory: Essays on Verbal and Visual Representation*. Chicago: University of Chicago Press.

Miyoshi, Masao. 1993. "A Borderless World? From Colonialism to Transnationalism and the Decline of the Nation-State." *Critical Inquiry* 19, no. 4: 726–75.

Mondzain, Marie-José. 2005. *Image, Icon, Economy: The Byzantine Origins of the Contemporary Imaginary*, trans. Rico Franses. Stanford: Stanford University Press.

Morgan, David. 2005. *The Sacred Gaze: Religious Visual Culture in Theory and Practice*. Berkeley: University of California Press.

Morin, Edgar. 1957. *The Stars*, trans. Richard Howard. Minneapolis: University of Minnesota Press.

Mukherjee, Bharati. 1999. "The Saint Mother Teresa." *Time 100*, June 14, 10–12.

Mukherjee, Sutapa, et al. 2001. "The Bullet-Riddled Biography." *Outlook*, August 6, 51–53.

Nancy, Jean-Luc. 2000. *Being Singular Plural*, trans. Robert Richardson. Stanford: Stanford University Press.

——. 2005. *The Ground of the Image*, trans. Jeff Fort. Dartmouth: Fordham University Press.

Neuwirth, Robert. 2005. *Shadow Cities: A Billion Squatters, a New Urban*. New York: Routledge.

Olin, Margaret. 2002. "Touching Photographs: Roland Barthes' 'Mistaken' Identification." *Representations* 80: 99–118.

Pai, Sudha. 2001. "Phoolan Devi and Social Churning in UP." *Economic and Political Weekly of India*, August 11, 3017–18.

Pandian, M. S. 1992. *The Image Trap: M. G. Ramachandran in Film and Politics*. New Delhi: Sage Publications.

Panjiar, Prashant. 2004. *The Definitive Images: 1858 to Present*. New York: Penguin.

"Pankaj Has Criminal Record, Say Police." 2001. *The Statesman*, August 3, 1.

Panofsky, Erwin. 1924. *Perspective as Symbolic Form*, trans. Christopher S. Wood. Cambridge: MIT Press, 1993.

Panofsky, Erwin, and Gerda S. Panofsky. 1939. *Studies in Iconology: Humanistic Themes in the Art of the Renaissance*. Hartford: Westview Press, 1972.

———. 1955. *Meaning in the Visual Arts: Papers in and on Art History*. New York: Doubleday.

Parker, Andrew, and Eve Kosofsky Sedgwick. 1995. "Introduction: Performance and Performativity." *Performativity and Performance*, eds. Parker and Sedgwick, 1–18. New York: Routledge.

Parks, Lisa. 2007. "Obscure Objects of Media Studies: Echo, Hotbird and Ikonos." *Mediascapes: Journal of Cinema and Media Studies* 1, no. 3.

Peirce, Charles Sanders. 1867. "On a New List of Categories." *The Essential Peirce: Selected Philosophical Writings, Volume I (1867–1893)*, 1–10.

———. 1878. "The Probability of Induction." *The Essential Peirce: Selected Philosophical Writings, Volume I (1867–1893)*, 155–69. Bloomington: Indiana University Press, 1992.

———. 1885. "On the Algebra of Logic: A Contribution to the Philosophy of Notation." *The Essential Peirce: Selected Philosophical Writings, Volume I (1867–1893*, 225–28.

———. 1903. "The Harvard Lectures on Pragmatism." *The Essential Peirce: Selected Philosophical Writings, Volume II (1893–1913)*, 133–257. Bloomington: Indiana University Press, 1998.

———. 1996. *Charles S. Peirce: Selected Writings*, ed. P. Weiner. New York: New York University Press.

"People Sneak Past Police." 1997. *The Statesman*, September 10, 3.

Phillips, Melanie. 2003. *The Ascent of Woman: The Suffragette Movement and the Ideas Behind It*. London: Abacus.

"Phoolan Case: Cops Settle for Revenge Motive." 2001. *The Statesman*, August 1.

"The Phoolan Phenomenon." 2001. *The Hindu*, July 27, 10.

"Phoolan Supporters Come to Blows." 2001. *The Statesman*, July 8, 1.

Pietz, William. 1985. "The Problem of the Fetish I." *Res 9* 13: 23–45.

Pinney, Christopher. 2001. "Piercing the Skin of the Idol." *Beyond Aesthetics: Art and the Technologies of Enchantment*, ed. Christopher Pinney and Nicholas Thomas, 158–80. London: Berg.

———. 2002. "The Indian Work of Art in the Age of Mechanical Reproduction: Or, What Happens When Peasants 'Get Hold' of Images?" *Media Worlds: Anthropology on New Terrain*, ed. Faye Ginsburg, Lila Abu-Lughod, and Brian Larkin, 355–69. Berkeley: University of California Press.

———. 2004. *Photos of the Gods: The Printed Image and Political Struggle in India*. New York: Reaktion.

Prasad, Gargi. 2003. "Arundhati Roy Donates Rs.1.67cr Award Money." *The Hindu*, January 23, 3.

Prasad, Madhava. 2004. "Reigning Stars, the Political Career of South Indian Cinema." *Stars: The Film Reader*, ed. Lucy Fischer and Marcia Landy, 97–114. New York: Routledge.

Primlane, Ritu. 2000. "Vandana Shiva and Globalization." *India Currents*, August 6, 6–8.

Racine, Josine, and Jean-Luc Racine. 2004. "Beyond Silence: A Daily Life-History in South India." *Telling Lives in India: Biography, Autobiography, and Life History*, ed.

David Arnold and Stuart Blackburn, 252–80. Bloomington: Indiana University Press.

Rai, Amit. 2009. *Untimely Bollywood: Globalization and India's New Media Assemblage*. Durham: Duke University Press.

Rai, Raghu. 1996. *Faith and Compassion: The Life and works of Mother Teresa*. London: Element.

———. 2005. *Mother Teresa: A Life of Dedication*. New York: Harry N. Abrams.

Rajagopal, Arvind. 2001. *Politics after Television: Religious Nationalism and the Reshaping of the Indian Public*. Cambridge: Cambridge University Press.

Rajagopal, Balakrishnan. 2003. *International Law from Below: Development, Social Movements and Third World Resistance*. Cambridge: Cambridge University Press.

Rajan, Gita. 1992. "Subversive Subaltern Identity: Indira Gandhi as Speaking Subject." *De/Colonizing the Subject: The Politics of Gender in Women's Autobiography*, ed. Sidonie Smith and Julie Watson, 196–222. Minneapolis: University of Minnesota Press, 1992.

Ramaiah, A. 1992. "Identifying Other Backward Classes." *Economic and Political Weekly*, June 6, 1203–7.

Ramaswamy, Nimmi. 2004. "Making the Dravidian Hero: The Body and Identity Politics in the Dravidian Movement." *Confronting the Body: The Politics of Physicality in Colonial and Postcolonial India*, ed. James H. Mills and Satadru Sen, 135–45. New York: Anthem.

Ramaswamy, Sumathi. 2003. "Visualizing India's Geobody: Globes, Maps, Bodyscapes." *Beyond Appearances?: Visual Practices and Ideologies in Modern India*, ed. Sumathi Ramaswamy. New Delhi: Sage.

Ramesh, Randeep. 2007. "An Activist Returns to the Novel." *Sydney Morning Herald*, March 10, 2.

Rao, Anupama. 1998. "Understanding Sirasgaon: Notes towards Conceptualizing the Role of Law, Caste, and Gender in a Case of 'Atrocity.'" *Signposts: Gender Issues in Post-Independence India*, ed. Rajeswari Sunder Rajan, 103–36. Delhi: Kali for Women.

Rao, Malathi. 2002. "Voices to Be Heard." *Deccan Herald*, October 27, A42.

Rao, S. L., and I. Natarajan. 1996. *Indian Market Demographics: The Consumer Classes*. Delhi: Global Business Press.

Ravi, Srilata. 1999. "Marketing Devi: Indian Women in the French Imagination." *Alif* 19: 131–50.

Ravindran, Visa. 2001. "Canonising Crime." *The Hindu*, October 28.

Reddy, Rammonahar C. 2001. "Deconstructing a Legend." *The Hindu*, August 1.

Reddy, Vanita. "The Nationalization of the Global Indian Woman." *South Asian Popular Culture* 4, no. 1 (April): 61–85.

Roach, Joseph. 1996. *Cities of the Dead: Circum-Atlantic Performance*. New York: Columbia University Press.

Robinson, Cedric J. 2000. *Black Marxism*. Chapel Hill: University of North Carolina Press.

Rojek, Chris. 2001. *Celebrity*. London: Reaktion Books.

Roy, Arundhati. 1996. *The God of Small Things*. Delhi: India Ink.

———. 1999a. *The Cost of Living*. New York: Modern Library.

———. 1999b. "The End of the Imagination." *The Cost of Living*, 91–128.

——. 2002a. *Power Politics.* Boston: South End.

——. 2002b. *The Algebra of Infinite Justice.* London: Flamingo.

——. 2003. *In Which Annie Gives It Those Ones.* Delhi: Penguin.

——. 2004a. *An Ordinary Person's Guide to Empire.* Boston: South End.

——. 2004b. *Public Power in the Age of Empire.* New York: Open Media Series.

Roy, Bharati. 2002. *Early Feminists of Colonial India: Sarala Devi Chaudhurani and Sokeya Skhawat Hossein.* New Delhi: Oxford University Press.

Roy, Parama. 1998. *Indian Traffic: Colonial and Postcolonial Identities in Question.* Berkeley: University of California Press.

Rushdie, Salman. 2002. "Gandhi Now." *Step across This Line: Collected Non-Fiction, 1992–2002,* 165–68. New York: Random House.

Sahay, Uday. 2006a. "Empires and Communications Strategies." *Making News: Handbook of Media in Contemporary India,* ed. Uday Sahay, 8–12. New Delhi: Oxford University Press.

——. 2006b. "Preface." *Making News: Handbook of Media in Contemporary India,* ed. Uday Sahay, xvi–viii. New Delhi: Oxford University Press.

Said, Edward. 1983. *The World, the Text, and the Critic.* Cambridge: Harvard University Press.

"Saint in the Making." 2003. *Times of India,* October 21, 1.

Sarkar, Bhaskar. 2008. "The Melodramas of Globalization." *Cultural Dynamics* 21, no. 1: 31–51.

——. 2009. *Mourning the Nation: Indian Cinema in the Wake of Partition.* Durham: Duke University Press.

——. 2010. "Grounding the Global: Malegaon Video Aesthetics." Talk presented at the Crossroads conference, Hong Kong, June 17–21.

Sarkar, Tanika. 2002. *Hindu Wife, Hindu Nation: Community, Religion, and Cultural Nationalism.* Bloomington: Indiana University Press.

Saxena, Deshdeep. 1996. "Voices from the Chambal." *Sunday,* April 30–May 6, 10–12.

Schechner, Richard. 1989. *Between Theater and Anthropology.* Philadelphia: University of Pennsylvania Press.

Schickel, Richard. 1985. *Intimate Strangers: The Culture of Celebrity in America.* New York: Doubleday.

Schulze, Brigitte. 1995. "The Cinematic 'Discovery of India': Mehboob's Re-invention of Nation in Mother India." *Social Scientist* 30, nos. 9–10: 72–87.

Schweitzer, Arthur. 1984. *The Age of Charisma.* Chicago: Nelson Hall.

Shears, Richard, and Isobelle Gidley. 1984. *Devi: The Bandit Queen.* London: George Allen and Unwin.

Sebba, Anne. 1997. *Mother Teresa: Beyond the Image.* New York: Random House.

Sekula, Allan. 1982. "On the Invention of Photographic Meaning." *Thinking Photography,* ed. Victor Burgin, 84–109. New York: Macmillan.

Sen, Mala. 1991. *India's Bandit Queen: The True Story of Phoolan Devi.* New York: Pandora.

——. 2001. "Phoolan, Point Blank." *Outlook,* August 6, 10–16.

Sharan, Awadhendra. 2002. "Claims on Cleanliness." *Sarai Reader 02: Urban Morphologies,* ed. Ravi Vasudevan, 31. Delhi: Centre for the Study of Developing Societies.

Shaviro, Steven. 1993. *The Cinematic Body (Theory Out of Bounds)*. Minneapolis: University of Minnesota Press.

Shershow, Scott Cutler. 2005. *The Work and the Gift*. Chicago: University of Chicago Press.

Shih, Shu-mei. 2004. "Global Literature and the Technologies of Recognition." *PMLA* 119, no. 1: 16–30.

Shiva, Vandana. 1997. *Biopiracy: The Plunder of Nature and Knowledge*. Boston: South End.

Short, T. L. 2004. "The Development of Peirce's Theory of Signs." *The Cambridge Companion to Peirce*, ed. Cheryl Misak, 214–40. Cambridge: Cambridge University Press.

Silverman, Kaja. 1984. *The Subject of Semiotics*. New York: Oxford University Press.

Sinha, Arvind. 2006. "The Growing Need for Alternative Media." *Making News: Handbook of Media in Contemporary India*, ed. Uday Sahay, 120–24. New Delhi: Oxford University Press.

Sinha, Mrinalini. 2006. *Specters of Mother India: The Global Re-structuring of Empire*. Durham: Duke University Press.

Sivathamby, Karthigesu. 1981. *The Tamil Film as a Medium of Political Communication*. Madras: New Century Book House.

Smith, Sidonie, and Julie Watson, eds. 1992. *De/Colonizing the Subject: The Politics of Gender in Women's Autobiography*. Minneapolis: University of Minnesota Press.

Sobchack, Vivian. 2004. *Carnal Thoughts: Embodiment and Moving Image Culture*. Berkeley: University of California Press.

Sommer, Doris. 1988. "Not Just a Personal Story: Women's *Testimonios* and the Plural Self." *Life/Lines: Theorizing Women's Autobiography*, ed. Bella Brodzki and Celeste Schenek, 107–30. Ithaca: Cornell University Press.

Spink, Kathryn. 1997. *Mother Teresa: The Complete Authorized Biography*. New York: HarperCollins.

Spivak, Gayatri. 1988. "Can the Subaltern Speak?" *Marxism and the Interpretation of Culture*, ed. Cary Nelson and Lawrence Grossberg, 271–316. Champaign: University of Illinois Press.

———. 1997. "Diasporas Old and New: Women in the Transnational World." *Class Issues: Pedagogy, Cultural Studies, and the Public Sphere*, ed. Amitava Kumar, 87–116. New York: New York University Press.

Srinivas, S. V. 1996. "Devotion and Defiance in Fan Activity." *Journal of Arts and Ideas* 29: 67–83.

———. 2006. "Hong Kong Action Film and the Telegu Action Hero." *Hong Kong Connections*, ed. Meaghan Morris, 111–25. Durham: Duke University Press.

———. 2009. *Megastar: Chiranjeevi And Telugu Cinema after N. T. Ramo Rao*. Oxford: Oxford University Press.

Srivatsan, R. 2000. *Conditions of Visibility: Writings in Photography in Contemporary India*. Calcutta: Stree.

———. 2001. "Imaging Truth and Desire: Photography and the Visual Field in India." *Interrogating Modernity: Colonialism and Culture in India*, ed. Tejaswini Niranjana, Vivek Dhareswar, and P. Sudhir, 155–98. Calcutta: Seagull.

Stiglitz, Joseph. 2005. *Globalization and Its Discontents*. Ann Arbor: University of Michigan Press.

Stoller, Paul. 1997. *Sensuous Scholarship*. Philadelphia: University of Pennsylvania Press.

Sunder Rajan, Kaushik. 2006. *Biocapital: The Constitution of Postgenomic Life*. Durham: Duke University Press.

Sunder Rajan, Rajeswari. 1993. "Gender, Leadership, and Representation: The 'Case' of Indira Gandhi." *Real and Imagined Women: Gender, Culture and Postcolonialism*, ed. Rajeswari Sunder Rajan, 99–122. London: Routledge.

——. 2004. *The Scandal of the State: Women, Law and Citizenship in Postcolonial India*. Durham: Duke University Press.

Suraiya, Jug. 1997. "Mother Always Did Something Beautiful for God." *Times of India*, September 6, Q45.

Tagg, John. 1982. "The Currency of the Photograph." *Thinking Photography*, ed. Victor Burgin, 110–41. New York: Macmillan.

——. 1988. *The Burden of Representation: Essays on Photographies and Histories*. Amherst: University of Massachusetts Press.

Tarrow, Sidney. 2005. *The New Transnational Activism*. Cambridge: Cambridge University Press.

Taussig, Michael. 1991. "Tactility and Distraction." *Cultural Anthropology* 6, no. 2 (May): 147–53.

——. 1999. *De/Facement: Public Secrecy and the Labor of the Negative*. Stanford: Stanford University Press.

Taylor, Charles. 2004. *Modern Social Imaginaries*. Durham: Duke University Press.

Taylor, Diana. 2003. *The Archive and the Repertoire: Performing Cultural Memory in the Americas*. Durham: Duke University Press.

Taylor, Woodman. 2001. "Penetrating Gaze: The Poetics of Sight and Visual Display in Popular Indian Cinema." *Pleasure and the Nation: History, Politics, and the Consumption of Public Culture in India*, ed. Rachel Dwyer and Christopher Pinney, 298–322. London: Oxford University Press.

"Tears Mingle with Pain." 1997. *Asian Age*, September 1, 1.

Thacker, Eugene. 2006. *The Global Genome: Biotechnology, Politics, and Culture*. Cambridge: MIT Press.

——. 2008. "Uncommon Life." *Tactical Biopolitics: Art, Activism, and Technoscience*, ed. Kavita Philip and Beatriz da Costa, 304–22. Cambridge: MIT Press.

Thapar, Romila. 2004. *Somanatha: The Many Voices of History*. London: Verso.

Tharoor, Shashi. 2005. "The Great Digital Divide." *The Hindu*, November 20, 2.

Theodore, Stanley. 2001. "Bandit Queen, the Legend Lives." *The Statesman*, July 28, 1.

"Three Husbands and Phoolan's Mother Battle It Out for Her Crores." 2001. *Times of India*, August 21, 1.

Tomlinson, John. 2009. "Global Immediacy." Held and Moore ed., 80–87.

Tripathi, Salil. 2001. "Culture Clash: The Limits of the Imagination—America Haters Are Blaming the Victim." *Asian Wall Street Journal*, October 5, 4.

Tsing, Anna Lowenhaupt. 2004. *Frictions: An Ethnography of Global Connection*. Princeton: Princeton University Press.

Turner, Graeme. 2004. *Understanding Celebrity*. Sage Publications.

Uberoi, Patricia. 2006. *Freedom and Destiny: Gender, Family, and Popular Culture in India*. Delhi: Oxford University Press.

Vachani, Lalit. 1999. "Bachchan-alias: The Many Faces of a Film Icon." *Image Journeys: Audio-visual Media and Cultural Change in India*, ed. Christine Brosius and Melissa Brosius, 199–232. Delhi: Sage.

Vanaik, Achin. 1997. "No Sense of Proportion." *The Hindu*, December 9, Q5.

Van Asselt, Willem, Paul van Geest, and Daniela Müeller, eds. 2007. *Iconoclasm and Iconoclash: Struggle for Religious Identity*. Leiden: Brill.

van der Veer, Peter. 1994. *Religious Nationalism: Hindus and Muslims in India*. Berkeley: University of California Press.

Varner Gunn, Jane. 1992. "A Politics of Experience: Leila Khaled's *My People Shall Live: The Autobiography of a Revolutionary*." *De/Colonizing the Subject: The Politics of Gender in Women's Autobiography*, ed. Sidonie Smith and Julie Watson, 65–80. Minneapolis: University of Minnesota Press.

Vasudevan, Ravi. 2000. "The Politics of Cultural Address in a 'Transitional Cinema': A Case Study of Indian Popular Cinema." *Rethinking Film Studies*, ed. Christine Gledhill and Linda Williams, 130–64. London: Edward Arnold.

Verdery, Katherine. 2003. *The Political Lives of Dead Bodies*. New York: Columbia University Press.

Wallerstein, Immanuel. 1979. *The Capitalist World-Economy*. Cambridge: Cambridge University Press.

Warner, Michael. 1993. "The Mass Public and the Mass Subject." *The Phantom Public Sphere*, ed. Bruce Robbins, 377–401. Minneapolis: University of Minnesota Press.

——. 2002. *Publics and Counterpublics*. Cambridge: MIT Press.

Weaver, Mary Ann. 1996. "India's Bandit Queen." *The Atlantic Monthly Magazine* 278, no. 5 (November): 89–104.

Weber, Max. 1968. *On Charisma and Institution Building: Selected Papers*, ed. S. N. Eisenstadt. Chicago: University of Chicago Press.

Werbner, Pnina, and Helen Basu. 1998. "The Embodiment of Charisma." *Embodying Charisma: Modernity, Locality, and Performance of Emotion in Sufi Cults*, ed. Pnina Werbner and Helen Basu, 3–30. New York: Routledge.

Wharton, Annabel. 2003. "Icon, Idol, Totem and Fetish." *The Icon and the Word: The Power of Images in Byzantium*, ed. Anthony Eastmond and Elizabeth James, 3–11. Burlington, Vt.: Ashgate.

"When the Rich and Poor United." 1997. *The Statesman*, September 7, 1.

Wilkinson, Tracy, 2003. "Confirming Miracles Is Art and Science." *Los Angeles Times*, October 14.

Williams, Linda. 1991. "Film Bodies: Gender, Genre, and Excess." *Film Quarterly* 44, no. 4: 2–13.

Willis, Andy, ed. *Film Stars: Hollywood and Beyond*. Manchester: Manchester University Press.

Wolfe, Charles. 1991. "The Return of Jimmy Stewart." *Stardom: Industry of Desire*, ed. Christine Gledhill, 92–106. Berkeley: University of California Press.

Woodward, Richard. 2002. "Iconomania: Sex, Death, Photography, and the Myth of Marilyn Monroe." *All the Available Light: A Marilyn Monroe Reader*, ed. Yona McDonough Zeldis, 10–35. New York: Touchstone.

Wyschogood, Edith. 1990. *Saints and Postmodernism: Revising Moral Philosophy*. Chicago: University of Chicago Press.

282; activists as, 302; outlaw as, 291; saint as, 292

Cuny, Marie-Thérèse, 189, 337 n. 8, 338 n. 9

Currier, Erin, 150–51, 333 n. 19

Curtin, Michael, 7, 158, 333 nn. 25–26

Daku Hasina (1987), 170, 244

Dalit, 108, 131, 223, 241, 265, 275, 311 n. 2, 329 n. 37, 338 n. 11, 348 n. 23, 351–52 n. 13; as citizen subject, 209–12, 284–91

DAM/Age: A Film with Arundhati Roy (2002), 196, 285–86

Dársan, 82

Daulin, Amy Marie, 237, 239

Davis, Carol Boyce, 187–88

Davis, Richard H., 80–82, 322 n. 17

Dean, Jodi, 178–79

Death of Icons, 206–7, 212

De Certeau, Michel, 33, 97, 99

De Cordova, Richard, 153, 162

De Darkar, Bishaka, 131

Defacement, 54

Deleuze, Gilles, 97, 320 n. 2, 325 n. 37

Democratic state, 284–91

Derrida, Jacques, 44, 59, 87, 183, 213, 224, 323 n. 27, 342 n. 42, 352 nn. 14–15, 352–53 n. 20

Dickey, Sara, 247–48, 334 n. 43

Diprose, Rosalyn, 98

Documentaries, 196

Dutt, Sanjay, 60–61

Dyer, Richard, 144, 155, 248, 336 n. 65, 345 n. 25

Eck, Diana L., 80–82, 90, 322 n. 17

The Electric Moon (1992), 111

Eley, Geoffrey, 260–61, 347 n. 9

Embodiment: consumption and, 38, 65–67, 85, 97, 207, 215, 224; difference and, 29–31; sensation and, 7–8, 44, 105; synaesthesia and, 8, 44, 66, 85; visuality and, 70–71, 78–79, 82, 96, 321 n. 13. *See also* Corporeality

Exem, Celest Van (priest), 201–3, 341 n. 32

Exorbitance, 183–84, 197, 207–8

Expressivity, 226

Fan cultures, 247–48

Fernandes, Leela, 170–71, 299, 335 n. 54

Fischer, Lucy, 144, 194, 331 n. 3, 339 n. 18

Flexible accumulation, 13

Fractal personhood, 94–95, 174–77

Frain, Irene, 337 n. 8, 338 n. 9; *Phoolan* (1992), 189

Francis of Assisi, St., 148, 206, 342 n. 39

Fraser, Nancy, 261, 346–47 n. 8

Freadman, Anne, 63–65, 316 n. 3, 319 n. 33

Freedberg, David, 72–73, 80, 321 n. 6

Freedom fighter, 306

Freitag, Sandra, 30, 245

From Saint to Sainthood (2004), 128

Fuller, Matthew, 161, 172, 184, 235, 331 n. 4

Gaines, Jane, 175, 344–45 n. 22

Gallagher, Mark, 173, 349 n. 57

Gandhi, Mahatma, 55–62, 86–87, 104, 319 n. 27, 350 n. 36, 352 n. 16, 354–55 n. 31

Gandhi (1982), 194

Gandhy, Behroze, 165, 169, 247, 334 n. 43

Garbo, Greta, 79, 154–55

Gatens, Moira, 98

Gell, Alfred, 76, 94–96, 174, 177–78, 218, 233, 246, 312 n. 8, 323 n. 28

Gere, Richard, 106, 256

Ghosh, Rupali, 266

Gjergji, Lush, 190

Gledhill, Christine, 144, 173–74, 244, 336 n. 59, 336–37 n. 65

Global green, 109, 113–20, 300–304, 307–8. *See* Activists

Global icons, 16; globality of, 11, 23, 26, 303; translocality and transnationality of, 237, 269, 300–303; universalism of, 14, 21–22, 26, 33, 140, 155

The God of Small Things, 111

Gombrich, Ernst, 90

Google Earth, 37–38, 310

Gordon, Avery, 4, 104, 229

Grable, Betty, 175

Gramsci, Antonio, 19–21, 217, 313 n. 21, 314 n. 23, 350–51 n. 4

Bishnupriya Ghosh is a professor of English and affiliated faculty in the departments of Film and Media Studies, Comparative Literature, and Feminist Studies at the University of California, Santa Barbara. She is the author of *When Borne Across: Literary Cosmopolitics in the Contemporary Indian Novel* (2004).

Library of Congress Cataloging-in-Publication Data
Ghosh, Bishnupriya.
Global icons : apertures to the popular / Bishnupriya Ghosh.
p. cm.
Includes bibliographical references and index.
ISBN 978-0-8223-5004-0 (cloth : alk. paper)
ISBN 978-0-8223-5016-3 (pbk. : alk. paper)
1. Popular culture. 2. Signs and symbols. 3. Celebrities.
4. Mass media. I. Title.
HM621.G47 2011
306.01—dc22   2011010761